This book is for my mother,
Eileen McKay,
who bought me my first magazines

Gladly wolde he lerne and gladly teche

Geoffrey Chaucer

The Magazines Handbook

The Magazines Handbook has firmly established itself as the essential introduction to the theories and practices of the modern magazine industry. This fully updated third edition comprehensively examines the business of publishing magazines today and the work of the contemporary magazine journalist.

Jenny McKay draws examples from a broad range of publications to explore key jobs in the industry, covering everyone from the subeditor to the fashion assistant, as well as analysing the many skills involved in magazine journalism, including commissioning, researching, interviewing and production.

Updated specialist chapters discuss the growth and development of electronic publishing and online journalism, new directions in magazine design, photography and picture editing, and the most up-to-date legal frameworks in which magazine journalists must operate.

The Magazines Handbook includes:

- interviews with magazine journalists, editors and publishers
- advice on starting out and freelancing in the magazine industry
- an analysis of 'new journalism' and reportage
- a glossary of key terms and specialist concepts
- information on contacts, courses and professional training.

Jenny McKay MA (Oxon), has worked as a journalist in magazines, newspapers and television. She has extensive experience of the university-level teaching of journalists and is currently Senior Lecturer in magazine journalism at the University of Sunderland, UK. She was a founding member of the Association for Journalism Education and the International Association for Literary Journalism Studies and is an editor of the journals they publish: *Journalism Education* and *Literary Journalism Studies*.

Media Practice

Edited by James Curran, Goldsmiths College, University of London

The *Media Practice* handbooks are comprehensive resource books for students of media and journalism, and for anyone planning a career as a media professional. Each handbook combines a clear introduction to understanding how the media work with practical information about the structure, processes, and skills involved in working in today's media industries, providing not only a guide on 'how to do it' but also a critical reflection on contemporary media practice.

The Advertising Handbook
3rd edition
Helen Powell, Jonathan Hardy,
Sarah Hawkin and Iain MacRury

The Alternative Media Handbook
Kate Coyer, Tony Dowmunt and
Alan Fountain

The Cyberspace Handbook
Jason Whittaker

The Documentary Handbook
Peter Lee-Wright

The Fashion Handbook
Tim Jackson and David Shaw

**The Graphic Communication
Handbook**
Simon Downs

The Magazines Handbook
3rd edition
Jenny McKay

The Music Industry Handbook
Paul Rutter

The New Media Handbook
Andrew Dewdney and Peter Ride

The Newspapers Handbook
4th edition
Richard Keeble

The Photography Handbook
2nd edition
Terence Wright

The Public Relations Handbook
4th edition
Alison Theaker

The Radio Handbook
3rd edition
Carole Fleming

The Sound Handbook
Tim Crook

The Television Handbook
4th edition
Jeremy Orlebar

The Handbook

Third edition

Jenny McKay

Routledge
Taylor & Francis Group

LONDON AND NEW YORK

Third edition published 2013
2 Park Square, Milton Park, Abingdon, Oxon OX14 4RN

Simultaneously published in the USA and Canada
by Routledge
711 Third Avenue, New York, NY 10017

Routledge is an imprint of the Taylor & Francis Group, an informa business

First edition published 2000 by Routledge
Second edition published 2006 by Routledge

British Library Cataloguing in Publication Data
A catalogue record for this book is available from the British Library

Library of Congress Cataloging in Publication Data
McKay, Jenny
   The magazines handbook/Jenny McKay. – 3rd ed.
   p. cm. – (Media practice)
   Includes bibliographical references and index.
   1. English periodicals–Handbooks, manuals, etc. 2. Periodicals –
   Publishing – Great Britain – Handbooks, manuals, etc. 3. Journalism
   – Vocational guidance – Great Britain – Handbooks, manuals, etc.
   I. Title.
   PN5124.P4M39 2013
   052 – dc23   2012031305

ISBN: 978-0-415-61756-7 (hbk)
ISBN: 978-0-415-61757-4 (pbk)
ISBN: 978-0-203-14327-8 (ebk)

Typeset in Helvetica Neue and Avant Garde
by Florence Production Ltd, Stoodleigh, Devon, UK

MIX
Paper from
responsible sources
FSC   FSC® C004839
www.fsc.org

Printed and bound in Great Britain by
TJ International Ltd, Padstow, Cornwall

Contents

Contributors

Tom Ang is author of 22 books on digital photography, including the award-winning *Digital Photography Masterclass*. He was editor of *Photography* magazine, picture editor of *Sunday Correspondent Magazine*, and has served on international picture juries in London, Cannes and Prague. He is based in New Zealand. Website: www.tomang.com.

Phil Cullen is a journalist and photographer who lectures in media photography and journalism at the University of Sunderland, UK. He has served time as a magazine designer, newspaper editor and exhibiting artist, among other things.

Lee Hall edited national news-stand magazines for Future Publishing and is now a senior lecturer in magazine journalism at the University of Sunderland, UK. As a freelance journalist he has contributed to a range of titles, including *FourFourTwo*, *The Guardian*, *Edge* and *BBC Focus*.

The day **Tim Holmes** started on his first magazine the management decided to close it down. Fortunately he found a better job on a bigger title, working with talented people who taught him all he needed to know to start his own publishing company. He now runs the magazine courses at Cardiff University's journalism school and publishes in the field of magazine studies. His most recent book is *Magazine Journalism*, published by Sage in 2012.

Anthony Richards LLB (Hons), BEd, MA, barrister-at-law (non-practising) was lecturer in journalism and law at Lambeth College, London, UK, and a former Press Association Law Service reporter. He is now retired.

Mark Robertson is a communications officer for the Edinburgh International Festival. He was music editor and deputy editor of *The List* for several years and was the first winner of the Scottish Periodical Publishers Association's Award for Feature Writer of the Year.

Linda Ventry LLB (Hons), MLitt, is a writer and editor specialising in Scots law. Based in Edinburgh, she is currently working as an editor for law publisher LexisNexis UK.

Carole Watson is Senior Lecturer in journalism at the University of Sunderland, UK. She was formerly a journalist and executive at the *Daily Mirror*, *Grazia* and *News of the World*.

Acknowledgements

In preparing this book I have benefited from membership of two academic organisations – the Association for Journalism Education and the International Association for Literary Journalism Studies – whose members, journals and conferences have helped to shape my thinking about the significance of magazines.

I have been generously assisted by staff of the Professional Publishers Association, in particular Kathy Crawford and Loraine Davies, Tom Hawkins and by the many magazine journalists and publishers who have fielded my questions. They may not agree with my conclusions but I hope they will recognise the picture of the magazine world that I have tried to draw. I am grateful to the journalists who agreed to be interviewed and to those writers who contributed chapters or interviews. The many students I have taught and been challenged by also deserve my thanks, especially those who keep in touch with me as their careers progress.

I'd like to thank my colleagues at Sunderland University for sharing with me their knowledge of and interest in magazine journalism. Alison Barratt, Ian Blackhall, Julie Bradford, Phil Cullen, Neil Farrington, Lee Hall, Alex Lockwood, John Price, Alistair Robinson, Chris Rushton, Caroline Sword and Carole Watson have all helped in various ways, as have Andrea Robertson and Lianne Hopper.

For their tolerance of my magazine habit I thank my children Jack Archer, Alfred Archer, Barnaby Archer and Cressida McKay Frith, as well as my husband Simon Frith, whose delight in discussion and support for this project in every way could not have been stronger. Finally, I'm grateful to Louise and Paul Howard who know that without their warm hospitality in London this book would have been impossible to write.

CHAPTER 1

Introduction

Magazines have been part of my life since I bought my first pocket-money copy of *Robin* to read about the latest adventures of Andy Pandy. From Andy I moved on to *Bunty* with her cut-out paper dresses, and I remember my first disappointment with cover mounts when a magazine called *Princess* was launched with TV adverts promising a princess outfit to wear. This, as it turned out, was only for a competition winner and not something you could pick up at the newsagent.

Illustrations in another girls' magazine for a story called 'Judy swims to Fame' left me thinking for months that men with chiselled features and blonde hair were apt to be called 'fame', a word I hadn't hitherto encountered. A magazine called *Petticoat* left me with the conviction that every girl in the world but me had a collection of 20 pairs of identical court shoes in different psychedelic colours. With further dismay I learnt from grown-up magazines that one of the world's ten best-dressed women spent at least ten minutes every day plucking the individual hairs on her legs. Fortunately, I'd already discovered *OZ* and *New Society* by this time, so I was able to change to a better kind of magazine.

At school I worked on the staid annual magazine. The editorial dilemma we faced was whether to abandon the old-fashioned printer and move to a new printing company that could do exotic things with photographic reproduction. A school cruise saw my contributions appear in a magazine called *Aqueous Humour*, devised as a way to keep us amused for the ten days' uninterrupted sail at the end of the trip. This magazine was reproduced on an antiquated Gestetner machine. From there to university, where I regularly read *Spare Rib*, obscure journals about medieval literature, *Vogue* if I could borrow a copy, the Survival Society newsletter and *Isis*, the student magazine I would eventually edit.

Anyone who has worked in student journalism will know what it is to go without sleep for three nights in a row, to beg multinational companies for money, to encounter the joys and limitations of PR at first hand, and to argue about who spilled the Cow Gum over the typewriter or, the modern equivalent, beer over the keyboard. Student journalism convinced me I wanted to work in magazines and left me with that inability to walk past a news-stand without stopping that will be familiar to readers. If it's not, then maybe you're reading the wrong book.

I live in a house filled with magazines of all sorts. A five-minute survey revealed the following titles in a list which does not include any that are here for research purposes alone, nor does it include newspaper supplements: *Adbusters*, *Ms. Brill's Content*, *Time*, *The New Yorker* and *Bust* from the United States; *Oh Comely*, *The Big Issue Scotland*, *Is This Music?*, *Muzik*, *M8*, *The List*, *Radio Times*, *Muso*, *NME*, *Reportage*, *Granta*, *High Life*, *Total Film*, *The Spectator*, *Music Week*, *European Journal of Cultural Studies*, *Screen*, *Popular Music*, *British Journalism Review*, *Product*, *Hello!*, *Condé Nast Traveller*, *The Beano*, *London Review of Books*, *Critical Quarterly*, *The Wire*, *Red Pepper*, *New Statesman*, *Prospect*, *Mslexia*, *Birds*, *Private Eye*, *The Skinny*, *Official Playstation 2 Magazine*, *Soca News*, *BBC Music Magazine*, *The Journalist* and *New Internationalist*.

Maybe such a range is not typical, but I can think of homes that come close. Nor is it that surprising when you consider the average newsagent stocks about 450 titles and even that's only a small fraction of the total number of titles published in the UK. So what is it about magazines that there are so many and that they are being bought in huge numbers, even when finances are tight for so many readers and there are so many increasingly appealing digital rivals to print?

WHY ARE MAGAZINES SO POPULAR?

The most immediate answer is that people like to read magazines for information and entertainment. The popular illustrated general magazines such as *Picture Post* may have gone (although *Reader's Digest* still sells 383,650 in the UK alone, 17 million worldwide, according to June–December 2011 figures) but in Europe there is still life in the general weekly magazine formula, as the continued success of *Paris Match* and *Stern* shows. Nowadays, what magazine publishers claim as one of their strengths is their ability to identify niche markets. They can profitably produce publications for quite small groups of people whose shared interest may be as obscure as smoking cigars (*Cigar Aficionado*) or keeping carp (*Koi Carp*). More popularly they can produce magazines such as *FHM* which, within a few years of its launch, reached a circulation of three-quarters of a million, and *Glamour*, which went from launch with the April 2001 issue to become the UK's best-selling women's monthly glossy in just 16 months. Four years on, its circulation was still rising and it had become the best-selling women's monthly glossy in Europe, as well as the UK.

Information may be anything from how to choose a bridesmaid (*Brides & Setting Up Home*), the best place to go to learn kitesurfing (*Kiteworld* magazine) or the latest political scandal (*Private Eye*). Nor is the information all in the editorial. Many magazines provide a wealth of information through their adverts, particularly the classified ones. Sports magazines list dealers specialising in arcane equipment; interior decoration magazines are good places to look for suppliers of furniture or flooring; wildlife magazines provide useful addresses for ecotourist travel and suppliers of birdseed.

The magazines which cater for special interests or hobbies act as a substitute or extension of the reader's own social circle of like-minded people: if you're the sole 14-year-old fan of hip-hop in your village, then you catch up on the general gossip with your copy of *Source*. This function is also part of the appeal of the internet, and Facebook or Twitter in particular, where there is the added advantage of more direct contact with other people. The business or trade press, equally, circulate information to those who share an interest in a particular field.

What constitutes entertainment is even more varied. It might be joky pictures of celebrities (*More!*), pin-ups of bare-breasted women (*Front*, *Loaded*, *Nuts*) or of red-breasted mergansers (*Birds*, *BBC Wildlife*), profile articles about politicians (*New Statesman*) or sportsmen (*Shoot*), romantic fiction (*The People's Friend*), quizzes, horoscopes, personal columns or real-life stories of the 'My best friend stole my husband so I bedded hers' variety (*That's Life!*). Sometimes reading magazines even becomes a group activity when friends choose to chat together about what they've read.

Another appeal of magazines is that they act as a badge of the reader's allegiance to certain values or interests. Just as a rap fan wouldn't be seen dead with a copy of *Top of the Pops* under his arm, so a reader of the feminist magazine *Ms.* would know she had wandered into alien territory if she found *Playboy* on the coffee table next to *Penthouse*. This aspect of magazines is not confined to readers with minority interests. Jane Reed, who was editor of *Woman*, put it this way: 'A magazine is like a club. Its first function is to provide readers with a comfortable sense of community and pride in their identity' (Winship 1987: 7). There's a lot of truth in this idea that magazine readership can create a sense of belonging to a wider group, although what she says is not quite right in that the first function of most commercial magazines is to make money for the publishers: a loyal readership is essential for this and what Reed describes is just one strategy editors have as they struggle to create and maintain that readership. There are, of course, also magazines whose publishers don't have any interest in making money. Fanzines in music and sport, for example, are usually put together by fans for other fans, simply to share the love of a particular sound or club. But even these have a connection with the commercial world of magazine publishing: James Brown, who was editor of *Loaded*, *GQ* and then *Jack*, began his career by publishing his own fanzine and in 1999 set up his own company, I Feel Good Publishing, which was later sold to Dennis Group.

WHO SHOULD READ THIS BOOK?

This book is for people who want to work as magazine journalists. It's also for people who don't yet know which branch of journalism they want to work in. The uncertainty doesn't matter. As the chapters on careers and training make clear, career paths are now far more flexible than a generation ago, and there is a lot of movement between the various media and indeed within the media: publishing is such a multiplatform undertaking, with print brands usually providing audio and video editorial and advertising material for readers too. All of this means there may be people who have been working as journalists in one of the other media who find themselves joining a magazine or looking for work on one. The book should be useful for them too. While writing it I have tried to keep the requirements of these different kinds of readers in mind, while aiming to write a book which university tutors in journalism will find useful both for the information it provides and for the issues it raises.

Where information is concerned one problem is that the detail changes very fast, as with any twenty-first-century industry that is subject to market forces. I'm thinking here of things like who edits or owns which magazine and which sectors of the consumer market are flourishing or wilting, rather than what constitutes a good piece of feature writing. For this reason, where I have given examples from specific magazines or companies I have tried to place them in a general context and also tried to make clear where the kind of information I am discussing comes from so that students can trace the most up-to-date titles and figures for themselves.

Where issues are concerned it is important to make clear that such discussion has not always formed part of a journalist's training. Increasingly it does, since university courses in journalism got under way in the UK in the early 1970s. But there is still suspicion in some editorial offices that training, even for graduates, is about teaching people how things are done (and have always been done) rather than allowing any discussion about why they are done that way and whether there might be other ways of working. Academics have been criticised for asking too many questions about the practice of what I would call a craft or trade but some like to call a profession. I wouldn't deny that some theoretical academic debate can miss the point either through being too earnest or through a lack of common sense. However, my own experience as one who trained and worked as a journalist, who has taught journalism skills for many years and has also read much of the recent academic work on journalism, is that some of it can be of great help to trainee journalists, even if that's not its purpose. If someone had offered me Galtung and Ruge's article on the structuring and selecting of news while I was training as a reporter, I would have understood much more quickly what the news editor was trying to say about news values (Chapter 7; see also Galtung and Ruge 1973). Ben Crewe's book, *Representing Men*, is a theoretically grounded account of cultural production based on interviews with several editors and publishers of men's magazines, including James Brown (*Loaded*, *GQ*, *Jack*), Ekow Eshun (*Arena*) and Piers Hernu (*Front*).

It provides a useful insight into the unprecedented development of the men's magazine sector in just over ten years. Besides, the media are influential both in determining what issues get a public airing and in the way they comment on and shape the discussion of those issues. It is important, therefore, that the choices they make about what is significant, the agenda they help to set for the rest of society, should be open to question from both those who want to work as journalists and those who, as media commentators or as academics, study what journalists do. With the revelations about phone hacking and all-round bad behaviour that are emerging in evidence to the Leveson Inquiry, it is becoming clear that more and earlier self-scrutiny would have been of benefit to the press.

MAGAZINE OR NEWSPAPER JOURNALISM?

One curious thing about magazine journalism is how much less academic attention it has attracted than newspaper journalism. (This holds true for all aspects of magazines that academics might study: history, ethical issues, influence of regulatory bodies, language, sociology and so on.) Even attention from the general public is comparatively limited unless there is the spectacular firing of an editor or a fashion spread which causes offence or, as in the case of *The Spectator* in 2004, a series of salacious, gossipy stories about the private lives of a succession of senior staff and writers. This neglect is reflected in the relative numbers of university training courses devoted to newspaper and periodical journalism. Never has journalism been so popular as a career choice for graduates, but for most of them – and their careers advisers – journalism still means chasing fire engines to daily deadlines or following politicians on the campaign trail.

There are understandable reasons for this. Hard news is seen as exciting, frontline and edgy, largely about war or crime or affairs of state. Magazines, with their less frequent deadlines, are thought to be light, less important and soft – largely about things that don't matter quite so much. Countless films and television shows, from *The Front Page* to *Drop the Dead Donkey*, feature wise-cracking, cynical, hard-nosed newshounds. But the magazine offices portrayed by popular culture are filled mainly with the fragrant folly of the television show *Absolutely Fabulous* or the film *The Devil Wears Prada.*

Part of the problem may have been that the word 'magazine' used to imply 'women's magazine' to many people. This has been changing since the launch of *Loaded* in 1992. Its pioneering path was soon followed by the success of several other monthly titles for men (*Maxim*, *Arena*, *GQ*, *Front*) and then, in 2004, the unexpected but quickly established challenge from men's weeklies, *Nuts* and *Zoo*, even if their success is now on the wane. Anything produced specifically for women has tradi- tionally been accorded less value than that which is otherwise regarded as the mainstream. But the consumer magazine market includes a majority of publications not targeted at women and is too important to dismiss. Consumer magazines, according to the Professional Publishers Association (PPA), are those that provide leisure-time information and entertainment. In the UK there are more than 3,000 publications that fall into this category, but almost double that number of magazines fall into what's known as the business-to-business sector and used to be called the trade press. That's another 5,000-plus titles. Clearly this is a substantial market, but it is much less visible than the consumer market because so many trade publications are sold by subscription: people see only the ones related to their own fields of interest.

Taken together, then, these two sectors (consumer and business-to-business), with a total turnover of around £6.4 billion, form a strong magazine industry. And it's not just in the UK, but also in many other countries where new markets are opening up (see Chapter 16). According to government figures the periodicals and journals sector of the UK publishing industry provided employment for more than 53,400 people at the end of 1996, compared with the newspaper industry which employed around 47,000. The trend here is significant too: for magazines the 1996 figure is a rise of more than 9,000 in three years; for newspapers it represents a fall of 6,000 (Department of Culture, Media and Sport 1998: 86).

Another under-reported statistic is that in 1997 around half of all journalists in the UK were employed in magazines rather than newspapers (Delano and Henningham 1997), a proportion that is likely to have increased thanks to the large number of redundancies the newspaper industry has seen in the years since then. In his book *News and Journalism in the UK*, Brian McNair (2009: 9) looks as if he is about to redress the balance of significance as between newspapers and periodicals: 'No overview of the British print media would be complete without some reference to the periodical sector: those weekly, fortnightly and monthly publications which straddle the boundaries between journalism, leisure, entertainment and business.' Yet there is something dismissive in that phrase, 'some reference', given that the periodicals industry is considerably bigger than the newspaper industry, however you measure it (Department of Culture, Media and Sport 1998: 86). McNair notes the journalistic emphasis of both *Private Eye* and *The Economist*, but again with the idea that these are journalistic because they are about the common hard news preoccupations of economics and politics. This implies that much of the written material that finds its way into the approximately 3,500 consumer titles and the 5,000-plus trade titles is not journalistic. I wouldn't challenge that view by citing the frothier lifestyle magazines or the sillier celebrity titles, but I would argue that there is a lot of excellent journalism being pursued in periodicals, even if some of them are little-known trade publications such as *The Engineer* or what could almost be called 'alternative' magazines such as *New Internationalist* and *The Big Issue*. There are plenty of magazines which deal with serious subjects and demand of their writers the highest standards in writing and research (McKay 2004/2005). Peter Preston, former editor of *The Guardian*, argued that the future of newspapers, as they compete with electronic news, lies 'in targeting, in niche markets, in an extension of newspapers' attitude towards features' (Preston 1999). These are precisely the things at which the best magazines already excel.

Even if you use McNair's own criteria to define news, there are stories with economic and political implications being broken or followed through in the trade press with more expertise or thoroughness than many newspapers can manage (*Computer Weekly*'s tracking of the evidence surrounding the Chinook helicopter crash on the Mull of Kintyre is a good example). Furthermore, journalists who work for specialist publications are constantly asked by reporters who work for general newspapers to give quotes or background briefings, or even write articles when a story breaks in their field of expertise. Journalists with *Flight International* gave about 100 interviews in the two days following the attack on the World Trade Center in 2001, according to the magazine's editor, Murdo Morrison. Also, Stephanie Hawthorne of *Pensions World* says she is regularly invited to give expert commentary for stories about pensions in the general press (PPA Magazines 2004 conference).

At the lighter end of the news agenda it is common to find that editors like Martin Daubney, when he was editor of *Loaded*, and Celia Duncan of *CosmoGIRL!* were called upon by other journalists to share the expertise they have acquired as part of the job. Editors often say it is an enjoyable part of their work and a useful way to promote their publications (PPA Magazines 2004 conference).

Magazines have other uses too – as agenda-setters. In areas such as medicine, the journals *The Lancet* or *BMJ* are regularly the sources of news for all other media. In the entertainment and lifestyle fields the same thing happens. For the past 35 years at least, newspaper journalists have been dependent on music magazine brands, ranging from *NME* to *Mixmag* and *fRoots* for their understanding of musical trends. The *Radio Times* finds the interviews it runs are often picked up by other publications as source material for their stories about television and radio personalities.

WHAT EXACTLY IS A MAGAZINE?

There are other reasons, too, for suggesting that newspaper and magazine journalism should be accorded more equal status. Journalists now move freely between the two media (see Chapter 2) and almost all daily and weekly national newspapers now bring along in their wake a selection of what can only be described as magazines. *The Sunday Times*'s colour magazine, launched in the early 1960s, was the first UK example and was soon copied by most of the other weekend newspapers. These colour supplements contained a miscellany of articles including, typically, some hard-hitting coverage of social problems or of wars. But their stories were not tied to the same daily or weekly deadlines as the news sections and so gave their writers and photographers the chance to produce a more considered kind of work. The supplements were also printed on better-quality paper. This, along with the coloured inks and the different size, meant that readers of the colour supplements, in the early days, would always have known that what they held in their hands was a magazine.

How much more confusing the situation is now. Many papers publish subsidiary sections which aren't glossy, which may be daily, which are a different size from the main paper and which, by virtue of not being tied to the hard-news agenda, have a magazine 'feel' to them. Take *The Guardian*'s 'Weekend' or the *Mail on Sunday*'s 'Night and Day' sections: are they magazines? If not, why not?

For a definition of a magazine or periodical we could look to the industry body for help, but it doesn't provide a full answer. The members of the PPA are companies that know they produce magazines. But those newspaper publishers who produce publications such as *The Times Saturday Magazine* (a weekly with heavy, glossy paper, full-colour photographs and illustrations, and a miscellany of stories) do not belong to it. So membership of the PPA can't help much with definitions. Whereas everyone knows more or less how to define a newspaper, the definition of magazinehood is much less distinct – so many kinds of journalism are published in magazines, so many kinds of journalists are employed on them.

If there can't be an exact and limiting definition of what goes into a magazine it is perhaps because the word was first used to imply something miscellaneous. Edward Cave, a printer and publisher, is usually credited with being the first to use the word 'magazine' in the title of a periodical when he launched his *Gentleman's Magazine* in 1731. There were publications that we now would describe as magazines before that date, notably Defoe's *Review* and the first women's magazine, launched in 1693, called *The Ladies' Mercury*. But these were not, as far as we can tell, referred to as magazines. Gradually, after Cave's venture became well enough known, the word magazine, which is related to the French word for shop, *magasin* (which in turn derived from the Arabic for emporium or warehouse of goods), acquired its modern meaning. Not only that, it has come to be used in other media, such as television and radio, to refer to programmes which provide a miscellany of stories within a limited field: *In Touch* is a radio 'magazine' programme for the blind; *Top Gear* is a television magazine programme about motor cars. Perhaps the description given by Ruari McLean in his book about magazine design is as helpful as any: 'A magazine is, usually, less ephemeral than a newspaper, less permanent than a book' (McLean 1969: 1). No one could quarrel with that as the 'usually' allows for exceptions to the rule.

LOOKING AHEAD

The magazine industry in 2012 appears to be in not bad shape, even if it is recovering after a period of economic recession that continues to affect both advertising and circulation and, by association, undergoing an almost unprecedented level of scrutiny thanks to the Leveson Inquiry into press standards. The introduction of computer technology to print publishing during the 1980s breathed new life into magazines, allowing them to experiment with design, to cut costs and, in theory at least, to shorten lead times. As so often happens with technological innovation, some predictions did not come true. It was assumed that as desktop publishing (DTP) became a financial possibility there would be a burgeoning of cheap, alternative magazines produced by anyone who had something to say and the hope that someone would want to read it. This hasn't really happened and you could certainly argue that the development of the photocopier actually made more difference to the publication and distribution of alternative publications than did computerised setting (Atton 1999).

In the 1990s the great change was the arrival of the world wide web and the internet. Forecasts about the possible effects of this on magazine publishers were at wild variance. Some heralded it as the start of the collapse of magazines and even newspapers: who would need them once they could have a tailored digest of news and features stories ('The weekly/monthly Me') sent directly to their desks in digital form? The funny thing about how wrong this prediction has so far turned out to be is that digests of the contents of magazines have appeared (*The Week* is one such successful publication), but provided in hard-copy form as yet more magazines.

Publishers were then worried that they ought to be keeping up with everyone else by getting into web publishing but without really knowing what to do with a website or whether they could make money with one. As Tim Holmes shows in Chapter 12, publishers have more than come to terms with the digital communication revolution – they have embraced it wholeheartedly and there can't be many print publications that don't also have a web presence. Some are generating extra business or building up databases, and it's now clear that there is money to be made in digital publishing, especially in the business information field, either through advertising or through the direct selling of knowledge or products. Some publishers are merely providing an extra service to readers through their websites, but by doing so are learning more about their readers' interests and improving public recognition of their brands.

The mood of the magazine industry in the UK was more positive than might have been expected at the 2012 annual conference of the PPA, which represents 80 per cent of the UK market. While the men's market (with one or two exceptions) was showing signs of strain during 2011, current affairs titles such as *Private Eye* and *The Week* were putting on significant circulation. The business-to-business sector, which suffered the most during the economic recession, was discovering cause for cautious optimism and there was continued talk of activities such as brand extension, exhibition organisation, database provision and the exploitation of content in media other than print. Many publishing houses are turning to global markets where there is continued launch activity. By 2012 the newish, free titles from ShortList Media – *ShortList* for men (launched 2007) and *Stylist* for women (launched 2009) – had established themselves with circulations of around 513,000 and 424,000, respectively: in 2012 *Stylist* editor Lisa Smosarski was voted consumer media Editor of the Year by the PPA.

In early 2005 *Easy Living* and *Grazia* entered the crowded women's monthly and weekly markets, again with great success. And new titles continue to emerge. In July 2010 the fresh-looking magazine *Oh Comely* appeared and in 2012 *LandScape* was launched by Bauer. The story is not always good, however, and in 2004 some high-profile publications folded; among them were *J17*, *19*, *The Face* and, within a few months of its launch, *Cut*. Music titles and those aimed at teenage girls were under particular pressure (Alden 2004). Since then there have been further casualties, including *Smash Hits* (in 2006), *Sugar* (in 2011) and *The Word* in August 2012.

Magazine publishers and editors have long liked to say that there is a magazine for every taste. Marie O'Riordan, then editor of *Marie Claire*, is typical. She says that for readers the only difficulty 'lies in multiple choice' (Alden 2004: 27). However, it's just not true that there exists a magazine to suit every taste. There certainly is a magazine for many hobbies (unusual pets in *Practical Reptile Keeping*, embroidery in *Cross Stitcher*) and for weird sexual obsessions as in, for example, *Leg Sex*. These publications represent niche marketing in the extreme. Some mainstream subject areas are hardly touched by magazines because their potential target audiences are not sought by advertisers. One obvious gap in the current marketplace is for magazines which deal intelligently and wittily with a much broader range of subjects for women and for girls than any of the current British ones do, although relative newcomers *Oh Comely* and *Stylist* do, in their different ways, offer some relief from the usually limited content. Given that there are more than 80 magazines for women on the news-stands, it is surprising how similar groups of them are. No amount of advance hype about how different new magazines such as *Grazia* and *Easy Living* were going to be could disguise the truth, when they arrived, that their content is utterly predictable as a product for the current women's market. The competition in all sectors of the consumer market is fierce (there are at least 20 UK magazines devoted to home decoration, for example) but for publishers the remedy seems to lie in further fragmentation of the market, rather than in consolidation of their products.

SCOPE OF THIS BOOK

Business and industry perspectives are dealt with in Chapters 15 and 16. For some reason these aspects of publishing life are largely ignored in the training of newspaper journalists, but are thought by many to be essential for magazine journalists. I think it is useful for workers in any industry to have some idea about how it is financed and what problems are currently worrying the owners and managers. For magazine publishers the impact and potential of the internet is one concern. So too is the effect that changes in the pattern of retailing in the UK may have on magazine distribution. Will supermarkets drive local CTNs (the industry's name for confectioner, tobacconist, newsagent shops) out of business? Will they be willing to stock such a wide range of magazines as the CTNs? Another concern, raised by Felix Dennis of Dennis Publishing, is what he describes as the functional illiteracy of one-quarter of the UK's teenagers: 'How many magazines will they be reading in ten years' time?' he asks. A further worry, voiced by Dennis, is the environmental impact of destroying so many trees to produce magazines. Even if publishers don't worry too much about that, he implies, the environmental lobby will and this could eventually have an impact on sales, especially now that an electronic alternative is available (Dennis 2004: 45–50).

From outside the industry concern is regularly expressed about the content of magazines. There has long been discussion about the limitations of the material published specifically for women. Criticisms include worries about the possible negative effect on women (especially young women) of a literary diet of little but beauty, fashion and titbits of gossip, whether about celebrities or 'ordinary' people. This kind of argument can be patronising to women, assuming as it sometimes does that they read little else or that they need more protection and education than men.

There is, too, a strong strand of feminist criticism which argues that by their very nature magazines aimed at women do acquire a role as shapers and definers of what women are and how they are perceived (Ferguson 1983; Greer 1999; Macdonald 1995). If that's so, then it does matter what images of women are provided by these publications and what social roles women and girls are seen to play in them and in the magazines aimed at men. Some commentators have also analysed why the subject matter of commercial women's magazines is, on the whole, so limited, and have looked at what this means in terms of what is left out of magazines (Steinem 1994).

There are also commentators who have decided that consumer magazines are not influential because their readers don't take them seriously, using them merely as light relief from busy lives (Hermes 1995). These ideas will be discussed further at appropriate points in the following chapters, although I'll now declare my own position. First, I believe magazines do wield a strong influence over their readers. I base this on common sense, my own experience and, much more convincingly, on the research undertaken by publishers and advertisers. Second, I am on the side of Cynthia White, who argued in her Royal Commission report that magazines should cover a much wider range of subjects the better to prepare girls and women for life in a real world instead of one bounded by agonising over how they look and how to cope with domestic drudgery. She was writing in the mid-1970s. Her conclusions are, regrettably, still valid in 2012 (White 1977).

Third, I take a feminist position in that I find the picture of women's lives to be gleaned from reading many women's magazines disheartening as well as unrealistic, even allowing for a bit of fantasy and plenty of light-hearted fun. The underlying assumption of so many publications is that women are obsessed by their appearance and with good reason, as that is what will define them in the eyes of the world. The argument here is also commercial as American feminist editor Gloria Steinem described in 'Sex, lies, and advertising' (Steinem 1994): lack of confidence about looks leads to expenditure on clothes and cosmetics, without which consumer magazines would not exist. It will be interesting to see whether the newer, more narcissistic men's lifestyle magazines such as *Shortlist* and *Men's Health* will convince men to spend as much time, energy and money on their appearance as women are now expected by editors, and encouraged by advertisers, to do. That this matters is the point made by Nichols and McChesney, who observe that: 'This is a generation that is under pressure from the media it consumes to be brazenly materialistic, selfish, depoliticized and non-socially minded. To the extent one finds these values problematic for a democracy, we all should be concerned,' (Nichols and McChesney 2000: 63; quoted in Davies 2008: 396).

While it's true that romance and marriage have been pushed aside since White was writing, these topics have been more than replaced by sex dressed up in various guises on the problem pages, the fashion pages, the general features and the health pages. Nothing wrong with that if people want to read about it, but it is the fact that there is so little in the way of debate about anything vaguely contentious (as opposed to prurient) that gives rise to criticism. Two relatively recent trends in women's magazines are that the stories about the personal lives of so-called celebrities which dominate are written in an increasingly bitchy, almost vicious tone, and that radical cosmetic surgery is written about with alarming acceptance and frequency. Added to these is the well-publicised concern over the way increasingly explicit sexual material is being used in magazines for young men and women, as a means to boost circulation.

In one book it is not possible to discuss every aspect of writing, editing and publishing that might interest journalists who want to work in magazines. This is because the range of titles is so varied that there are not many general points that cover every case. Consequently, it is not really possible either to give representative examples of texts. Instead, I have referred to a wide variety of periodicals on the assumption that where this book is being used as part of a course, tutors and students will want to find their own examples to illustrate (or, indeed, challenge) the points made here. What I have tried to do is to concentrate on the areas that are most important for a beginner to know about.

One of the differences between newspaper and magazine journalism is that there are certain agreed things that news reporters need to know how to do. Among these, apart from news writing, are included some features writing and some subbing. Even within newspaper offices, though, basic reporter training will not now make provision for all the kinds of writing and editing that the magazine sections of newspapers require. Yet most journalism training is taken up with the inculcation of news values and the skills required to write hard-news stories. This book doesn't, therefore, seek to cover the same ground as newspaper journalism training books for the simple reason that there are several of these and there is much less available to the magazine journalist.

An elementary knowledge of government is an essential part of a news journalist's training. While it may well be useful knowledge for magazine journalists, no one could argue that they all need it, and indeed most editors and publishers say that if there has to be a choice they think it is more important for all their staff to know something about the magazine publishing industry than about the mechanics of government. Again, the ground is covered in most newspaper training books as well as in the book by John Morrison and others recommended at the end of Chapter 5.

There is, however, no disagreement at all among editors about how important it is for all their staff to have a knowledge of the law as it affects journalists. For this reason Chapter 18 is devoted to the subject. Although many magazine journalists will pass an entire career without attending a criminal court or an inquest, there are nevertheless aspects of the law about which everyone who ventures into print ought to know.

This book is written primarily for journalists who work in magazines, so it doesn't attempt to explain how advertising sales executives do their job or indeed what magazine designers or photographers or stylists need to know. It does, however, include chapters on magazine design and on picture editing and illustration. These chapters provide an introduction to how the experts in the visual aspects of magazines approach their tasks so that the writers and subeditors who work with them will have an informed understanding of how certain decisions are made. Many magazines have small staffs, and writers and subs on magazines are therefore more likely to be involved in decisions about the look of their publications than they would be on many newspapers.

Chapter 11, which looks at subediting and production, concentrates on writing and presentation. It does not venture into the realms of computer software. It's true that many subs these days will need to know how to use Adobe InDesign, but it would be impractical for a general book such as this to attempt to teach it. The practicalities of an individual system are best taught by computer specialists, so the aspects of subediting covered in Chapter 11 are, broadly speaking, the ones that apply to whatever software (or indeed whatever technology) is being used to produce a magazine.

Because there is so much variety in magazine content, readers will find plentiful references to further sources of information and an extensive bibliography to help them explore the areas that interest them most. At the end of each chapter is a list of books and websites that are recommended to supplement the points made in the text. Full bibliographical references for these are provided in the bibliography. I have included wherever possible references to examples of good journalism in the hope that these will act as a kind of inspiration of what it is possible to achieve as a journalist. One thing that puzzled me as a trainee journalist on a hotly competed-for graduate training scheme was that there was no discussion of the best journalistic writing or of the literary value of journalism. In my own teaching I have always tried to go against this tradition by urging journalism graduate students to read good journalistic writing, whether from among what is current or from anthologies. So I make no apology for including in these pages references to writers who with courage, grace or skill open windows on the world, which is the most important thing a writer can do for me.

I would like to be able to recommend a comprehensive history of periodical journalism, but it doesn't yet exist. Those who are interested to know what has gone before, once they have exhausted Cynthia White on women's magazines (White 1969) and David Reed on popular magazines from 1880 to 1960 (Reed 1997), will have to browse in general press history journals and books, some of which are listed at the end of this chapter. For current coverage of the magazine world, students should look regularly at *The Guardian*'s media section, *Private Eye*, the *Press Gazette* and *Media Week*, magforum and PPA websites. The American monthly *Brill's Content* is not too hard to find in the UK and provides information and comment about what is going on across the Atlantic.

The only other thing to do is to explain how I came by the information and opinions that are set out on the following pages. The reason this is necessary is that there is, as I have already hinted, a lingering suspicion among some journalists that anyone who doesn't make a living as a journalist has nothing useful to teach about journalism. I would counter that argument, in my own case at least, by saying that I was a journalist for ten years, and part of me still is. Almost more important than that is the fact that I have taught a lot of journalists. They keep me informed about current practice. So too do the journalists who kindly accept invitations to speak to my students and the editors I talk to on a regular basis. So, in addition to the sources in published material (books, magazines, industry documentation, websites), my most important sources are journalists, the men and women whose job is an important and a fascinating one if not in every circumstance an enviable one.

RECOMMENDED READING

Armstrong, L. (1998) *Front Row*.
Ballaster, R., Beetham, M., Frazer, E. and Hebron, S. (1991) *Women's Worlds: Ideology, Femininity and the Women's Magazine*.
Benwell, B. (2003) *Masculinity and Men's Lifestyle Magazines*.
Braithwaite, B. (1998) 'Magazines: the bulging bookstores' in *The Media: An Introduction*.
Conboy, M. (2002) *The Press and Popular Culture*.
Crewe, B. (2003) *Representing Men: Cultural Production and Producers in the Men's Magazine Market*.
Davies, N. (2008) *Flat Earth News*.
Dennis, F. (2004) 'The Four Horsemen of the Apocalypse', *British Journalism Review*.
Frith, M. (2008) *The Celeb Diaries: The Sensational Inside Story of the Celebrity Decade*.
Griffiths, D. (ed.) (1992) *The Encyclopaedia of the British Press 1422–1992*.
Holmes, T. and Nice, L. (2012) *Magazine Journalism*.

Johnson, R. (2011) *A Diary of The Lady: My First Year and a Half as Editor*.
Johnson, S. and Prijatel, P. (2006) *The Magazine from Cover to Cover*, 2nd edition.
Kelsey, L. (2003) 'Introduction' in *Was It Good For You, Too? 30 Years of 'Cosmopolitan'*.
Long, P. (2012) *The History of the NME: High Times and Low Lives at the World's Most Famous Music Magazine*.
McKay, J. (2004/2005) 'The invisible journalists', *Media Education Journal*.
MacQueen, A. (2011) *Private Eye: The First 50 Years – An A–Z*.
Nichols, J. and McChesney, R. (2000) *It's the Media Stupid*.
Reed, D. (1997) *The Popular Magazine in Britain and the United States 1880–1960*.
Reeves, I. (2005) 'Say it loud, I work in mags and I'm proud', *Press Gazette*.
Smith, A. (1979) *The Newspaper: An International History*.
Weisberger, L. (2003) *The Devil Wears Prada*.
White, C. (1969) *Women's Magazines 1693–1968*.
Wolf, N. (1991) *The Beauty Myth*.

Periodicals

Adbusters, *Brill's Content*, *British Journalism Review*, *Campaign*, *Media Week*, *Private Eye*.

Websites

Association for Journalism Education: www.ajeuk.org
British Society of Magazine Editors: www.bsme.com;
http://magculture.com/blog
Magforum: www.magforum.com/0vanda/visual_history_of_UK_magazines.htm
Media Guardian: www.guardian.co.uk/media/pressandpublishing
Professional Publishers Association: www.ppa.co.uk
Press Gazette: www.pressgazette.co.uk
For a list of magazines published in the UK: www.magazine.co.uk/magazines/a_z/

Films

The Devil Wears Prada, dir. David Frankel, DVD release 2007.
The September Issue, dir. R.J. Cutler, DVD release 2009.

CHAPTER 2

Training for magazine journalism

For many careers the route to a job is clear. Even if competition for jobs is fierce there is often a recognised qualification you must have before you apply for a first post. After that the contacts, the determination, luck and the job market all play their part, but that vital first step is to get the basic training.

The position in journalism is different and confusing, not only to outsiders hoping to get in but also to many of those who already work as journalists and are in the position of hiring recruits. In this chapter I will concentrate on entry into magazine journalism, but much of what I cover applies to other aspects of journalistic work in the media.

QUALIFICATIONS

There are no minimum qualifications for journalists, so in theory you could get a job without an A-Level or a GCSE. And however many training courses there are available, there will always be some magazine editorial staff who get in by informal means: by talking their way into a job as an editorial assistant perhaps, by going to an office for work experience and contriving to become indispensable, by bombarding an editor with such good cuttings or story ideas that in the end a job has to be offered. This is anathema to those who believe that journalism is a profession, but it is a fact of journalistic life. If you write well enough and are able to convince an editor of your worth, the lack of a paper qualification in anything, let alone in journalism, is no barrier to success. Except, of course, for the fact that so many people, including some of the best graduates, want to be journalists too, many of them in magazines. They will be competing fiercely for jobs and so editors can look for flair in addition to educational achievement, not instead of it.

In practice, then, almost all entrants to journalism nowadays have been to university or college; often that includes a postgraduate vocational qualification after a first degree in some other subject. Of those currently working in magazine journalism, about 90 per cent are graduates and for all journalists, including newspapers, the figure is about 80 per cent. This change has come about in the course of a single working generation and the obvious reason is the huge growth in the proportion of the UK population that goes to university.

If you're unlucky as a new journalist you might come up against older journalists who say journalists are born, not made, and that training is unnecessary, beyond some media law and shorthand. For those who think in this way there is only one thing worse than training, and that is training that takes place in a university. Luckily this approach is not as common as it was even 25 years ago. If you find yourself in an editorial office where this view still prevails, you are likely to find your life made miserable if you ever make the slightest mistake or ask a simple question about practice. Luckily, too, for readers of this book at least, this attitude is less prevalent in magazine offices than it is, or at least was, in newspapers, particularly the regional dailies and weeklies. If you do come up against it, being astoundingly competent at your job is usually a good way to silence critics, but if you're a beginner there will be things you still need to learn even if you've completed a course of training.

The truth is that journalism is madly competitive: staff jobs are increasingly hard to come by and so the more training you have the more employable you are likely to be. From the 1960s to the 1980s it was virtually impossible, thanks to agreements between unions and management, to get a job on a national newspaper without first serving an apprenticeship on a regional daily or weekly paper. Whatever else recruits had done before, those indentured years helped them to learn under the guidance, in the best offices, of experienced reporters and subeditors. Of course, in-house, on-the-job training was, and still is, a lottery, since it was unsystematic and depended on the editor allocating good members of the editorial team to the job, rather than the less good, whose time could be spared from more important duties. During this period and beyond there were pre-entry courses that school-leavers or graduates could take at colleges or universities, some lasting just a few weeks, others up to an academic year and leading to the award of a diploma or even a Master's degree. The pioneering courses in the UK were at Cardiff University and City University in London. Not only did they train graduates for newspaper journalism, they realised that there was scope for training graduates in other kinds of journalism too – periodicals as well as broadcasting. What many entrants to the trade of journalism had in common was that at some point they would sit examinations organised by the National Council for the Training of Journalists (NCTJ). These gave newspaper editors (and other employers) guidance about whether certain skills and knowledge had been acquired, but they were never an absolute requirement for entry into journalism, however much the NCTJ and some editors would have liked them to be.

JOURNALISM IN UNIVERSITIES

Until the early 1970s, there was no formal route into magazine journalism at all. This may be why careers advisers often assumed that journalism as a career meant newspaper journalism, because there was at least some kind of pattern to training for this. Journalists who wanted to join magazines from newspapers would some-times find their qualifications helpful, but equally could, and still might, encounter magazine editors who had never heard of the NCTJ. A similar problem arose as the various further education and higher education courses in journalism got under way. They don't all teach exactly the same things or at least don't emphasise the same skills. The qualifications are at differing levels (from certificate, through HND to graduate diploma and MA or MLitt or even MSc) and there is no consistency in the level at which applicants join. Some universities cater only for graduates, some teach undergraduate journalism degrees, some further education colleges cater for school-leavers on block-release courses. You can see why this is confusing already, before we even get to the vexed subject of media studies.

To digress for a moment. There is often contempt shown by senior journalists (who really should be better informed) about media studies. The distinction is clear to university staff, but perhaps they have not made enough effort to explain it to those outside the academy. Put simply, media studies is the analysis of what media practitioners and others who work in the media produce. A media studies course may or may not contain some elements of media or journalism practice, but in essence it is an academic study in the same way that English literature is the study of what novelists and poets produce, not a training in how to write novels or poems. A journalism degree by contrast is more likely to include vocational training for those who want to be journalists. In universities this will certainly involve some academic analysis of what journalists produce, but the point of journalism courses in many universities is to train journalists, not to train academics, even if those journalists are able to reflect critically on what they do for a living. Just to confuse things, some degrees are called journalism studies, and these are likely to resemble media studies in that they are more about the academic analysis of the field than about learning to practise the skills required to become practitioners. The key is in the word studies, and the advice is to look carefully at what a given university course claims to be offering.

Much of the prejudice about media studies comes from those who are ignorant of this distinction – their comments about media studies being a bad preparation for a media career are therefore not worth listening to. Those who graduate in any aspect of media or journalism are, if they are any good, very successful indeed at finding jobs. There are a few who decide that they don't want to be journalists after all, but the skills they acquire on university journalism courses should prove valuable in many other careers.

However, even those critics who can see the distinction between media studies and vocational journalism training are wrong when they argue that students who take degrees in media or communications are misled into expecting to work in the media afterwards. First, no one deliberately misleads them and, second, lots of them do, in fact, go on to be successful in the media. Michael Jackson, with a glittering career in television, went on to head BBC2, then Channel 4: he studied communications. Mark Daly, the award-winning investigative reporter who worked under cover for the BBC's documentary series *The Secret Policeman*, was a student of film and media at Stirling University, before taking a postgraduate diploma in journalism. Just two examples, but there are many more. Media studies courses do not necessarily provide much training in practical skills, but for many students that suits well. If you're passionate about television, radio or the printed mass media, what is wrong with devoting a period of academic study to their critical analysis? They are worthy fields of study in their own right, and if by the end of a degree the student decides to try to work in the media, then what's wrong with knowing how to write a feminist critique of women's magazines or how to deconstruct a television documentary in the manner of Raymond Williams or John Fiske? As an intellectual training at undergraduate level (always assuming the course is a good one) study of the communications media is as good an intellectual training as any other more traditional degree. So long as there is no confusion for students or teachers about what practical, vocational training is, then there shouldn't be a problem.

For those who want to do journalism studies courses at undergraduate or graduate level that are vocational and therefore a direct preparation for work in journalism, there are certain indicators to look out for that the right kind of work will be done and assessed on the course.

ACCREDITATION

What could be the simplest check is to look for accreditation by an industry body. Accreditation ideally follows an examination by industry and training professionals of the way that a course is run. For magazines, any courses which are accredited by the Periodicals Training Council (PTC), the training arm of the Professional Publishers Association, are likely to be worthwhile, as are those accredited by the NCTJ. This doesn't mean that all of those which are not accredited are not good, as newer courses will not yet have arranged for the expensive and time-consuming visits and assessments to take place. Nor, if they are very new, will they have been able to provide the accrediting body with a list of graduates and their employment records. Perhaps the thing to do is to check whether an application for accreditation has ever been turned down.

The PTC does not set exams for students to take. It monitors, on behalf of its member magazine publishers, the efforts of those who do and there is therefore no conflict of interest with the education providers. It also provides support, speakers and advice to universities and colleges where magazine journalism is taught. It runs an annual award scheme for magazine students from accredited colleges, as well as a Magazine Academy day when students attend masterclasses by leading players in the magazine world. At the time of writing the PTC accredits nine BA and five MA degrees, two postgraduate diplomas and one postgraduate course. It also runs MagNet, a mentoring scheme which enables ethnic minority students to be teamed up with a professional mentor from the industry. In a recent development the PTC now also offers two online qualifications, the PPA Foundation Certificate in Journalism and the PPA Professional Certificate in Journalism which may be taken by staff members as well as those hoping to get into magazine journalism.

The NCTJ's interest in magazines is more recent. Its original purpose was the training of local newspaper journalists, who would work for at least two years before they could move to national papers. When universities became involved with journalism the NCTJ found itself, in effect, in direct competition with them because it provides its own training courses, as well as setting its own examinations which students at accredited centres are obliged to sit, often at their own expense, if the university is to gain and keep accreditation. The expense of taking these exams runs into hundreds of pounds and this can act as a deterrent for students. The NCTJ now also offers accreditation for magazine degrees as well as those dedicated to sports or fashion. Students taking these three routes to the NCTJ's diploma can expect to cover many of the same skills and knowledge as those taking the more traditional route, but with the added opportunity to develop their specialist knowledge in the field of their choice.

If accreditation is a useful but not an infallible guide, what else can you look for? Check in the course literature whether those who teach the practical journalism aspects of the course have worked as journalists. It's also worth checking how much experience they have of teaching, as it's not every former journalist who can teach well without some practice. Check the timetables to see what proportion of time is devoted to developing practical skills. Ask to see the facilities that will be available to you as a student and find out how much time you will have with them. A Mac-filled newsroom with all the latest software is only as useful as the amount of access to it students have. Ask to see samples of student work and perhaps a list of assignments set in any given year. You might also ask to see a list of the career paths of graduates if the course is well established.

For some candidates there won't be much choice, as they will be offered only one place. Competition for the good journalism courses in universities is strong, certainly, but the number of applicants alone is not always a reliable guide as most serious candidates will apply to several courses. Universities, too, are in competition for the really good candidates who will therefore be likely to have a choice about where to go. There may be overriding personal reasons pointing a student in one direction or another, but if there aren't then the considerations I have listed above should influence the decision. Financially, a graduate course is a big investment, so you have a right to make sure you will get value for money. There doesn't seem to be much conformity about the costs of courses at graduate level, largely because they are all funded in different ways by their host universities. It's a point to watch out for. The cheapest course might just be less good. On the other hand, it may offer less in the way of equipment, but for the difference in fees you could buy yourself what is needed (laptop computer, appropriate software, mobile phone, camera, etc.) and still have them to use at the end of your year's study.

Students aiming at careers in magazines will probably try to choose the periodicals courses in universities, but newspaper training will almost certainly contain many of the same elements (with perhaps less emphasis on production). Career paths are not tightly fenced into one medium and so if money dictates that you study at the nearest college and that offers only newspaper journalism, by taking up a place there it doesn't mean you can't expect to work in magazines. Apart from anything else, it could depend on what kind of magazine job you aspire to. If you want to be a South-east Asia correspondent of *The Economist* then news training would be the most useful thing.

The point about career paths is important. It is increasingly rare for journalists today to make a career entirely in one medium. They move jobs from television to newspapers to magazines or the other way round, or while having a job in one they do freelance work for another. As well as this, any given journalism brand such as *Cosmopolitan* or *The Guardian* will have developed a wide range of multimedia platforms by which they appeal to their readers. This means that throughout your training and your career you should be aware of the developments in all media and how they will affect your own work. In addition to further and higher education institutions and the accrediting bodies I've mentioned, there are also private providers of training for the industry. PMA Training in London is one that is well established. It runs short courses of interest both to those already in the industry and those hoping to get in. A new entrant to this field at the time of writing is the Condé Nast College that is due to open in London in 2013. It will offer a *Vogue* Fashion Foundation Certificate (ten weeks at a cost of £6,600) or Diploma (one year at £19,560) and is for those who want to work in the fashion media. Eventually the intention is to add a *House and Garden* diploma.

ON-THE-JOB TRAINING

One disadvantage with any on-the-job training for beginners is that it means employers are having to pay people who are not yet fully competent. They may not pay them much, but any salary is a drain on resources, especially if the post-holder is completely untrained and untried. One reason that many publishers of newspapers gradually defrosted their attitude to university journalism courses was that they realised the cost of initial training was being shifted to the pockets of students. Publishers used to have to pay while trainees learnt the elementary skills as well as paying fees for the block-release courses. Now they start to pay the graduates, at least, when they already have a good knowledge of all the basics, plenty of practice as reporters, and probably some worthwhile cuttings to prove they have what it takes to get published.

One of the best options for an aspiring magazine journalist, especially one on a limited budget or one who is simply tired of classrooms, is to be taken on by a magazine publisher as a trainee. There will be a salary, formal training, the chance to practise straight away and under guidance what has been learned in training, and the immediate opportunity to start building up a portfolio of cuttings and a list of contacts. Unfortunately, the days when big companies regularly took on groups of trainees on these terms have now more or less gone, although IPC and Incisive Media continue to run graduate trainee programmes as of 2012.

One way to find out about courses run by universities, colleges or private companies is to check the PTC or NCTJ websites, which have lists of those they accredit. A fuller list of courses, whether or not accredited, is to be found on the *Press Gazette* website; on www.magforum.com you'll find a list of UK magazine publishers and magazine titles. Traineeships are more likely to be found these days in the trade or business press. Such publications are not so easy to find in newsagents, but can be an excellent way into the world of magazine publishing, provided you have no objection to becoming, for a year or two at least, an expert in finance, cement mixing, print buying, the timber trade, dentistry or insurance (see Chapter 3 on careers).

COSTS

If you do decide to train at your own expense, there is an enormous range in how much you might have to spend. This partly reflects a lack of agreement over what you need to know to work as a journalist on any magazine compared with what you need to know to work on a specific one. My own list would run like this. For any magazine: the skills of touch-typing; shorthand; Word; Adobe InDesign and Photoshop; written English; subediting; research (online, paper-based and inter-personal such as interviewing face to face, by telephone or using social media); and basic knowledge in the fields of business, government and media law. Beyond those (and I recognise how arguable this list is) it would be desirable for most if not all magazine journalists to have some knowledge of the history, business and design of magazines, as well as an understanding of the media studies approach and a developed interest in the field they hope to write about, whether it is fashion or economics or fishing for trout. In practice, this last point is almost the least important, as many journalists find themselves writing about subjects in which they have no expertise.

The courses run by colleges, universities and private organisations vary wildly in the prices they charge, as I have noted. Some examples, correct as of early 2012, are as follows. For £4,050 students from the UK or Europe can take a one-year MA course in magazine journalism at Sunderland University. Students from abroad pay £9,400. At City University in London the figures are £9,000 for UK and EU students, £18,000 for international students. For an undergraduate degree the fees at Sunderland University are £8,500 per year – that's £25,500 in all. At Cardiff University the undergraduate degree is £9,000 per year for UK and EU students, or £11,900 for overseas students. And if these figures seem high, it's worth comparing them with private providers of journalism education. PMA charges £816 for its two-day introduction to journalism skills, or £486 for a one-day introduction to media law. The journalists' union, the NUJ, also runs a suite of training courses that are open to non-members, although they have to pay more. For example, a two-day feature-writing course is £275 for members, but £495 for non-members. In addition, there are a range of other educational institutions offering further education-level courses open to graduates and non-graduates.

For some aspiring magazine journalists these sums sound impossibly high, especially when you take into account the modest salaries that are paid for first jobs and out of which you might be expected to pay off a student loan or a career development loan. Note, though, that first pay at the junior level in magazines is likely to be higher than in local weekly newspapers. For a few students there is help in the way of scholarships to study at certain universities. The Association of British Science Writers has substantial awards available for those with a science background, and at Cardiff University there is a bursary from the *Radio Times* available for study on the periodicals journalism course. All organisations will have details about fees and funding on their websites and that is where you should check for the latest information.

PREPARATION FOR FINDING WORK

Some graduates decide to break into magazine journalism as freelances. This kind of work is discussed fully in Chapter 4, but here it is worth outlining the pitfalls for the beginner. To be a successful freelance you have to be sure that the work you produce is of a professional standard and is properly presented, and you also need contacts who have responsibility for commissioning copy. A new freelance can build up the contacts by pitching exciting ideas and producing good copy. But if you have never worked as a staff journalist and you've had no training, then the problem is going to be the quality of your work. If, in the early days, you offer commissioning editors work that is not up to standard then it will deter them from looking at your ideas in the future. The warning here is against trying too soon to make a living as a freelance. Many are the staff journalists with years of experience who decide to make a go of the freelance life, perhaps after redundancy or even just because they fancy being in charge of their own lives. A history graduate with a couple of music review cuttings from the student paper or website is unlikely to be able to compete. Having said all this, if you are determined that you must work as a magazine journalist and that you can't afford formal training, then you'll have to train yourself. Spend time on the BBC College website. It's a fantastic resource for all journalists, not just those who want to work in broadcasting. Read Chapter 4 of this book, on freelancing, read other relevant books, read and analyse successful magazine journalism, study the markets, get some work experience – unpaid if necessary – practise writing and interviewing even while you carry on with the day job. Invest in the most up-to-date equipment you can afford – phone, laptop, camera, and so on. Pin two notes above your desk to remind you: 'You're only as good as your last by-line' and 'Features editors are always short of ideas'.

If you nevertheless decide to try for a job or place on a course, there are certain things editors and lecturers will be looking for in candidates. The personal qualities likely to characterise journalists are well enough known (curiosity, competitiveness, plausible manner, good memory) and the skills that are needed you will be acquiring as a trainee. Beyond this the things that influence those with the power to pluck you from obscurity are, in the end, all things which show you have talent, persistence and an absolute commitment to being a journalist. So a portfolio of cuttings from student papers with perhaps a couple from your local weekly paper or specialist magazine and ideally one from a regional or national would be standard. They show that other people think your work is worth publishing and that you have the nerve to persuade them to do it. They may also be evidence that you have spent some time doing work placements – this is, again, almost a standard requirement. To get a placement you need persistence and possibly contacts. It shows not only that you are keen enough to arrange the placement, but that, having done one (or several), you really know what you are talking about when you say you want to be a journalist. Otherwise an interviewer might suspect that you think magazine journalism is all glamour and no graft, more about drink, drugs and missed deadlines than about chasing late copy, reading proofs or devising workable flatplans. If you are applying to the 'abfab' world of the women's fashion glossies or to a depraved den of laddishness you will have to convince the editors in your own personal way that you know enough about the content of their publications to be able to contribute. There are some aspects of journalism that can't be taught and the patience you need to interview soap starlets about their sexual preferences is probably one of them. Likewise, the imagination to think up new ways of describing the comeback of the little black dress. Most journalists would also recommend that you have your own blog and keep it updated. It will demonstrate the quality of your work and that you are committed to producing journalistic material on a regular basis.

WORK EXPERIENCE

Work experience is a relatively new concept in the world of UK journalism, although in the past 25 years it has become fairly essential for anyone hoping to make a career as a journalist, for some of the reasons given above. It can be a great disappointment to employers and students, and most often if it is, this is because there has been a lack of clarity about what is expected. This can be due to a muddle about the very term 'work experience', so it is important to have a clear idea of what you mean by it. At the simplest level there is the kind of work placement where youngsters, probably still at school, go into an office for a week or so. The point of this is exploratory – to get some idea of what journalism and journalists are like, to see if it's the kind of work that might be of interest. Later, when it is clear that they want to be journalists, perhaps because they've had work published in student papers, they might take on longer work placements where, as well as being allowed to shadow reporters, they may be allowed to do some research or caption writing or try writing simple stories.

On longish work experience periods, especially over holidays when there may be a shortage of staff, students can find they are gradually entrusted with tasks of considerable responsibility. At a more advanced stage still, those students who are studying journalism for degrees or postgraduate qualifications will almost certainly be required to undertake periods of work experience. What they are entrusted to do here will depend on the competence of the trainee and the confidence shown in him by the editor. Up to this point there is unlikely to be much in the way of payment. I believe that if student work is published by a magazine or paper, then a lineage rate should be paid as it would for any other journalist: copy that's good enough to publish is good enough to pay for. A few publishers do give their students on work experience some financial help, in recognition of the fact that they are trained and experienced enough, especially at graduate diploma level, to make a worthwhile contribution to the editorial team.

A note of caution here about what some organisations call work experience – it can often seem like exploitation. When students have gained their qualifications in journalism they may be offered unpaid work experience or internships for weeks if not months, with the incentive that a job could be coming up in the near future and they would be ideally placed to get it if they have already been around in the editorial office. It's understandable that new journalists accept this, but they shouldn't have to. Apart from anything else it makes a nonsense of that case made by some editors that they don't get enough recruits from poorer families. You already need quite a lot of cash behind you to study for a degree, then a post-graduate diploma which almost always has to be funded personally. Even quite well-off families baulk at the idea of a substantial period of unpaid labour for a profitable publishing house, especially as these kinds of jobs usually leave little time for the part-time, cash-gathering jobs in bars or shops that students now regularly do. The issue of internships has caused a lot of controversy, and not just in journalism. Law and banking firms, fashion companies and many others now almost depend on 'workies' to do the kinds of tasks that would once have been the responsibility of paid employees.

When work experience as part of a course goes well, the student returns to class with renewed enthusiasm for the job, new contacts and some worthwhile cuttings. Sometimes, too, a work placement may have the effect of convincing a student that a field they'd thought about is in fact not for them. Work experience goes badly when the student expects too much of it, complains of being ignored by staffers, of not being allowed to do anything useful, or of finding too many other work experience people sitting around the newsroom at the same time. From an editor's point of view a student on work experience can seem too demanding, or not well enough informed about the content of the publication to be of much help. The faults can lie on either or both sides. Some senior staff have students assigned to them unasked by editors and simply can't be bothered finding time to help them, either because they are too busy, or perhaps because they feel threatened by them. Or they may not fully realise how much training and experience a student already has, they may not distinguish between the school student making initial enquiries about a variety of careers and the graduate student who is much further on in her career planning. Equally, some students expect to be given stories to write without having to go to the effort of thinking up any leads for themselves. The PTC has recognised this problem and it now publishes a booklet called 'Guidelines for organisation of work experience placements', which helps both employers and students to get the most out of the arrangement. The NUJ similarly offers advice and has in fact helped to establish that young people who work as interns for more than a short, limited period are in fact legally entitled to pay and other benefits enjoyed by employees. There are also some magazine publishing companies that employ interns on proper contracts. *Cosmopolitan* is one – an intern there can expect enough pay to live on in London, nine months' experience on one of the leading national women's magazines, and the chance to build up a portfolio and to acquire a wide range of professional contacts.

A positive note on which to end a discussion on training comes from Dylan Jones, editor of *GQ*, former chairman of the British Society of Magazine Editors and winner of its coveted Editor of the Year Award four times. 'There are few things more exciting than seeing someone come in on work experience and a few months later they're writing cover stories,' he says. 'And there's no reason why that shouldn't happen.' Consumer journalism is competitive, he acknowledges, but says 'the quality of young people coming in at entry level is incredibly high. There's a lot of jostling for position but that obviously benefits the magazines' (Reeves 2005: 22–23). At a time when the magazine publishing industry is changing very fast indeed, new entrants to the field have certain advantages, as Gill Hudson, editor of *Reader's Digest*, told the PTC's Magazine Academy in 2012. The main one is that most editors are not digital natives, whereas young people coming into the industry are. She said: 'We need their skills digitally. They're better equipped than we are', adding, though, that they need to show all the classic journalism qualities too.

CONTACTS

In this chapter it only remains to stress the importance of making and maintaining contacts, something a student can begin to do from day one. Journalists need contacts first as part of the reporting process, as sources of quotes, background information and ideas. In the context of getting jobs, however, the more important sort of contacts are those in a position to hire, or to commission, or even to hint that work might be available in a given office. The lucky student will know some journalists anyway, but others will have to find ways of getting to know some. Work experience plays its part. Shameless phone calls asking for a few minutes of someone's time to gather advice or pitch a features idea are another way to get through the door. When it comes to making contacts, your imagination and your personal level of shyness are the only limits.

RECOMMENDED WEBSITES

Association of British Science Writers: www.absw.org.uk
Condé Nast College of Fashion: www.condenastcollege.co.uk
International Federation of Periodical Publishers (FIPP): www.fipp.com
Guardian: www.guardian.co.uk/media
Incisive Media Editorial Training Programme:
　　www.incisivemedia.com/static/editorial-training-programme
IPC Media training scheme: www.ipcmedia.com
Magforum blog: www.magforum.com
National Council for the Training of Journalists: www.nctj.com
PMA Training: www.pma-group.com
Press Gazette directory of journalism courses:
　　http://blogs.pressgazette.co.uk/wire/7142
Professional Publishers Association: www.ppa.co.uk/training-and-
　　careers/careers/magscene
Periodicals Training Council: www.ptc.co.uk
Work experience guidelines: www.ppa.co.uk/training-and-careers/hr/ptc-work-
　　experience-guidelines

CHAPTER 3

Jobs and careers in magazine journalism

The number of full-time staff journalists a magazine employs varies enormously from one publication to the next. An international news magazine such as *Time* has the budget to pay the huge staff it needs to provide in-depth global news coverage. The emphasis is on writing and reporting with high-quality photography and graphics. Gathering news widely for a publication with several geographically separate editions as well as several websites is a labour-intensive task.

More commonly, however, magazines have what looks almost like a skeleton editorial staff, supplemented by freelances. Most often these freelances are the writers and photographers, but in addition magazines are likely to employ a battery of casual subs when edition times are close or there's an outbreak of flu. The most senior jobs – such as editor, fashion editor or features editor – are usually done by members of staff or employees on substantial contracts, as these are the people who determine the tone and quality of the magazine. But with the increasing trend within all journalism towards the slenderest of staffs, even senior roles may be performed on a consultancy basis by those from outside. Almost at the other extreme is a monthly magazine such as the *London Review of Books*, where the editorial team consists of about six people even though it is a dense, wordy, lengthy publication to read. This is because the editorial staff write almost none of the content. What they do is commission contributors to write reviews of books in their special fields of interest.

CONSUMER MAGAZINES

It's not so different on a typical consumer magazine such as *Cosmopolitan*. The masthead (or staff box) reveals a features editor, a senior features writer and a features writer, all of whom are on the staff. The subeditors department has three people in it, although it is likely that on smaller magazines there would be fewer subs, so other staff – such as the deputy or assistant editors – would tackle some subbing. In the fashion team of four there is no one whose title includes the word 'writer', and the same is true of the three-strong health-and-beauty team. Below these in the list are the 11 contributing editors, who are usually freelance writers paid retainer fees to supply a regular number of features each year. Even including non-staffers and the editorial secretaries, there are, on most consumer magazines, considerably more names listed under the business functions such as advertising, marketing, promotion and publishing than there are among the writers, artists and production types. On newspapers, by contrast, there is not likely to be a staff list published in this way.

In bigger publishing houses some staff do the same job for a number of publications. A publisher, for example, may cover four or five publications in the same field, and it's quite common in the business-to-business (B2B) press for designers or subs to work on a range of titles. This makes sense as smaller publications don't necessarily generate enough work for full-time employment, but the publishing house can nevertheless offer attractive full-time jobs by combining work on more than one title.

From the perspective of the young journalist who wants to work in magazines this can be disheartening. The excitement and buzz of working for a title like the award-winning *Glamour* is not going to be part of the life of many writers, who are more likely to be at home awaiting commissions from a range of publications. On *Glamour* there is more chance of a job as a stylist or as a subeditor. It makes sense, therefore, for those who know they want to work in magazines to ask themselves what it is about magazine journalism that appeals. Is it the opportunity to write features about sex for lads' magazines? Is it the chance to write about economic news with the luxury of weekly deadlines? Is it the attraction of writing scintillating headlines while surrounded by fashionable young creatures dressed in exotic clothes? Is it the prospect of heading towards mainstream news journalism, using the specialist press as a training ground? Is it the desire to write about a specific field that is covered properly only by magazines?

The answers to these questions will help an aspiring magazine journalist to focus on the kind of work to which he is most suited. For instance, a newshound who wanted to work on *The Economist* would be well advised, if unable to get a traineeship there, to try for one of the national or international news agencies or else get into financial journalism, perhaps through financial newsletters or the B2B press. Someone who wants to write general consumer features needs to consider whether she is suited to life as a freelance because so much of the copy that glossy consumer publications use comes from out-of-house sources. If that is her ultimate aim it might make sense to take a first job as a sub or an editorial assistant as a way of making contacts and learning from the inside about how such magazines work.

CAREER PATTERNS

What should be clear is that a career in magazine journalism means a varied set of possibilities. For many journalists in the twenty-first century a career almost certainly will not be confined to one medium. Reporters and subeditors may be poached from *The Big Issue* or the *London Review of Books* by *The Guardian*, or move from *The Big Issue* to the German edition of *Sugar*. Charles Moore, former editor of *The Sunday Telegraph*, worked on *The Spectator* magazine first. Tina Brown, former editor of *Tatler*, and in 1999 the launch editor of the US magazine *Talk*, began her career writing for *The Sunday Times*. Julie Burchill, who started out on *NME*, moved from there to *The Face*, has also been a columnist for the *Mail on Sunday*, *The Sunday Times*, *The Times* and *The Guardian*, as well as founding and folding a magazine, the *Modern Review*, along the way. Journalists now move far more freely between the media than used to be the case, whether that's from one job to another or within one job, writing material for print, audio, video, websites and social media. Gill Hudson, editor of *Reader's Digest* and former editor of *Radio Times* reminded delegates to the PTC's Magazine Academy in 2011 that 'the industry is changing at an unprecedentedly fast pace', and that it's only eight years since Facebook started, seven since YouTube and six since Twitter.

There is also now the possibility of travelling to other countries to work on local publications. There has been a British invasion of American journalism in recent years. As more companies expand their operations abroad, more opportunities exist for moving to other countries on behalf of UK companies such as The Economist Group, which does 80 per cent of its business outside the UK. This is true in the B2B sector as well as consumer publishing. VNU Business, for example, moved from no overseas editions to 57 editions in just six years. On the subject of location, aspiring journalists should note that although London is the centre of the UK magazine publishing industry, there are other places such as Manchester, Glasgow, Edinburgh and Dundee with thriving magazine publishers: Future, one of the UK's largest consumer magazine companies, is based in Bath.

This means that journalists should be ready to seize opportunities wherever they present themselves. As John McKie, former editor of *Smash Hits* and *Q*, said: 'I got my dream job on a music magazine by casting the net wide, writing news and features and whatever else came up.' For others, seizing opportunities might mean that if you work for *OK!* you could slide into television as the magazine launches a broadcast spin-off, while if you work for *Eastenders* at the BBC you could slip into magazine journalism through the magazine *All About Soap*. And that's without looking at the potential for online or electronic journalism as outlined in Chapter 12.

PROFILE

John McKie, columnist for the *Daily Record*, former editor of *Smash Hits* and *Q*[1]

There aren't many journalists who get to do their dream job, but John McKie, who edited *Smash Hits* for several years, was that lucky. Yet his achievement is also the result of hard work, determination and an obsession with music that he'd had for as long as he can remember. 'I grew up with *Smash Hits*, *Q*, *Select*, *NME*, *Melody Maker*. I read all the pop magazines,' he says. But although his older brother always wanted to be a journalist (and became one), schoolboy John had no thoughts of a career. 'When I was a kid I didn't know what I wanted to do. It was at university that I started to get a passion for journalism.' He wrote regularly for the *Glasgow University Guardian* and to no one's surprise became music editor.

From Glasgow he studied journalism at Strathclyde University, where he wrote about pop when he could but also learnt to write news and features as well as picking up the essentials of law, government and production. Armed with his diploma he started to do shifts for the Scottish *Sun* and then the freelance jobs 'just came up'.

McKie also wrote and printed in full colour a glossy magazine which he called *CV*. It contained interviews with celebrities he had not published before, including ones with Marti Pellow, Harriet Harman and Jeremy Paxman. He sent the 350 copies to newspaper editors, magazine editors and section editors, particularly hoping, he says, 'that a magazine editor would pick up on it'. It helped to land him a job with the *Mail on Sunday*, first as a features writer and after a few months on the news desk, working at the hard end of Sunday tabloid journalism.

'You've got to be really tough to do that kind of hard news,' he says, recalling the journalist friend who got beaten up and his own experiences of being threatened. 'I don't know if I'd want to do it again. At the time it was a challenge. I was keen to get on and I got to work on big stories.'

Then there was a stint at *The Independent*, before going back to the game of freelance, this time with regular shifts on the *Standard*'s Londoner's Diary. 'My aim was to do it for about six months. A diary job is a good way to get contacts and meet people,' McKie says. He did plenty of freelance work for other pages of the *Standard* and for many Scottish and English newspapers.

Just when he'd begun to think his career could do with a change of gear (and just when a 'horrific tax demand' began to loom) McKie saw the advert in *The Guardian* about *Smash Hits*. His reaction was 'that would just be the best fun of all jobs. I wasn't particularly confident of getting it but I thought, I'm nearly 27 and I need to go for it now or I'll be too old.'

Emap obviously thought he was young enough to do the job and he joined almost immediately. There was a handover period for his first few weeks when the acting editor put the magazine together, but after that he was in charge. Not only had he never worked for a magazine before, he'd never been the editor of one.

'Every day I was surprised by the job, by how tough it is. You grow into it though,' says McKie. He compares the job to that of a football referee: 'That old thing about the ref having to take 500 decisions in ninety minutes. I took decisions all day long.' What he was deciding about was design, layout, pictures, stories, ideas, who gets the record company freebies, how to fix up deals with artists or wholesalers or TV programmes. He also had to manage a team of people – which means earning the respect of those already there, recruiting new staff, nurturing talent, coping with egos, or just making sure everyone gets along together.

Some people who become editors, McKie says, soon discover that they really want to be writers after all. Not him. 'I decided I really want to make a go of it.' That meant he had to take on the business aspects of magazine publishing too. 'Support from the publisher is vital,' he says. So too is careful study of the competition. (The main rivals to *Smash Hits* for its readers aged between eight and fourteen were *TVHits* and *Top of the Pops Magazine*.)

So McKie had to think about circulation figures and marketing and branding and websites. 'It was a famous brand so all eyes were on us. I had to court the industry assiduously.' The lighter side of this (and one of the best parts of the job for McKie) was getting to meet popstars and to see them getting onto the front cover of *Smash Hits* for the first time. It also explains why he had to be involved in so many day-to-day decisions. 'Dealing with the record industry, tying in maybe a gift idea with the editorial and the cover. The editor's authority is needed for a lot of the deals,' McKie says.

The drawbacks of the job were that there was no time for a social life outside work. He'd be in the office from half past nine in the morning till nine or ten every night, and otherwise out at record industry events. 'You need massive energy levels for the job,' he says, 'and you also need a thick skin. You have to be able to ignore the music industry slagging you

PROFILE

off behind your back. You have to be tenacious about what you're doing and not panic if the circulation figures aren't soaring.'

Apart from going to parties where he'd meet the Spice Girls, and getting popstars to make funny faces during photoshoots, the very best part of the *Smash Hits* job was 'hearing a record that you know is going to be huge months before it's released'.

He also loved 'putting pages together, coming up with ideas like a Steps karaoke track on a CD cover mount, thinking up silly jokes and funny cover lines, writing the Editor's letter'.

Sometimes he even managed to write a story. 'I'd try to write features if there was time. Sometimes I had to. I was the only one in the office with shorthand.'

Who does what?

There are some job titles which may need explaining. What is the difference, for example, between an editor and a managing editor? Each magazine will have its own system, but a common one is to have an editor who is the creative whizz-kid behind a title. She's good at ideas, at dealing with people, possibly at writing and probably at editing copy. She's also good at being the public face of the magazine. She may, like Rachel Johnson the columnist from the *Sunday Times* who was appointed editor of *The Lady*, be fantastically well connected in the right social circles for the magazine's readership. Behind many such a charismatic editor is a thoroughly well-organised managing editor who does not feature so much in the limelight but who is there to make sure the magazine comes out on time and is run as smoothly as possible. In the case of Rachel Johnson this is Carolyn Hart, who carries the title of editorial consultant. Then there are deputy and assistant editors who share some or all of the tasks of the editor, and in some cases will take responsibility for a particular section of the magazine: at *Marie Claire* there is an assistant editor for features and another for production. A contributing editor is not a full-time member of the staff, but is a regular freelance. A features editor or commissioning editor will, on some publications, write but more often will be responsible for coming up with story ideas and matching them to writers. They are also the people to whom freelances pitch suggestions. News and feature writers will do exactly as you'd guess. Some magazine job titles use the word director rather than editor as a mark of seniority if there is a big team. So on *Harper's Bazaar*, for example, the fashion director will be senior to the fashion editor, who is senior, in turn, to the fashion assistants.

Fashion and beauty

Fashion editors and directors, or their equivalent in beauty or even in a home and interiors department, will not necessarily do any writing. They get their jobs because of their knowledge of fashion or make-up or furnishings. Some can and some can't write well, but for most magazines the only writing required for those departments is the work of the subs in producing headlines, captions and standfirsts or sells, usually written in consultation with the stylists, who will explain what the 'story' is behind a series of photographs. Even *Vogue*, which is a kind of reference magazine for the fashion industry, offers almost no analytical writing about its main subject.

What these staffers do is research the themes and merchandise they want to promote in their pages. Research can mean anything from attendance at the seasonal clothes shows in the fashion capitals of the world such as London, New York, Milan and Paris, to visiting a fabric trade show, to being bought lunch by a make-up company PR executive, to trailing round stores looking at china or shoes, to talking to specialist location researchers for suggestions about where to shoot. The fruits of the research are crystallised into a 'story' idea. These stories may be more or less comprehensible (sometimes more or less offensive – the 'heroin chic' look in the mid-1990s was notorious, for example) but they provide a theme around which everyone involved (fashion team, art director, photographer, stylists, writers) can think imaginatively. The clothes and accessories then have to be called in through the relevant press offices and models, hairdressers, make-up artists, photographers, studios, set-builders, airline tickets, hotels and so on have to be coordinated and booked. (The documentary feature film *The September Issue* follows the preparation of the September 2007 edition of American *Vogue* and is a good way for an outsider to get a sense of this process.)

Once the pictures are chosen and the layouts designed, the fashion, beauty or home staff might write the captions. Otherwise they would be responsible only for giving the subs full information about which products are included in the photographs. Publications which take this function most seriously may have a merchandising editor whose working life is spent making contact with press offices and shops to check price, size, colour and availability of the goods which feature on the editorial pages.

Travel

Some of the most envied journalists are those who carry the title of travel editor. Research for their pages may involve a few tedious press lunches, but in the end you can't write about exotic holidays unless you go on them and that's what makes these people so envied. If they have a lot of pages to fill they will almost certainly have to do some commissioning and editing of copy as well, but it's not as if freelance journalists are likely to quibble at the prospect of a free holiday for four in Greece at the expense of the travel company. In fact, much travel writing in magazines and newspapers is produced by freelances or by staffers from other departments of the publication or publishing house, or even, as Rachel Johnson found out to her surprise when she took on the editorship of *The Lady*, 'travel freebies were used – like MPs' expenses – in lieu of income, and were handed like sweeties as rewards for good behaviour to the various office pets' (Johnson 2011: 47).

Other roles

An editorial assistant may be a trainee who is learning how to do a variety of journalistic tasks, or in some cases it may mean being, effectively, a secretary who can be trusted to undertake editorial tasks such as research or keying in copy.

Many magazines have agony aunts or uncles, or even advisers on other kinds of topics who answer readers' questions in print. These are, more often than not, freelance contributors from outside the staff, although some of the higher-circulation women's magazines do employ whole teams to deal with the agony aunt's correspondence.

One women's magazine, *Good Housekeeping*, has a long-established and well-regarded product- and food-testing department, which is devoted to doing just that. Called the Good Housekeeping Research Institute (GHRI), it is staffed by scientists, engineers, nutritionists and researchers whose job is 'testing everything from moisturizers to bed sheets to mobile phones', as well as every recipe that appears in the magazine. On any magazine staff where there is food copy there are likely to be home economists. In general the food stylists and cooks are freelances who work for a variety of companies, both journalistic and commercial.

For many other publications the job titles are more or less self-explanatory. The crucial point is that the smaller the magazine the more blurred is likely to be the boundary between tasks performed by different members of staff. On some magazines everyone may take a turn at subbing, proofreading, commissioning or writing. This is particularly true in the B2B sector.

Publisher is another key role that journalists tend not to know much about. The publisher is responsible for the finance and the strategic planning which support the publication of a magazine. Although publishers are often drawn from the ranks of advertising and marketing staff, there are notable exceptions such as Nicholas Coleridge at Condé Nast, Alan Lewis at IPC and Ian Birch at Emap. And, of course, publishers are sometimes journalists who have decided to set up their own companies of which they remain proprietors. Robin Hodge of *The List* is one (see Chapter 16).

Also significant is that much of the writing on all kinds of magazines is done by freelance contributors. *The Spectator*, for example, has a small staff and commissions most of the material for any issue from among a team of regular columnists, commentators and reviewers. *The Condé Nast Traveller* commissions celebrities as well as journalists to review hotels and travel services.

One obvious problem, then, is that it is hard to get a staff job as a writer, although there are more full-time posts for writers in the B2B press. Another is that on magazines where staff numbers are at a minimum it can be hard for a new member of that staff to get any training. However much a junior journalist has learned in advance of the first job, there comes a time when the regular advice of a more experienced colleague is essential. Even if no one is actually delegated to do this, it will happen naturally in a good, well-staffed office, but may be forgotten where pressures of time and rivalry are too great.

News

In this discussion of magazine jobs there is not much about news. This is not because there aren't good jobs involving news to be had on magazines. There are, and some of the healthiest titles in the UK at the time of writing are the current affairs publications *Private Eye* and *The Economist*. But news-based titles are more likely to function like newspaper newsrooms, even if the deadlines are further apart. Careers for general news reporters tend to follow the pattern outlined above – movement between one medium and another. More often than not, though, news in magazines is related to a specific field of interest. In the business press this may be nursing or banking or insurance; in the hobby or specialist consumer press it may be knitting or bikes or boats. In magazines like *Chat* or *That's Life!*, which feature real-life stories of the triumph-over-tragedy sort, most of the features are written by journalists who either work as freelances or, perhaps more typically, work for news agencies. In this case they may be employees whose work is sold through the news agency to newspapers or magazines that may have commissioned it or will consider it as speculatively written copy. Increasingly, such agencies act more like brokers and do not actually employ writers whose work they sell, but take a commission on what is sold. Young journalists who aspire to write features are now finding that a stint working for a news agency is an excellent way to learn how to produce stories for a wide range of publications and to build up contacts on commissioning desks in newspapers and magazines leading, possibly, to a full-time features job (see Chapter 8).

OTHER MAGAZINE PUBLISHING SECTORS

The discussion in this chapter so far has used consumer magazines as the model, partly because these tend to be better known and partly because much of what has been said about them applies to the other magazine publishing sectors (for a full discussion of these sectors see Chapter 15). Here I want to draw attention to them because of the wide range of journalism jobs they can offer.

I take the largest of all magazine publishing sectors first – the B2B or trade sector.[2] This covers many more titles (around 5,000) than the consumer field (around 3,000), but its titles are not so well known because they are produced for circulation groups linked by a narrower range of interests (often professional) than many consumer titles, particularly the lifestyle ones. Indeed, they may have tiny circulations in which case they are more likely to be called newsletters.

From the careers point of view, magazines such as *GP*, *Flight International* and *The Banker* may look as though they'd be of interest only to journalists who would really prefer to be doctors or pilots or bankers. Not so. Many of these magazines come from large publishing companies. When they take on a trainee reporter for one magazine she doesn't have to stay there forever. Careers with trade magazines can move fast, as companies that have tested out an employee are likely to look favourably on promotion or internal moves to other publications. Specialist knowledge is not usually required, although it could be an advantage. What employers look for is a willingness to learn about the field and all the basic journalism skills useful to any publisher. Once the specialist knowledge has been acquired, of course, then there is no reason why it shouldn't be used to build up a special expertise as a reporter, whether for other, more general magazines (an oil-industry expert joining *The Economist*, for example) or for other media such as newspapers, radio or TV. The business sector can be a worthwhile route into journalism and is beginning to lose its image as being slightly unglamorous compared with 20 years ago. Publishers and editors working in it say they put a lot of effort into staff training and development as they want to hold on to the expertise their staff acquire in their specialist fields.

The same advantage of building up expertise can go with a job on an in-house publication such as a staff magazine. You may not want to spend your entire life writing for the staff journal of an international oil company, but a couple of years doing it could leave you with a marketable knowledge of the oil industry from the inside. Pay and conditions on company magazines can be very good compared with commercial consumer publications.

Another kind of commercial publishing that can offer good prospects is contract publishing. A contract publisher such as Redwood produces magazines (some regular, some one-offs) for other organisations. It offers the publishing and editorial expertise and its clients will brief them as to the kind of publication they want, whether it's an in-house annual publication or a shopper's magazine such as those available at supermarkets or which come through the mail to store-card holders. In some ways these magazines don't carry so much kudos for the individual journalist – especially if bylines are not used, or if they are largely marketing vehicles – but again they can provide valuable experience. Customer magazines, such as those provided to airline passengers, may have the highest standards of writing and illustration and use the best writers and photographers to freelance for them. So too can the best of the retail store magazines. Overall, the customer publishing sector has seen considerable expansion in recent years, and at the start of 2012 included five out of the UK's seven top magazines, measured by circulation.

Another field to consider, especially for a writer who has a mission to make the world a better place, is a non-governmental organisation or public information publication. Someone who wants to write exclusively about development economics, for example, might find a job as a writer within the publications department of a charity such as Oxfam or Christian Aid much more attractive than a typical regional newspaper, or even many national newspapers, either as a career goal in itself or as a way of building up expertise in a particular field.

MONEY

So far I have not said much about pay. In Chapter 4 on freelance work the point is made that most (although not all) of the journalists who make fabulous sums work as freelances and that when the money reaches dizzy heights then the lucky earners have moved beyond mere journalism into the realms of showbiz. True, some of them may still be doing journalistic work, but if that's all an employer wanted he wouldn't need to pay huge sums to get someone to do it. The big-name, starry journalists earn showbiz fees and pay some of the showbiz price as far as privacy is concerned. But then there are other ways in which journalism as a career resembles one in showbusiness or even the arts. On the whole, starting salaries on magazines are likely to be higher than on newspapers. At the top executive end of the scale, salaries are of course negotiable and could run into hundreds of thousands of pounds.

THE SIGNIFICANCE OF TALENT

Many journalists harbour notions about a mysterious thing called talent that someone either has or does not have. Nowhere is this view more prevalent than among old-school journalists who think their trade can't be taught. And nowhere is it more clearly expressed than in the labels that are attached to individuals such as 'She can really write' or 'He couldn't write to save himself'. Substitute 'dance' or 'sing' for 'write' and you can see why the analogy works. This also helps to explain why some journalists, particularly young ones, seem to be waiting, as if for their talent to be discovered. Luck, it seems to them, plays a huge part in shaping the career of a journalist. While this is true, up to a point, of the news journalist who just happens to be in the right place when a huge news story breaks, on the whole journalists create their own chances. The lucky-number attitude prevails, I suspect, because of the huge differences which exist in pay and conditions between people who are doing the same kind of job and in a trade where merit or skill or experience do not necessarily determine who earns most or even who gets promoted. In many careers there is a clearer path to advancement (all else being equal) which does not depend so much on luck and talent but more on skills, aptitude and hard work.

Test the talent theory out by asking journalists about other journalists they admire. Ask them what in particular they admire and as often as not the answer will be vague and unmeasurable. 'He writes like a dream' – well, yes, but what does that actually mean? 'She's a great editor' – again, yes, but in what sense exactly? 'She really understands her readers' – but does that make someone great or merely able to read market research reports, a competence that would be taken for granted in any other commercial setting?

Of course, there are great journalists. But there are also ways in which those who work as journalists are ill served by these notions of talent and luck. For one thing it leaves many of those at the beginning of their careers uncertain about their capabilities and therefore pathetically grateful for jobs with laughable rates of pay and lamentable conditions which are tolerated because of the lingering hope of outlandish rewards or at least a serviceable gravy train at some later point in the career. I'm happy to argue that pretty well anyone with certain qualifications, reasonable intelligence and the right skills could work effectively as a journalist if they put their mind to it and were properly trained. Is journalism really so different from the civil service, or teaching or nursing or medicine or the law or retail management or commerce? In other careers people perform with different levels of success and their performance is attributed to a variety of factors. But it is not common in these jobs to act as if all the problems at work will be sorted out when a stroke of luck occurs like a lottery win.

ABSORBING THE CRAFT MYSTERIES

Another thing that distinguishes journalism, perhaps to its detriment, is the way in which preference is given in the selection of new recruits to those who have already absorbed many of the craft mysteries of the trade by doing unpaid work experience. Some work experience is a good idea (see Chapter 2) but one adverse effect of the emphasis placed by editors on work experience and on something as indefinable as talent is to absolve themselves of responsibility for some aspects of effective training. The risk is that certain of those craft mysteries are perpetuated beyond their useful life as they are handed on, without much question, from one generation to the next. This, I suspect, is why there was initially so much resistance to the teaching of journalism in universities from those journalists (particularly in newspapers) who did not like the idea of journalism being taught in an atmosphere of intelligent enquiry, in case the questioning undermined some of their most cherished beliefs and habits.

NOTES

1   John McKie was appointed editor of Q magazine in February 2001. He then
    moved to the *Daily Record* as a columnist.
2   For a while, around 2005, there was a move to rename the sector as 'the
    professional media' but this didn't seem to take hold. It remains, in 2012, the
    B2B or trade press.

RECOMMENDED READING

Bradford, J. (2013, forthcoming) *Fashion Journalism*.
Crewe, B. (2003) 'Editors and magazines', in *Representing Men: Cultural
    Production and Producers in the Men's Magazine Market*.
Edwards-Jones, I. and Anonymous (2006) *Fashion Babylon: From High Fashion to
    High Street – Looking Up the Skirts of the World's Most Glamorous Industry*.
Frith, M. (2008) *The Celeb Diaries: The Sensational Inside Story of the Celebrity
    Decade*.
Holmes, T. and Nice, L. (2012) 'The magazine workforce', in *Magazine Journalism*.
Johnson, R. (2011) *A Diary of The Lady: My First Year and a Half as Editor*.
Long, P. (2012) *The History of the NME: High Times and Low Lives at the World's
    Most Famous Music Magazine*.
McKay, J. (2004/2005) 'The invisible journalists', *Media Education Journal*.
Morrish, J. and Bradshaw, P. (2012) *Magazine Editing: In Print and Online*.
Reeves, I. (2005) 'Say it loud, I work in mags and I'm proud', *Press Gazette*.
Southwell, T. (1998) *Getting Away With It: The Inside Story of Loaded*.
Thurber, J. (1984) *The Years With Ross*.
Tomalin, N. (1969) 'Stop the press I want to get on', in *A Journalism Reader*.

Websites

Gorkana, media job alert service and database: www.gorkanajobs.co.uk
The Guardian: www.jobs.guardian.co.uk/media
Magforum: www.magforum.com
Professional Publishers Association: www.ppa.co.uk/training-and-
    careers/careers/magscene

Film

The September Issue, dir. R.J. Cutler, DVD release 2009.

CHAPTER 4

Freelance journalism

Most journalists at some stage wonder if they would be better off as freelances than working in their regular jobs. The appeal is obvious, and freedom is the most important part of it: freedom to choose your own hours, freedom to work on stories that interest you, freedom to work with people you respect. No more rigid office hours. It sounds good but it isn't quite like that.

There are people who make a good living as freelances and almost any journalist who makes a spectacularly good living will be freelance, even if that means being hired by the season rather than to do individual stories. However, the life of most freelances is not all rosy when compared with that of other journalists. Experienced former staff journalists often report their shock at discovering they have to work 24 hours a day at first to make ends meet. Whether someone can make a go of it comes down to ability, of course, as well as to temperament, health and domestic circumstances.

Leaving aside ability for a moment, the significance of temperament is that if you work entirely freelance you have to enjoy lack of routine and to revel in uncertainty: not just at the level of not knowing what story the features editor will allocate today, but at the level of not knowing whether you will earn anything in the next month. Then there's health. Freelances can't readily afford to turn down work, at least at the beginning of their careers and so should, ideally, be in the pink of health. Employees can make up for a bout of flu or a migraine by catching up when they return to work, but the freelance is vulnerable to the natural preferences of commissioning editors for freelance staff to be available on demand. Lastly, there are domestic circumstances by which I really mean dependants and financial commitments: far easier to take the plunge as a freelance if you have no children and no mortgage.

STARTING OUT

To become established as a freelance is far harder for those new to journalism than it is for those with experience. All the advice from old hands is that if you want to be freelance it is much easier when you have a range of contacts both as potential commissioners on magazines and as potential sources of stories. This is understandable. From a commissioning editor's point of view an experienced journalist can be depended upon to produce copy to professional standards. Someone unknown (even someone with experience but who is not known to the editor) does not bring that guarantee until several pieces have been written. References or introductions can help, so if you are starting from scratch make shameless use of successful journalists you know. Ask if you can mention their names when making an initial approach to an editor to pitch an idea. Do this, however, only when you are sure you can produce publishable work.

Some novice journalists want to be freelance for the reasons outlined above or because they want to live in a particular place far away from the hub of the magazine publishing industry, or even because they want to write about a subject in which they have a developed interest. This last reason is the one most likely to lead to success. The world is short of science journalists, for example, so a new journalist who has training behind him might find it relatively easy to break into the freelance market by virtue of that training combined with the specialist knowledge. The same may be said of numerate graduates, or better still those who train as journalists after working in a different field. Teaching or accountancy are the most common and this experience combined with journalism training can lead to good freelance careers writing about education and money.

Otherwise the difficulty for beginners is how to convince editors to take their work and, at least initially, they may have to pitch ideas on the understanding that the editor will have a look at the finished piece with no obligation to buy. If copy is competently written for the target market an editor may be willing to offer a proper commission another time. If the copy is used a freelance fee should be paid, even if the editor did not commission it. Young journalists are often so desperate to get cuttings that they accept much lower fees than the National Union of Journalists (NUJ) agreed rates, or even no fee at all. Yet if a publication uses copy it is because the copy is of publishable standard and so there should be no reduction in fee just because the writer is not yet fully established in a career.

In the case of a novice the issue of a kill-fee is more complicated. If an established journalist is commissioned to write a piece that is not used, perhaps for reasons of space, the normal practice is for what's known as a kill-fee to be paid. How much this is will depend on the circumstances and whatever was negotiated at the time of commissioning, but half of the agreed fee would be normal, assuming the writer had some chance of selling the material elsewhere. If the piece is unlikely to be usable elsewhere perhaps because of timing or because the writer has an exclusive contract with one publication, then it is reasonable for the kill-fee to represent the full fee, as the work put in by the writer is the same whether or not the publisher uses it. A grey area here might be if the copy was simply not good enough to be published – in these circumstances an editor might feel justified in refusing to pay.

Kill-fees are not, however, paid when a piece has not been commissioned by an editor, who has merely agreed to look at copy to see whether it might be publishable. This does not count as a commission. If beginners whose copy turns out not to be usable can nevertheless get some comments on their work from the commissioning editor, then they will have gained something from the experience. Most editors have no time to give this kind of help and may not even have the courtesy to let writers know what has happened to their copy, let alone advise about how to improve it. Fair enough in a way. That's not what they're paid to do.

THE COMMISSIONING EDITOR

What a commissioning editor is paid to do is to seek out lively copy from interesting writers. Many features editors say that one of the most difficult parts of their job is maintaining a steady flow of exciting ideas with which to fill their pages. The puzzle is then why so many of them are not more receptive to ideas when freelances pitch them. Not only are many of them unreceptive, some are actively hostile, some are even rude and discourteous. Even well-established freelances, not just the unknown newcomers, find this curious. From an editor's point of view the problem may be that they are sent more unsolicited, unprofessional stories written speculatively than anyone could possibly be expected to deal with politely. In her published account of her first year as editor of *The Lady*, Rachel Johnson invites readers to share the contents of her inbox, allowing them to see the kind of uninspiring articles amateur or semi-professional writers send in. She bins almost every unsolicited feature and all of the short stories (Johnson 2011: 191–193). However, when ideas are professionally written and presented, even by newcomers, the writer should be treated with the basic courtesy of a reply, however brief. What so many freelances experience, until they are well known and valued by a particular features editor, is no reply at all, then curtness or evasion when they try to elicit a response.

What this reflects is the curiously unprofessional way in which many publishers behave in relation to freelances. They expect publishable standards of work, but many of their transactions with freelances are undertaken without written contracts in advance and with little guarantee of anything for the journalists. There may be understandable historical reasons for this, but the effect is that freelances other than those at the top suffer greatly from the insecurity of not knowing whether or how their work will be used. In many cases there is a sense that the journalist is lucky to have her work published, that it is somehow an honour rather than a business transaction for the copy to be included in a magazine. This may be true for the student journalist placing her first or second piece, but after that the feeling of gratitude should pass. Publishers say that they run businesses not charitable foundations, and so it is not unreasonable for journalists to expect to be treated as valued producers of the product which publishers make their money by selling.

There are some signs of change, however. Recent debates about copyright have brought the subject of contracts to the fore. The NUJ now encourages its members to get written contracts before they undertake a freelance commission and even provides a model confirmation of commission form for its members.

PERSONAL SAFETY AND INSURANCE

Related issues about professional practice are those of safety and insurance. Here, too, it used to be common for both employers of freelances and the freelances themselves to have an almost amateurish approach to personal safety while working on a story and to the insurance implications if anything should go wrong. It goes without saying that journalists may have accidents or be attacked while working, whether or not they are covering wars or riots. Even those who set out to cover wars have been known to think they are adequately covered by travel insurance (if they have thought of insurance at all!). They are not. Employers are legally required to have rigorous health and safety policies that include appropriate insurance, as well as training in risk avoidance and in first aid. But these requirements don't always cover freelances, who are in any case likely to be more vulnerable as they won't necessarily have the back-up of an office team knowing where they are meant to be and when. Journalists are beginning to take these issues more seriously, although the macho image of the newshound has perhaps hindered progress. Advice is available from the NUJ, whose London freelance branch website is particularly helpful, the Brussels-based International Federation of Journalists, and the International News Safety Institute.

MAKING A LIVING

At the top level, freelances can be extremely well treated. Some command high fees and for the London-based national magazines and newspaper supplements there can be lucrative contracts. Journalists who are in a position to command a fair deal from a good editor don't really have a lot to worry about. Except, that is, for the worry of falling out of fashion. Life on a magazine or a newspaper can be very like life in a traditional royal court. Rulers come and go, and along with them come and go their favourites. The features freelance or fashion stylist who is favoured by one editor may fall from grace and find a regular contract coming swiftly to an end when that editor moves on. It follows that a freelance should ideally build up a number of regular commissioning contacts so that if one editor leaves, the writer is not left without work.

Even when a piece has been used and there is a written or verbal agreement about how much is to be paid, writers can find it difficult to get at the money. This delaying of payment is perhaps less unusual as a business practice than the lack of contracts, but for the freelance who is trying to survive on modest fees it can make life intolerable to have to waste time chasing up uncontentious payments. There never seems to be a good reason. When freelances phone up to chase their fee, the editorial department always blames accounts and, guess what, the accounts department always blames editorial. The loser is always the writer. Why should it take three months for an agreed fee of £150 to be sent to a writer by a highly profitable publishing company?

The other point about income is that unless writers enter the showbiz league, they are not likely to be paid well. Certainly over a period of 15 years or so the fees that can be expected hardly seem to have risen at all at the lower end of the range. The best way to find out what it is reasonable to expect for a particular commission is through the NUJ's freelance branch website. There's a guide to the various rates that can be expected from the various publishers, as well as examples sent in by members of actual fees recently paid. Examples at the time of going to press are: in the UK between £250 and £700 per 1,000 words, depending on the size and circulation of the magazine. Of course, such figures don't take account of the starry names in the profession who are likely to be able to name their own price.

Another thing to take seriously at the commissioning stage is the increasingly vexed issue of copyright. If you sell your work, what rights are you prepared to release? How many uses does the commissioning publication buy from you? Does it have the right to sell your work on to other media such as the internet? If it does, will you have any say in how it is used even if you are not paid more than once? As a freelance your aim should be to regard what you're selling as a licence for a particular use and to aim to hold on to control over material you have produced. Writers are, however, under ever-increasing pressure to sign away all rights. This is a complex issue and advice should be sought from the NUJ or other professional organisation before signing contracts.

None of this is meant to discourage young journalists from being freelance, merely to prepare them for some of the realities of this existence. The fact that pay is not high on individual publications makes it the more important for journalists to ensure that they use the fruits of one piece of research as widely as possible, targeted at different readers. Assume, for a moment, that you sell an article to a trade magazine about the fishing industry. In the course of your research you get to know quite a bit about the life of a fisherman and discover (hypothetically of course) that (1) they earn huge sums and (2) they spend a lot on cars. Scope here for a straight news feature on the money angle, a motoring feature perhaps on the type of cars they like to buy, a woman's magazine article if you discovered that women are now going to sea along with their menfolk. The possibilities are, in fact, endless, and are discussed further in Chapter 8.

FREELANCING ON THE SIDE

So far it may sound as if working freelance is a choice willingly made by journalists, but that's not always the case. For many journalists in staff jobs freelance work is their bit on the side, the bit which makes the difference between a living wage and an unrealistic one if they happen to work on weekly provincial newspapers. A problem can arise if the day job demands total commitment. Some papers, for example, forbid their reporters to work for anyone else even when the work they want to do overlaps in no way with their full-time job.

Other employers accept that their employees will work freelance elsewhere in their own time if there is no conflict of interest with what they are already contracted to do. Indeed, for many journalists this is the established route to promotion or at least better pay. Working casual shifts or taking on freelance commissions in order to get a foot in the door of another editorial office is a normal strategy in a career where jobs are rarely advertised and usually filled by those whose work is already known to the editor.

Shifts are important. If a writer or subeditor does the kind of work that is measured in shifts, then so long as they turn up for their shifts, most of what they do as casuals for other employers outside couldn't reasonably be seen as detrimental to their main job. There is a problem, however, with the kind of job where an employee is hired to be more than a presence performing a particular task. A valued fashion staffer, for example, brings contacts, experience and creativity to the magazine, which it would not be acceptable for her to share with a rival while she remains on the staff.

What sometimes happens, though, is that even such staffers can take on freelance work which is not necessarily related to journalism or not to the same kind of journalism. The magazine sent to customers of the Standard Life insurance company contains articles by several well-known newspaper financial journalists whose home papers would not want to see them writing for other newspapers, but presumably don't object to seeing them write for a customer magazine. (Other publishers would, of course, object to this and it certainly raises eyebrows among discerning readers who like to think that reporters are not beholden to outside commercial interests.) Some writers may work for other media with the blessing of their main employer. The magazine financial journalist who is invited to participate in radio or television discussions, for example, is regarded as drawing welcome attention to his publication by virtue of the expertise he is being asked to share. Or to take an example in the other direction, Maggie O'Kane, *The Guardian*'s highly acclaimed news reporter, wrote a piece for *Red* about what it was like to leave her young baby for the first time when she went back to work to cover the war in Afghanistan. The other variation on this theme is for writers to take on freelance commissions from completely different sorts of organisations: writing speeches for politicians perhaps, or copy for publicity material or books. Many specialist music critics, for example, supplement their newspaper and magazine work by writing CD liner and concert programme notes.

FREELANCE BY NECESSITY

Those freelances working to supplement their income could be said to be willing. Less willing are the journalists who are freelance out of necessity because they don't have a regular full-time job. These may be recent graduates who are searching for a post and who are well advised to think of themselves (and set themselves up) as freelances from the minute they leave college until they find a job. Some of them will discover that they can survive successfully and stop the hunt for a job. Some just use the cuttings they acquire as freelances to help them into that first job. But there are also those who lose their jobs at the midpoint or later in their careers and have to set up as freelances because journalism is what they know how to do best. Often this proves to be a way of bridging the time before a new job is found, but again, as with the college-leavers, there are those who find they enjoy the freelance life and can earn enough to live on. These latter freelances have all the advantages when it comes to attracting good commissions because they have the contacts, the experience, the cuttings and the inside knowledge of how magazines work to be able to approach editors with confidence.

CASUAL SUBBING

So far I've talked about freelancing as if it were just writers who do it, but in fact most of the editorial functions, except the most senior – those that set the tone of the magazine – can be performed by freelances. Writers are usually commissioned on the basis of individual articles, or series of articles or columns, whereas subs will be hired by the day. Indeed, they have to be. Unlike writers, subs are needed in the office at specified times and so if one of the staffers is ill or on holiday it is likely that a freelance will be brought in, perhaps at short notice. Most chief subs will have a list of regular casual subs on whom they can call during busy periods and most, too, will be willing to try out new ones in order to keep their list up to date. This can be a good way to break into subbing or into a particular magazine, although it's not necessarily a sure route to a writing job. Many magazine editors, while entrusting subs with the most precious of copy to edit, will nevertheless ignore the possibility that their subs could write material of equivalent standard themselves. Ultimately, whether freelance subbing can lead to commissions for writing depends on the publication and the writer. That's not a problem for subeditors who like subbing and don't indulge in daydreams about the glory of being a writer.

PAYING TAX

One problem for casual subs is the way they get paid. They are hired by time rather than by piece of work and this very roughly means that the Inland Revenue likes to see tax deducted by the employer, even where the sub is working for a range of different employers and is, therefore, genuinely freelance, not someone masquerading as freelance in order to benefit from more generous tax allowances. In practice this is a problem only if a sub doesn't realise it in advance and expects to be paid in full, saving up for a schedule D, self-employed tax bill to be paid at the end of the year.

Tax is a vexing topic for all freelance journalists because it is so easy to forget how much money is likely to be needed to pay that tax bill when it arrives. The temptation is there, too, to delve into whatever funds have been put aside for the taxman to tide the journalist over a bad couple of months. The advice most experienced freelances offer is to get an accountant as soon as is practical, which means as soon as you earn enough, from all sources, to interest the tax man – £8,105 for 2012–2013. Accountants can advise about the demands the Inland Revenue is likely to make and about whether it's necessary to register for VAT. They will advise about national insurance and how to prepare for retirement or sickness, parenthood or holidays. If you're self-employed you don't have the comfort of an employer in whose interest it is, or at least whose duty it is, to look after you.

Another advantage of using an accountant is that if you have a phobia about brown envelopes filled with instructions about tax, you don't even have to open them. You can just send them on to your accountant and wait for the information to reach you in a more palatable, more constructive tone. Accountants know what it is acceptable to claim in the way of allowances. They know, for example, that you may set against tax a drink bought for a commissioning editor from abroad but not one from the UK. They may even be able to explain the logic of this. They know also that certain expenses can count as legitimate business expenditure – a computer, perhaps, or a proportion of the phone contract. And they are used to filling in all those forms so they do it without getting into an emotional state (helped, of course, by the fact that it's not their own money they are signing away). Lastly, what many people don't know until they hire their first accountant is that the fee for the accountant can be set against tax, making the arrangement an even better investment.

ORGANISING YOUR WORK

For young journalists this talk of accountants may seem premature, but if they are going to attempt to live by freelance work then this is a serious professional consideration. Some students approach freelance work in a dilettante fashion, thinking they will just do a bit of work here and there and see how it goes. Those are the ones who give up soonest and resort to staff jobs if they can. The successful beginner journalists who make it as freelances tend to be those who are deadly serious in their intentions. From day one they are at their desks at 9 a.m., pitching ideas, writing, building contacts and so on, generally behaving like any other person who is determined to succeed in a self-employed enterprise. They buy the best equipment they can afford and once the work starts to come in they are methodical in their office habits. Records of correspondence, invoices, expenditure, ideas and cuttings should all be kept tidily and backed up so that the process of chasing up payments can be as painless as possible. And like any other journalist they should file all the versions of their stories and their notes, whether recorded or written, so that legal problems can be sorted out swiftly.

However well intentioned new freelances are, things can go wrong. To begin with, most feel that the problem is going to be finding enough work, not having too much to do. They accept everything that comes their way, knowing that reluctance on their part is unlikely to be rewarded with a second offer. This means, of course, that far from avoiding the unattractive jobs, they may have to take them on, these being the ones that may be offered to freelances because no one on the staff wants to do them. It is difficult to get the balance right, especially at first. As the work pours in a freelance can find herself taking on far more than is reasonable because she is aware that next month there may be nothing at all on offer. Forward planning is difficult and the stress level can be high, especially for those who find they are not brave enough to take a break either at weekends or even for a holiday.

Another difficulty with the freelance life is that if you work on features which require a lot of research, the amount of time spent is most unlikely to be reflected in the fee you earn. Two hundred pounds may be okay for an opinion piece that you hammer out in a couple of hours once a week, but reporting is more demanding than that. It takes hours of trouble – tracking down interviewees for example, visits to get eyewitness evidence, research and so on. All of this takes time. Staffers will say that they don't get enough time allocated to do proper research either, and it is true that productivity rates – if measured by output of words – have risen in the past two decades to the detriment, many would argue, of serious investigative reporting or even competent thorough reporting, both of which suffer when reporters are rushed too much. So staffers have a point, but how much more keenly are these pressures felt by freelances who are merely selling a finished product, with little account taken of the amount of time their product will take to create.

There is another myth about freelancing – that freelancing particularly suits women who want to combine a career with bringing up a family. The problems with this proposition start before the first child is born. No maternity leave for the freelance. Then there is the uncertainty of income. Fine to be freelance if you are attached to someone who earns a regular sum. More difficult if both parents are freelance and not at an advanced stage in their careers. This is where temperament comes in. More clearly a problem for all is the notion that a freelance writer can just potter about doing bits of journalism between bathing the baby, cooking meals and supervising homework. Some miracle-workers can and it depends a bit on what kind of freelance work you are trying to fit in. The reality for most working parents is that a full-time job, or at least a part-time staff job, is more practical because if there is a regular income then arrangements about childcare are easier to make. Childcare is expensive and it usually has to be regular (childminders, nannies and nurseries all have their financial commitments too and want a regular, not a sporadic income). Clearly this is a point that won't affect all journalists, but young women journalists are so often told they will be able to do a bit of freelance work when they have children that it is worth noting the difficulties.

PITCHING IDEAS

I turn now to some of the practicalities of doing the work itself. For the sake of the discussion here we'll assume that a new freelance is used to producing work of a professional standard as it's a bad idea to offer work before you are ready to sell it on equal terms with established journalists. The main exception to this would be where you have some inside knowledge – about what really goes on in student union bars would be one example, or about trout-fishing, if that's your obsession. Another possible exception would be if a journalist had seen some of your work and suggested you submit it on the off-chance that it might be acceptable.

Assuming the work is good enough, your first task is to come up with suitable ideas that you can pitch. 'Suitable' applies in various ways. The proposal must be one that you could reasonably tackle with your experience and contacts and, unless you are already well known to the editor, one that is not going to cost the magazine a fortune in expenses. Yes, it might be interesting to talk to Cubans about the cigar trade in the light of the Clinton sex scandal, but few features editors would have the budget to send anyone, let alone an untried freelance, to Cuba to have the conversations. So the ideas must be suitable for you, but they must also be suitable for the magazine for which you are aiming to write. As Chapter 16 shows, one of the most significant things about magazines is the way many of them are so tightly targeted at groups of readers. They have their niches, and the successful freelance knows how to write copy that is appropriate for them. The ability to pitch ideas successfully is increasingly important for all journalists, as staffers will be required to pitch to features editors in much the same way as freelances, so it's vital that all journalists develop this skill.

Choosing your subject

This brings us to subject matter. If a freelance has an unusual hobby or interest she should capitalise on it by trying to write about it for the relevant magazines. Many publications depend on freelances to contribute copy, some on a regular basis. This is not a bad way for a journalist to start selling freelance work. Even if you don't want to spend your whole career writing about horses, the fact that there are several magazines devoted to the leisure riding market means that all those years you spent hanging around the local riding school could be put to profitable use at the start of your career. The more unusual your interests the more use this approach is likely to be. Football and pop music, by contrast, are much less help because so many journalists want to write about these subjects. Some will get to do it, but the competition is fiercer than it would be for, say, the writer with a first-class degree in biochemistry who wanted to sell stories about health issues. If, for whatever reason, you have good access to a celebrity then you should make the most of the fact when you are pitching ideas.

What the freelance writer must do, then, is study the publications she wants to write for, whether or not they reflect any particular interest of her own. It's not a bad idea to start with a magazine that you especially enjoy reading because then, as a typical reader, you can develop ideas based on what it is you yourself would like to read. This may be impractical if your favourite reading is *The New Yorker* or *Vanity Fair*, but if you have wide reading habits (and you should have) then there ought to be some publications you see regularly for which you feel you could write well enough to chance a proposal.

Presenting your idea

The question of coming up with ideas and developing them is covered in the next chapter. For now we'll assume you have worked up some good, relevant ideas and want to know what to do with them. The first question is how to make contact with a commissioning editor. These days email is the norm and it is vital that the pitch is made as efficiently as possible.

There are some basic rules for when you send in an idea. Make sure that the presentation and writing are immaculate. You could get away with the odd typographical error if the editor knew your work well enough to realise this represented an unusual slip rather than a slapdash approach to all your work, but if you are unknown then any evidence of inattention to detail will count against you. A common fault among freelances, especially new ones, is to treat the outline of ideas much more casually than they would any writing they do for publication. This is a mistake as the email is a sample of your work and will be treated as such by whoever reads it. A writer who is new to the publication should include a short covering paragraph to explain who they are, why they'd like to write for the magazine and what relevant experience they have. If you have a blog or website then links should be clear in the email.

A second common mistake is to write too much. A good features idea should be capable of summary in one paragraph. If an idea is to look professional it ought to say why the writer thinks it is suitable for the target market and make clear what the angle is. It's not enough to say 'I'd like to write an article about sunbathing'. That's a topic not an idea for a feature. Better to find an angle: 'In the decade or so since doctors began to link sunbathing with skin cancer cases of the disease have risen dramatically. Why is this and are there many people who have stopped sunbathing as a result of the warnings?' That's more like an idea that could be developed into a feature. The initial idea should be kept short and simple and should include some information about how the piece would be researched, who you would interview, what other sources you would use. It should also show that you have some ideas about how the piece could be illustrated, such as what could make a good photograph or where relevant library pictures are held. Your picture ideas will show that you are thinking about journalism as a professional writer should. Many features editors advise sending in two or three ideas at once, if each one is kept brief. This can give an editor an indication of the range of your ideas, which might work in your favour: even if the current ideas are not wanted it may be obvious from the spread of proposals that you are thinking along the right lines for the editor's publication and she may be inclined to look favourably at your other suggestions.

Beginner journalists are often worried about having their ideas stolen by commissioning editors to whom they offer stories. This certainly does happen and not just to novices, although sometimes there is a genuine misunderstanding: an idea may have already been commissioned from someone else, which an outside freelance would not know. Given that journalists are trained to recognise stories and develop them in particular ways, it is not at all surprising that more than one of them will produce the same idea for the same publication at around the same time. However, there is no copyright on ideas and so a features editor who is slightly less than scrupulous, faced with a great outline idea from an unknown freelance, just might turn it down and quietly ask a more experienced writer to tackle it. There is no obvious way to stop this happening, although it is worth making clear to the editor that you've noticed and if it happens more than once to look elsewhere to sell your work. The most encouraging point to be made when this happens is that if your proposals are being lifted by commissioning editors, it does at least mean your ideas are right for that publication. A slightly jokey email to that effect might produce a commission. Some editors are prepared to pay for an idea even if they then ask their own writers to develop it.

What you have to do next is wait, although probably not for too long, certainly no more than a week. If your email has reached the features editor's inbox it has either been rejected or is waiting for a decision. That decision may never come if you don't take steps to have it dealt with. You have to tread the delicate line between being a nuisance and being a seasoned professional trying to get a decision. Many young journalists err on the side of timidity, forgetting that commissioning editors are tough and entirely used to people phoning up to complain, whinge, make demands or simply to exercise their egos. You have every right to offer a piece to an editor (unless you've been asked not to submit any more), just as she has every right to refuse it without explanation. But you are a professional, not someone looking for a favour, so if your work is not wanted by the first magazine you'll be keen to try to sell it, perhaps in a modified form, somewhere else.

One dilemma for freelances is whether to have their ideas out for consideration in different editorial offices at the same time. Where there is a tight deadline for the relevance of the piece this may be essential, but it is probably best to be frank with the editors that this is the case. What you don't want is for both to accept and publish the same piece. (A writer might not mind this but editors would and the next commission might be hard for a writer in this position to secure.) With less time-sensitive pieces the advice most features editors give is to send to one publication at a time, which will cut down on the danger of two editors using your work at the same time. If you adopt this approach it gives you a perfect excuse to demand a fairly quick decision, so that you can take an unwanted idea to another editor. In reality things are not that straightforward. An editor may simply not be able to make a decision quickly – the planning meeting for a given issue may be three weeks away – and if that's the case you will just have to weigh up whether it's better to leave it there or offer it elsewhere as well. Once you are established as a freelance it will become clear that there are no fixed rules about any of this, so much depends on the individual editors and on the quality of the relationship freelances establish with them.

THE BRIEFING STAGE

If an idea is accepted in principle and a commission offered, then a briefing discussion should take place either by phone or in person. For the first time with a new publication it is worth trying to arrange a face-to-face meeting so you can get to know the person who is commissioning you. However, editors are busy and writers just have to take what time is offered.

What is vital at this stage is to get a clear brief and to make sure it is understood by both sides. It is worth writing up a note of the discussion and copying it to the editor. It may be that your idea has turned out to be the basis of a feature with a different emphasis to that which the editor wants, but in the excitement of having a piece accepted you think what is wanted is what you proposed. A good commissioning editor will thoroughly talk through the angle, the research, the quotes, the length. A good writer adheres to this and if tempted to change much of it because of what is discovered during the research process will contact the editor to talk over any proposed change of emphasis.

It is also vital to get an agreement about the fee for the piece and to have this established in writing if at all possible. Something else which beginners don't always think to discuss is expenses. These are not handouts based on an editor's generosity, but a reimbursement of what you have to spend in order to write the piece. Examples would be transport costs to the homes of interviewees, drinks for the main contact and so on. An editor must be given the chance to agree to this in advance; to save aggravation at a later stage it is worth having an upper limit written into the contract or letter of agreement.

Other points to get straight at the commissioning stage are the desired length of the piece, whether sidebars or boxes are needed, the deadline and how the copy is to be supplied. The writer must stick to the length where possible or else discuss any changes in advance. Partly this is what is expected of a professional journalist and partly this is to protect your own copy. If you submit far too much then someone will almost certainly have to cut it and they may not have enough time or attention to do it justice. A journalist knows that the deadline is sacrosanct. If there is an unarguable reason for seeking to extend it (the prime source of information has at last agreed to talk but only on the day after the piece is due), then contact the commissioning editor. Monthly magazines are more likely to be able to allow a little leeway, depending on which section the piece is commissioned for. On weeklies it may simply depend on which issue the story is intended for.

SENDING IN COPY

In the old days of hard copy, it would have been on paper, obeying all the basic rules of presentation in hard copy – double spacing, one side of the paper only, paragraphs not to run over from one folio to another, generous margins, catchlines on each folio, 'more' or 'ends' at the end of a folio. These rules still apply where offices require hard copy or for journalists who have no alternative means of supplying their work. In the past, too, there was the option of telephoning copy and reading it out to a copytaker who typed it up there and then. Otherwise email is now the norm. It is essential to make clear on the document how you can be contacted during the editing period and if the story is such that the editor will want to contact someone mentioned in it – to arrange photos perhaps – then contact details for that person must be supplied too.

ACCEPTANCE

Once a story has been accepted by a magazine or a website the writer more or less loses control over it unless she is a star name. There may be an email from the office to check facts or ask for supplementary information, but it is not common for the writer to be involved in the process of preparation for press or to look at either text proofs (galleys as they used to be called) or page proofs. In some ways this is a pity, especially where complicated photo captions are required, because subs can make mistakes which the writer would pick up instantly. If you know a story is complex in this way and you have the time you might offer to go into the office and check, but don't be surprised if the offer is turned down.

One of the most disappointing things that can happen to a new freelance is to have their copy used but without a byline. More distressing still is to have their work used but see someone else's name at the top of it. This happens more in newspapers than in magazines. The lesser crime of omitting any byline may occur because the story is short or not of much importance – the same treatment would be given to copy from a staff journalist. Sometimes, though, the name is just left off because the writer is not on the staff. There is no acceptable explanation for putting someone else's byline other than a genuine mistake. If it happens you could write to the editor of the publication and make a complaint. Whether a freelance can afford to risk offending the commissioning editor in this way is a matter for individual judgement, but it wouldn't do any harm for freelances to be more vociferous when they are badly treated whether over pay, contracts or treatment of their copy.

UNSOLICITED COPY

Behind much of this chapter is the assumption that a writer is not going to submit unsolicited, completed articles. Editors do, just occasionally, read these, but mostly they don't. Unless a magazine makes it clear on the editorial pages that it welcomes uncommissioned contributions the best advice is not to waste your time by sending them. About the only exception that might be worth a try would be to write sample material if, say, you were trying to interest a publication in taking a regular column from you. Here you would not be expecting what you send in to be used, but would be aiming to give the editor a flavour of what you might be able to write on your chosen topic in a given month or week.

CONCLUSIONS

The freelance life is not for everyone, but it can be a rewarding way to pursue a career in journalism. It can be a stressful existence, but it can also enable a successful freelance to have more control over the kind of work undertaken than staffers usually have. In addition, there are probably a majority of journalists for whom freelance work forms part of their whole career, either at particular times or throughout as a means of varying the work they do on a daily basis or merely as a means to earn more money or write about different subjects. However, for anyone who likes freelancing either as a career or as a supplement to a career, the future is currently very uncertain. Publishers continue to pare down full-time staffs to the minimum, which ought to mean they are using more freelance contributions, but the fact is that budgets for freelance contributions are also being slashed, partly because advertising revenue is stretched ever more thinly between publications. This means writers have to be flexible and creative about how and for whom they produce their work. The word entrepreneurial is often used nowadays in relation to young journalists who are encouraged to think in terms of setting up their own publishing operations using blogs and websites to develop their businesses and writing profiles. At the very least this gives them the chance to develop contacts, to practise their journalism skills and to establish a journalistic profile.

RECOMMENDED READING

Dunn, S. (2008) 'Would you be better off hiring an accountant?' *Guardian*.
Leverton, M. (2010) *How to Work as a Freelance Journalist*.
Quinn, C. (2010) *No Contacts? No Problem! How to Pitch and Sell Your Freelance Feature Writing*.
Rudin, R. and Ibbotson, T. (2002) *An Introduction to Journalism*.
The Writers' and Artists' Yearbook, 2013 (July 2012).

Websites

The Guardian freelance charter: www.guardian.co.uk/info/guardian-news-media-freelance-charter
International Federation of Journalists: www.ifj.org
International News Safety Institute: (INSI) www.newssafety.org
London freelance branch, fees information: www.londonfreelance.org/feesguide
National Union of Journalists: www.nuj.org.uk
Reporters Without Borders (Reporters Sans Frontières): http://en.rsf.org

CHAPTER 5

Ideas and information

Ideas and information are the raw materials of a journalist's craft, which involves coming up with ideas on a punishingly regular basis. Much of the rest of the job is about seeking out information so that it can be marshalled into shape for the use, or the entertainment, of the reader. Here I will look at these two processes before a brief discussion of commissioning. This is relevant in this chapter because it affects and is affected by what happens to the ideas and information: it is relevant in this book because a magazine journalist is more likely to be given some responsibility for commissioning early in a career than would be the case in newspapers.

Once again the immediate difficulty is how to say anything general about such a diverse product as magazines. How can you compare the creative and research skills needed by a writer for *Heat* with those required by an investigative reporter on *Private Eye*? You can't as far as the actual ideas or the specific information are concerned. But if you think in terms of processes, rather than of end-products, then there are certain things in common. It's a question of emphasis: some tasks, a beauty photoshoot is one, require more in the way of ideas and less in the way of information research and manipulation or curation; other tasks, such as an analysis of the impact of the Eurozone crisis on high-street shoppers in the UK, clearly depend on extensive research and understanding of data and information of various sorts. (For a fuller introduction to reporters' research skills, see 'Researching the Story' in Frost 2010.)

For many people the range of sources of information has proliferated so wildly in recent years that they depend on journalists to guide them through the maze of nets, webs, books, advertising, broadcast media and so on. Some have argued that the accessibility of information might mean there is no longer a role for journalists. I argue the opposite. The more information we all have access to, in whatever medium, including the web, the more there is for journalists to do in the way of making sense of it all. As Nick Davies argues: 'Bloggers and citizen journalists do uncover untold stories . . . But, against that, the Internet is also functioning as a kind of information madhouse, frantically repeating whatever fragments of "news" happen to make it into the blogosphere, much of it nonsense' (Davies 2008: 395). Many readers, for many purposes, need information filtered by a journalist or by a publication they can trust. They simply haven't time to research at first hand everything they might want to know about and there is plenty of evidence that readers trust magazines (Consterdine 1997, 2002). In this respect a magazine is a brand that is able to develop loyalty in its readers (and in almost all cases has now been extended to include a related website, Facebook page, Twitter feed, etc.). Journalists can also give readers ideas about what they might want to know about, whether it's a new product for salmon farmers or guidance about car maintenance. The world is a complicated, information-filled space and part of the job of journalists is to act as navigators through this space – an important job given that many sources of information have their own perspectives which they are seeking to impose on others. This is partly what the processes of producing ideas and researching information are about. When writers choose to pitch one idea rather than another, or editors choose to commission one feature rather than another, they are already selecting which information their readers will have access to. Even where the subject matter is the frothiest of entertainment the same holds true, although it may matter less in absolute terms.

What follows will not be relevant to every journalist on every magazine, but it aims to provide guidance that could be of use to any student or new journalist who is not committed to a lifetime on one publication.

WHERE DO IDEAS COME FROM?

There is a proportion of news that, in a way, declares itself: a city-centre bomb, for example, the publication of a report about the poor health of schoolchildren, the death of a celebrity. As Chapter 8 shows, features are less tied to time and to the daily news agenda, so there is more flexibility regarding their subject matter and the way it is treated. This means there is more pressure on feature writers and editors to produce ideas. Using their imagination in this way is something many journalists love. For others it is a challenge. They'd rather be given a story lead and then get on with finding out what they need to know in order to write it. Journalism needs both sorts of people. It is important, though, to realise that the creative part of news and feature writing doesn't stop when an idea for a story has been agreed. The success with which a writer tackles her research can be equally dependent on the freshness of her ideas: thinking up a new angle, finding new people to talk to, or asking them questions they have not been asked before.

All of this is just as creative a process as thinking up ideas in the first place. As Andrew Marr, broadcaster and former political editor of the BBC, argues: 'Journalism needs the unexpected. It needs the unpredictability and oddness of real life.' For these to surface in newspapers and magazines it is necessary for reporters to be 'inquisitive, energetic and honest' and for them to have time to do the legwork out of the office, in the world they hope to report. He laments the blandness of so many publications where journalists are deskbound and 'vulnerable to the PR machines' (Marr 2004: 384–385). This last point was demonstrated forcibly by Nick Davies in his book *Flat Earth News*, in which he argues that journalists are more than merely vulnerable to the machinations of PR workers; rather, they are increasingly dominated by them to produce the raw material and prompts for their stories (Davies 2008: chs 2–6).

In an ideal world, for strong news and features the most important things a journalist needs in order to produce a continuous flow of usable story ideas are these: insatiable curiosity, an excellent memory, good general knowledge, strong powers of observation and meticulously maintained filing systems and contacts books. Story ideas are not floating chimeras that occasionally materialise in the brain of a lucky hack. Ideas for stories can be thought up by the dozen in minutes by any experienced journalist worth the name. They wouldn't all be equally marketable, but the point is that the generation of ideas is not as mysterious or as difficult as beginners often think. So where to start?

The diary

Many editorial offices start with the diary. In a newsroom the diary, whether on paper or screen, is the focus around which reporters are organised by their news managers. Into it go all the regular meetings and events, as well as the press conferences, visits by politicians or celebrities, anniversaries and so on. The diary should contain a note of every news event of interest to that publication that can be predicted. On magazines of whatever kind there is likely to be an equivalent – news-based for *The Economist*, recording the international dress shows for a fashion magazine such as *Elle*, tied to the relevant sporting fixtures for a sports magazine such as *F1Racing*, noting the wedding dates or birthdays of celebrities in *Hello!*. Freelances create their own diaries so that they can keep track of developments in the fields they write about.

Diaries can also be used to look backwards. Journalists like to have a 'peg' on which to hang stories. In the case of stories not tied to the hard-news agenda this can be expressed another way as 'an excuse to run the piece'. This is not meant as a criticism. My own impression, though, is that journalists are far more attached to the idea that a feature needs a peg than readers, who will happily read a story with no peg at all if it's good. By looking backwards I mean the use of anniversaries of events as reasons to run features that perhaps assess the long-term effects on a community of a tragic accident such as the Paddington rail crash; consider the mood of the nation one year after the death of Diana, Princess of Wales; a music magazine might write about the status of Purcell in the tercentenary of his death. Instantly, a long list could be produced, the key ingredients being the date and the questions a reporter might ask about the significance of that date. Many editorial offices pay companies to produce lists of dates that are of interest in this way, and there are other services to help editors compile their diaries. Arts editors make use of FENS, an online forward-planning database or the directory London at Large, which has notes about which celebrities are travelling through the city. A useful agency is Celebrity Search. As a last resort journalists can trawl through the archive of their own publications to find less well-known stories to update or even to run regular columns of material based around what happened 50 years ago, for example.

When looking for ideas it is vital to keep in mind who the readers are and what they are interested in – know your market, in other words, and know how the magazine is to be branded or sold to that market. What image is it trying to create? Editors and senior staff often have firm convictions (perhaps unjustifiably firm in some cases) about what is right for their publications.

Other people

Moving on from the diary, don't ignore your most easily accessible resource. Ideas can arise from everywhere and everyone – any conversation you have or overhear might give you an idea for a question that needs asking or a trend that can be spotted. We all have differing concerns, experiences and approaches to the world: for a good journalist this means that there is an infinity of informal resources in addition to all the formal ones.

Contacts

Another important source of ideas for journalists is the contacts book, whether in paper or digital form. At its simplest this is a record of names and extensive contact details. Because journalists can't predict what stories they might work on or even which publication they might eventually join, a worthwhile contacts book is likely to be comprehensive. A reporter on a local weekly might think she'll never need to interview a butcher again after covering the launch of a brand of sausages. But 18 months later, in her new job on *Meat Trades Journal*, she could find it useful that there is a friendly butcher who knows and trusts her as she researches stories about the possible causes of *E. coli* or BSE.

For most journalists their contacts book is their most valuable possession. They don't want to share its contents with anyone, nor can they afford to lose it. Computers can be replaced, so can mobile phones, but a contacts book is a personal creation that can't be quickly or easily reproduced. A well-organised journalist must keep a duplicate and this is much easier to do if the information is held electronically – in a personal digital assistant (PDA), for example. An actual book, such as a loose-leaf personal organiser, is in some ways more reliable, as will agree anyone whose electronic equivalent has crashed and taken with it all the data it contained. A book can be carried about and used in awkward places where a computer would be intrusive. Nor does it have to be woken up when all you want is to check a phone number. The loose-leaf format is essential though, as sooner or later the pages will fill up and need to be replaced.

The reason a contacts book is so precious to a journalist is because so much journalism is written on the basis of quotations (see Chapter 9). Reporters use their contacts to get quotes, to get background information and to get stories. This might be when a contact rings up and alerts a journalist to something that is going on. But it might also be that a journalist, looking for ideas, will use social media to follow contacts, or even phone them and ask what is happening in their field of expertise, or what the general concerns are at the moment among their colleagues. It's a good idea for journalists to keep in touch with contacts regularly anyway and to use any opportunity to trawl for ideas.

Other journalists and media

It should be apparent that there is no magical art to this. A great deal more help, however, is available so long as the writer has the approach I've just outlined. Still without leaving the editorial office, a writer is likely to refer to the work of other journalists in the pursuit of story ideas. There may be something in his own publication that could be followed up or approached from a different angle. Other comparable magazines have to be scrutinised anyway, to check they are not providing their readers with a better service, so it makes sense to apply the same curiosity to their stories in case a new angle could be used with the same material. Apart from that, any other publications or indeed the broadcast media can be sources of ideas. All journalism feeds off other journalism and so the business-to-business (B2B) press, for example, will be combed by the newspapers and consumer magazines; local newspapers will be scanned by regionals; regionals by dailies; and websites, Facebook and Twitter by all other media.

There is an inherent danger in this approach, however, which must not be overlooked. It's easy to slip into whatever bad habits or errors other journalists or publications have demonstrated when they researched and wrote their stories.

Even so, ideas are picked up from specialist publications by less specialist ones and so on: for example, a story about hip-hop might surface in *The Source*, be taken up by *NME*, and then by the national press or by general magazines. Indeed, periodicals about style and the arts are regularly devoured by arts journalists on newspapers looking for story leads (Dawson Scott 1997). Academic and medical journals such as *The Lancet* are routinely studied by journalists looking for stories they can translate into terms their readers will understand.

Equally, newspapers will be read by magazine journalists who may spot stories that could be developed and adapted to suit their readers' interests. An announcement about mortgage rates, for example, could be developed for the estate agents' or builders' trade magazines to show exactly what effect it might have on their businesses, while *Homes and Gardens* could research the effects on behalf of ordinary home owners. A good example of this in action was the story by Lorna Gray in *Cosmopolitan*'s December 2011 edition about the increasing number of young women being admitted to hospital with hypothermia as a result of being out in the cold at night wearing very skimpy dresses and no coats. She noticed a small nib (news in brief) in a weekly paper about a girl who had died from hypothermia and discovered that alcohol can mask the symptoms by making the sufferer feel too hot. She asked around and found young women to talk to who had suffered in this way themselves or knew people who had. She talked to doctors too, and soon she had plenty of material for a couple of spreads in the magazine.

Your publication

As a useful source of ideas, don't forget the magazine you work for. Back issues can be exploited for stories relating to anniversaries or even just for past–present comparisons. Even in the current editions, however, there are bound to be good starting points for stories. The letters page is one, partly because an individual letter might raise an issue that your magazine ought to be covering or because cumulatively the letters might reveal a general concern among readers that could be explored. If so, you have a ready source of names as initial contacts for your research.

Market research

Market research is a way in which the response of readers can be gauged and suggestions gathered about what readers would like to see. This information may not be quite as specific as a feature idea, but it can give an idea of the kind of topic that is popular. Personally I'm very suspicious of this use of market research and I think journalists should be wary of it too, as it undermines the professional skills for which they are hired in the first place. There is greater use of market research in television than in magazines, but the question remains: which focus group could ever have dreamt up programmes that became as popular as *Monty Python's Flying Circus*, *Dr Who* or *Changing Rooms*? And, as John Morrish says in his guide to editing magazines, 'no survey would ever have given any support for the creation of *Private Eye* or *The Spectator*'. Morrish notes the danger of research becoming 'an expensive distraction' if it doesn't have a clear purpose, and makes the point that research findings 'can act as a mirror to prejudice' as everyone who uses the documents will find within them material to support their own views. There is also a problem with the quality of the information: 'What people say they want is not actually what they buy . . . people do not always tell the truth to researchers' (Morrish 1996: 26–36). He is not the only person to believe that strong editorial ideas come from an imaginative, creative, confident editorial team.

If an editor doesn't have this she would be better to try to build one than to spend all her time studying market research reports. Gill Hudson, then editor of the *Radio Times*, summarised the views of many editorial teams when she said at the PPA's Magazines 2004 conference that 'as a market we are in danger of being market researched to death. Market research belongs in a box marked "to be looked at from time to time".'

Adverts

Another occasionally good source for stories, especially in lifestyle magazines, can be the advertisements, large or small, display or classified. A story may emerge from the advert itself – Benetton has capitalised on its use of controversial photographic images to make sure the press prints stories about how wrong it is to do so. Or there may be information contained in the advert which allows a sharp reporter to identify a story. To make up an example: a writer on *Bicycle Monthly* might notice in the small ads that there is a bike shop for sale in Anytown. He remembers that the UK's greatest ever cyclist lives there, where he owns a bike shop. A couple of phone calls and a visit later the writer has a big feature article with photos about the retirement plans of the famous cyclist. He's planning to cycle alone around the world at the age of 65. It's also the basis of regular features over the coming 18 months as the magazine monitors his progress, maybe even agreeing to sponsor the trip.

From this fictional example you'll see the personal qualities referred to above have come into play. If our *Bicycle Monthly* reporter was not observant or did not have a good memory he might not have thought there was anything worth pursuing in that unobtrusive small ad.

Curiosity

The quality of curiosity speaks for itself. Journalists must be the kind of people who want to know as much as possible about anything and everything. They should always be asking questions; that way they will always have ideas for stories. To go back to the cycle shop example: the question that occurred to the reporter is 'Why would Tony Wheels, the cyclist, be selling up?' The answer (he's retiring to cycle the world) provokes a lot of further questions in the curious mind and out of them grows the story.

Established sources of information

There isn't space in a book of this size to consider reporters' work on serious, hard-news stories, as these are well covered by a range of news-oriented books. As a general principle, journalists should all be asking questions of whatever ideas and information they come across and should be seeking out material wherever they can. To take a simple example: a reporter could make freedom of information requests about almost any topic and find that a worthwhile story emerges, not necessarily because any corruption is uncovered, but simply because the information is new. Heather Brooke's persistence in asking questions revealed the scandal of the kind of claims MPs in the UK Parliament were making in relation to their expenses. She demonstrated that the UK is a remarkably and unacceptably secretive society and until the implementation (in 2005) of the Freedom of Information Act (2000), the public had no right of access to information about publicly funded bodies, even though such information is gathered at public expense (Brooke 2010: ch. 8).

Press officers, of course, try to ensure only the information they wish reaches the public domain, but thanks to the Freedom of Information Act it is now possible for reporters to get access to a huge range of information that would simply have been off-limits in the UK until the Act came into force. The Act allows any member of the public to request access to information held by any public body. In practice, though, there are restrictions, with delay or cost barriers put in the way of those seeking to research a topic, as Brooke shows in *The Silent State*.

Press officers and press releases

Journalists are more than ever bombarded with information by those who want to attract their attention and gain publicity for their cause or their activity (Davies 2008: 157–204). Sometimes this is done openly, sometimes with little regard for the truth in an attempt to manipulate the thinking of the public. No editorial office is properly established until it becomes the target for press officers sending out announcements as hard copy or email about anything from a summary of a cabinet minister's speech to the launch of a new face cream. Journalists seem to divide into those who delete press releases unread and those who merely rewrite them slightly for inclusion in their pages (some don't even rewrite them).

What press officers do is usually less proactive (their word) than what most PR people do, which is to say they are more likely to react to events than to act as agents trying to get free advertising space in editorial pages. Press officers do rather less of contacting the press and trying to sell a client, and rather more of responding to enquiries from the press. These enquiries may be for the clarification of facts, for quotes, for access to the right person in the organisation, for background guidance about lines of thinking, or requests for press releases, for books to review, tickets to concerts and so on. Press officers do take the initiative too, of course. They send out press releases, organise press conferences and photo-opportunities, and collate information and cuttings. They also try to interest the press in stories relating to their organisation, but in general the reporter at the receiving end of a call from a press officer feels less pressured to respond positively. Good press officers who tailor a story to the publication are successful because once journalists realise that the material they send is likely to be of interest they are more inclined to read it.

Most journalists, quite rightly, are sceptical, if not cynical, about both sets of people, because so often what the PR and press officers seem to be doing is preventing journalists from getting at the information they want. The ones who are good at their job are masters of manipulation in all kinds of ways that the average hack, at least at the beginning of a career, would probably never think possible (Michie 1998; Davies 2008). What I want to suggest, though, is that a journalist, when seeking ideas or pursuing research, may take help from wherever it is available so long as he is sure of exactly what he wants and is able to separate his agenda from that of the press officer. There's no point in dismissing all press officers just because some PRs are so indiscriminately pushy as to be complete time-wasters.

Some press releases may contain good ideas for stories, but these will not necessarily be the stories the press officers are pushing. As ever, it's up to the journalist to ask questions of the material. For example, if a police press release glows about a fall in the number of street-crimes committed against pensioners in the past year, our observant reporter might recall that following two murders the previous year most pensioners in the town no longer go out at night. Yes, the crime figure has fallen but this is because of an unacceptable if self-imposed restriction on the liberty of the over-65s, not because the police have persuaded muggers to drink cocoa in front of the TV of an evening instead of going to the pub. In this case, what the press officer could certainly supply is the crime statistics and some police officers to interview or at least some quotes. In addition, the press release would have alerted the reporter to the fact that there is a story to be investigated.

Many press offices are sound sources of facts and figures, and of cuttings or information on websites on relevant topics taken from a range of publications, something that can be hard to pull together otherwise, especially in the heat of researching a story on a deadline. Most press offices will supply photos, video and audio material to accompany stories; some will also let journalists into their libraries or archives. With luck, press officers will be well informed about the work of their organisation and those working in the same field. This is particularly true of well-run non-governmental organisations (NGOs), including some charities. The journalist just has to remember that every organisation or company has its own priorities when producing information. This means that when researching a story, one strategy is always to ask yourself: who will have an alternative slant on this information? Who might have the counter-arguments? Which press office will have the information to back that up? Of course, you would do this in the interest of balance and of finding people to quote, but you can also do it in the early stages of research in order to find basic information. Crime reporters, for example, will nearly always talk to pressure groups like the National Association for the Care and Resettlement of Offenders or the Howard League before assessing Home Office reports, just as environment reporters will get story ideas from Greenpeace and Friends of the Earth (Schlesinger and Tumber 1994). Lobby groups, NGOs and government departments all have information offices and they are worth approaching unless you have discovered one in particular to be unhelpful or short of the kind of information you need.

Public relations

In all of the suggestions so far the writer is the initiator of the idea. In reality that is less and less likely to be the case, as Nick Davies shows in his discussion of lobbyists and press officers:

> So, the picture emerges. Journalists who no longer have the time to go out and find their own stories and to check the material which they are handling, are consistently vulnerable to ingesting and reproducing the packages of information which are provided for them by this PR industry. At the very least, this involves their being directed into accepting stories and angles which have been chosen for them in order to satisfy somebody else's commercial or political interests. At the worst, this embroils them in the dissemination of serious distortion and falsehood.
>
> (Davies, 2008: 203)

The functions of a PR officer and a press officer overlap to some extent and vary from one organisation to another. A PR officer is more likely to take what's known as a 'proactive' role towards the media, which is to say she will be expected to initiate contact with journalists and try to persuade them to give favourable editorial mention to whatever product, line or person she is pushing. She will, of course, be on hand in case of emergency or adverse news about her client or employer seeping out to the press. Often, though, in times of crisis, a company or celebrity will call in a PR consultant who specialises in crisis management. One peculiarity about PR is that in many organisations which otherwise take their public profile seriously, no PR people sit on the board of directors and so are not in a position to advise in advance about the way the media will interpret certain policies. The PR staff are depended upon to deal with problems after the event, but not always to comment on which managerial decisions are likely to cause problems in the first place.

More generally, though, PR officers are the ones with expense accounts for taking journalists out to lunch to sell them ideas. They are also the ones who organise press trips to sun-soaked resorts for the test-driving of cars or launching of new perfumes. To someone who hasn't worked in the media before, the array of inducements which flow in from businesses through PR agencies or in-house PR offices can be bewildering. Is it really necessary for journalists to have lunch on the Orient Express to discover the merits of a new range of fashion watches, for example? A range of sun lotions would surely do their job just as well if beauty editors did not meet it for the first time at a lavish champagne reception. At their most powerful, and useful to their clients, PR officers can manage any aspect of an encounter with the media, whether it is the press in pursuit of a sex scandal or a magazine editor seeking access for an interview, although the more famous celebrities are likely to have agents to look after this kind of bargaining, and these agents have increasing influence over what finally gets into print (see Chapter 10).

The other side of their job is less visible: preventing stories detrimental to their clients getting anywhere near the press in the first place. Max Clifford, a celebrity publicist, has said that this aspect of his work is as important as the more visible ways in which he manages publicity for his clients by manoeuvring them into the press.

More seriously, PR specialists are involved in the manipulation of political, environmental, economic and business news agendas, as Davies (2008) describes. In addition, most areas of consumer journalism are now unthinkable without the support of PR professionals and their extravagant budgets. PR has been defined as 'a deception designed to exploit public opinion for political ends' (Anderson and Weymouth 1999: 16; see also Michie 1998). These writers are reflecting the view of cultural historian Jürgen Habermas that 'the corporate art of public relations' is part of the process by which information in the public sphere is manipulated in favour of those whose wealth or other forms of power gives them privileged access to the media; Nick Davies' forensic account of how effective this is should be read by every beginner journalist. At a more trivial level, in the consumer press for example, the general point holds good that money buys influence through favourable editorial mention (see Chapter 15). For a useful insight into the way PR people think about the media and try to manipulate journalists, try consulting Theaker's *The Public Relations Handbook* and Phillips and Young's (2009) *Online Public Relations* as, whatever else they do, PR staff still spend most of their time engaged in media relations (Theaker 2011: 148). Perhaps in the case of pushing new products in the consumer magazine sector this doesn't matter too much because it's what readers expect. But as Heather Brooke observes about more important topics, PR 'is essentially taxpayer-subsidised propaganda . . . Public relations is about controlling the flow of information in order to sell products. PR has no place in public institutions and drastically damages democracy' (Brooke 2010: 37, 256).

RESEARCH

For some journalists the research stage of a story is by far the most interesting, assuming they have adequate time to do any. In Chapter 9 there is a discussion of how information is put together through interviewing and contacts with people, and for some reporters that is the basis of most of what they write (Schudson 1995: 72). For others, particularly those working in the serious news press, research means different things depending on the story. Jessica Mitford wrote with relish about researching stories. For her the goal, when gathering background information,

> is to know, if possible, *more* about your subject than the target of the investigation does. To this end, I soak up books and articles on the subject, type out relevant passages, and accumulate a store of knowledge before seeking an interview with said target.
>
> (Mitford 1980: 5)

Journalists all have their own methods of working, but Carl Bernstein points to Mitford's introduction to *The Making of a Muckraker* as being 'as good a primer on reporting' as he's ever read (Mitford 1980: 263).

Libraries

Magazine and newspaper publishers have their own libraries or archives of cuttings and reference material and all journalists should be familiar with how to access and use them.

Digital sources

The internet has transformed the research process, as Tim Holmes explains in Chapter 12, and this applies equally to the search for ideas. Think of a word, preferably one for a weird activity such as trepanation. Key it into your search engine and off you go on the trail of ideas, quotes, books, contacts. The possibilities provided by the internet only reinforce my point about how easy it is to come up with ideas for feature stories. Chris Frost goes so far as to argue that 'the Internet, particularly the world wide web, is now the sensible starting point (but only the starting point) for any research' (Frost 2010: 52). One problem, though, is that every other journalist working on the story may consult the same starting point so you need to consider what you can bring to a story that is richer and more engaging than they, or indeed your readers, can get access to instantly. That will depend, as often as not, on the quality and originality of your questions as well as the reliability and way with words of your sources.

Frost notes, correctly, that a careful journalist has to be wary of the pitfalls of using information acquired through the internet, as Chapter 12 explains, but the internet has undoubtedly transformed the work of journalists. Apart from providing access to websites, it makes it much easier to conduct interviews with busy people, as well as to access a huge range of information on every conceivable topic. It also makes the process of checking facts much quicker, again so long as dependable sources are chosen. And it provides extensive opportunities for crunching numbers to produce or verify stories that emerge out of statistical analysis.

Styling for photography

So far it may seem as if all magazines are full of words, which of course they are not. The people who style fashion photos or create the sets for magazines about food or homes and decorating don't usually write much, but they do have to generate ideas about the 'stories' for the pictures, the copy that will go with them, and to help decide which merchandise to call in. Here it can be more difficult to pin down where the concepts come from, although it often is simply a development of what is going on in the relevant industry. If grungy clothes in grey are on all the catwalks then grungy clothes in grey will permeate the fashion pages. And if designers of household fabrics are suddenly showing animal prints at the international exhibitions, you don't have to wait long for jungle decorating themes to hit the magazine racks. But beyond the ideas currently being pushed by designers and manufacturers, stylists take their inspiration from anywhere, whether it's the music scene, classical painting, graphic design or the latest film. (There was a plague of khaki safari kit on almost every fashion page while the film *Out of Africa* was on general release in the UK.)

CONSTRAINTS ON RESEARCH

Research can be the most enjoyable part of the journalistic process, but it can also be the most frustrating. There aren't many kinds of research in any field that operate entirely without a deadline – even PhD candidates have a time limit – so not many pieces of research have the luxury of being allowed to continue until all the questions have been fully explored. However, in journalism the time constraints are usually extremely tight and often unrealistic. Features writers may regularly have to write several thousand words a day, all of which need 'researching'. Journalists have to research their stories at such speed that they can't afford to check much, or to follow up leads which might yield a new angle. Anyone who is on the receiving end of calls from journalists who are looking for information will be familiar with their plea to talk to you that minute – later this afternoon or even tomorrow morning is just not possible, whatever else you might have in your diary. When the topic under research is not tied to a particular day in news terms, why is there not more scope for forward planning? Even in well-run offices journalists often work to time constraints which are more to do with editorial office custom than pursuit of the best story, and which are undoubtedly detrimental to the quality of the information that reaches their readers.

Part of the cause of this is money. A reporter's time is expensive. Speculative research that might produce nothing or research which yields results slowly is, as many editors freely admit, just not affordable. That's partly why there are now so many columns based on personal opinions: these usually require no research at all. It's also the reason for the increasing prevalence of what Nick Davies calls 'churnalism', 'the heart of modern journalism, the rapid repackaging of largely unchecked second-hand material, much of it designed to service the political or commercial interests of those who provide it' (Davies 2008: 60). Many journalists now hardly leave the office and are in no position to check anything adequately, let alone ferret out their own stories by use of their own contacts. Davies is writing about newspapers, but the situation on magazines is not necessarily different, and where features are concerned, in the weekly real-life and celebrity sectors, there is much the same relentless churn of stories, many of which come from the pressurised working environment of news agencies.

Journalists should be aware of the risks of working at speeds too great to allow for adequate research, especially when they are writing about specialist fields.

Davies recounts in his chapter about the so-called millennium bug how false stories are able to dominate the journalism agenda because no one understands enough to challenge them. And Ben Goldacre, a doctor who writes about the media's coverage of science stories, produces a continuous stream of examples to demonstrate how inadequate that reporting is, even in the serious press (Davies 2008: 9–45; www.badscience.net; www.guardian.co.uk).

The limits to the amount of time available to work on stories, to check facts and test ideas, have, among other things, led Nick Davies to the conclusion that we are now in an 'age of falsehood and distortion'. The problem, as he sees it, is that 'the primary obstacles to truth-telling' by journalists are now enshrined in the way the industry works. So the problem lies not so much at the point of publication 'but also at the earlier and even more important stage of gathering and testing raw information' (Davies 2008: 23).

Secrecy

For journalists to gather information successfully it is not just a question of knowing what to ask and who to ask, or where to turn for written or online sources. Yet this has been far from true in the UK, as compared with some other Western democracies, and very far from true in countries where censorship of the press is a significant political tool. The popular conception of censorship is of a process that happens after the journalist has produced the story but before it is published. In fact, the restrictions start much earlier and indeed censorship (with its close co-conspirator, secrecy), at the enquiry stage can be more effective since it prevents journalists getting at information in the first place, rather than discovering information but then not being allowed to publish it.

'Secrecy', according to Davies, 'is one of the great British diseases. It's so secret that we don't even admit we suffer from it.' His comments come from his endorsement of Heather Brooke's book, *The Silent State*. In the UK journalists have had to struggle to unearth all kinds of information to which, in other countries such as the US, there would be a right of access. An example of this, which relates to a tragic story, appeared in *The Guardian* (7 October 1999: 4). In its coverage of the Paddington rail crash it noted:

> Safety warnings kept by Railtrack which could have alerted the public that trains had overrun signals outside Paddington Station before Tuesday's crash are protected by Whitehall's draconian secrecy laws . . . Members of the public cannot even ask the company . . . to release the reports or minutes of its safety committee.

So British journalists, like the British public, until recently have had no right of access to information even where, as in the above example, such information is of unquestioned public interest and may involve public money or, in some cases, public appointments. This gives rise to concern, particularly in areas of public administration, responsibility for which has increasingly been shifted by government to the rather grey area of rule by quango, as John Turner explains (Turner 1998: 186). The acronym 'quango' stands for quasi-autonomous non-governmental organisation and includes such institutions as Trinity House (the lighthouse service), NICE (the National Institute for Clinical Excellence), and the Office for Budget Responsibility. One concern is how accountable they are, given that the members are responsible for spending public money but are not elected, and many of the posts are filled by government appointees without an open selection procedure.

The centralised nature of British political life, the secrecy that pervades politics and government, can make life difficult for the reporter who simply wants to find out what is going on in a particular government department. As historian Bernard Porter noted, although there are other societies which are or have been as secretive as Britain, the British are peculiar for the depth of their secrecy: 'Not only are we secretive, we are secretive about how secretive we are' (Porter 1999: 13). The Official Secrets Acts ensure that questions are not answered freely and that those who are employed in all manner of capacities by the Crown must sign a document preventing them from disclosing any information they have gathered during their service. Stories, possibly apocryphal, abound about some of the sillier restrictions this imposes, such as the gardener refusing to reveal what plants are grown at Windsor Castle or whether Prince Charles prefers China or Indian tea.

The worrying side of this, though, is that workers in industries such as the nuclear industry are not at liberty to voice their concerns, and documents which are essential to the work of a serious news reporter are simply unobtainable. Employees in occupations as diverse as health and education are now contractually bound not to talk to the press. An account of how these restrictions can affect the work of a journalist, and one which along the way compares the situation in the UK with that in the US, is provided by Marilynne Robinson in her article 'The Waste Land', about Sellafield nuclear reprocessing plant. She points out that the *sub judice* rule, which prevents open discussion of any issue about to become the subject of legal action, can keep serious issues out of the press. (The Paddington rail crash in October 1999 reminded us how little information could be made public during the two years following the Southall rail crash, while criminal proceedings were under way.) Robinson gives the example of Thalidomide, the drug implicated in the birth of children with serious deformities. Its manufacturers managed to keep the question of their liability before the courts for 17 years and therefore out of public discussion until *The Sunday Times*, then under the brave editorship of Harold Evans, broke the story in defiance of the law.

In the US the British climate of secrecy provokes puzzlement. For Americans 'a democracy without the means of public information is but a prelude to farce or tragedy' (Evans 1999). As Bernard Porter argues, great advances in access to information have been made in recent years (for one thing, it is now acknowledged that the UK has secret services) but the secret services were 'expressly exempted' from the Blair government's Freedom of Information Bill: 'Secrets . . . are still regarded as the property of the secretive; there is no presumption of a public "right to know" ' (Porter 1999: 15). In January 2005 the situation began, gradually, to change for the better when the Freedom of Information Acts became law throughout the UK, a development that is obviously helpful to journalists although, as Heather Brooke pointed out, it took the best part of five years for this key piece of legislation to be of practical day-to-day use.

Many journalists accept that there have to be some constraints on the publication of information. The issue is at its clearest during a time of war, when in the interests of security governments traditionally clamp down on what can be published. Fair enough, perhaps, not to broadcast to the enemy that they can expect a 'surprise' bombing raid tonight or that troops are being massed on the border ready for an invasion. But things are less clear cut when it comes, say, to reporting the number of casualties. Governments prefer to keep quiet about their own losses in case morale is affected. They also like to keep quiet about civilian casualties on the opposing side – again out of a wish to carry public opinion with them.

Privacy

There has been much debate recently about privacy, prompted by the more unpalatable excesses of the media. While it is easy to see why people should want aspects of their lives to remain private, it can also be argued that privacy laws protect the wicked from discovery. A fuller discussion of these issues is to be found in Chapter 17 and of the relevant aspects of the law in Chapter 18. For the purpose of this chapter it is important to point out that any journalist who works in news and on sensitive issues must be well acquainted with the regulations, partly to know what not to do and partly to be aware of what rights do exist so that when organisations try to restrict freedom in ways beyond what is legally accepted they can be challenged. Useful guidance to the workings of local and national government is provided in John Morrison's (2011) book, *Essential Public Affairs for Journalists*. Apart from the legal restrictions on the work of journalists, there are codes of practice to guide them in what is acceptable behaviour. These are published by the National Union of Journalists (NUJ), the Society of Editors and, for now, the Press Complaints Commission. In mid-2012 the latter is in a transitional phase but whatever body replaces it will no doubt be a similar source of guidance.

TURNING IDEAS INTO STORIES

There are two other processes connected with ideas that need to be mentioned in this chapter. One is the pitching of story suggestions and the second is commissioning them. However good an idea is, it has no real value unless the writer knows how to sell it to someone else. The word 'sell' is clearly appropriate when a freelance is offering ideas to a commissioning editor, but it also describes what writers on the staff of a magazine have to do. Money may not change hands for staffers in the way it does for freelances, but the process of persuasion is the same. Because pitching ideas is such a vital part of a freelance's job it is covered in detail in Chapter 4.

The commissioning process

Magazine editorial teams are often small, and in many cases staff have to undertake a variety of tasks, so it can fall to the lot even of beginners to be responsible for commissioning other writers. It's useful, therefore, to think about what the task involves.

By far the most grief between commissioning editors and writers occurs because of misunderstandings: the writer wrote what she thought she was asked to and the editor disagrees entirely. One way to minimise the risk of this is for the commissioner to note down what has been decided at the meeting or during the telephone call and send a copy to the writer. That way misunderstandings can be caught at an early stage. The problem with this is that it is not always the case that a written agreement will exist between magazine and freelance for a particular feature. Anyone who is commissioning should note down exactly what they want. If they don't know exactly then that can be made explicit. It's also helpful to say which are the essential ingredients of a story and which are less crucial but nevertheless desirable. Naturally, during the research stage, what a writer uncovers may alter the direction or significance of the story. It makes sense for the commissioning editor to encourage writers to make contact regularly during the research stage or just before writing up.

It's not easy to say what makes a good commissioning editor. Being full of ideas or knowing how to find them is clearly essential, as well as knowing how to match the idea to the writer, whether staff or freelance. Just as important is being able to recognise the quality of the ideas put forward by others, as well as being able to spot the strength hiding in a mediocre idea, to see how it could be developed or how the questions could perhaps be asked in a different way to yield more interesting material. A good commissioner, then, is open to new ideas and also, I would argue, to new writers. She should be on the lookout for new talent, whether this means paying some attention to the speculative approaches which all commissioning editors receive or actively studying the writers who are already in print in her field to see if anyone is better than the writers she is currently using.

Commissioning editors also need a talent for pitching ideas, just as freelance writers do. The bigger the magazine the more likely it is that the process of selling ideas happens in a kind of chain. The writer sells ideas to the commissioning editor, who then has to sell them either to the editor or to an entire senior editorial team, which may operate rather like the news conference on a newspaper, where the heads of each section meet to offer their 'list' of stories.

One of the most satisfactory parts of the commissioning process can be reading the copy when it arrives – if it meets the brief exactly and is well written. There will be cases, however, when the copy doesn't meet the brief or, for whatever reason, has to be either rejected or sent back for rewriting. This is when a commissioning editor needs reserves of tact. Editorial judgement is important too, because distinctions have to be made between the piece which can't be saved, the piece which needs reworking by the writer, and the piece which needs substantial reworking by the editor or subeditors. Magazines have different approaches and money plays its part in the decision making. If the story is important for the magazine, is it quicker to get a sub to rewrite it than to ask a disgruntled freelance to spend more time on a piece that he regards as finished? If the story is well written and could be even better, is it worth the editor's time to make the improvements? The answer really depends on the standards to which the magazine aspires and the generosity of the editorial budget. For a good account of the interventionist approach James Thurber's biography of E.H. Ross is hard to beat. It's true that the skills of a great editor such as Ross can't be taught. The mechanics of editing can, and so can some of the criteria for selection of stories. What can develop only with experience is the ability to get the best out of writers and then to work at their copy until its best qualities emerge. Legendary editors such as Ross have this ability, and although it doesn't always make them popular it certainly helps to make them great.

RECOMMENDED READING

Baggini, J. (2002) *Making Sense: Philosophy Behind the Headlines*.

Brooke, H. (2007) *Your Right to Know: A Citizen's Guide to the Freedom of Information Act*, 2nd edition.

Brooke, H. (2010) *The Silent State: Secrets, Surveillance and the Myth of British Democracy*.

Brooke, H. (2011) *The Revolution will be Digitised: Dispatches from the Information War*.

Davies, N. (2008) *Flat Earth News* (chs 5–6).

Frost, C. (2010) *Reporting for Journalists*, 2nd edition (chs 3–4).

Goldacre, B. (2009) 'Bad Stats' in *Bad Science*.

Marr, A. (2004) *My Trade: A Short History of British Journalism*.

Michie, D. (1998) *The Invisible Persuaders: How Britain's Spin Doctors Manipulate the Media*.

Mitford, J. (1980) *The Making of a Muckraker*.

Morrison, J. (2011) *Essential Public Affairs for Journalists*.

Robinson, M. (1985) 'The Waste Land', in *The Granta Book of Reportage*.

Theaker, A. (2011) *The Public Relations Handbook*, 4th edition.

Thompson, D. (2008) *Counter-knowledge: How We Surrendered to Conspiracy Theories, Quack Medicine, Bogus Science and Fake History*.

Wheen, F. (2004) *How Mumbo-Jumbo Conquered the World: A Short History of Modern Delusions*.

Websites

Heather Brooke: http://heatherbrooke.org
Nick Davies: www.nickdavies.net
Ben Goldacre: www.badscience.net
Freedom of Information: www.foi-uk.org.uk

CHAPTER 6

Writing
Where to start

Just as there is no such thing as a typical magazine, so there is no single way to write for magazines. What is an appropriate style will depend on the purpose of the magazine and who its readers are. To a more limited extent this applies to newspapers, and accounts for the differences between, say, a lead news story in *The Independent* and the way the same story might be written for *The Sun*.

VARIETY OF STYLES

In magazines things are not so straightforward: the material they cover is varied, the purposes for which they are written are diverse and the readerships are, in many cases, tightly defined in terms of interests, class or age. This means magazines adopt a much more individual approach to the style of writing they publish. Furthermore, there are magazines which intentionally use a style which acts almost as a way of excluding those who don't understand it. Their aim is to give readers the sense of belonging to a club or at least that the magazine is read only by people like themselves who share the same tastes in music or in fashion.

Examples can be found in magazines aimed at teenage girls and young women which use words like studmuffin, hunk, vidfest, snogfest, tongue sarnie (this is a French kiss, for those who don't know!) and so on. Alliteration is rampant (TV totty, fact files, plump up your pout, bag a boy, lassoo a lad); second syllables are abandoned (sesh for session, fave for favourite, gorge for gorgeous, pash for passion, bod for body, vid for video, ish for issue); apostrophes proliferate (L'il cutie, chillin', hoo-bloomin'rah!). In the drive for high circulations such writing could be counter-productive in that some of the slang vocabulary is not widely used even by the target age range and certainly not throughout the UK. That, however, may be the point. By reading these words as if they were the in-words in the metropolis, readers can get a vicarious sense of being part of what is cool. Using, or at least understanding, this kind of language helps readers to differentiate themselves from their less cool peers as well as from parents or other figures of authority like teachers. Turn to the hipper fashion, music, lads' or sports magazines to see no end of examples of language used in this way to draw the readers in. Apart from helping to brand readers as cool, it contributes, no doubt, to the entertainment value of the publication both by the jokiness of its tone and by the sheer fun of playing with words, which has long been part of the English tradition of writing. In the satirical, political magazine *Private Eye* language is used to parody styles of journalistic and other writing both as a source of entertainment but also to make serious points about political and social issues.

This use of style is also intended to differentiate the magazines from one another. Publishers see this as an increasingly important task in the crowded consumer magazine marketplace, although I'm not sure the strategy necessarily works, as all the magazines aimed at particular groups seem to pick up the same linguistic quirks, probably from each other.

Which style to use

What this book can't do, then, is provide a comprehensive guide to writing in the styles that consumer and lifestyle magazines use. For one thing a list of appropriate vocabulary would be out of date within a few months, and in any case colloquial style is written, at its most convincing, by those for whom it grows naturally out of their own way of speaking. What any good magazine writer will learn, and any good features editor will explain, is that the writer must always have a clear idea of the market for which he is writing. Viewed positively this merely reflects what all competent writers (and speakers) do: they adjust the style of the language they use according to who they are writing for or talking to. We all do this as part of the daily communication we have with other people. So thinking of the market is not necessarily much more than good manners, although obviously it is a more difficult undertaking if you are writing for the many readers of a high-selling monthly than it is if you are talking to a few people you've just met on the beach.

Viewed less positively, however, there are some problems. The first is for journalists who write for readers who are not like themselves either socially or in educational terms, or even just in age. In newspapers this matters less because they mostly strive to cater for a broader range of people. But in magazines, where the readerships are identified so narrowly in the terms listed above, it does matter. If you are writing for young teenage girls it is most unlikely that you are yourself a young teenage girl, so how do you know the peculiarities of their language? You might have been a teenage girl quite recently and that would help, although colloquial language changes even in a few years, so you're likely to be out of date. Or you might have friends and family who are teenage girls. You could talk to them. You could go out deliberately to meet some, perhaps even formally through a focus group. You could read the magazines they read, watch the television and listen to the radio. The problem with this, though, is that any of these strategies brings with it a level of artificiality, as well as carrying the risk of circularity: magazines are written in a certain style because that's how other journalists are writing for the same audience. And this problem doesn't just apply to a teenage readership. There's the problems of age and class. Even if journalists are from a working-class background (and many aren't), by the time they've landed well-paid jobs on a London-based glossy they are encountering a different kind of language every day. What are they to do? How do they know the right language to use for C2, D, E readers (see Chapter 15) outside London? One of the conflicts this can give rise to within a magazine office is when the various writers and editors assert that they know best about aspects of language which can never be established with absolute certainty, such as whether particular words would be used by, say, teenage boys in Liverpool.

The regional consideration is significant too. For all that consumer journalists say they try to tailor their words to their readers, they are apt to ignore the different usages that are common in different parts of the country. There is a strong metropolitan bias in almost all consumer magazines. This bias may be inevitable, given that London is where most magazines are based and therefore where most magazine journalists live. But it's something to consider when you hear journalists talking about the importance of knowing the market.

Some good examples of the muddled thinking in editorial offices about appropriate language were collected by Sheena-Margot Gibson. She asked a selection of editorial staff working on magazines for teenagers why they used certain slang words like 'totty' and so on. In several cases senior staff said the quoted words were not used in their publications and so were astonished when Gibson quoted page references from their current issues. More intriguing still was an air of defensiveness. Gibson was simply trying to find out where the more arcane words came from. But some editors said they were actually trying to cut back on this kind of language and one said, puzzlingly, that the word 'totty' had now been banned from the publication (S.-M. Gibson 1999). The question is why they should feel the need to do that if it reflects street language. The problem, for a writer, is how to follow the vagaries of the thinking about language in a particular editorial office.

A skilful writer, with an observant eye and ear for language, can learn how to repro-duce the required style. If you want to write for a particular magazine, or if you've landed a job, the trick is to study carefully the way it is written and note the characteristics in the same way you would if you were learning a foreign language. Points to watch for include rhythm, rhyme, length of sentences and paragraphs, alliteration and vocabulary, some of which are usefully described by Linda McLoughlin (2000) in her book *The Language of Magazines*. House-style guides can help and so too can the subeditors, as they are the people who are charged with establishing the linguistic style of the publication or website, although what you do when confronted by conflicting advice from different sections of the magazine is something your own diplomatic skills will have to resolve.

Individual magazine styles

Style does not, however, just refer to the quirky use of language common to popular youth culture. Many magazines have their own tone – *Time* magazine is a good example of a news magazine with a recognisable style for its news pages, even if the opinion essays are allowed more variety. Other serious publications such as news or industry or professional magazines strive for what is generally thought of as a neutral voice in their news pages at least, and probably with features too, although with features in whatever kind of publication there is always more scope for the individual voice of the writer to be heard. This is in fact one of the attractions of feature writing for some journalists, and in particular one of the attractions of writing features for magazines, some of which not only tolerate but actively nurture the individuality of their writers. *The New Yorker* or *The Spectator* or *Rolling Stone* are not bought because readers want to read reportage or opinions expressed in a corporate monotone: they are bought precisely for the variety and literary quality of voices they offer.

LEARNING TO WRITE

One question that arises in any discussion of writing skills is whether they can, in fact, be taught. The view that writers are born not made is still common, as is the notion that there is an absolute distinction between literary writing and journalistic writing. Literary writing, the thinking goes, is creative, imaginative, of enduring quality and written by a human being blessed with some mystical quality. Journalistic writing, by contrast, is mundane, dull, lacking in creativity and written by a tired cliché-monger who has no sensitivity to the nuances of language.

The idea that writing can't be taught is gradually going out of fashion as formal training for journalism becomes more widely accepted and as more creative-writing courses are established. In the old days many good journalists managed well enough without training, but what happens now, in universities and colleges, helps to speed up and formalise a process that would once have taken place in an ad hoc way in magazine and newspaper offices. Some writers are more naturally fluent or sensitive to language than others, but that doesn't mean they will somehow be damaged by doing a little systematic thinking about their main means of communication.

The second point, that literary writing is a separate undertaking from journalistic writing, is, I think, most easily belied by making a list of highly regarded literary writers who have also worked as journalists. Starting with Daniel Defoe, a random list might include Samuel Johnson, Charles Dickens, George Eliot, Mrs Gaskell, Arnold Bennett, Oscar Wilde, George Orwell, Tom Stoppard, Joan Didion, Tom Wolfe and James Fenton. The focus of this debate is one that underpins discussion in many areas of cultural endeavour: is there a qualitative difference between high and low culture (between literary imaginings and factual reporting, for example), or is there merely writing, some of which is better than the rest? The better does not always have to be the fictional or lyrical; it might be a highly crafted piece of reportage based on detailed documentary research and extensive interviews (McKay 2011). This is not a debate that needs to detain all readers, although it does have direct ramifications for features writing at least, and will be touched on again in Chapter 8. The debate was widened beyond university classrooms by Tom Wolfe in his introduction to an anthology of mainly American writers called *The New Journalism* and given an additional lease of life here in the UK by the increasing respect given to reportage in recent years, as exemplified by the publication of anthologies such as *The Faber Book of Reportage* and *The Granta Book of Reportage*.

One of the most common reasons given for dismissal of news writing is that it is hackneyed and formulaic. This is sometimes true and not surprising given how much journalism is written every day. Sometimes the cause is not that the writer doesn't have a way with words. It may be because of the constraints that surround the writing of news. If everything has to be done quickly, under pressure and with minimum fuss, then it's quick and easy to adhere to the formula, and that may be what editors want. It doesn't necessarily follow that other kinds of writing by the same person under different constraints can't be written to the highest literary standards.

While flair, talent, genius, individual voice – whatever you want to call it – can't be taught, certain technical skills can. Some of these can be prescribed in advance of the writing, although it is much easier to indicate what to avoid than it is to give firm guidelines that will produce workable prose. One of the best ways for anyone to improve what they write is to read as widely as possible, reading with a questioning eye to analyse how writers achieve certain successful effects or what is wrong when the writing is dull. Everyone has their own tastes, and so there is little point in recommending here particular authors; the names of revered writers are easy enough to come by. There are some books about the English language that are worth recommending because they are readable, entertaining and informative – these are listed at the end of the chapter.

GENERAL WRITING SKILLS

It is to some of the general skills I want to turn now, hoping the reader will recognise that they don't hold good for all magazine writing but can be a touchstone. Given the scope of this book, it is not possible to go into detail. Two of the most useful books for journalists are *English for Journalists* by Wynford Hicks (2006) and *Essential English for Journalists, Editors and Writers* by Harold Evans (2000), which cover grammar, syntax, punctuation and so on, but always from the perspective of a journalist and using examples from journalism. A useful online resource is the BBC College's website, which offers tutorials on many aspects of journalistic writing.

Spelling

Spelling is one technical aspect of writing that can't be taught by someone else, but a writer who is determined can usually improve it. With modern computer spellchecks it may be argued that it is not necessary for a writer to spell correctly. In fact, it saves a lot of time if she can: spellchecks have limited capabilities and produce delightful misreadings thanks to the number of homophones in English; but also, if a deadline is very tight, spellchecks force more pauses for questioning over proper names than is ideal. They also don't help much at the final proof stage, when an eagle eye can spot a misspelling before it makes it into print. Someone who knows their spelling is weak and who wants to make a living as a writer would be advised to work at it, to learn the regularly used vocabulary in the same way as they might learn foreign words in language classes.

Punctuation

Another technical skill that can give trouble to new writers is punctuation. This can be taught and no doubt has been to all journalists throughout their schooldays: taught, learned and more or less forgotten in some cases. The apostrophe is the most confusing it seems and it wouldn't surprise me if this punctuation mark disappeared altogether over the next few years, so many are the people who are unable or unwilling to learn the simple rules by which it should be used. This is not the place to go into them. You'll know you have an apostrophe problem if you would have difficulty writing phrases to do with 'books belonging to many children' (children's books) or 'fleeces from many sheep' (sheep's fleeces) or something belonging to 'it'. ('It's a girl', cried the midwife. 'Its hair is black' is one way of trying to remember this one.) The general advice here is to look carefully at what appears in print and try to understand why an apostrophe or a hyphen is used where it is, as these are the two most regularly misunderstood marks of punctuation. A full exposition of the accepted conventions of punctuation is available in G.V. Carey's (1976) book *Mind the Stop* and *The Oxford Dictionary for Writers and Editors* offers a succinct guide under the entry 'Punctuation'. Anyone who knows their punctuation is shaky must chain a copy of this book to their desk, open at the punctuation page. Lynne Truss's best-selling book, *Eats, Shoots and Leaves*, is a light-hearted but informative look at the rules of punctuation. Lastly, bear in mind that conventions in punctuation do gradually change over time.

Jargon

Publications like *Rolling Stone*, *The Spectator* and *The New Yorker* are a long way, stylistically, from the mass-market consumer weeklies and monthlies. Situated half way between, perhaps, are the professional and trade publications which use their own vocabulary, although not in the light-hearted way of the teenage magazines and not to act as a badge of cool. What they use, which would not necessarily be acceptable on the pages of general newspapers, are jargon words.

Jargon often gets a bad name for reasons that are not altogether fair. What jargon describes, essentially, is a set of words or ways of speaking that are used and understood by particular groups of people when talking about their shared interest. So if a group of academics are at a meeting and talk about the SHEFC, the REF, staff–student ratios, sabbaticals, PhDs and FTEs, no one will think them rude or incomprehensible, although if the same people were holding a general conversation at a party (it has been known!), where other guests were not involved in university life, then to use the same language would be rude as well as pointless, because the outsiders would not understand.

Jargon, then, has its place and in the right context – at a meeting of colleagues or in a publication aimed at a particular group of people with shared knowledge – it is the correct language to use and may have a precision that day-to-day words would lack in this context. In the wrong context – in a publication for a wider group of people than those who might readily be expected to understand it – jargon words go against all the principles of good journalistic writing, and in particular the rule that journalism should be easy to understand.

It follows, then, that one of the jobs of any journalist, whether in magazines or newspapers, is as a translator of jargon. So many fields of interest these days do have extensive vocabularies of words and acronyms which would mystify those outside, that journalists must be careful not merely to reproduce the jargon. If they do they may lose their readers and, worse, they may misunderstand the story if they themselves do not understand the jargon. This is why it can be helpful to look at the task as one of translation, since you can't begin the process unless you understand what you hope to translate. Another advantage of thinking in terms of translation is that it helps the writer to distinguish between jargon and gobbledegook.

The difference is that with jargon a meaning can be tracked down by the non-specialist; with gobbledegook there is no discernible meaning. A definition of gobble-degook nowadays is generally that it is pompous-sounding rubbish. It may sound like official jargon (and that was once its official meaning) but when submitted to scrutiny it turns out to be more or less devoid of meaning. The writers who are most tempted to produce this are politicians, officials and bureaucrats in complex organisations such as the BBC. So prevalent was gobbledegook in official documents that an organisation called the Plain English Campaign was set up to work for improvements. Partly as a result of that, documents like tax returns or passport application forms have been made much clearer in recent years. Examples of gobbledegook are easy enough to find and *Private Eye* regularly publishes some of the worst excesses, particularly from the BBC and local authorities. For an explanation of how the style is arrived at and also avoided, it's worth reading George Orwell's essay 'Politics and the English language'. Written in 1946, it shows that the tendency towards deadly obfuscation is not just a late-twentieth-century problem in English. It's also worth reading because much of what he said in the essay is accepted as gospel by writers, editors and those who teach English generally (Orwell 1946: 127). Even if you don't agree with all his points, as a journalist you will inevitably encounter those who do.

Journalism style

Clarity, economy and simplicity are the three most important characteristics of journalistic writing and with good reason, even if they were not always accorded the value they are now. It was towards the end of the nineteenth century, when the mass-market publishing of journalism really began to get under way in America and Britain, that emphasis began to be given to what was regarded as the more masculine style characterised by terseness and brevity: the idea was that men were much too busy to waste time reading magazines or newspapers in which unnecessary words were employed (Garvey 1996: 178).

This has become the predominant thinking behind all of the news writing and much of the feature writing in the UK today. Readers are thought to be in a tearing hurry and to have the attention-span of grasshoppers: in the case of tabloid papers or the most popular mass-market magazines for women this means editors offer readers a large number of short stories, all screaming for attention. In the case of the more serious magazines and newspapers it means that although stories aren't necessarily short, they must still be regarded as competing with all the other stories on the page or in the publication, and display techniques are used to attract the notice of readers. I wouldn't necessarily argue with any of this – many of us do lead busy lives – but it's worth drawing attention to the assumptions that are handed on to each new generation of journalists as if there were no other way. It's worth noting, too, the extremes to which this case has now been pushed in even the most serious of radio and television journalism where interviewees and contributors are constantly being interrupted and cut short because of the acute pressure of time, making an intelligent exposition of a complicated issue increasingly difficult to find.

Nevertheless, clarity, economy and simplicity are meant to prevail. By striving for clarity the journalist tries to avoid any ambiguity and not to test the reader's patience with unnecessary allusions. (This is one way in which journalistic writing differs from some literary writing, in which ambiguity is valued and indeed may be part of the literary point.) In striving for economy, journalists aim to tell their stories in the shortest possible way, using short words, short sentences and short paragraphs. Of course, all this is relative and journalism that deals with complicated technical material for a well-informed audience such as the readers of *New Scientist* can afford to use longer, more abstract words than would be appropriate for the triumph-over-tragedy human-interest narrative in a weekly such as *Chat*. The principle holds true though, it's just that the target audience has also to be borne in mind. In striving for simplicity the journalist is taking the most direct route through her material, keeping subordinate clauses to a minimum and avoiding anything which might distract the reader from the main purpose of the story.

We've looked at some of the reasons for the establishment of these principles of writing and these were to do with the readers. There are others that have more to do with the way journalism is produced. Journalists usually work under severe time pressure. Magazines and newspapers also set a premium by space. Copy has to compete for the limited available space and this has implications for the way journalists approach their work. These constraints do not necessarily apply to all magazines, of course, and for some magazine writers, particularly the writers of longer features, there is the luxury of being able to write to a length the material seems to merit rather than an arbitrary length decided by the page layout or the quantity and quality of other material that week.

I turn now to simplicity. New journalists, especially recent graduates, often take time to work free of a more leisured, academic style in which they aim to cover all the possibilities or nuances of an argument. Journalists have to learn to be brutally selective in what they try to include in their stories. They can't put in everything they have discovered during their research, and the point of what they write is not to show that they have done enough reading, as it sometimes is with student essays. What matters in journalism is that a story is told and that it is told quickly. A narrative thread is vital to most journalistic writing. One way to move towards this style is to imagine you meet friends at the bus stop and you've just heard some news. Ask yourself: what is the first thing you would say about a particular incident? What sort of language would you use?

Another technical point to do with simplicity has been touched on already: subordinate clauses can slow the narrative process down. By this I mean the kind of sentence that starts with the less important information first, as in this example:

> 'Having settled down in the armchair, Jemima read her copy of *The Economist* from cover to cover.'

This sentence structure is all right to use now and again, to vary the rhythm of the language or to affect the emphasis, but, because the reader has to wait so long for the subject of the sentence (Jemima) and for the main verb to appear, it does make the reader work harder than he would if it were written in the more straightforward way:

> 'Jemima settled down in the armchair and read her copy of *The Economist* from cover to cover.'

The first sentence is longer and the information is offered in a more complicated way than is necessary.

More problematic, however, and yet increasingly common, is for the subordinate clause to confuse the writer so that she forgets altogether what the subject of the sentence is supposed to be:

'Having settled in the armchair, Jemima's magazine fell on the floor.'

The mistake here is that the subject of 'having settled' is Jemima, but this gets forgotten by the second half of the sentence, which reads as if the magazine had settled in the chair rather than its reader.

'Freezing cold and hungry, the boy's coat was no protection against the rain.'

Here, the boy is the subject of the first part of the sentence, but the second half reads as if the coat were.

The point about narrative does not just apply to straightforward news or news feature writing as you might expect. In those cases it is obvious that stories are being recounted, but in other sections of magazines, too, the story model is used. Advice articles might use a fictional narrative thread, or real-life case histories, or be framed round a countdown to an event. Even the picture-led sections of the consumer press are thought of in terms of stories (see Chapter 3).

The advice always given to news writers does not apply to every kind of magazine work, but is useful to bear in mind. If you are telling a story there are six questions that will need answering at some point: who, what, where, when, why and how. In literary writing the answers to these may not all be offered at once (or even at all), but in news journalism it is usual to provide them as soon as possible. Certainly by making sure you answer these you will ensure that the essential information is given.

RETAINING THE HUMAN INTEREST

Another important point about much journalism is that it is, ideally, about people. Even quite abstract information will almost always be told in terms of the people who are affected, in all but the driest of magazines. So, if an announcement is made about the closure of a radio station, it is likely to be written about in terms of job losses. If a new, environmentally friendly nappy is designed, it will be featured in terms of happiness for green parents or the potential for discomfort among babies.

This point goes well beyond the simple techniques of language use – it is about deciding what is a story in the first place or at least deciding how a story should be framed. This is why interviewing is so important (see Chapters 9 and 10). In order to produce accessible narratives, people have to be involved. This gives rise to the phrase that you will hear anywhere there are journalists: 'human interest' is what makes readers read stories and journalists must therefore learn how to provide it.

When most people talk to each other, or when fiction writers tell us stories, they tend to use concrete words rather than abstract ones. This can be a useful guide to journalistic writing. To oversimplify: concrete words describe tangible things such as desks, chairs, people, hair; abstract words are the intangibles such as love, kindness, philosophy. If a novelist simply wrote that a couple were 'in love' her career would not take off. It's when the love is described in terms of the concrete that the picture emerges: red roses are sent or red traffic-lights are ignored, a red dress is worn to attract. This is not to deny that writing about abstractions in abstract terms can be done and done well, but to indicate that mostly in human-interest journalism it has no place, and also to suggest that when a reporter is struggling with a piece of journalistic writing this might be a key with which to start the diagnosis.

A related point is the old one about descriptive writing needing to take account of all the five senses if it is to be vivid. Most school pupils are taught this at some stage, but many forget during the undergraduate years of wrestling with argument and the exposition of ideas in their essays. Orwell makes this point in his essay. His suggestion is that a writer should not even begin to think about words until he has established as clearly as he can through pictures and sensations what he wants to say (Orwell 1946: 139).

Another test with which to diagnose problematic writing would be to look at whether too many verbs are being used in the passive voice. Orwell draws attention to this too, and he would have had all the more cause to do so if his essay had been written 50 years later (Orwell 1946: 139), as the growth of officialese in that time has been huge and it is here that the tendency to overuse the passive voice is most prevalent, especially what might be called the dangling passive, which is where the subject of the sentence is not made explicit.

First, an explanation of the passive voice. A simple sentence in the active voice runs 'subject, verb, object', as in 'The dog bit the girl'. Changed into the passive voice, and with no loss of meaning, this becomes 'object, verb, subject', as in 'The girl was bitten by the dog'. The problems here for journalistic writing, if we bear in mind the points about clarity, simplicity and economy, are as follows. First, the passive phrase works almost back to front. It is slightly less clear to the reader, perhaps not in this example, but in more complex sentences. The reader has to do more work to understand; and as we have seen, the reader of journalism can't be counted on to do anything but lose interest at the first sign of difficulty. Second, then, this means the sentence is slightly less simple than the straightforward active one. Third, and this is the clinching one for journalists, the second sentence is longer than the first. It takes up more space and more of the reader's time.

This does not mean the passive voice should never be used in journalism, merely that it should be used sparingly to vary the rhythm of sentences, perhaps, or to shift the emphasis from the perpetrator to the victim of the attack in this case, from the subject to the object.

The incomplete passive, however, is more problematic and I would advise journalists to avoid it if possible. Here's an example: 'Manolo Blahnik's latest shoe designs were praised.' The crucial information here is missing, because we don't know who did the praising: was it the fashion editor of *Vogue*, a medical foot specialist, or even a foot fetishist? The quoted sentence is much more interesting to the reader as soon as the identity of the praiser is known. In this example it may not seem to matter much, but if you move on to items of government policy and discussion of it then you can see why a great deal of official writing is done in this uninformative way – it avoids the question of responsibility. The serious reason, then, that the dangling passive voice should be avoided in journalism, is that its use means the writer or whoever she is quoting is not telling the whole story.

There will be occasions when this kind of language is unavoidable. In the UK we have a tradition of off-the-record political briefing which functions by not assigning responsibility for statements to any individual. There may be a good case for this system (although I can't see it), but all journalists, whether in favour or not, should be aware of the way that language works to support it.

AVOIDING LOOSE ENDS

Where a dangling passive is used out of carelessness rather than out of an attempt at obfuscation it is an example of something else that journalists should avoid – the 'loose end'. (Literature, again, may be different as in literary writing ambiguity may be part of the effect the writer is trying to achieve.) Loose ends are merely gaps in the information the writer is providing. In the dangling passive examples the subject of the verb is missing, but in other examples it may be a bigger chunk of the narrative that is missing or, and this happens more often, something is mentioned in the story which is never properly explained, leaving the reader feeling puzzled or cheated or both. As often as not this is a result of lazy reporting and not a problem of language use, but sometimes the two are connected and since it is a problem that could emerge at the writing stage and should definitely be picked up by either the writer or the subeditor it is worth mentioning here.

One example is where a mother was interviewed about the effects on her family of an accident her toddler had while in the care of a nanny. The child was badly injured. The mother was quoted as feeling guilty about having left the child in the care of someone else and said she had vowed never to leave the child in the care of another again. The story concluded by reminding readers that the mother had a demanding career. The loose end here is that given the vow and given the job, what arrangements has the mother made for the child? Does it come to work?

Does the father look after it? The granny? Does the mother have the freedom to work always at home? Will she ever leave it with a babysitter or is the child inseparable from its mother until it reaches adulthood? What about school? The underlying point of the story was to undermine the confidence of mothers in those whom they trust to care for their children. It left open many questions about what that might actually mean in practical terms, but even within its own limited narrative did not address the questions it gave rise to.

This kind of omission is much more common than it should be in journalistic writing and arises when journalists are working too quickly, for whatever reason, or when they are not asking enough questions, not thinking through the consequences of what they write. Another factor can be that they are simply trying to include too much information. The point made earlier about journalists having to be selective is relevant here. It may be that a story contains a loose end that doesn't need developing, and therefore the easiest way to deal with it is to cut the reference out altogether. In the example I've given this wouldn't have worked because it was intrinsic to the story that a career woman was the subject, but in other cases it is simply a question of limiting the points that the writer is trying to make, to keep the main story as straightforward as possible.

ORWELL'S SIX RULES

In his essay on language Orwell gives six rules, including a reminder that no rules to do with the use of English should be regarded as absolute. The first rule, that you should not 'use a metaphor, simile, or other figure of speech which you are used to seeing in print', refers to ways of describing one thing in terms of another, as in 'She was a dove', meaning she had a peaceful manner like a dove (metaphor, where something is described as if it were something which in fact it merely resembles); 'He was like an elephant', meaning he was very large (simile, where one thing is compared directly with another); 'He's been off the bottle for a while' (metonym, meaning he has stopped drinking). All these ways of using language contribute to the richness of English, but Orwell's point here is that once they become over familiar they lose their strength and become clichés. So 'avoid him like the plague' no longer has any vitality to it as a simile; nor does 'pretty as a picture' or 'cool as a cucumber'.

Clichés

A cliché is an expression that has become so familiar that it has lost its freshness and therefore its strength. Whoever first used 'tip of the iceberg' or 'level playing field' or 'crystal clear' was using figurative language to try to make what he was saying more vivid. Phrases like that get taken up by other language users, though, and after endless repetition they no longer carry figurative force and simply act as verbal padding, whether in spoken or written language. If we were considering worn-out figurative language only as a kind of failed attempt at last-minute decoration this might not matter, as the reader could quickly learn to ignore it. But language is not that. It is the essence of what is being written or said, as Orwell suggests: 'If thought corrupts language, language can also corrupt thought' (Orwell 1946: 137). If you agree with Orwell it's clear why clichés should be treated with suspicion or at least circumspection. The risk of using clichés is that your writing will be dreary and will therefore not be read by people who have anything better to do. More seriously, the danger of writing clichés is that they can come to shape the way you think. If you're used to writing about teenagers as bored, or footballers as brainless, or blondes as bimbos, then it takes a big effort to notice that the ones you actually talk to are none of those things. I have slipped, here, from the individual cliché of expression to the stereotyping of people or ideas, but that is deliberately to demonstrate the problem with clichés: how quickly they can slide from one thing to the next and establish or perpetuate a bad habit of thought.

There are two further points to make about clichés and journalists. From a charitable point of view it can be said that one reason clichés creep so widely into news and news feature writing is the pressure of deadlines. Not a bad excuse, although this and some of the other points made in this chapter about the constraints of time and space should perhaps raise questions about why these pressures are so often allowed to excuse so much slack practice. From a less charitable point of view it has to be recognised that clichés are what many editors want both in the words and the thoughts of their writers. Anyone who has written for a variety of publications will know that some subeditors have a licence to inject clichés into the writers' copy. It's as if editors fear readers won't be able to follow the story or the line of thought unless they have the well-trodden mental footprints of clichés to guide them.

Euphemisms

Closely allied to the idea of the cliché – in that it also helps to deaden the impact of language and therefore to conceal precise meaning – is the euphemism. In war reporting we read of 'collateral damage' and 'ethnic cleansing', both in themselves innocuous phrases, but ones which refer to the killing of human beings either by accident or design. Terms like these are not usually made up by journalists, they are used by officials and then taken up by journalists whose job really ought to be to write and speak more clearly. 'Collateral damage' is military jargon and as such has no place in an account of war written by a journalist for the general reader unless she wants to draw attention to the euphemistic way in which soldiers refer to what happens in wars. 'Ethnic cleansing' is vicious, racist murder; the adoption of a word like cleanse, which has so many other, positive connotations, assists readers in denying what it is they are actually reading about.

These are extreme examples, and there are others: 'child abuse' sounds mild enough compared with the systematic torture or rape to which it routinely refers; 'sexual harassment' sounds blandly bureaucratic compared with the actuality of the incidents reported; discussions in the UK about the rights of parents to use 'corporal punishment' on their children might be more honestly discussed if more precise words such as 'hitting' or 'beating' were used. In these cases journalists may try to excuse themselves by saying that the reality is too unpleasant to spell out – an excuse that would be more convincing if the media were not otherwise filled with stories and examples of cruelty and horror.

Less extreme examples of euphemisms may be less significant, but they nevertheless lend an air of unreality and untruth to the journalism which perpetrates them. Those more high-minded journalists who see part of their job as being to struggle against lies and evasion should keep at the forefront of their minds the way that language contributes to exactly these twin barriers to the truth, just as it always has.

All journalists at the beginning of their careers should be encouraged to reflect on what exactly they are doing with language when they use it. It is not the job of a book like this to dictate the purpose to which language should be put, but language is the tool of the trade which journalists use most, whichever medium they work in, and, to judge by the strong feelings that are aroused in any discussion of its use, it's a tool which is believed to carry immense power.

Political correctness

On a related note we need to look briefly at what some writers call political correctness, but which could, less controversially, be called courtesy. In many publications a writer goes against the house style if he refers to women or any other group which is thought to be disadvantaged in such a way as to enhance that disadvantage. So, for example, only a well-established feminist could nowadays get away with writing about girls when she meant women.

In the early days of the struggle by ethnic minority groups and women for social equality many journalists dismissed the idea that choice of words made any difference. (This was perhaps surprising since they had staked their lives and livelihoods on the fact that words did matter.) Now, however, many of the bigger publishing houses have recognised that there is something excluding about, for example, writing which uses the male pronoun, he, all the time when the people who are being described are in fact a mixture of he and she. For that reason they recommend a variety of strategies such as always using 'they' to describe undefined people or, as I have done in this book, varying at random the use of he and she.

When you write for a publication you need to find out from the house-style guide what its policy is on this as there is still considerable variety and the phrase 'politically correct' is often used to denigrate worthwhile attempts to think about the full significance of a writer's choice of words. Of course, the prescriptive aspect of this can be taken too far, but the underlying motive is, in many cases, less sinister than polite.

In her discussion of house style, linguist Deborah Cameron makes clear how arbitrary are some of the precepts laid down by style guides and by chief subs (Chapter 11; see also Cameron 1996). These precepts do, nevertheless, have to be accepted by those who want to write for a publication. This is where the Orwell essay can help as it has formed part of the received wisdom on language in journalism circles for many years.

One of the things Orwell most hated was pretentiousness. The journalist has to work at avoiding this in two ways – there's her own writing and then there's the writing or speech of others whose views she is responsible for reporting. If self-important or obfuscatory language is used by others, it is the job of journalists, as I have suggested, to translate it into everyday language that is accessible to the audience they are writing for. Orwell's essay gives many examples of how language can be used to confuse rather than illuminate in the way the writers 'dress up simple statements and give an air of scientific impartiality to biased judgements' (Orwell 1946: 131).

Orwell recommends choosing short words, and although this advice should not be taken to extremes, it isn't a bad beginner's exercise to try to rewrite a piece of serious journalism from, say, a political or business magazine, in words of one or two syllables. Impossible, of course, but good practice in the discipline of writing for a mass audience. The point about cutting out words, too, is a good one. Anyone who has worked as a subeditor knows how easy it is to trim down the words of someone else and yet how difficult it is to do the same for your own work. It also makes sense to practise rewriting material from a print source as if for online publications as, increasingly, writers are being asked to do this professionally (see Chapter 12).

Perhaps the last word should go to Samuel Johnson. He is often quoted for the following suggestion which, in my experience, proves especially helpful to writers who are struggling in the early days of features writing: 'Read over your compositions, and where ever you meet with a passage which you think is particularly fine, strike it out.' Naturally it is better if the writer can do this striking out for himself, but if he fails to then he should remember there is always a subeditor to do it for him – the danger is that the sub might choose the wrong fine paragraph and ruin the sense.

RECOMMENDED READING

Bryson, B. (2009) *Mother Tongue: The English Language*.
Bryson, B. (2009) *Troublesome Words*.
Butterfield, J. (2008) 'Style wars: usages people hate', in *Damp Squid: The English Language Laid Bare*.
Cameron, D. (1995) 'Civility and its discontents: language and "political correctness"', in *Verbal Hygiene*.

Carey, G.V. (1976) *Mind the Stop: A Brief Guide to Punctuation.*

Curtis, S. and Manser, M. (2006) *Penguin Pocket Writer's Handbook.*

Dignall, C. (2011) *Can You Eat, Shoot and Leave?* (Workbook).

The Economist (2012) *The Economist Style Guide*, 10th edition.

Evans, H. (2000) *Essential English for Journalists, Editors and Writers.*

Harcup, T. (2009) *Journalism: Principles and Practice*, 2nd edition.

Hicks, W. (2006) *English for Journalists*, 3rd edition.

Hicks, W., with Adams, S., Gilbert, H. and Holmes, T. (2008) *Writing for Journalists.*

McKay, J. (2011) 'Reportage in the UK: a hidden genre?', in *Literary Journalism Across the Globe: Journalistic Traditions and Transnational Influences.*

McLoughlin, L. (2000) *The Language of Magazines.*

Marsh, D.R. and Hodsdon, A. (2010) *Guardian Style.*

Oltermann, P. (2009) *How to Write.*

Orwell, G. (1946) 'Politics and the English language', available at www.mtholyoke.edu/acad/intrel/orwell46.htm

Phillips, A. (2006) *Good Writing for Journalists.*

Ritter, R. (ed.) (2000) *The Oxford Dictionary for Writers and Editors.*

Strunk, W. and White, E.B. (2008) *The Elements of Style.*

Truss, L. (2009) *Eats, Shoots and Leaves.*

Venolia, J. (2001) *Write Right! A Desktop Digest of Punctuation, Grammar, and Style*, 4th edition.

Waterhouse, K. (1991) *English our English (and How to Sing It).*

Whale, J. (1999) *Put It in Writing.*

Websites

www.bbc.co.uk/academy/collegeofjournalism/how-to/how-to-write

www.correctpunctuation.co.uk

CHAPTER 7

News writing

Most books for journalists assume that news is what journalism is about – a variety of definitions of news are accordingly offered. A book about magazines doesn't need to repeat these since in general magazines are not in competition with the other news media to be first with anything. They sometimes are but that's not usually their prime aim. Trade or professional publications do bring new knowledge to their subscribers – for example, a new surgical technique – but it seems to matter less whether this information is exclusive. Magazines and periodicals are likely to be less urgent in their approach, and all the better for it, as Martha Gellhorn – legendary war correspondent and writer of news, features and fiction – believed: 'The trouble with writing for any newspaper is lack of space: I feel as if I am talking at top speed in one breath' (Gellhorn 1989: 171). Something of the same works for readers who may feel, as they read a magazine piece, that they are not being hustled from one point to the next with quite the haste that a newspaper report would employ. One of the advantages of the internet is that the space available for a story can be expanded as necessary, and in this respect it is a hybrid: it is faster and more up to date than a newspaper can be, but also offers infinite space if required by a particular story.

Space is not the only constraint on journalists: shortage of time is another. And time is also significant within the story itself. Almost every news intro you read in a newspaper will mention time in some way, to make clear to the reader when an event happened as well as to convey the impression that the paper is as up to date as possible. If an event took place at one minute past midnight, then an evening paper (or a morning paper, supposing they still have deadlines so late) would refer to it as taking place 'early today' not 'late last night'.

Yet even where that pressure does not exist, on a monthly or a weekly periodical for example, it is normal to include a reference to time in almost all stories. If a product is being launched then the readers want to know when. Writers would be wrong to assume that magazine stories do not need to be precise about time if they relate to events that were widely covered in the daily news media. Each story has to be complete in its own right. Another reason for this is that many stories are covered by virtue of when the event happened. If that's recently, then good enough, but otherwise a story is most often tied to a 'peg', which means it is seen to have relevance to the readers because of a date. This may be an anniversary – for example there was a mass of journalistic material produced to mark the tenth anniversary of the end of the destruction of the Twin Towers in Manhattan. To some this may seem an artificial requirement. If a feature about the aftermath of an event is worth reading, is it really worth reading only on the tenth anniversary? A good question, which not only those outside journalism might ask. However, journalists do like to stick together and do what the others do (unless they are in a position to scoop the others exclusively), and so the peg prevails, even if ordinary readers don't accord it nearly as much importance as journalists do.

NEWS IN MAGAZINES

For the purpose of a book about magazines, though, there is no need to look into all aspects of hard news. Those reporters who cover general news, even for magazines, will find plenty of books about news to explain how to go about collecting and writing it. There are magazines devoted to news and these have developed their individual styles of writing and presenting stories according to their deadlines, audience and purpose. *Time*, *Newsweek*, *The Economist* and *Private Eye* are all well known. And *The Week* has proved successful in the UK with its provision of a range of news stories, reviews and features collected together in summary form. In this chapter, though, we will think of news in consumer and B2B magazine terms, where it is the imparting of new, or newish, information relevant to the audience of a publication. In the previous chapter some general aspects of journalistic writing were covered, but there remain a few to consider which relate to the newsier pages. It's also worth indicating some of the common assumptions about and techniques of news writing for newspapers as the writing style on many trade and professional papers is modelled on these. So, too, to some extent are the principles of news selection.

LENGTH

In Chapter 6 we saw that in journalism, words, sentences and paragraphs are kept relatively short. This was explained as part of a striving to use words clearly and economically, without looking at some of the practical, production-related reasons

PROFILE

Nicholas Robinson, multimedia reporter for *Meat Trades Journal* and *Global Meat News*

Nicholas Robinson works for William Reed, a large publishing house that specialises in B2B or trade magazines. These are the kind of publications that aren't so obvious on the news-stands because they are often distributed by subscription to readers who seek access to news and features related to their occupations. Nicholas works for publications aimed at those involved in the meat trade.

He came to the idea of training for journalism later than many who choose it as a career. There were no journalists in his family and it wasn't until he'd been working for over a year in retail that he discovered his talent for journalism and his determination to try to do it for a living.

While employed as an assistant manager for House of Fraser he came across the website myvillage.com. 'You could put yourself forward to write articles about where you lived,' he says, 'and so I wrote a piece about a graffiti artist called Hush who happened to live near me in Newcastle.'

When he saw it published, Nicholas says, 'I just thought – this feels right.' And he soon realised he'd prefer to be doing that kind of work than to be making a career in retail management.

It wasn't straightforward though. He'd left college after a year to start work, and so had to do an access course at Middlesbrough College before gaining a place at Sunderland University to study for a degree in Magazine Journalism. He specialised in magazines because he felt it was a diverse field and he didn't know what kind of journalism he wanted to end up doing. He chose to train in a university because he felt he needed to acquire as many skills as possible before being ready to look for work as a journalist. He picked the Sunderland course, he says, because it offered the National Council for the Training of Journalists qualifications alongside his degree. 'That was a useful added extra for me,' he says. So too was the encouragement to get as much work experience as possible.

At that stage he assumed he would work on consumer magazines mainly, he says, because he didn't really know much about the B2B sector. 'It was only when we discussed the trade press as part of our introduction to the magazine publishing business that I realised what a wide-ranging sector it is and how I might be able to capitalise on my retail experience if I worked in it.'

His luck was in. William Reed advertised for a journalist just before Nicholas completed his degree and his application was successful.

He was able to join the company as soon as he'd finished his studies and found somewhere to live near the West Sussex company offices.

Readers of B2B publications are experts and so Nicholas had to learn quickly. 'It was quite surreal at first,' he says. 'From the first day I was writing about things I knew nothing about and I had to sound authoritative. But there was plenty of help available in the office and I just had to get on with it.' After nearly three months he wouldn't claim to be an expert but even by the second month, he says: 'I felt I was able to go to work feeling I knew more about some parts of my subject than some of the readers did.'

One way he acquires his expertise is through the day-to-day writing and research he does. 'If I'm reworking a story from the magazine for the website I'll read all the recent related stories and talk to some of the people involved, to bring the material up to date.'

He also makes the best use he can of the events he attends as part of the job. Many reporters in general news nowadays claim they never get out of the office. Not so for Nicholas. He spends a fair bit of his time meeting people and making visits. An important and expanding revenue stream for B2B publishers is the organising of events, and William Reed is no exception. So Nicholas attends industry award ceremonies and exhibitions such as The SuperMeat and Fish Awards, where he'll be reporting as well as making the most of the opportunity to meet the people he's writing about on a daily basis. 'It's about putting names to faces,' he says, 'and also helping to promote the magazine brand in the industry.'

In some ways, he says, reporting for a B2B publication is similar to working in general news and features. Nicholas writes and produces video for the print magazines *Meat Trades Journal* and *Meat Trades Journal Extra* and the websites Meatinfo.co.uk and Globalmeatnews.com. Most news items go online first and are then updated for print, he says, although for features it is the opposite – they go to print first. 'There are intensive press days as with any publication,' he says, 'but there's also time for senior staff to work on copy with me so I can develop my skills.'

In the long term Nicholas is optimistic about the future of magazines, especially in the B2B sector because, as he says, many people who are working in the retail sector of whatever kind are just not free to be reading online during working hours, but they can pick up a print publication and dip into it. He's keen to make a career in the trade press and says that eventually he'd like to be responsible for his own title and make use of the management skills he developed in his first career.

PROFILE

for keeping things short. (Some of these practices evolved thanks to old printing methods, and yet in the digital age several of them hold good for online technology.) The first of these is to do with the length of lines typically used to print journalistic writing. Few magazines are printed with lines as long as those in books. These lines, for example, have an average of 14 words or 84 characters in them. In *Chat* a typical story would have five words to the line (roughly 30 characters if you count the spaces between words as one character), while in *Time* a typical line is about seven words (42 characters) long. A tabloid newspaper would have maybe three or four words to the line, and short words at that. This explains why paragraphs whose length is acceptable in books may seem too long if translated into journalistic print: the columns turn into long slabs of grey print without that rest for the eye provided by an indented new paragraph. The same is true of words. In short lines, long words can take over almost the whole width of the column and lead to an excessive number of lines ending with hyphens: yet another reason why journalism has a tendency to favour short words.

STORY STRUCTURE

If journalism is about telling stories then one thing that distinguishes it from more literary writing is the regularity of the way news stories are structured. The thinking on most newsdesks is that all the important points of a story should be included in the first paragraph, or perhaps the first two if the story is complicated. From then on the story should be told in descending order of importance, bringing in the relevant supporting evidence from quotes as soon as possible. This structural formula is usually referred to as an inverted pyramid.

Another reason for using this shape relates to the readers who, as we have seen, are assumed to be always in a hurry. They may not want to read to the end of stories but want to get the gist of an event by quickly reading the intro and first few paragraphs. An underlying problem with this model, which is not much voiced in newsrooms except perhaps when it causes problems for a trainee, is how to assess that descending order of importance. For many seasoned reporters, who have absorbed thoroughly the values of their publication, or indeed of the prevailing journalistic traditions, it may seem obvious which points are more important. Journalists sometimes refer to this as having a 'nose for news' or, more formally, 'having news sense'. Many practitioners will argue that this sense is innate and can't really be taught, even though it is possible to list the characteristics which are typical of news stories, and to analyse both the process and the outcome of news selection (Galtung and Ruge 1973).

There is another structure used regularly, although more often in features writing and in American journalism. It is what is known as a 'delayed drop'. Instead of starting with a bald statement of what has happened the writer eases into the story, with some lines of description perhaps, or some other tangential information.

In this kind of introduction the most important information may not be offered first, but what is presented needs nevertheless to intrigue the readers enough to make them read on. The introductory paragraph, or intro, is sometimes known as a lede, to use the American term. It is regarded by journalists as the most important paragraph by far. In striving to get it right journalists are in the process of identifying the most important elements of the story and many will say that, at least as far as news is concerned, once they have settled on a good first paragraph the rest of the story falls into place. How the rest of the story is written depends on the magazine and the sort of news pages for which it is written. Broadly speaking, though, the basis of a great deal of news journalism is the quotation from verbal sources or, as Michael Schudson phrases it from the American perspective, 'The interview is the fundamental act of contemporary journalism' (Schudson 1995: 72). How quotes are acquired is covered in more detail in Chapter 9, but how they are used will be discussed here.

FACTS ARE SACRED . . . OR ARE THEY?

It is an axiom of British and American journalism that news is not meant to be biased in any way and presents a balanced account of any story. This is the 'comment is free but facts are sacred' line of the late C.P. Scott, former editor of the *Manchester Guardian*, that is usually quoted to new journalism students. (Martha Gellhorn said that her own journalism tended to take the opposite stance. This may be why she was, in the eyes of many, such a great reporter.) Clearly magazines and newspapers do not, in practice, take the Scott approach or, to take an extreme example, we'd never have seen headlines such as *The Sun*'s infamous 'Gotcha', which heralded the sinking of the *Belgrano* during the Falklands War in the early 1980s. Many young reporters find it confusing to be told repeatedly and categorically by senior journalists that objectivity is the name of the game and yet to read, in every publication, reporting that is not objective at all.

There is nowadays a more open debate among both practitioners and academic commentators about this contradiction, although it is a debate which can become irrational and defensive if participants from the two groups find themselves together in the same room. Arnold Wesker, who studied the workings of journalists in preparation for writing a play, touches on the reason: 'Journalism intimidates because its currency appears to be irrefutable fact and the great myth about himself and his profession to which the journalist succumbs is that he is engaged mainly in the communication of objective fact' (Wesker 1977: 105). There is still reluctance among journalists to recognise that, as Wesker puts it, 'fact may not be truth, and truth, if it has any chance of emerging, may rest in the need to interpret those facts'. One understandable reason for this reluctance is that there is security and simplicity in the idea that to report is merely to chronicle events using an agreed set of criteria by which to judge what matters to readers. If journalists admit that by their choice of stories or angles they are exercising not only a personal choice but their power over the way readers view the world, then by implication they carry more responsibility than most would want or admit to. The tension with academic discussion of journalism practice is therefore predictable. Schudson suggests that the notion of objectivity as a professional value in journalism was from the moment it was articulated as an ideal nevertheless recognised to be a myth 'because subjectivity had come to be regarded as inevitable' (Schudson 1978: 57). Yet Wesker's evidence, and much research, suggests that what commentators observe is not always the same as what practitioners see. Rather than being defensive, practitioners might do better to acknowledge what is obvious to everyone else and continue to do their job with an open acknowledgement of how difficult it is.

Common sense (another ideological position!) ought to show how impossible it is for reporters to write anything but the simplest of hard-news stories without at least an attitude of mind contributing to the shape of the final story. At its most transparent this is because reporters develop their stories by asking questions, and as soon as they begin to consider who to ask or indeed what to ask they have begun to shape the outcome.

To give an example, if a bomb explodes in a city street and four people are killed, the story so far is straightforward and can be reported in one simple sentence without any point of view slipping in (unless, of course, an official tries to block the publication of the story as a means of preventing the public from panicking). If, however, the reporter covering the story asks the police if the event can be linked to the Hamster Liberation Army, then an element of bias has already crept in, with the suspicion that the HLA may be involved. If he further seeks quotes from the city's leading hamster-hating pressure group then their view is accorded an importance which may, or just as easily may not, be justified. (For a discussion of how linguistic choices, too, can reflect the ideological position of journalistic writing, see Fowler 1991; Cameron 1996.)

The hamster example may be light-hearted but the point is serious and has attracted wide academic attention, the best introduction being Cohen and Young's reader in which they make the point:

> There is a common conception of news as an objective body of events which occur and which the journalist pursues, captures in his notebook or newsreel and takes back triumphantly to his editor. Objectivity consists in reproducing the real world as faithfully as possible. But even within the boundaries of this rather simple conception, it is obvious that it is not technically possible to reproduce all the events, to tell all the stories, to give every bit of information. So some selection must take place.
>
> (Cohen and Young 1973: 15)

Several essays in their book examine how this selection process works, based, as it is so often, on the journalist's 'news sense' – that is, her skill in predicting what readers want to know. This does, inevitably, lead to bias as events are always interpreted in the light of what a given group of people perceive to be of importance and this is in turn affected by their own views about 'how things happen' in society and what that society is like. Cohen and Young are careful to point out that this bias is not *necessarily* 'impelled by a conscious machiavellianism' of the sort that censorship exemplifies (Cohen and Young 1973: 19). It can be just the result of habits of mind (or, I would add, the absorption of craft skills and norms) which mean that journalists and editors endeavour to 'fit' events into a particular world view.

The American journalist Pete Hamill has argued persuasively against the current trend in news writing towards 'salacious soap opera' of which the increasing obsession with z-list celebrities and the burgeoning of the women's weekly celebrity titles filled with mindless and often nasty tittle-tattle are current examples. For Hamill the best news writers 'provide knowable facts . . . and separate the knowable from the speculative'. He said that this approach would give print media such as newspapers and magazines the strength to see off the competition from TV news and the internet, although he wasn't to foresee some of the excesses of bad or at least careless treatment of the facts that would be unearthed in the UK a decade after his book was published (Hamill 1998: 99). The flaw in his argument is perhaps that what is actually being trusted by readers is a writer and not a medium. If a trusted, methodical, accurate writer set up a website or a blog or a Twitter stream, then readers could look at her work there instead of, or as well as, in print. It so happens that print journalists like to think that the unregulated nature of the internet means that the material is not sifted and assessed by journalists and therefore is unreliable. Given the low levels of trust the public seem to have in what they read in newspapers, it's hard to see quite where journalists like Hamill get their confidence that the public trusts them to gather and process more accurate information. Nevertheless, Hamill is aware that there will always be some limitations. In his plea for higher-quality news publishing he argues that journalists 'must ensure their stories are true, or as close to truth as the imperfect tools of reporting can make them' (Hamill 1998: 88–89).

For Hamill that means quoting from as wide a variety of sources as possible, which few news editors would quarrel with, even if the usual constraints of time and money mean that 'as possible' takes on a less than desirable regulatory function. Academic discussion of the use of quotation in journalistic writing draws attention, as you might expect, to aspects of the practice journalists take for granted but which observers are freer to question. Schudson, for example, notes that American journalists did not routinely ask questions until the early nineteenth century, that interviewing did not become common until the late nineteenth century and now, according to American research into Washington reporters, 'journalists depend so heavily on interviews that they use no documents at all in nearly three quarters of the stories they write' (Schudson 1995: 72–73). He notes that journalists use quotations to establish their credentials, to demonstrate that they are doing their job properly, are in touch with the right people. The interview can be viewed positively, perhaps, as a 'means of cultural control over people in the public eye', but it nevertheless continues to raise uncomfortable issues of whether an interviewer makes news or reports it, 'of whether the journalist is responsible to the interviewee . . . or to some other force – "truth" or the "public" or the news institution' (Schudson 1995: 88–92).

QUOTATIONS

For reporters, the quotations they gather are part of the process of telling a story: they are used to gain responses to events, to report announcements, to make a case, to illustrate a predicament, or to describe what an eyewitness saw (see Chapter 9). One of the frustrations for new journalists is to discover that however worthwhile a point of view or a line of argument about a particular event may be, it can't usually be argued on the news pages except through the words of people other than the reporters. There are exceptions to this: *Time* magazine labels its opinion pieces as such at the top of the page.

The position in consumer magazines, however, is different. Some of the human-interest feature articles in both women's and men's consumer magazines are written on the quotation principle as this is thought to be the best way to tell the story. But much of the rest of what is written in consumer magazines is opinion of one sort or another and that is almost certainly what readers enjoy about them. Don't look to *Company* for a balanced news item assessing the merits of a new line in bubble-bath, or even a discussion of whether bubble-bath might be harmful to the environment or the skin: equally, don't read *Loaded* for a balanced assessment of the dangers of drinking too much beer.

Presenting the quotes

Common as quotes are in journalism, the technicalities of using them can be confusing for a beginner. First, punctuation. House style will determine whether the quotation is to be indicated by single quotation marks 'like this' or with double quotation marks "like this". Whichever is the style the opposite will be the case for a quotation that is used within a quotation, as in this example:

> The editor said angrily to the writer: 'I told you if someone you interview says "don't quote me" then you mustn't give their name.'

In this example you will notice that 'said' is in the past tense. This is usual when a quotation is said on one occasion, when it relates to a particular event or even interview. Often, however, 'says' in the present tense will be used instead:

> The editor says 'It's quite wrong to publish the names of those who want to remain anonymous.'

Here she is reported as expressing a generally held view or policy, one she might be expected to hold again tomorrow or next week. The present tense gives the feeling of continuity, whereas the past tense, in the first example, implies that the quotation was taken from a single conversation. This is not a firm rule but a useful guide. The other thing that the present tense does is to convey immediacy, in a way that we are all familiar with in ordinary conversation. In an account of an evening out on the town a friend might say:

> 'So I go up to the bar, order my drink. Next thing the barman pours a beer over my head.'

The speaker and the listener know that the events took place in the past, but the present tense brings the story to life.

This pursuit of immediacy is one of the reasons that quotations are so widely used in journalism, a point to remember when trying to decide which bits of a story should be put into direct speech (a quotation) and which should be put into indirect speech, as in:

> She said she had gone into the bar and ordered a drink.

When the material gathered by interview is put together into a story by journalists it is usual to use a mixture of direct speech and indirect speech, linked together as appropriate, perhaps by narrative, perhaps by linking phrases. If an eyewitness account of a big story is being given, direct quotation may take up more of the story, but a less dramatic story – especially one where the interviewees have not had much that is interesting to say – will be better written with more reported (indirect) speech. The advantage of direct quotation is vividness, especially true if the speaker has a way with words, but even if she hasn't there is a liveliness about direct quotation which is lost in any other way of reporting what is said. Against that, however, it should be said that direct quotation can slow down the progress of a narrative or argument if it is used too much.

Journalists therefore try to achieve a balance. In selecting which words to quote directly they seek out the most individual or personal phrases and leave the more general points or those which act more as a kind of summing up in reported speech. So, in the above example, the speaker might have said by way of introduction to her anecdote about what happened in the pub: 'It was a really good night out.' This bit could be written indirectly in the interests of moving the story along as:

> She said it was a good night out until things went wrong in the pub. 'I went up to the bar. . . ' and so on.

Some writers would do this naturally, but it's a point which can cause confusion among new writers and subeditors. Indeed, fiction writers who use dialogue have to make similar choices when considering how to tell their stories, so there is no harm in looking to novels and short stories for examples of how to do this.

On the more technical aspects of punctuating quotations, I have mentioned the two different kinds of quotation marks and that their use is a matter of house style, but a point which gives a lot of trouble is whether to put other marks of punctuation such as commas and full stops inside or outside the quote marks. There are some house styles which are slightly quirky on this point, but in general the advice is to be logical.

If a full sentence is in the quotation then the full stop comes within the quotation mark:

> The stylist said: 'I am not going to feature white shoes, whatever they're showing on the catwalks this season.'

Notice here, too, the use of the colon before the quote. This is, again, partly a matter of house style but is commonly used where a quote is of a substantial length. If the style of a publication is chatty and colloquial then the colon might not be used as it can be thought of as implying a longer pause and therefore a slight slowing down of the reading process. It would also not be used where the quotation is short:

> To conclude the meeting, the editor said 'No cigarette ads'.

This example also shows that it is correct to put the full stop outside the quotation marks, where the quotation is just a phrase rather than a sentence, or even sometimes if it is a sentence but a very short one.

Things get more complicated here if there is a quotation within a quotation, but armed with logic the writer should not have too much difficulty:

> The subeditor said: 'This headline doesn't work. How can the writer argue Elvis Presley is "not really dead"?'

The single quotes are put around the whole sentence. The double quotes around the quote within a quote. The question mark relates to what the subeditor is asking, not the writer, and so it has to be outside the double quotes but inside the single one to show that it relates to the whole sentence. If a question mark had not been needed here then a full stop would have been used in its place, like this: dead".'

It's even more confusing if you start breaking up quotations, as journalists often do, to make clear, early on, who is talking or even just to vary the rhythm of the sentences:

> There was a lot of confusion after the press conference. 'I couldn't find the photographer,' said the reporter, 'so I just had to do the interview and hope the editor didn't want a photo.'

The second half of the quote doesn't need a capital letter at the beginning, as the whole quotation is being seen as one statement. If a full stop was used after the word 'reporter' then the second half of the quotation would need to begin with a capital letter.

One final point about quotation is that when a lengthy quote is used it may run on for more than one paragraph. The convention in English, although not in other languages, is that where this happens quotation marks should not be used at the end of a paragraph, but they should be used at the start of the next one to indicate clearly that the direct speech continues. This does not apply if the speaker changes. A new speaker gets her own punctuation.

OTHER WAYS OF WRITING NEWS

The guidelines for structuring a news story – important information first, basing it around quotations – are not strict rules, although they are widely used. Whether they are adhered to too rigidly by news reporters is a question raised when you see the styles adopted by other media. There are magazines that offer digests of the week's news. *The Week* is one. *The Spectator* has long published, at the beginning, a succinct summary of the week's general news. None of these have space for the full treatment that a story is accorded on the news pages (or even in the news in brief columns that many papers have), but it is possible that as readers become accustomed to reading these terser versions of stories so fashions in general news writing will change. Regular readers of 'alternative' magazines will already be familiar with more variety in the way news can be treated as will those who are used to reading the news pages of magazines and newspapers from other countries or even community newsletters from nearer home that are written by those who haven't been trained as journalists. And now many of us get our news delivered via Twitter or online sites through mobile phones or tablets. For these methods, succinctness is more important than ever. And at the same time the multiplatform environment offers readers the opportunity to pursue an interest in a story through video or audio material and a wealth of links to further content.

WHAT IS NEWS?

So far in this chapter we've looked at the writing of news stories, but not much at what actually constitutes news in the first place. Again, for newspapers this would be a simpler task. As Galtung and Ruge quantify, and almost any newspaper demonstrates, there are certain conditions that hard-news stories satisfy to a greater or lesser extent. These include, about any given event, its frequency, its relevance to the audience, its proximity, the extent to which it is exceptional, and so on (Galtung and Ruge 1973: 70). In magazines with specialist readerships, news could be almost any piece of information or opinion that might be of interest to the readers and that they did not know before, although even the second part of that statement shows how much scope there is for interpretation here: unless readers can be depended upon to read every page in every issue of a publication it may well be that editors have an excuse (or, more positively, a duty in the case of trade and professional publications) to keep certain types of information before their audiences. The readers and their interests must always be at the centre of any journalist's thinking. Readers of a bike magazine are likely to be keen cyclists, so stories about changes in the laws which affect cyclists would be more prominent and be written about in much more detail than they might in a magazine for policemen or car-owners, or even a general news publication. For readers of *BBC Wildlife* a news story might be about the opening of a hedgehog sanctuary. For readers of *Coast* it could be about the opening as a heritage centre of a decommissioned lighthouse. For readers of *Bliss* it might be the launch of a range of lipsticks, although this is a good example of how news selection is an ideology-laden process, whatever journalists like to think. The news about the lipstick would be little more than free advertising of a product and the perpetration of the views that, first, girls should wear lipstick to enhance their appearance and, second, that they should regularly buy new lipsticks even before the old ones are finished. There are any number of things that teenage girls might be offered in the way of news: the choice is made according to an ideological position, clear to the observer if not to all editorial staff and readers. If the topics which constitute news are so varied, it's no surprise that the approaches to writing differ too. Much the same may be said of feature writing for magazines – but that's another chapter.

RECOMMENDED READING

Cameron, D. (1996) 'Style policy and style politics: a neglected aspect of the language of the news', *Media, Culture and Society*.
Cohen, S. and Young, J. (eds) (1981) *The Manufacture of News*, 2nd edition.
Evans, H. (2000) *Essential English for Journalists, Editors and Writers*.
Fowler, R. (1991) *Language in the News: Discourse and Ideology in the Press*.
Frost, C. (2010) *Reporting for Journalists*, 2nd edition.
Hamill, P. (1998) *News is a Verb: Journalism at the End of the Twentieth Century*.
Harcup, T. (2009) *Journalism: Principles and Practice*, 2nd edition.
Hicks, W., with Adams, S., Gilbert, H. and Holmes, T. (2008) *Writing for Journalists*.
McKane, A. (2006) *Newswriting*.
McNair, B. (1996) 'Journalism and the critique of objectivity', in *News and Journalism in the UK*.
Reah, D. (1998) *The Language of Newspapers*.
Rudin, R. and Ibbotson, T. (2002) *An Introduction to Journalism*.
Schudson, M. (1995) *The Power of News*.

Website

www.bbc.co.uk/journalism/skills/writing

CHAPTER 8

Features writing

Lord Northcliffe, founder of the *Daily Mail*, believed: 'It is hard news that catches readers. Features hold them.' It's a positive view although not one echoed by all journalists. The view that real journalism is 'hard news' and that its opposite is 'soft features' still prevails on some newspapers. This – even though Northcliffe's point has probably been true for as long as there has been mass-market journalism, and in particular since the broadcast media, later joined by the internet – took over the job, in most homes, of bringing in the hard news. Northcliffe's point is that hard news is much the same wherever you read it, but that features create a unique tone and character. If that is partly true of newspapers, it is much more true of magazines, many of which contain almost entirely features material.

Let's take the exceptions first. News magazines such as *Newsweek* or *The Economist* all have news pages, but as they are not published daily it is not usual for readers to get their first information about big events from them. That comes from the daily press, from radio, television, or the internet unless the subject is of interest only to specialists. This means that even in news magazines, stories are written as background to the news or as a development of it. Accordingly, a more accurate name for some periodical news writing would be news backgrounder, a term that is familiar on newspapers too. It's one kind of features writing, as we shall see. It's also a kind of features writing that can't be dismissed as 'soft'. A news backgrounder differs from straight hard news in that it offers more information and greater length and space than is available for the writer to explain the issues or cite examples. So it follows that to write news features is at least as demanding, if not a whole lot more demanding, than to write news.

For the reader, features may be more interesting to read because they offer a deeper and wider coverage of their subjects. Peter Preston, former editor of the

Guardian, went so far as to say that the public's appetite for topical features is 'ravenous', and this may help to explain why the publishers of periodicals currently seem less pessimistic than their newspaper rivals.[1] While futurologists like to argue that the printed word is on the way out, magazines continue to be launched, sold and licensed throughout the world, and one of the sources of their appeal is the quality and range of the features they contain.

WHAT ARE FEATURES?

We have noted that news is written about in terms of people as far as possible, and that it tells stories about human beings, that a strong narrative thread is important and that news writing should contain references to time. A great deal of news writing is constructed around quotations, ideally from people as living sources, but also from written sources, particularly and increasingly press releases. Much of this is true of features writing, but there are several differences between features and news and therefore between what writers specialising in these types of writing are expected to do.

One thing that will be obvious to anyone who reads a lot of journalism is that the distinction between the content of periodicals and newspapers is increasingly blurred. I stress content because there is still plenty to separate the two kinds of publications in terms of design, paper quality and so on. But where content is concerned newspapers nowadays provide readers with a wealth of feature material, whether in the main news sections or in the burgeoning number of supplements and specialised sections they produce. This is of interest to magazine journalists because in many ways these supplements are simply magazines – the weekend newspaper colour supplements, for example – or if not they may be using exactly the same kinds of stories and styles of writing as publications which are more usually thought of as magazines. Even on the traditional news pages it is true to say that much of what appears could actually be called features writing rather than news.

It's also true that the word journalism in its broadest sense has always covered a variety of types of writing, including reporting, essays, descriptions of people and places, gossip, reviews, advice about how to do any number of things, comment on current events or indeed on events which are not all that current. Among all this we would recognise news by the fact that it is new information and, almost always, that it is being reported as soon as possible after the event. It's also a word that has been used in English in its more or less modern meaning for many more centuries than 'features'. Features writing is topical as well, but it is much less anchored to the moment than news. Editors like to have the security of writing about the same topics as everyone else (unless they have an exclusive), and so if there is an event such as the break-up of a pop star's marriage or the murder of a ten-year-old by another child, these stories are likely to prompt hundreds of stories on related topics.

However trivial some features topics are, there is a significance to the best features writing which should not be ignored. John Pilger refers to what he calls 'slow news' and his book *Hidden Agendas* is devoted to it. The phrase is usually used disparagingly among journalists to mean a day when the 'authorised sources of information' such as governments and corporations are out of action and there has not been any act of God or calamity to interest the hard-news hacks. Pilger's positive use of the term is to describe the stories that take longer to uncover, which are less immediately tied to the daily or even weekly agenda, and which are often ignored altogether by most news media. In his book there are good examples such as his revisiting of East Timor and his account of the sacking of dock workers in Liverpool in 1996. Pilger's journalism is passionate and committed – passionate about humanity, particularly the underdogs of humanity, and committed to telling the truth, or at least a version of the truth different from those which predominate in most of the mass media. Even those who don't share his political convictions can learn from his methods. He asks questions about events and received wisdom that lead him to uncover new ideas and information. Viewed even just as good examples of the practice of features journalism, his books are worthy of study, while for those who share his convictions he is one of Britain's current journalism heroes.

I've mentioned that features are less tied to time than news and are likely to be longer than news stories, but these are not absolute rules. A news story in *The Economist* is likely to be longer than many a feature in *That's Life!* or *Grazia*. What almost always holds true, though, is that a feature story is likely to be longer than a news story in any given publication.

Another distinction between the two kinds of stories is that in features there is often more scope for the writer to develop or use an individual style of writing, as well as to allow for more of the writer's personality to show through. Indeed, one American textbook's definition of features writing takes this point further than most British features journalists would when it says 'A good feature story is a creative work of art.' The same book suggests that in features writing 'to make a point the writer controls the facts – by selection, structure and interpretation – rather than the facts controlling the writer' (Metzler 1986: 190). This is a useful way to begin thinking about features, where more emphasis is put on writing style and tone, even if it is rather naive about the extent to which facts stand by themselves on the page, unimpeded by anything the writer might do to them.

So far I have perhaps implied that magazines are filled with either news or features, and indeed that would be one way to summarise even if it is too simple. News or trade magazines are easier to divide up in this way than consumer magazines, which contain a wide range of material, some of it written by journalists, some not. Typical things to find in consumer magazines are interviews, gossip pages, competitions, advice columns written by agony aunts or uncles, reviews, listings, surveys, crosswords, fashion and style pages, cookery, home interest, horoscopes, personal opinion columns or columns recounting some aspect of life, whether it's daily home life or some other kind. Many magazines carry letters pages and these are often good indicators of the tone of a magazine. The problem for monthly magazines, however, is that by the time a letter has arrived in the office and found its way into an edition of the magazine, several months may have passed because of the long lead-time to publication.

CONSUMER MAGAZINES

It is not my intention here to explain how writers or editors produce all this material, as in many cases the way this is done is entirely individual to a publication or, as in the case of horoscopes or fiction, is really beyond the scope of what journalists are expected to do other than sub them. There are, however, a few points worth making about consumer magazine journalism.

Fiction

The first is that whereas fiction used to be a prominent part of many magazines, particularly those for women and girls, it no longer is. *The People's Friend* still runs romantic stories, but many other publications have phased them out. What seems to have replaced romantic fiction is realistic, explicit sex. Indeed, the prevalence of articles about sex in many consumer magazines is enough to prompt the suggestion that recruits to these publications had better make sure they have learned by heart Alex Comfort's *The Joy of Sex*. Agony aunts who discuss personal relationships have been a staple of consumer magazines for centuries, even if the material they now discuss is more openly about sex and less about romance or strategic marriages than once it would have been.

Horoscopes

A second point is the popularity of horoscopes. If an aspiring journalist had a gift for writing these the success of her career would be assured, provided the fashion for them didn't change. The trouble is, as with any branch of popular entertainment, trends change unpredictably but inevitably. Linda McLoughlin (2000) has a useful analysis of horoscopes in women's magazines in her book *The Language of Magazines*.

Listings

An increasingly common part of the contents of many consumer magazines are listings connected with entertainment. Some magazines, such as the *Radio Times* and *TV Times*, are based almost entirely around listings for broadcast programmes. Yet other magazines such as *Hello!* list television programmes too. Newspapers and the internet all do this as well, and there are entire magazines such as Scotland's

The List devoted to arts and entertainment listings. Perhaps the continued popularity of these paper lists is evidence that electronic journalism is not yet in a position to replace the more traditional paper journalism in the daily habits of readers.

Reviews

Reviews and event reports are a staple of many magazines, whether they cover the arts, sport or politics. For some young journalists writing reviews can provide a useful way into print, but the bigger and more established a publication is, the more likely it is to want to engage big names to write reviews. Reviewing or match reporting rarely pays well, although it can bring other rewards such as free books or tickets to events you would otherwise have to pay to see. A regular reviewer for a good publication must build up her own relationship with record or publishing companies so that even if the reviewing work dries up on one magazine, enough of the raw material continues to be sent to provide ideas and subjects on which to base pitches to other publications. Reviewing is hard to break into in one way, as arts or literary editors tend to use their own coteries of writers. However, it isn't time consuming or expensive for someone who wants to review to write a couple of sample pieces to offer to an editor.

Quizzes

Quizzes, with titles such as 'Are you way too good for him?' (*Cosmopolitan*), which form such a staple part of journalism for women, are included as entertainment and are often written in-house by the editorial team, and with a great deal of amusement. Readers enjoy playing games like this, even if the pop-psychological approach of most of them is more light-hearted than seriously informative.

Photography

Another vital part of many magazines is the photography. The days of the general photojournalism magazines such as *Picture Post* have gone, although photographers are still despatched on stories with reporters for news and some documentary work. It is rare for articles in consumer magazines to devote much space to documentary photography, although there are exceptions: the colour news magazines such as *Time*, *Newsweek* and *Paris Match* or the specialist publications such as *National Geographic*. What is increasingly popular, however, is what could loosely be called pin-up photography, whether it is portraits of bare-boobed babes for the men's magazines, men unzipped for the women's market, 'delish' hunks for the girls' magazines or, less lasciviously, footballers or cyclists in the sporting magazines, horses in the horse magazines, model railway kit in the railway magazines or animals and birds in the many publications now devoted to wildlife. Fashion, beauty, food and interiors style photos are, of course, a significant part of the content of glossy magazines, but they are not photojournalism (see Chapter 14).

PROFILE

Lorna Gray, features writer, *Cosmopolitan*

Lorna Gray 'absolutely loves' her work as a features writer at *Cosmopolitan* magazine. 'It's my dream job,' she says. 'I am a *Cosmo* girl. I am the typical reader.' But that's not the only reason. 'It's the best of the glossies,' she says. 'It has so much personality and heart and is right down there with the readers.'

This closeness to the readers is important to her so the very best part of the job is that she gets to meet them. *Cosmo* has specialist entertainment writers and editors and so Lorna doesn't get to mix much with the stars. 'I've interviewed Russell Brand, Channing Tatum and Matthew McConaughey although I do prefer my real-life work!' she says. Instead she concentrates on the features that are not about celebrities, and that's just fine with her. She interviews ordinary people for the more investigative, issue-based pieces. 'I love writing real-life stuff', she says. 'I find it really gripping to hear people's stories. And then it's lovely thing if you get a letter saying they liked the piece.'

Lorna discovered her taste and developed her undoubted talent for real-life reporting by working for London-based news features agency Famous Features, which sold her work to the weekly women's magazines and the tabloids. This gave her the practice she needed at interviewing, pitching ideas and writing up stories in a wide range of styles. It didn't take more than a few months for her to be offered a full-time job writing for *Chat* and *Pick Me Up!*, where she additionally found herself taking responsibility for the work of others by having to commission and edit stories as well as write them.

The surprising thing is how quickly all this happened. Within two years of leaving Stirling University Lorna had achieved her current job. She had studied for a journalism degree that included one module in magazine journalism. 'That's how I discovered I really liked magazines,' she said. 'We had to do a celebrity interview and I got hold of Cameron Stout from *Big Brother*. I really liked doing that. It was great trying my hand at feature writing for the first time.'

Work experience was not compulsory but it was strongly encouraged on her course, and so Lorna arranged some with local radio in Scotland, where she's from, and with *More!* magazine, as well as a month with *Cosmopolitan* – time she was able to put to good use for her academic dissertation as well as for developing her professional skills. Then, as she was about to graduate, she was offered an internship by *Cosmopolitan*

PROFILE

and was in the fortunate position of having to choose between that and an offer of work from Central FM.

There's a certain amount of controversy about internships these days, but *Cosmopolitan* treats its interns properly: they are paid just about enough to live on and the contract lasts for nine months. During that period Lorna worked as the features intern. While she was there she was learning how to do the job (research, writing, pitching), amassing some cuttings and establishing plenty of useful contacts among the kind of people who are responsible for commissioning features for newspapers and magazines.

It was through those contacts that she found the job at Famous Features, and once there her work was particularly in demand by IPC's *Pick Me Up!*, which eventually offered her a job.

A few months later, *Cosmopolitan* advertised for a features writer through the industry jobs website Gorkana. Lorna was encouraged to apply and found herself having to go through an intense selection process. She had to pitch in detail several features ideas, write a column, complete several research and writing tasks within a week and then undergo a searching interview by three senior members of staff. That got her through the first round! There was more to come in the shape of tests of her ability to generate ideas, write and edit.

'I'm just so lucky,' Lorna says of her success at getting the job, although you could say that after such a gruelling set of tests maybe luck doesn't come into it – talent and hard work obviously do too. One of the ideas she pitched, about young women and hypothermia, was so good she was asked to write it up the same week and it appeared in *Cosmopolitan* just a couple of months later. She's sure that the time she spent working on real-life stories for the tabloids and women's weeklies helped her to be selected for this job.

In the end, luck is partly what you make of it, according to Lorna. She expresses amazement at how some people who come into magazines for work experience just don't really make enough of what's on offer. 'They turn up late, don't offer to make the tea, don't ask if anyone needs help,' she says. 'They waste a fantastic opportunity.'

She, on the other hand, made herself known to as many people as possible and was keen to turn her hand to anything, including photocopying and distributing the post. 'That's a very good way to meet everyone,' she says, 'and then it's up to you to take the initiative, be willing to do whatever comes up.' One thing that came up in her case was the chance to write bylined copy for the 'Sex and Single Girl'

PROFILE

column – an article about what it's like to share a flat with your male best friend.

Now on the staff of a famous women's glossy, Lorna recalls that as a child she 'always, always wanted to be a journalist'. There are no journalists in the family but her aunt clearly remembers that Lorna used to make her own magazines and wrote a book, as well as producing/editing a newspaper while she was in the last year of high school.

Given that *Cosmopolitan* is one of the most famous magazine brands in the world there must be some perks in addition to the job satisfaction that goes with writing features. 'Well I am in charge of the books coverage,' says Lorna, 'so I get lots of books. Then there are the beauty and fashion freebies, not to mention all the parties and events I get invited to.'

For now, then, Lorna is very happy where she is. As she's only just settling in she hasn't had time to think far ahead into the future. 'I'm loving this right now,' she says when asked about her ambitions. And she's optimistic that print publications will survive the competition from other media while making good use of them to extend and enhance their brands. 'I hope print doesn't die out in my lifetime,' she says, 'and I don't think it will. There's nothing like reading a magazine in print.'

PROFILE

Personal columns

What is true of all these aspects of magazine content that are not strictly to do with journalistic writing is that they help to create a context for the journalism. They also help to create the tone or atmosphere of the publication, and this in turn, editors believe, helps to inspire the loyalty of readers.

This tone is further established by the personal opinion columns, whether they are openly labelled as such or whether they appear as a 'letter from the editor' or in some other guise. Whereas, in news, there is a tradition of journalists attempting to write impartially, in consumer magazine journalism this is not the case. Within such a magazine there may be pockets of reportage that do aspire to impartiality, but much of what surrounds these will be opinion in one form or another.

At its most journalistic it may be the sort of column that tells the story of the writer's week or some domestic incident, or it may be almost an essay on a topic likely to interest readers. It would be hard to train a writer to produce this sort of thing. If you think you can do it, try it out, several times, and then test it out first on non-journalists and then, if you're going to try to sell it, on editors. The mistress of the domestic life column was Alice Thomas Ellis who wrote the weekly 'Home Life' in

The Spectator for several years and published collections of these columns in book form. She was, however, one of our leading novelists, as well as someone who had an unusually rich home life (seven children, famous and interesting or weird friends) and so the fact that her column about daily life was so readable is not surprising. Sandi Toksvig is another daily-life columnist whose writing is readable and funny, although we shouldn't forget that she too has another professional life, in her case as a stand-up comedian. The problem with this kind of column is that while many journalists are capable of producing half a dozen of them, far fewer can sustain the effort, so the material begins to wear thin. To write one should not be seen as an easy option. The best are informative even if they are also entertaining.

THE JOURNALISTIC FEATURE

If we turn now to what journalists would consider to be features proper, rather than all those items other than news with which magazines are filled, there is no set of formulae to learn as there is for news. Far more flexibility is allowed in structure, style and tone and, as I have noted, there is more scope for the writer's voice to emerge. (Indeed, some editors would say that a voice has to emerge or the writing will remain too flat and too bland to sustain the reader over the greater length at which features are published.) There are, nevertheless, certain types of feature which are common and which can be used in many ways and to cover many different topics.

News backgrounder

The news backgrounder I have mentioned, and this is probably the most common kind of feature. It is very much what its name suggests – a look in more detail at some aspect of a story beyond the hard-news element. Take the example of the week that three bombs exploded in areas of London with large ethnic minority communities – Brixton and Brick Lane. That's the hard news. A news backgrounder might look at the groups who are suspected of planting the bomb – what motivates them? How big and influential are they? Another might examine the recent record of racially motivated crime in those areas. Another might interview residents to find out what their daily experience of racism is. There are no real restrictions to the kind of question that can be asked in a news backgrounder, giving the reporter scope to think through the implications of an event and use the usual reporter's techniques to find the answers, opinion and descriptive colour.

The interview or profile

The interview or profile is one of the most common types of magazine features, whether it is hung on a topical peg or not. Interviews may be with celebrities or with ordinary members of the public who are in the news in their own right, or whose job or field of interest is in the news. There are many ways of conducting and writing interviews or profiles, and for a fuller discussion of the history and techniques see Chapters 9 and 10.

The composite interview

Closely allied to the interview with one person is what might be called a composite interview feature. That is where a number of people are asked about a particular topic and their views or their stories are told in separate pieces of copy, each of roughly the same length, often with a picture at the top. The series of interviews would be introduced with a few paragraphs to explain the purpose of the piece and why it is topical. There is no limit to what this kind of feature might be about. Three examples: young men who earn their living as rent-boys; women who became Labour MPs in the 2009 general election; four men who quit their jobs and then got rich.

The point of composite features is to tell a story about people, what journalists call a human-interest story. Many of the most readable human-interest stories are those about people who are not in the public eye. Pete Hamill, in his lament about the state of journalism at the end of the twentieth century, was scathing about how overshadowed ordinary lives are by the predominance of the famous. 'The print media are runny with the virus of celebrity' is how he puts it, noting that among the celebrities who are most often written about 'true accomplishment is marginal to the recognition factor' (Hamill 1998: 79, 80). Others feel differently, as the contents lists of most magazines show. And Lynn Barber says she writes about famous people precisely because she finds fame to be a subject of fascination in itself (Barber 1998: xi).

Human-interest stories

The term 'human interest' covers a huge range of material, and at its simplest means the telling of any story through the eyes of the people who are involved or affected by it, although often it is the people who are the point of the story rather than any independent event. An example of a typical weekly women's magazine human-interest story would be an account of a woman whose teenage son caught her as she fell out of a burning building, saving her life. The narrative would be broken up by quotes from her to give a vivid account of the fear and then the gratitude she felt. What the reader gets out of an account such as this is not altogether clear. For journalists it is obvious that as human beings we are all interested in what befalls other human beings. From a literary perspective it could be said that the stories journalists write are the close relations of any other stories that people like to tell and have always told each other, whether fictional or factual or somewhere in between; whether spoken, sung, filmed or written down.

In his anthology of reportage, John Carey suggests that one of the pleasures of reading accounts of the tribulations of others is that it 'places him continually in the position of a survivor' (Carey 1987: xxxv). His view is coloured by his arguable (not to say blinkered) suggestion that good reportage is largely about death and war. Good reportage can, in fact, be written about almost anything. The preponderance of death and war in the press and in his anthology has, I would argue, more to do with the interests and, just possibly the gender, of those doing the commissioning and selecting of articles than with any absolute notion of what it might be worthwhile to read. Nevertheless, Carey is making a brave attempt to understand why it is that we should want to read lengthy accounts, which go well beyond the bare facts, of what has happened to people we have never met and never will. There would, after all, be little journalism and few journalists if nothing more had been written about, say, that famous car accident in 1997 than: 'Diana, Princess of Wales, died in a car accident in Paris early today.' Readers do want to know more, editors are paid to predict (or perhaps dictate?) how much more, and journalists do want to make a living.

Within the broad category of human interest you could certainly include all celebrity coverage and many interviews with those who are not famous, if they are talking about their lives in general. One subdivision of the interview category, for example, is the interview series based around one aspect of the lives of a range of people. 'A life in the day' in *The Sunday Times Magazine* is a well-known example of this, and a tribute to its success is the number of copycat regular features it has prompted both in the same magazine ('Relative values') and in others: for many years *The Observer* ran a series called 'A room of one's own', and the *Radio Times* a regular piece called 'My kind of day'. These are all shortish and are not designed to probe the depths of the subject's psyche. As often as not they are written in the first person, although usually as filtered through a journalist to make it readable. The point of these is, very simply, to give an insight into one or two aspects of the lives of others partly through an examination of their 'daily rituals' as Hunter Davies, whose idea it was in the first place, puts it in the introduction to the anthology of some of the best examples from the first 25 years (Stafford-Clark 2003).

The triumph-over-tragedy piece

Another staple of human-interest journalism is what is known as a triumph-over-tragedy (TOT) piece. The nickname is self-explanatory: a true story is recounted about some brush with horror or death or embarrassment or disability. The gravity of the circumstances varies and the style in which it is written up varies too, according to the magazine. There are those who assume that TOTs are found mainly in the down-market press, in particular the weekly women's magazines. In reality there is no such restriction. Up-market magazines and broadsheet newspapers all have their own ways of presenting what is in essence the same kind of story.

If TOT stories are one step away from fictional narratives, there is another staple of features journalism that is perhaps two steps away. This is the personal column through which the writer tells the story of his life week by week, weaving into the broader narrative momentous life events which can't be recounted in a jokey tone just for their entertainment value. Reading these columns is like reading a novel in real time, so at each sitting there is only a limited amount that can have happened to the writer as the illness progresses, or the divorce proceeds. For many readers these narratives are much more gripping than the best fiction for the uncomplicated reason that they are true and in the most extreme cases because far from being triumphs over tragedy they provide a detailed account of the tragedy as it unfolds. Ruth Picardie wrote about and then died of breast cancer; John Diamond was treated for and died of throat cancer; Kathryn Flett told readers about getting divorced and then being ditched by a new lover. The most up-to-date version of this kind of writing appears not in print but in personal blogs which allow anyone to 'publish' the story of their lives on a regular basis. The quality of the writing is variable, but at its best this kind of writing can give an invaluable insight into the lives of those who wouldn't otherwise necessarily have a voice. It can also be available almost immediately instead of having to negotiate a print publication schedule. (See Chapter 12 for a fuller discussion of blogging.)

Some readers complain that this kind of writing is self-indulgent and too personal. Its supporters argue that it's the personal nature of it that makes it so worthwhile to read. John Diamond, who was already writing a regular column before he became ill, merely mentioned the diagnosis one week and found himself inundated with letters from readers who wanted to sympathise or advise, or who took strength from the writing, but who most definitely wanted to read more, which perhaps bears out Carey's point about the pleasure readers get from being in the position of survivors. It goes without saying that this isn't the kind of writing a journalist can set out to base a career on, but it should be noted as a trend because of what it says about readers.

In many cases the TOT narrative does involve the account of an event, whether it's a train crash or being stuck on a snowy mountain for three days with no food. Part of the piece therefore would be a simple narrative account of the event leading up to the tragedy and its eventual overcoming. Many features, though, are based just on the account of an event or a set of circumstances. An event such as a political demonstration might be written up as part description, part narrative, part quotation from participants or observers, and with some explanation of the political purpose.

Essays

Another feature type, although one more often found in serious magazines such as the *London Review of Books* or *Prospect*, is the essay. Here the writer takes a topic such as racism, the death penalty, secondary school education, begging, one-night stands and writes a considered piece based on research and reflection. The research separates this from a straight opinion piece, though the distinction is not absolute. In a more essay-like article the journalist might start the research phase with a question rather than a point of view, whereas most opinion pieces start from a premise that the writer researches only to find supporting evidence. By opinion pieces I don't just mean the kind of polemic that takes a stand on matters of political or ethical importance. In some of the more light-hearted magazines an opinion piece might argue the case for staying single or avoiding football matches on television.

Advice

It would be impossible to discuss features writing without mentioning the 'how to' feature. In one form or another these fill the majority of pages in magazines aimed at women and girls, and that's without including the agony columns giving advice about specific problems. There are, of course, feminist accounts of why it is that females are thought to be so incompetent at leading their daily lives that they need a limitless supply of advice about how to do it. 'Look great naked. The lazy girl's workout for a sexy body'; 'How to find your mate a boy', are some examples. Sociologist Marjorie Ferguson argues that much of what is going on in the pages of the magazines for women and girls is comparable to what happens in religious cults: just as newcomers are initiated into the rites of a religious sect, so women and girls learn the rituals associated with the 'cult of femininity', such as how to cleanse, tone and moisturise their skin, among many other things (Ferguson 1983: 5). Harmless enough advice is offered in some cases, but as feminists of the more traditional sort argue, the range of topics on which advice is offered is narrowly limited to beauty, fashion, home making and sex (Greer 1999: 312; McKay 1999; White 1977: 46–47). The reason the range is so limited is that these are the topics on the strength of which advertising can be sold (see Chapter 15).

The overnight success of men's lifestyle magazines suggested that boys and men need help with learning the basics of daily life, just as women have always been thought to. Or, at least, it showed that publishers have decided there's money to be made out of telling them they need such help.

The 'how to' feature appears in almost every kind of periodical publication. Financial magazines tell readers how to purchase pensions or choose a stockbroker; parenting magazines explain the intricacies of nappy-changing; mountain-bike magazines give guides to bike maintenance. The writer's imagination is the only limit to what could be turned into a serviceable 'how to' piece. The same could be said about features in general. There is not really a restriction on subject matter other than the preferences of the editor and the bounds of good taste – not even that in some magazines.

REPORTAGE

Another type of feature, reportage, is in fact the vaguest, because the word 'reportage' covers so many possibilities and forms part of so many kinds of journalism. At one level the word simply means journalistic reporting, and in that sense it should cover straight news writing too. However, most British news reporters would not think of applying the word to what they do. If they used the word reportage at all they might use it to mean something more like a news background feature, something that contains elements of descriptive writing and the other various reporting techniques. That's too simple, though, as reportage does not have to be tied to subjects which are currently in the news. Ian Jack, former editor of *The Independent on Sunday*, discusses the way the French word 'reportage' carries a weight that the English equivalent, 'reporting', does not and suggests that this has something to do with the limited status of journalism in the UK: 'Reporting never did have much in the way of social status in Britain, where deference and privacy were valued more than "people poking their noses in".' This only gets worse, he argues, the more journalism becomes a branch of showbusiness. For him, 'good reporting/reportage means to describe a situation with honesty, exactness and clarity, to delve into the questions *who, what, when, why* and *how* without losing sight of the narrative' (Jack 1998: v, vi).

Some of the best reportage starts not from an event that has taken place by chance, but from an interest of the journalist, a question she wants to explore. Jessica Mitford's *The American Way of Death*, an exploration of how the funeral industry works, is as good an example as any. So is the more recent exploration of poverty in the UK by Nick Davies, published as *Dark Heart*. Andrew O'Hagan wrote an article for *The Guardian*'s 'Weekend' magazine which traced the journey of a lily from the field in Israel where it was grown, through the flight to London, the wholesaler, the packaging, the florist, to the purchaser. In a long article such as this, a variety of subjects were touched on, giving the reader an insight into many aspects of life: commerce, mourning ritual, the logistics of the florist's trade (O'Hagan 1998).

One of the best writers of this kind is the American John McPhee. He takes a subject such as oranges (in *Oranges*) or the mercantile marine (in *Looking for a Ship*) or man's struggle against nature, as exemplified by attempts to reroute rivers or calm volcanoes (in *The Control of Nature*). He then sets out to find out what he can about his chosen topics, using all possible methods of research, and weaves the information into fascinating narratives incorporating history, biography, economics, geography, sociology, geology and psychology (McPhee 1989). Ryszard Kapuściński is another well-known writer whose piece 'The soccer war', about the war over a football match which broke out between El Salvador and Honduras in 1969, has found its way into anthologies. The idea for reportage may grow out of the hard-news coverage of a story that a journalist then decides to revisit. A good example here would be 'Inside Iraq' by James Buchan, published in 1999, which is an account of a visit to the country several years after the war which followed its invasion of Kuwait to see what life was like in the aftermath. Åsne Seierstad's books *The Bookseller of Kabul* and *101 Days in Baghdad* are recent examples of book-length reportage produced by a journalist who was otherwise working to daily news deadlines.

What Mitford, McPhee, O'Hagan, Kapuściński (and, indeed, all the best journalists since Defoe) demonstrate is a strong curiosity. They want to know how things work, why things are done as they are, how people and places and systems fit together. For some writers the obsession with wanting to know more leads them to do their research undercover, by joining an organisation or pretending to be someone they are not. The most famous English example of this is George Orwell's account of living at the margins of society in *Down and Out in Paris and London*, but there have been several other notable examples: Gloria Steinem's account of life as a Playboy bunny (Steinem 1995: 29); Günter Wallraff's description of living as a Turkish migrant worker in Germany (Wallraff 1985); and, going back to the turn of the twentieth century, the American journalist Nellie Bly ('the most famous journalist of her time') who feigned insanity as a teenager so that she could find out what life was like in a hospital for the insane (Kroeger 1994). The ethical questions raised by this kind of work are similar to those faced by sociologists who seek to gain access to institutions or groups in order to study them (McKay 2012). There are many occasions when journalists do this kind of undercover reporting in a minor way – the reporter who spends a day on the streets of London begging (Gerard Seenan for Glasgow's *The Herald*) or rather longer doing the same thing and backing up the account with research and interviews (Andrew O'Hagan for the *London Review of Books*). It will be obvious why undercover reporting is so often done at the lower end of the social and income scales: much easier to bluff your way through a day as a homeless beggar than as a stockbroker.

For the reader, features like this have the same appeal as any other journalism – entertainment or information as well as the literary pleasure, if the piece is written well, in both the way language is used and the narrative structure. Or, as one of the great journalists, Martha Gellhorn, put it:

> A writer publishes to be read; then hopes the readers are affected by the words, hopes that their opinions are changed or strengthened or enlarged, or that readers are pushed to notice something they had not stopped to notice before.
>
> (Quoted in Jack 1998: xi)

Unfortunately, the kind of reportage in which she specialised is not as common as it once was or as it might be, given how many millions of words of journalism are put together each month. One reason is that it is expensive to produce because of the amount of time it takes to research. Few magazines can afford the luxury of time for their reporters – a week nowadays would count as generous, at least in Britain, but a feature writer who wants to spend time investigating a subject or a group of people fully will not acquire much material in such a limited time if he also has to produce a lengthy article. This is one explanation for the increasing prevalence of the personal life or personal opinion columns: little time needs to be 'wasted' in research (Jack 1998: vii, viii).

THE NEW JOURNALISM

This point was anticipated by Tom Wolfe in his introduction, 'The new journalism', to the anthology of the same name he edited with E.W. Johnson. Published first in 1973, and reissued regularly since, the writing it contained and the writers for whom it was a showcase became the inspiration for many journalists, especially those who wanted to write features. One characteristic of their writing was the use of techniques more usually associated with the writing of fiction to produce articles which in many cases read like novels or short stories, even though they were tightly tied to factual reporting. Another characteristic was the depth of the research they were able to undertake. They stayed with their subjects for longer than most reporters can now expect to do.

There was never really a movement called 'new journalism', but what Wolfe and Johnson did was to identify a kind of journalism, aspects of which had, in fact, existed quietly for almost as long as journalism and which was becoming fashionable in the US in the 1960s and 1970s. Some of the writers included in the anthology were or became famous: Joan Didion, Hunter S. Thompson, Gay Talese, George Plimpton, Truman Capote and Tom Wolfe himself.

The only British writer to be included was Nicholas Tomalin, a hard-news man who was killed in the Yom Kippur war. His piece, 'The General goes zapping Charlie Cong', became a model for other writers who wanted to write about media events as they really were, rather than just writing about what the media managers wanted to convey to the readers. Tomalin seems to have written down exactly the words the general used to describe why and how he was killing Vietnamese peasants. The more typical journalistic approach would have been to protect readers from the man's bluntness, perhaps in the General's interest, perhaps to spare the readers the unpalatable truth about what was really happening in South-east Asia. 'There's no better way to fight than goin' out to shoot VCs. An' there's nothing I love better than killin' 'Cong. No, sir' is the quote with which Tomalin finishes the piece (Wolfe and Johnson 1990: 227).

In his article there is virtually no comment by Tomalin apart from the briefest of asides about his 'squeamish civilian worries', and certainly none of the generous use of the first-person viewpoint which has provoked not only criticism of the new journalism style, but also some self-indulgent emulation from less talented writers. The article's strength is in the way it conveys the emotional reality of war. It was also important, in Wolfe and Johnson's eyes, because it proved that the techniques they had identified as characteristic of the new journalism could be used not just by grand feature writers who had plenty of time at their disposal for research and writing. Tomalin was working to a weekly deadline.

For much of the rest of what came to be called the new journalism, time was an important factor. Writers had to argue for enough time to research their subjects, to stay with the people they were profiling over a period of days or weeks rather than just meet them briefly to ask a few questions. They also needed time to write, as what they were doing aspired to the condition of the best literary writing, even if the writers themselves might not have expressed it in quite that way.

In search of emotional reality

The two most common criticisms of this kind of writing are, as I have noted, that it can be self-indulgent and that it makes false claims to be true. The self-indulgence criticism can be answered simply by saying that when good writers allow themselves into the story then it is for the benefit of the narrative: it is a choice the writer makes for good literary reasons. Journalism, however, like any other craft or art, is not always successful. As Paul Scanlon put it in his introduction to an anthology of writing from the American magazine *Rolling Stone*: 'Until you have mastered the basics of good writing and reporting, there is simply no point in trying to get inside a movie star's stream-of-consciousness, take an advocacy position on dog racing, or invent some new punctuation' (Scanlon 1977: 9). Even among the more seasoned reporters a generally good writer may misjudge her work on some occasions, or less skilful writers may attempt to use techniques which they are not capable of using well. In journalism a tradition has grown up that the story should be told in an impersonal third-person voice, so when the first-person viewpoint was used for telling stories rather than in clearly labelled opinion pieces there was bound to be resistance from editors. There was also bound to be a flock of journalists who seized on the technique, thinking it was an easier way to write than striving for objectivity. So, yes, it can be lazy and self-indulgent for a reporter to write more about her own feelings than to report those of others, but that's emphatically not what the new journalism, at its best, is about. It is, instead, about trying to use every means possible to get at different aspects of reality, both the circumstances of an event and the emotional or social reality that goes with it. Sometimes, because journalism is about human beings and the things that happen to them, allowing the reporter into the story can make it that much more vivid.

Getting at the truth

The other criticism, that exact accuracy can't be guaranteed, is one which can only be countered if the reader is able to trust the writer, and this is one reason why it matters if journalists are viewed as dishonest, as they increasingly are. Sebastian Junger, in his book *The Perfect Storm*, addresses the problem directly in the foreword when he discusses the various sources of information he has used 'to write a completely factual book that would stand on its own as a piece of journalism' but which would not 'asphyxiate under a mass of technical detail and conjecture' (Junger 1997: xi). In writing about the deaths of six fisherman at sea he had the additional setback of not being able to interview the men to find out about their personalities or ask how it feels to be dying in a storm. One of his several approaches was to interview those who had nearly died in storms at sea.

He resists the temptation to fictionalise any parts of the story, or dialogue, in his attempt to write 'as complete an account as possible of something that can never be fully known'.

The difficulty for sceptics arises when a reporter reproduces lengthy dialogue he has overheard, as Wolfe does in the extract from 'Radical Chic' in his anthology. How can he remember everything? The answer, given by Wolfe, is that he achieved this by using 'the oldest and most orthodox manner possible: . . . arrived with a notebook and ballpoint pen in plain view and took notes in the center of the living room through the action described' (Wolfe and Johnson 1990: 412). Another of the sceptics' questions relates to passages of interior monologue which some 'new journalists' write. Gay Talese's comments on this are illuminating. He says that as a writer he used the same techniques that his mother used in conversation with the customers in her dress-shop, which was a 'kind of talk-show that flowed around the engaging manner and well-timed questions of my mother'. She would simply ask 'what were you thinking when you did such-and-such' and she was a good and patient listener (Talese and Lounsberry 1996: 2–5). In other words he would ask, listen and make detailed notes.

This is where trust or faith comes in. You either believe that to be possible or you don't, but there is no real qualitative difference between trusting a reporter who writes in the new journalism style or one who writes in the more conventional way. Both kinds of writers include those whose work brings the business of reporting into disrepute, as well as those who bring it respect. What isn't in doubt, though, is that in as far as journalism is about 'getting at the truth' there exist several truths – social, psychological, emotional, economic – in addition to the events which are the narrative framework holding them together. To get at these various truths there is no reason why journalists, like fiction writers, should not experiment with a variety of techniques. Readers will make up their own minds if editors give them the choice.

In the UK, however, readers do not often have the opportunity to choose to read the kind of feature writing which in the US is now increasingly called creative non-fiction or literary journalism. These labels reflect the development of this kind of writing since the 1970s. Gone, more or less, are the pyrotechnics of punctuation for which Wolfe and Thompson (and indeed new journalism) became known. Accepted, though, is the more measured, often book-length reportage of Joan Didion, John McPhee, Gay Talese, John Berendt, Tracy Kidder, Calvin Trillin, Jonathan Raban and Gabriel García Márquez, among others.

It's not every aspiring journalist who wants to do this kind of writing. In the UK at least there is still a prevalent suspicion of what can be achieved, and many features editors would not want to publish features written in this way – just as they would not be able to pay for the time the research and writing processes would take. Although, as Carl Bernstein points out, Jessica Mitford achieved impressive journalistic results without a journalistic empire 'to back her up with clout and clips and cables and credit cards. Armed with a sturdy pair of legs, a winsome manner, an unfailing ear and an instinct for the jugular she sets on her merry way' (Mitford 1980: 262). It is, however, important for new feature writers to be aware of both the constraints and the possibilities of the genre. They may never have the freedom, as Gloria Steinem did for the piece entitled 'I was a Playboy bunny', to research a piece about the Playboy organisation by training and working undercover as a Playboy bunny for several weeks (Steinem 1995: 29). Or, as Pulitzer prize-winning journalist Tracy Kidder did, to follow a computer-design team to research *The Soul of a New Machine*, which in turn took over two years to write. Or, as John McPhee did, to spend several months living on Colonsay off the west coast of Scotland to write *The Crofter and the Laird*. Or, more recently, as Sebastian Junger did to write *The Perfect Storm*. But there is every sign that non-fiction has an increasing appeal for the public imagination, as the popularity of books such as Dava Sobel's *Longitude* or John Berendt's *Midnight in the Garden of Good and Evil* show, along with the popularity of confessional journalism and biography of various kinds. There is no evidence that the public's appetite for the drama of real life is waning, so it is perhaps surprising that magazine features editors have not chosen to offer their readers the literary equivalent. Much of what is commissioned is either the fantasy fodder of the lifestyle magazines (fashion, food, furniture, football and sex), straightforward news background, gossip about celebrities, practical advice about how to manage some aspect of life, or personal opinion.

PUTTING A FEATURE TOGETHER

Features, as we have noted, are likely to be longer than news stories. This usually, if not always, means that more material has to be researched and more sources found. The writer will need to knit together the facts and analysis, relevant anecdotes, case studies and plenty of colour (the journalist's word for description and eyewitness evidence). This raises the question of structure. News is almost always written to a formulaic structure, but features writers don't have similar formulae to provide the framework of their writing, and if they do make habitual use of one approach then their work will lose its edge. The truth is that what works at a length of 250 words will not be successful at 1,500.

There is no ideal way to structure a feature, so the best advice is for writers to analyse ones that seem to work well in the kind of magazine for which they want to write. It is common in many publications to see case studies based on interviews used even for stories about abstract subjects. For a piece looking at government pension policy, for example, it would be normal in many magazines (and newspapers) to start with a real-life case study or two as a way of attracting the reader's attention. Then the more abstract discussion or the quotes from financial experts can be woven into the whole piece. The problem is that although this is done for good reasons, it has, in its own way, become a cliché of feature writing. In general a features story needs a strong, intriguing introductory paragraph, although what that comprises varies according to the feature and the publication. In the introduction or the following paragraph or two, the writer should make clear what the story is about in a 'nub' paragraph which gives a brief explanation of the point of the piece. It's important not to be overambitious as most features work best if they are tightly focused on the particular rather than attempting to cover too much in a general way.

There are, then, no fixed rules about features, although individual publications may have their own. Even where there are rules, fashions in features style seem to change more quickly than those in news, depending on the publication, on its readers, and on the purpose for which the features are being written. It's easy to see, then, why journalists who like in-depth exploration of a topic choose to work on features, as do those for whom the literary aspects of writing are part of the attraction of journalism as a career. The broader scope and wider choices of subject matter and approaches to writing up the material can seem liberating to someone used to the constraints of hard news, just as they can also seem more bewildering to a beginner.

NOTE

1   Peter Preston, the Hetherington Lecture, Stirling Media Research Institute, Stirling University, 29 September 1999.

RECOMMENDED READING

Bergner, D. (2005) *Soldiers of Light*.
Carey, J. (ed.) (2003) 'Introduction', in *The Faber Book of Reportage*.
Carey, J. (2003) 'Reportage, literature and willed credulity', in *New Media Language*.
Davies, N. (1997) *Dark Heart*.
Ehrenreich, B. (2002) *Nickel and Dimed, Undercover in Low-wage America*.
Eisenhuth, S. and McDonald, W. (eds) (2007) *The Writer's Reader: Understanding Journalism and Non-fiction*.
Gellhorn, M. (1989) *The View from the Ground*.
Hennessy, B. (2005) *Writing Feature Articles: A Practical Guide to Methods and Markets*, 4th edition.
Jack, I. (1998) 'Introduction', in *The Granta Book of Reportage*.
Junger, S. (1997) *The Perfect Storm: A True Story of Man Against the Sea*.
Kapuściński, R. (1998) 'The soccer war', in *The Granta Book of Reportage*.
Keeble, R. and Tulloch, J. (2007) *The Journalistic Imagination: Literary Journalists from Defoe to Capote and Carter*.
McKay, J. (2011) 'Reportage in the UK: a hidden genre?', in *Literary Journalism Across the Globe: Journalistic Traditions and Transnational Influences*.
McKay, J. (2012) 'Åsne Seierstad and *The Bookseller of Kabul*', in *Global Literary Journalism: Exploring the Journalistic Imagination*.
McPhee, J. (1991) *The John McPhee Reader*.

Mitford, J. (1980) *The Making of a Muckraker*.

Pape, S. and Featherstone, S. (2006) *Feature Writing: A Practical Introduction*.

Phillips, A. (2006) *Good Writing for Journalists*.

Pilger, J. (1998) *Hidden Agendas.*

Pilger, J. (ed.) (2004) *Tell Me No Lies: Investigative Journalism and Its Triumphs*.

Scanlon, P. (ed.) (1977) *Reporting: The Rolling Stone Style*.

Seierstad, Å. (2003) *The Bookseller of Kabul*.

Seierstad, Å. (2004) *101 Days in Baghdad*.

Silvester, C. (1998) *The Penguin Book of Columnists*.

Sims, N. (ed.) (1984) *The Literary Journalists: The New Art of Personal Reportage*.

Stafford-Clark, H. (ed.) (2003) *A Life in the Day*.

Steinem, G. (1995) 'I was a Playboy bunny', in *Outrageous Acts and Everyday Rebellions*, 2nd edition.

Talese, G. and Lounsberry, B. (1996) *The Literature of Reality*.

Wheeler, S. (2009) *Feature Writing for Journalists*.

Wolfe, T. and Johnson, E.W. (eds) (1990) *The New Journalism*.

CHAPTER 9

Interviews 1
Chasing the quotes

No matter what kind of reporter you want to be, interviewing will form a large part of your work. This is because other people's words are the building blocks of so much journalistic writing. Writers of leader columns or opinion pieces do not need to use quotes, but almost all other journalism is based around quotes of one sort or another (Schudson 1995: 72). The way to get these is by interviewing.

A PROCESS AND A PRODUCT

To journalists, then, the word interview means two things – the conversation a reporter has with someone, as well as the copy into which the words may subsequently be shaped. Such conversations can cover a wide range of encounters. The news reporter's two-minute chat on the telephone to get an instant quote in reaction to an item of news is the quickest. Other news coverage might demand longer discussions by telephone, face to face, or even by email to get the outline of a new policy, details of a new product, or more extensive views about news events. Longer briefing discussions with contacts might take place over lunch.

Then there is the set-piece interview, whose purpose is to present the reader with an account of the personality of a celebrity or at least of one encounter with that celebrity. Interview features of this sort are also written about those who are not famous and often the journalist will get much more time with such a person than with someone who is in the public eye. Everyone has their own tastes, but for me too much space is allocated in magazines to predictable chats with celebrities and too little for interviews with people who have no claim to fame.

The late Tony Parker was so much the master of this type of writing in the UK that he can also be read as an ethnologist or oral historian. His work was published in magazines and newspapers, as well as books. One Sunday magazine article was entitled simply 'Smith' and was a series of interviews with women from varying walks of life, all called Smith. This kind of feature is entertaining and informative in the way that any sort of insight into the lives of others is, but it can also be as significant in its contribution to the readers' understanding of current affairs as more traditional news reporting and commentary. For example, Parker's collection of interviews *May the Lord in His Mercy be Kind to Belfast* (Parker 1994) is an illuminating introduction to the conflict between Catholic and Protestant and, by extension, between any warring parties. The material is presented in a direct manner, in the first-person voice of the interviewee with just a few details sketched in as background by Parker. The books of the late, great American journalist Studs Terkel have a similar appeal. Until well into his nineties Terkel was interviewing for radio, but collections of his interviews have been published and are compelling first-hand accounts of life in twentieth-century America.

THE ART OF EXTRACTION

One American journalism training manual defines interviewing as 'the art of extracting personal statements for publication'. The choice of 'extract', with its implication of drawing teeth, is appropriate for journalists. Another definition of news is that it is information others don't want you to print. If you accept that, you can see why interviews do not always go smoothly. Although an interview is in some ways like a conversation, there are significant ways in which it is not. Conversations can be relaxed, meandering, repetitive and ambiguous, but nonetheless enjoyable for the participants. A journalistic interview can rarely afford the luxury of any of this. As a journalist you have an agenda, a reason for talking to the subject, a set of questions you wish to ask or areas you wish to cover. It's likely that the interviewee will also have her own reasons for agreeing to meet you: your purposes may differ and this can be a source of tension, as Janet Malcolm outlines in her controversial book *The Journalist and the Murderer* (Malcolm 1990).

As a journalist you also have the pressure of time: the time you or your subject have allowed for your conversation, and the time you have available afterwards for further research or writing up the results. (Radio and television journalists are much worse off, at least on live programmes, because their efforts to keep to time are on such public display.) If you are doing a story which demands interviews with a number of people you also have to allow enough time to talk to all of them as well as to get back to earlier interviewees if in a later interview something is said that needs a response. It's the focused, purposeful aspect of a professional journalistic interview which differentiates it from much conversation. An interview may turn out to be an enjoyable dialogue, but the aim for the reporter is not to make or maintain friendships, even if a subsidiary aim is to make or maintain contacts.

Although the purpose is not social there obviously are sociable aspects to interviewing and for many aspiring journalists this is one of the attractions of the job. There are others, though, for whom the initial stages of developing the skill of interviewing can be trying. Someone who is naturally reticent or shy can find it takes real courage to phone a prominent person and ask them anything, whether it's the serious enquiry of a minister as to his views about the economy or the frivolous interrogation of a popstar as to which is his favourite shampoo. However, shyness is not necessarily a handicap. Provided it isn't crippling it can even work to your advantage. You are unlikely to irritate your subject by being too brash if you are shy, and you may even find it easier to establish a rapport as a result. Many of the people you interview in the course of your career will be more unsure of themselves during a journalistic interview than you are as the journalist. After all, they usually have more to lose if they say the wrong thing or if you twist what they say or report it inaccurately. If you interview politicians or popstars who are used to the media you will probably find they have been trained by experienced journalists or press minders in how to get the most from such encounters. The thing to remember is not to be intimidated. You have a job to do. They have agreed to be interviewed (usually). Either of you can bring the meeting to an end whenever you like.

If more comfort is needed then consider the words of American journalist Joan Didion, who has written some of the best journalism of the past 50 years. She says her shyness actually helps because her subjects grow embarrassed by the silent pall her nervousness tends to cast over the meeting and that this provokes them to fill the void by saying more than they might have intended (Didion 1974 [1968]: 13). This is not a technique available to all journalists for all kinds of encounter, but one perhaps even worth faking if the circumstances are right.

How to assess what circumstances demand is one of the skills a journalist acquires through experience. The problem arises out of that similarity with straightforward social conversation. We no longer study the art of conversation as once was done: being good at it is supposed to come naturally (Zeldin 1998). It follows, then, that being good at interviewing is regarded as a natural skill. Against this, though, any good journalist says that you must manipulate the circumstances of an interview to your advantage.

Personal attributes

Before we look at some of the techniques to use, let's consider personal attributes. Shyness, we've noted, need not be an impediment, whereas overweening arrogance certainly would be. The journalist interviewer is almost always just a channel for the flow of information: an irrigation channel directs and shapes the flow of water but is not the main point of the construction, the water is. In the same way a journalist is not usually the point of the interview. The person she is talking to, or at least his words, are the point. This means an interviewer must be good at listening and also at thinking quickly enough to be able to respond with relevant further questions. Whether you are already a good listener is hard for you to know, as most people like to think they are. You could try asking your friends.

Many experienced journalists say there is no such thing as a boring interviewee, only bad interviewers who encounter them. The belief behind this is one of the traditions of journalistic lore that everyone has a story worth telling. This may be true for the kind of interviews that could almost be classed as sociology or contemporary oral history, but it's too optimistic to assume that everyone you interview in the course of the mundane daily round is going to sparkle when questioned about some development in local government policy or even their latest role on the stage. Not everyone is fluent or relaxed enough to provide good quotes to order. It's up to the reporter to get the best material she can. The more imaginative the reporter and the more wide-ranging her own interests, the more likely she is to get good copy from those she interviews. (For a fascinating account of the importance of listening skills and how to develop them, see Gay Talese's introduction to *The Literature of Reality* (Talese and Lounsberry 2000).)

This touches on another common assertion about journalism – that you must have an unquenchable curiosity about everyone and everything to be a good journalist. I'm convinced this is true. It doesn't mean you can't develop a special interest in a particular field, but to interview well you must be driven by a desire to question, to find out, to fit together a picture or a narrative from what your subject is saying. Again, this is one of the attractions of journalism for many people: the journalist is paid to talk to an infinite variety of people about an infinite variety of subjects.

FINDING THE INTERVIEWEE

Concentrating first on advice that applies to all kinds of interviewing other than the celebrity sort, let's assume you know who you want to talk to and why. It may be that your news or features editor has suggested people to you as part of a briefing or that the person is in the news on his own account and is an obvious target. The first thing you'll need to do is get hold of the person you want to talk to, either to speak to straight away or to make an appointment if time allows. Where do you start?

Easiest to get is the person whose contact details you or a colleague already have. If your interview is with someone who is at work then you can usually find workplace numbers through the internet. If that fails then you have to start to think creatively. Might any of your contacts know your target? Are they likely to have an agent or publisher? Do they belong to a voluntary organisation? For many journalists the detective work is part of the fun. Bear in mind that most organisations will not give out the home phone number of a member of staff, but if you're tactful you may be able to persuade whoever is taking the call at work to contact your prey and ask him to call you back. If you leave messages on answering machines, voicemail, or through colleagues it is usually worth explaining who you are, what you want to talk about and what your deadline is. Those who work outside journalism don't always realise how quickly journalists have to produce their stories. If you can't get through in person you can additionally try sending emails. Depending on what you want to talk about you might try asking your subject if there is anyone else who could help if he is too busy.

When you make contact with the person who can help, you may want either to talk by phone or to arrange a meeting. At this stage you are a kind of supplicant, hoping for the co-operation of the subject in an undertaking which may be of no appreciable benefit to him. It pays, therefore, to be as polite as possible and as accommodating as your own deadline allows.

INTERVIEWING BY PHONE

If you're going to talk by phone, try to establish if it is a convenient time to talk and for how long the other person will be free. If necessary arrange a convenient time to phone back when you will be able to talk without interruption.

Don't forget when you are interviewing on the phone that it is more difficult to build up a rapport: your friendly smile can't be detected; the fact that you are small, gentle and unthreatening is known only to you, not necessarily to the person at the other end of the line, of whom you may be asking awkward, prying or embarrassing questions. The same is true in reverse: you can't see that your interviewee is responding with no irritation to your nosiness; you can't tell that he is trying to talk about a sensitive work issue just as his supervisor has walked into the office. As ever, the trick is to imagine yourself in the position of the interviewee and think how you would like to be treated. A telephone manner is as personal as conversational style but that doesn't mean you shouldn't reflect on how you tackle this aspect of your job. Make sure you don't keep interrupting. Think of ways to indicate that you are listening with interjections that don't disrupt, such as 'I see' or 'That's interesting'. Journalists spend increasingly large proportions of their time on the phone rather than going out to meet people, so it is worth learning how to get the most out of each call.

As a beginner this might mean making a note after a call that goes unusually well or badly and taking time to consider how you could have improved the results or what it was about your approach that worked well. In other fields where telephone calls are an essential part of the job – advertising sales or call-centres for example – the performance of staff is closely monitored and appraised, calls are listened to by supervisors and performance evaluated (Cameron 2000). This doesn't seem to happen in the newspaper or magazine industries, even though young or inexperienced journalists are often entrusted with sensitive calls and could perhaps benefit from the advice of their more experienced colleagues about how to handle contacts.

When you have finished the main part of your interview, don't forget to check the facts such as name, age, spelling of company name and so on. If you have a longish talk it can be easy to put the phone down, having forgotten these things. If your story is controversial or complex and you're working to a tight deadline you should ask where your interviewee will be later so that you can get back to him to check things if necessary. This is always worth doing if you are in doubt, as accuracy is important. With luck your interviewee will be more impressed by your attention to detail than irritated by having to take a second phone call.

MAKING NOTES

To be accurate you need to make notes. This is true whatever kind of interview you do, but on the phone there are special considerations. The first is that shorthand can be used freely to make notes without the worry of losing eye contact. Phone work is often done from an office, so there is a desk at which to work comfortably, pen in hand. You can also spread out notes about questions and shuffle them about and refer without embarrassment to notes of previous discussions, perhaps with different sources. One problem, though, is that writing shorthand or any other kinds of notes can be difficult if you're also holding a telephone receiver in the other hand. You may even want to be making notes directly by keyboard and this needs two hands. In other jobs where the phone is a vital tool, headsets which leave your hands free are the norm. Not so for journalists – most just have to get used to a crick in the neck.

The merits or otherwise of using shorthand are disputed by journalists, who divide into those who think it is essential and those who think it is unnecessary. My view is that it is extremely useful for any journalist, but that it would be wrong to pretend it is essential: many successful journalists don't have it. Another method of note-taking on the phone is to record the conversation, using a device that can be attached to the telephone. Some phones have these built in. At the time of writing the PCC says it is not necessary to say that a conversation will be recorded so long as it is made clear that the phone call is from a journalist and by implication notes of some sort will be taken. (An exception would be if the interview is being conducted as part of an investigation where subterfuge could merit a public interest defence.) Normally it would be polite to say that you would like to record the conversation, but it's easy to see how the right moment for this request might pass, especially in an interview with a busy person who doesn't much want to talk to you anyway. To raise the question of recording makes the encounter seem more formal and possibly more threatening than it otherwise would. Most people who are used to giving quotes will not object to being recorded, although it might be more difficult to get them to speak for some of the time off the record for briefing purposes unless you make it clear that you are switching the recording device off when they ask. Note that if you intend to broadcast the interview then you must tell the interviewee in advance.

INTERVIEWING BY EMAIL

Increasingly, email is used by journalists in relation to interviews. At the initial contact stage it has an obvious advantage over phoning – the message is dealt with by the recipient when it is convenient rather than causing an interruption at a busy moment. That can be particularly helpful if the interviewee is in another country. The drawback, of course, is that an email can be ignored, leaving the reporter unsure as to whether it has ever been read. When it comes to using email for the interview itself there can be advantages, depending on the kind of exchange that is being sought. If the writer is looking for information rather than colour, then clearly an email can be useful as it allows the interviewee to express ideas and information clearly and on the record. The reporter may then be able to copy the material directly into her story, always assuming she has made clear at the start that the response she is seeking is for publication. What it's not so valuable for is the kind of interview that is to be written up as a personality profile, as there is no illuminating human interaction taking place between reporter and subject.

INTERVIEWING IN PERSON

Now I turn to the interview in which you meet someone in person, either by appointment or by turning up on the doorstep or at the place of work. In the first case there is every chance that you will be met more or less on time, but again you must establish how long your subject has to spend with you. If you're preparing a several-thousand-word feature based on in-depth interviews with parents whose children have died of drug overdoses, for example, then each interview could take several hours if you want to build up the trust of your subjects and then to get the whole story from them. If, on the other hand, you are meeting a hospital consultant in her office you may have been allocated 20 minutes in her diary. Not much time and so you must make every second count. In cases like this it is worth asking if the subject can arrange not to be disturbed (except in life-threatening emergencies). To sit in the office of some frantically busy doctor or television producer while they field endless calls and then discover that your time is up is a frustration you can do without. You may learn a bit about their work through overhearing what they say and how they say it, but unless you're working on a personality profile this information is of no use. If your interview is meant to be about a new medical treatment or the latest announcement about TV schedules, it's not much help to be able to observe that doctor A is always rude to colleagues or producer B is patiently polite to anyone who happens to call.

If the meeting is in an office, circumstances should be conducive to your recording the conversation if there is not too much noise. If you're there just to get a couple of quotes it may be too cumbersome to start setting up recording equipment. However, it is easy when you start out to feel overwhelmed by the fact that someone busy and possibly important or at least senior in an organisation has agreed to see you. The risk is to be rather overawed and not assertive enough so that simple things which could help you to get the best out of the meeting don't happen, just because you were too shy to ask. Remember that if someone has agreed to see you it is their choice (almost always), and although they can choose to end the interview, you do at least have a right to be there asking questions.

So, if your interview is to take more than a few minutes, don't be afraid to take time to set up your equipment, placing it so that it records properly. Have an eye to seating arrangements so that you are at a comfortable height in relation to the person you are interviewing. If you want the meeting to be relaxed and informal because you don't intend to ask awkward questions, then that will affect whether you feel sitting at the opposite side of a power-desk is more appropriate than being side by side at a coffee table, for example. On the other hand, if you know you are going to be asking some difficult questions you might welcome the security of a formal set-up. In many cases you'll have no choice but always be alert to the possibilities. When someone has agreed to see you at home you may have to contend with the noises of family life or the television going on around you, and there will be nothing you can do to change it. The same is true of bars or pubs, hotel lobbies or factories, which can be noisy. These are the circumstances in which audio equipment simply is not much use except as a back-up to the written notes you take.

Once you are in the room with your interviewee and you know how long you've got, it's up to you to decide how to play the game, depending on the kind of information you're looking for. Advice from experienced interviewers varies. Some say that if you have a killer question you should get it in first so that the interviewee can relax a bit once it's out in the open. The drawback of this approach is that you might be shown the door before you have any material. Where an interview is not controversial, one technique is to ensure that you cover all the ground you intend to and that you are open to other ideas and themes that may arise in the course of discussion. These may be useful to broaden the story you are working on or may be stored up as material to pursue when you have a quiet afternoon.

Many interviews are not conducted in the best circumstances. You may be catching a head-teacher as she walks to her car and she agrees to talk for five minutes but no more. You may be kept waiting by someone with whom you have an appointment and then be told that there's not time after all unless you're prepared to travel in the taxi to his next meeting. These are yet more occasions when good shorthand pays off. Hard to tape well in a car park in a gale or in a taxi when the driver is an unreconstructed heavy metal fan.

Vox pops

There is one kind of interview that most journalists resist having to do. Many readers, listeners and viewers dislike them too. This is the vox pop, a term derived from the Latin for voice of the people. To produce vox pops a reporter (or sometimes a team of reporters) will simply head out into the streets and ask people what they think of a particular issue or event. The quotes are then more or less strung together by the reporters. If enough people are interviewed some interesting quotes may materialise and if they don't, the words may be rewritten or even invented on some magazines. Too often vox pops produce little that is worthwhile and are merely a cheap and quick way to fill space or air time, without the reporter having to make the effort to write a connected narrative or argument based on what she has found, or even to give much contextual information in which to set the quotes. Chris Frost, in his book on reporting, is more charitable. He suggests that vox pops can lend some colour to an otherwise dull report, but notes that as a form of interviewing it is slightly falling out of favour, in print at least (Frost 2002: 97). For fashion magazines, a close relation of the vox pop is the street-style piece, where photos are taken of the clothes people are wearing and a quote sought from the wearer (Bradford 2013).

RESEARCH

It's worth stressing the importance of research. Most people you interview will be busy and have better things to do than waste time with journalists, so to make the best use of your time you must prepare. If your story is for news or a news feature, you'll know why you are talking to that individual. The preparation you must do might involve checking the web, your magazine's cuttings files, talking to colleagues or contacts in other companies or organisations which might be affected, using the library and other digital research sources. Prepare and make notes on questions you want to ask, probably in order of priority. As the interview progresses you may not follow this exact order. If you did it might mean your interviewing style is inflexible in that you are not listening to the responses. But your list gives you something to refer to if the talk dries up and can also act as a checklist as the meeting draws to a close. There is nothing wrong with saying to your subject that you'd just like to check your notes to make sure you have covered everything. Again, thoroughness will probably be appreciated and a couple of extra minutes there and then could save you having to phone up later at a less convenient time to check a fact or two.

WHAT TO ASK

What questions you ask will depend on what kind of interview you are conducting. Do you want straight factual evidence with background detail and perhaps a human angle? Do you want a few good quotes to go with a story that in essence is more or less written? Are you trying to gather background material for a profile of a person or a market sector? When you are in pursuit of quotes there is no point in asking closed questions, ones to which the answer is yes or no. That might be acceptable as a way of getting at the facts, but if you want quotable material you must frame your questions to give the interviewee the best chance of expressing herself in her own language. 'What did you enjoy about your trip to Thailand?' will produce a more interesting response than 'Did you enjoy your trip to Thailand?'

The other thing to avoid (if you work for a reputable publication) is the loaded question. No one will respond positively to the 'When did you stop beating your child?' type of question, and interviewees will only think less of you for asking such a silly one. In the end, though, it doesn't matter what the interviewee thinks of you so long as you do your job in a professional manner. Like all journalists you are constantly looking out for and making new contacts, as well as nurturing the older ones, but this doesn't mean you have to temper the questions you ask if you think a story demands some awkward probing. Your reputation as a journalist depends on the quality of your stories and your writing. Many contacts are, in fact, replaceable.

OFF-THE-RECORD BRIEFING

When you interview for a news report or feature you may find yourself dealing with a conversation that your source wants to designate 'off the record'. It may not be the whole conversation – perhaps just a short part of a longer discussion that the interviewee does not want to have attributed to him. Information obtained in this way can be valuable as a pointer to the fact that you're on the right track and not wasting your time with a line of enquiry, even if the person you're talking to doesn't want to go on record with a comment. It can help you to find others who might. These sorts of comments, however, do have to be treated with care, depending on the subject. If they are not attributable there is always the possibility that they are malicious or ill-informed, so you should ask yourself why the interviewee wants to talk off the record. There may be good reasons, especially as increasing numbers of employees are prevented by their contracts of employment from having any dealings with the press, even over quite trivial issues. In many cases an off-the-record comment can give you guidance about what to ask those who have formal responsibility for, say, a company or a policy.

Can you write it up anyway?

Almost every beginner journalist will ask why, as a journalist, you can't just agree that the words are being spoken off the record and then ignore the agreement when it comes to writing up the story. The short answer is because this would be dishonest and therefore unethical. The longer answer is that if you don't respect your interviewee's wishes over this you are unlikely to be able to interview her again. In some fields this might not matter, but if you work in a specialist area (and particularly if you work in the trade press), you are likely to need to talk to the same people repeatedly. Your aim should be to treat them fairly. This doesn't mean you don't question them with toughness if the story merits it, or write pieces criticising their organisation when the time is right. But it does mean you need to be sure about the value of the story or the material before you sacrifice harmonious relations. And if you treat with contempt the confidences of one senior manager, say, then word is likely to get out. Others in the same industry will get to know that you can't be trusted and this could affect the reputation of your publications and all of its staff. This is typical of the kind of dilemma journalists regularly face.

An additional word of caution for the journalist who is genuinely trying to abide by the off-the-record agreement but nevertheless wants to use the points made by an informant. If the informant agrees to that, provided you don't actually attribute the words to him, you might settle on a form of words such as 'insiders say' or 'sources close to the band say'. The trouble here is that unless the pool of such potential sources is large you are in danger of naming the source by implication. Whether this matters to you depends on the circumstances, but it is a real danger that your source may not be alert to. The other danger is that someone who has not talked to you may be suspected of being the source, something your actual source may or may not be trying to bring about. Journalists should always be aware of the possibility that their contacts or sources might be trying to manipulate them. It's not easy to know how to prevent this happening, but a beginner reporter is particularly vulnerable in a field where there is so much received mythology about nods and winks and doing favours. Learning the rules of engagement for any given publication is one of the hardest things journalists have to do – largely because there are no rules about what would be acceptable behaviour in all circumstances for all journalists.

RECOMMENDED READING

Adams, S. (2009) *Interviewing for Journalists*.
Barber, L. (1992) *Mostly Men*.
Barber, L. (1998) 'Life', *The Observer*.
Barber, L. (1999) *Demon Barber*.
Bradford, J. (2013, forthcoming) *Fashion Journalism*.
Clayton, J. (1994) *Interviewing for Journalists*.
Davies, H. (1998) *Born 1900: A Human History of the Twentieth Century – For Everyone Who Was There*.
Fallaci, O. (2010) *Interview with History and Power*.
Frost, C. (2010) 'Interviewing', in *Reporting for Journalists*.
Hitchens, C. (2006) 'Oriana Fallaci and the art of the interview' *Vanity Fair*.
Malcolm, J. (1990) *The Journalist and the Murderer*.
Pape, S. and Featherstone, S. (2006) 'Interviewing', in *Feature Writing: A Practical Introduction*.
Parker, T. (1993) *May the Lord in His Mercy be Kind to Belfast*.
Silvester, C. (ed.) (1994) *The Penguin Book of Interviews: An Anthology from 1859 to the Present Day*.
Talese, G. (2000) 'Introduction', in *The Literature of Reality*.

Terkel, S. (2007) *Coming of Age: The Story of Our Century by Those Who've Lived It*.

Wolfe, T. and Johnson, E.W. (eds) (1990) *The New Journalism*.

Websites

www.bbc.co.uk/journalism/skills/interviewing/art-of-the-interview

CHAPTER 10

Interviews 2
Chasing the stars

There is an entire genre of journalistic writing devoted to the interviewing and profiling of celebrities – sportsmen, actresses, singers, presidents, television presenters, minor aristocrats, rock stars, even people who are famous just for being famous. The distinction between a profile and an interview is not entirely clear. At one end of the scale is the profile of the star in words that could be written without the writer ever meeting the subject. Such profiles are often anonymous and may be written by an acquaintance of the star, but are otherwise put together from cuttings and perhaps interviews with colleagues, friends and family. If written well these can give an insight into the celebrity's work or life, although the drawback is that the copy is secondhand and is unlikely to include fresh material in the form of revelations or even lively quotes.

At the opposite end of the scale is the interview which does not attempt to make any general points about the celebrity, merely to recount an encounter which took place for the purpose of the feature. At its most pared down this may take the form of a report, more or less edited, of the questions put and the answers given, with Q or A being included at the beginning of each paragraph. The depth and complexity of such interviews varies enormously from the level of the 'Biscuit Tin questions' in the now closed *Smash Hits* (where celebrities were asked random questions such as 'What's the perviest item of clothing you own?') to the extended conversations, allowed to run over several thousand words, made famous by Andy Warhol in his magazine *Interview*. In some magazines (*FHM* is one) two celebrities may be brought together to have the conversation rather than a journalist and a celebrity. From the reader's perspective this has the advantage of allowing him to eavesdrop, as it were, on the lives and thoughts of two celebrities at once rather than just the one, when the interview is conducted by a more self-effacing journalist.

WHY CELEBRITIES ARE HARD TO AVOID

Before we consider how to conduct and write up encounters with celebrities, it's worth thinking about how and why they have become such a staple of modern features journalism. Some are portraits of people like the actor Tilda Swinton or the politician Theresa May – written usually because they are in the news in some way, and based on a meeting or possibly two plus a trawl through the cuttings, a reading of any relevant books, watching of films, listening to music, and perhaps talking to enemies, colleagues or even friends. This material is then written up at varying lengths and with varying degrees of reference to the journalist's presence, a point I'll come back to. Apart from the big set-piece interviews taking up four or five pages and accompanied by specially commissioned photographs, in the weekend magazines which accompany newspapers there are smaller features based around the notion of getting to know a celebrity. The most famous and the most copied of these ideas is 'A life in the day' (see Chapter 8). These miniature interviews provide a short, readable insight into one aspect of the life of another person. The journalists are not trying to probe, but merely ask a few questions to fit a formula. This can mean the subjects are more relaxed in the way they talk. No hidden secrets are going to be revealed this way, but readers will be left with the feeling that they have had a brief but worthwhile conversation of the sort you might strike up on a bus journey with someone you've only just met, rather than the soul-searching psychological exposition that might go on between old friends who spend an entire evening together.

It's hard to imagine someone, especially a famous someone, choosing to reveal intimate secrets to a reporter they've just met, for publication to hundreds of thousands of readers. So why do stars agree to do interviews? The answer is usually to do with promoting a forthcoming tour or a new album or a policy decision. The more interesting questions are what does the journalist and her editor hope to get from these meetings and why the reader should want to read the results.

WHAT THE EDITORS WANT

Let's start with the editors. Editors believe readers want to read celebrity interviews and that these will help to boost or retain circulation figures. The success of magazines such as *Hello!* and *OK!*, which publish photographs accompanied by minimal interviews, shows that this is a fair assumption. A further positive reason is that a celebrity may have a genuinely interesting story to tell and has not already told it 20 times before in competitor publications. Then there is the thrill of the chase or the scoop: some kudos attaches to the journalist who can secure an audience with a star who doesn't normally give interviews. There is also the fact that publications help to establish their brand as glamorous and in touch with what is going on in a particular world by having the shining lights of that world grace their pages. Lastly, and less positively, is the way in which one publication doesn't want to be seen to be left out of the celebrity round: editors seem to think that if Helen Mirren is featured promoting a new film in one magazine then she has to be in all of them. Reporters may enjoy working with celebrities for the excitement that rubs off on their own lives. Or, more seriously, they may genuinely be fascinated by the whole business of fame (Barber 1998: x).

WHAT THE READERS WANT

Moving on to the reader. A good article based on an interview with a star gives the reader a feeling of greater intimacy with the subject. If you are a devoted fan of a singer such as Ian Bostridge, then it's interesting to learn something of his home life, what he reads, where he studied, whether he likes being on the road for concert tours, what he particularly likes about the music of Schubert. Sometimes, too, by reading an article about a celebrity you hadn't heard of, you can be drawn to their work and in the process discover a new writer or sportsman or popstar to look out for. At their best, interviews of this kind give the reader some idea of the work – the new album or film or book – and what it would be like to meet the famous person. This is why so many writers of profiles and interviews try to build up a picture of their subject so that they combine an account of a finite encounter with background information and observation to compose what is effectively a miniature biography.

In many cases the interviewer makes no pretence that the encounter has been for more than an hour or two, perhaps in a hotel or other public place, or perhaps over lunch. In these cases expectations can't be too high. An exchange of ideas on some topical subjects, some comments about the dress and manner of the subject and some biographical background sketched in. That's about all.

WHAT THE JOURNALISTS WANT

The psychological approach

Some interviewers are more ambitious. What they hope to get at is, if not intimate secrets, then a passably accurate analysis of the interviewee's character. This is what Lynn Barber, highly regarded and experienced interviewer in what has been dubbed the 'jugular' school of interviewing, sets out to do. She recognises that you can't make a profound assessment of someone's character based on an hour's talk, but argues that we do something like this in daily life: the difference is that she does it with famous people as part of her job. She is perhaps overstating the case. When you decide whether to hire a plumber or agree to work with someone else on a project on the basis of a short meeting, you don't do a profound character assessment, you merely decide whether you trust them. This is not quite the same as voicing publicly and in the permanence of print your conclusions about how the man's childhood experiences have affected his ability to mend burst pipes.

To entertain and be funny is Barber's declared aim and her method is to choose, wherever possible, difficult characters, mostly men, and to write about the encounters with a bluntness that leaves some readers surprised that she can ever find someone else to interview. What she writes can, of course, seem brutal in its frankness. For the reader the reward is that she is able to avoid the mindless puffery that PR people seem to think makes successful press exposure for their clients.

If avoiding the puffery is a laudable aim, the danger of Barber's approach is that her own personality and prejudices can get in the way of the subject. Her interview with Melvyn Bragg, for example, shows how she works on her material to produce a summary of his achievements and rather superficial assessment of where he has been misguided in his career (Barber 1992: 86).

Her occasionally clumsy probing and summarising can be compared with the approach of American journalists such as Rex Reed or Barbara L. Goldsmith, who make little comment, preferring to observe and let their subjects do the talking within the narrative framework they construct. This allows readers to draw their own conclusions about the characters depicted on the page (examples can be found in Wolfe and Johnson 1990: 72, 244; Silvester 1993: 556).

The observer

To write a piece such as Reed's 'Do you sleep in the nude?' or Goldsmith's 'La Dolce Viva' the reporters had to spend enough time with their subjects (Ava Gardner and Viva, star of Warhol's Factory) to be able to see them interact with several other people as well as the writer. Gardner is given time to talk and her monologue outpourings, while no doubt carefully edited by Reed, provide a wealth of verbal raw material on which the reader can reflect. The biographical information is included with deftness. The point about time is important. If a reporter is allowed several hours, or a number of meetings over a period of days (as Goldsmith must have been for her Viva piece), or even weeks, then the material is potentially much richer.

The promotional circus

Increasingly, however, press interviews with celebrities are arranged to a formal and frantic schedule – a film star may be flown into London from Hollywood to hold court for two days in a hotel room, with each of many journalists being given about 45 minutes with the star, whose PR minder is always present. It's not clear what is meant to come out of this sort of event other than a plug for the new film.

ORIGINS OF THE CELEBRITY INTERVIEW

In his anthology of journalistic interviews, Christopher Silvester dates the first example of a celebrity one at 1859, when the *New-York Tribune* published Horace Greeley's interview in question-and-answer format with Brigham Young, leader of the Mormon church (Silvester 1993: 4). The first record of the word as a journalistic term in the *Oxford English Dictionary* is in 1869. As Silvester shows, this new type of journalism was not universally welcomed, while those in favour pointed to the illusion of intimacy it offered.

An interview also allows a magazine to use the words and ideas of famous people who might otherwise expect to be paid. If you were to ask a scientist to write 2,000 words about the chemistry of the brain, say, then as an eminent academic she would reasonably expect to be paid; if she is interviewed about the content of her new book she will not be paid (Silvester 1993: 5).

Not all interviews with famous people are about the personality of the interviewee. A business journalist might try to interview the Chancellor of the Exchequer, George Osborne, about the state of the economy, or a media journalist might want to talk to James Brown, founding editor of *Loaded* and *Jack*, about the UK's men's magazine market.

PRACTICALITIES

The celebrity interview can be daunting. For one thing it's not possible to practise interviewing those who are in public life in advance of having to do it for real, unless you happen to have a famous acquaintance who is willing to give you a practice run. So a perfectly competent interviewer of schoolteachers, bus drivers, parents or any kind of ordinary person in the news, may find a celebrity interview much more difficult as fame, power or glamour can induce nerves in those who are not used to them. For those who make a career out of it, this problem soon resolves itself. Once you've met ten mega rock stars, including two of your own heroes, it's easier to face the next one: you know you can do it and you're no longer overawed by the expensive clothes and the entourage of flunkeys or doctors of spin. The other thing about megastars and politicians is that they have almost certainly been interviewed many times before, so they are likely to approach the job with a certain practised professionalism, even if this does mean some of them feel bored by the whole experience.

Where do celebrities come from?

How do you get your VIP to agree to be interviewed? If you are on the staff of a magazine, the problem may not be yours (Morrish and Bradshaw 2012: 147–180). A features editor may already have fixed the piece and will merely delegate to you the job of doing it. This arrangement might be the result of an approach by the star's PR handler to the magazine because there's a book, film or album about to be launched, or a politician's office may be keen to get her views on certain policies out into the open. Or it may have worked the other way – the magazine approaching the star, probably for the same kind of reasons of topicality, but possibly as part of a longer-term features strategy to get, say, the right mix of cover stories or range of celebrities across the year. Either way, if the agreement is in place all you have to do is confirm or arrange the time and place. If you've successfully pitched an idea, or if the features editor has had the idea but not yet taken it any further, you may have to do the fixing yourself.

In many cases, where a star is doing a publicity tour, this is not a problem, depending on the importance of your magazine and its reputation for the way it deals with celebrities – things you can't do much about. If your office doesn't already have the number for the celebrity then you can try various approaches: the record company, publisher, theatre, agent or other relevant professional contact of the star; your own contacts in the same field might let you have a number or address. It's quicker to phone, but there are people who prefer a written approach as they feel under less pressure to make an immediate decision. An email can be re-read and can give you space to explain exactly why you're interested in meeting the star. Also, the recipient can read it at a convenient moment, whereas a phone call can get you off to a bad start if it is an interruption.

Venue

If all goes well, and a meeting is agreed, you have to sort out the time and place. What is on offer is likely to be 40 minutes in an anonymous hotel room, whereas what you want is two hours at home. The latter would be preferable because it would allow you to pick up so much colourful material, ranging from how they treat their children to their taste in curtain fabric. However, the more famous the stars the less likely they are to let you anywhere near where they live. Understandable. A record company office, a dressing room, a constituency surgery or other place of work is still better than the hotel room because it allows you to get a sense of the atmosphere in which they work and can often reveal how the subject interacts with other people. In the end the choice is unlikely to be yours, but it's worth being prepared with suggestions in case for once it is. Where time is concerned you want as much as you can get.

Rules of engagement

There are a couple of other organisational points. It's increasingly common now for celebrities to specify in advance aspects of their life and work which are not to be discussed and those which may be. In fact, it's usual now for a list of pre-approved questions to be emailed in advance and for the writer to be denied all access unless this is accepted. As the interviewer you need to know what the restrictions are even if you then choose to ignore them during the interview. This is not to recommend that you do ignore their wishes, merely to recognise that for some journalists the areas that are off-limits are precisely the areas of most interest and so will be most vigorously pursued. One problem here for the celebrity interviewer is the power of PR handlers and agents, who will almost certainly insist on being present while the interview is taking place. It's all very well to offend one Hollywood starlet by not sticking to the agreement about the conduct of an interview if you know you'd never want to interview her again. But nowadays her publicist is almost certainly PR to a host of other celebrities and you could soon find yourself unable to get access to anyone at all for your next interview. As Lynn Barber says, editors whose publications depend on star-filled covers are powerless against the virtual monopolies created by publicists, whether acting for the individual celebrities or for record and publishing companies (Barber 1998).

THE IMPORTANCE OF RESEARCH

Once the interview is set up it's time for the research. How much you do will vary according to the time available, but most experienced interviewers would urge you to do as much as possible. What they mean by research is to find out, by as many ways as you can, information about the celebrity, their life, their views, their past and their work. The sources would obviously be the work itself – watching the films, reading the books, reading up about the sporting achievements – but would include looking at biographical information provided by the publicist, press cuttings, radio or television programmes, and in many cases would stretch to talking to friends, family, hairdressers and anyone who could shed light on the personality of the star. For any worthwhile interview, beyond the formulaic 'Biscuit Tin' type, this part of the job is vital. The more you know about someone you interview the more interesting will be the questions you can ask. Interviewees, famous or not, are irritated if interviewers haven't prepared adequately, although to be fair to journalists they are sometimes asked to do interviews at unreasonably short notice.

A further reason for being thorough in your research is that it will enable you to make the most efficient use of your allotted time with the interviewee. You won't waste ten minutes asking where they were born, how many sisters they had, or how many books they've written. All the factual information should be in your head beforehand so you can ask them the more interesting questions: 'You grew up in a family of nine sisters. Now you're grown up do you still see each other?' or 'Your wife is an airline pilot yet it's well known that you refuse to fly. Why is that?'

Indeed, it's not only the facts that are useful. From reading earlier profiles by other writers you may have gathered which topics your subject is good at talking about and others that he struggles with. Some interviewers think they should know roughly what most of the answers will be before they get anywhere near the meeting. This allows them to concentrate on the way the answers are given and on developing a line of questioning according to what the subject actually says.

ASKING THE QUESTIONS

This is an important part of any interview. Part of the preparation phase is creating a list of questions to which you'd like answers. Once you are with the subject you don't stick rigidly to this list unless you are paralysed with nerves. The questions are there as prompts and also for you to cast an eye over towards the end of the meeting to make sure the main points have been covered. But in a successful interview there will be a flow of ideas: the interviewer ought to be responsive to what is said, allowing answers to suggest new, related questions. Such a flow is not always possible. There's the time constraint, and there's the problem of the overenthusiastic talker who can easily distract you from your purpose. Sometimes this is deliberate: if there are topics your subject doesn't want to talk about then it makes sense for him to try to be lively and eloquent about other, less controversial ones. Sometimes, though, it may be just that your subject is a rambler and your task is to try to prune him into concise, quotable replies. Either way you, as the interviewer, must be prepared to interrupt if necessary to bring your subject back to what you want to talk about.

Power games

Taking control like this can be one of the most awkward things about journalistic interviews, which is why it is vital, in the early days, to keep reminding yourself that you are a journalist with a job to do, not a fan with a hero to worship or a would-be friend with a good impression to make. When you leave the meeting you will have a story to write, and your livelihood depends on it. There are many things you may not be able to control about the celebrity interview encounter, but where you can be in charge then don't shy away from the responsibility of directing what goes on so that you can get the best possible raw material for your story.

The awkward question

In many celebrity interview encounters there is the prospect of broaching a difficult, awkward or embarrassing question. Advice from the experts on this varies and you need practice to see which approach suits you best. Lynn Barber, for example, says that it can often pay to get the difficult question – the one your subject may be dreading – out of the way early on. They can then relax, knowing the worst is over. Others, however, recommend you wait until you've spent enough time with your subject for her to be at ease in your company and for you to have gathered enough answers to have something to write. If it's the one question that anyone would want to ask the VIP at a given moment, then I suspect the Barber approach would prove most fruitful. Also, most celebrities agree to give interviews to promote themselves or their work. It's not in their interests to send you away with no material.

There are ways of putting interviewees at ease where awkward questions are concerned. You could perhaps tell them at the start that if you do ask something they would rather not answer they can just raise a hand and that you won't interpret this in the finished copy as 'no comment'.

Is anything off-limits?

It can happen that when the awkward question is popped the subject will say things that she would prefer were regarded as 'off the record'. What is said off the record may still be useful, but this is less likely in the case of a celebrity profile when what you want is good, informative quotable material from the subject. Lynn Barber says she ostentatiously does not switch off her tape recorder when this request is made and she doesn't make agreements about treating the material as off the record because for her purposes such material would be useless. Other interviewers don't go so far but say they would never agree to comments being labelled off the record in retrospect.

Some journalists face a dilemma about whether they can use anything that happens during the interview. If, say, you overhear one side of a phone call, can you record what you heard or how the conversation affected your subject? The answer here, as ever, is that it depends on the circumstances and the importance of your future relations with the subject. In general, though, you probably should feel free to use the material: celebrities who would prefer to take a call in private can always ask a reporter to leave the room.

Another delicate problem is if the interviewee is not in control of himself because of drink or drugs. Whether to draw attention to this when writing up the interview is a decision for the journalist and editor. It may depend on what kind of publication the piece is for, and whether what is wanted is a no-holds-barred exposé of libertarian behaviour or a positive account of a man and his work.

What to ask the star

One thing that worries newcomers to celebrity interviewing is what sort of questions to ask, assuming they already have the main factual information. There is no simple answer here. Since the interview is usually prompted by the subject's career, then that is a fairly safe area to discuss, although the challenge is to get them to say something new or interesting. For the more psychologically probing interview, questions about childhood can produce revealing answers. In the end what you choose to ask can be as wild or random as is consistent with getting the best material from your subject.

Another worry that besets beginners is what to do if the subject is rude to them or starts to harass them in any way. This could happen in almost any interview, although it is less likely where a celebrity is concerned. What you tolerate will depend on how much you want the story and need the quotes, what kind of pressures await you from your commissioning editor if you return with nothing. The thing to remember is that you are as entitled to draw the interview to an early close as the interviewee is, but the ultimate power is yours because you are going to write up a story from what has happened. If you leave prematurely because the subject has been rude to you, he is the one left with the anxiety about how you will use the material, not you. Your responsibility is to your readers, your editor and yourself. Celebrities, whether they are artists, sportsmen or politicians, can usually look after themselves or else pay others handsomely to do this for them.

WRITING UP THE MATERIAL

For a beginner the actual encounter with a celebrity can be so much a focus for nerves that what follows may not be given much thought in advance. It should be. The writing up of your material is, in the end, what will make or break you as a journalist: a good writer can fashion lively, readable copy from a dull or even disastrous meeting with a celebrity, while a hackneyed writer who has seen it all before can render bland even the most sparkling personality.

Reflection

Build in some time for reflection immediately after the meeting. Don't rush to the next appointment or press conference. Set aside an hour at least to spend in a quiet place to read through your notes and sketch in details about the conversation, surroundings or events before you forget them. You might want to list what seem to be the most memorable points. Then, unless you have to write the piece the same day, you can allow your mind to absorb your material while you are thinking about other things, before you sit down to start to shape it into a readable feature.

Transcription

The next hurdle is transcription. If shorthand was your only means of recording the meeting then you must transcribe your notes as soon as possible. However fast your speed, your memory is an essential part of the shorthand process. You may not need to transcribe everything and as you transcribe you can be thinking about the material and making notes about what to use and how.

With audio recording there is less pressure to transcribe immediately as the words don't have to be recalled to mind. It is, however, worth checking immediately that your equipment has worked properly all the way through. If it hasn't, and you've just stepped out of the interview room, you may be able to salvage something by noting on paper all that you can remember. The drawback of recording is that you end up with far more material than is needed and it could take around five hours to type up an interview that lasted less than an hour, if you type every word. But you don't have to do that. As you listen you can edit and select the good quotes. And if, as is ideal, you have made written notes as well during the interview, you should be able to use these as a guide to when the best quotes or stories emerged.

Writing the copy

Once you've done your transcript and, if you're lucky, had a chance to reflect on the material, the time arrives to write. For a beginner this may seem less agonising than the meeting with a star, but it is nevertheless a challenging moment, especially if most of your journalistic writing to date has been the more formulaic news writing. If you have been well briefed by a commissioning editor then you should know what is wanted and in what style. This is helpful but still leaves you with a wide choice of structure as well as of material. One hour may not seem long when you are talking to your subject, but if it has gone well you'll have a lot of material. A common mistake is to assume that you just write this up in the same order as it occurred in the conversation. This may work well but there is no reason why it should. You are in charge of fashioning your raw material into something more than the mere record of a conversation; you are creating a piece which it is worth someone's while to read. Your aim is to find an angle, or point of view, or some kind of narrative around which to structure the quotes.

Sometimes, but certainly not often, this narrative might be an account of the interview process. In the hands of a skilful writer such as Hunter Davies an encounter which was unusual in some way, or one with a strong personality, can be brought memorably to life. I suspect, though, that the best examples of this kind of writing are based on lengthier meetings than average and where the writer has a chance to do more than merely perch on a hotel sofa for three-quarters of an hour.

Should the writer be in the story?

One of the things the so-called new journalism in the US in the 1960s and 1970s was trying to move away from, according to Tom Wolfe, was the blandness that deadened so much features writing and shackled its writers to a kind of numbing objectivity. It was as if interviews were written by an automaton: the fact that a meeting took place between the celebrity and a living, breathing, talking human being was somehow glossed over (Wolfe and Johnson 1990). He is generalising, of course. Good interviews have been published for as long as interviews have been conducted by journalists but so, too, have dull ones. When journalists use the first-person viewpoint and allow themselves into the story the result can be tediously self-indulgent, but for good writers the freedom to acknowledge their own existence can be positive.

Lynn Barber recounts that when she wrote about her former boss, Bob Guccione of *Penthouse*, for *The Sunday Times*, she made the case for using 'I' because the usual more objective 'we' sounded nonsensical when she referred back to her time as his employee. 'For the first time I felt I was writing the truth,' she recalls. For her there is no point in pretending that the subject is talking into a void (Barber 1998: 19).

The skill, whichever voice you choose, is in the judgement. If you write up a celebrity interview in the first person, remember that the reader is interested in you only as a piece of narrative furniture. Unless you are famous in your own right, readers really couldn't care less if you felt nervous in the lift beforehand or spilled your glass of wine, or hated the colour of the carpet. What might interest readers is whether the star made any effort to put you at ease, or threw your wine glass at his dog, or told you repeatedly how much the carpet cost.

One of the most common reasons for introducing the persona of the reporter into an interview is when the interview goes wrong. If it does the reporter could just give up and go home or not write up the encounter, but there is pressure to produce copy once an investment of time has been made. The story of disaster can be intriguing but it doesn't do to use this device too often, and to use it only if there is something genuinely interesting about what went wrong, perhaps because of the light it sheds on the character of the interviewee.

Another common reason for including the personal aspect of an interview is where the writer adopts the tone of the breathless fan meeting a lifelong hero. These features usually start by establishing the significance of the star both for the writer and for the reader, and then move on to an account in which the reality of the star's personality is revealed and compared with the writer's starstruck fantasy. Not many of these interviews get published outside student newspapers, but it is common for beginners to try this approach. A word of warning is that one of these pieces is probably enough for any single journalism career.

Inappropriate detail

A less common mistake is to use irrelevant information in an inappropriate way. If a journalist does an interview with someone well known, but it is meant to be about the person's professional views, not their personality, it can sound strange if a reference is made to the details of the meeting. So, to take a real example, an interview with a university vice-chancellor about his views on higher education policy was rendered farcical when halfway through the writer put in a sentence about how the man took another spoonful of chocolate mousse. Perfectly acceptable in another style of interview but completely out of place in this one.

How to shape the material

Apart from these approaches, the thing to do when you start to write is to be clear about what you're trying to achieve. If your aim is merely to give the reader an impression of what it's like to meet a gorgeous soap star between takes at the studio then things are not too complicated. If your aim is a quick, amateur psychological assessment of a personality, then the structure of your finished piece will require much more thought. A theme or angle will have to be decided upon: how much basic biography is needed to balance opinions about current issues or whatever takes place as you do the interview. There is no single correct approach to the writing of celebrity interviews. For the writer it is important to keep the readers and their interests firmly in mind and to remember that while any given reader probably has a variety of interests, they buy a magazine to find articles of a particular sort. For example, a reader of *Loaded* would probably expect an interview with an actress in that magazine to refer explicitly to her sex life, whereas if he also reads the *Radio Times* he wouldn't be at all surprised to find an interview with her contrasting her views on working in television and working in theatre. Readers of *Good Housekeeping* are likely to be interested in how the star runs her home and whether she likes gardening, while an article for *The Stage* might look at her early career and how she made such rapid progress to stardom.

One way to start (and this advice holds good for much journalistic writing) is to imagine you meet a reader on the train as you travel back from the interview. What would you say? What would be the most striking thing to recount? Thinking like this won't automatically suggest to you a structure, but it will help you to focus on what is significant. For example, if the biographical detail is fairly mundane (popstar comes from comfortable, happy, lower middle-class suburb, two brothers, early promise shown at guitar lessons), you might want to save this information until you have established in other ways what it is that makes your subject interesting today (he's just donated several million pounds to set up an orphanage in the Czech Republic). In this case you would probably fit in the biographical detail by summarising rather than by using extensive quotes.

Since there are no rules, the best advice is to read celebrity interviews systematically, making notes about what works and what doesn't, why you think a writer tackled the story in a particular way and whether, with the same quotes, you would have written the piece differently. Around the launch of a film or play or album, stars usually do several interviews for a variety of publications. Pick a name and look at all the interviews with that person so you can analyse the different written treatments and perhaps form some idea of which interviewers were best at extracting good quotes. As a beginner it would be worth trying to write several versions of your early celebrity pieces to experiment with different styles and structures.

Checking the facts

The last stage of journalistic writing is in some ways the most important – the stage at which you check and double-check for mistakes or for material which could get you or your paper into legal trouble. Celebrities are more likely to sue for libel than the rest of us because they can better afford the risk. They are also more likely to have reputations that merit the expense of defending in court.

Copy approval

One question this raises is whether in the interests of accuracy it is a good idea to show the finished copy to the celebrity before it is published. The answer is that in the UK this used not to be done, partly because it would be almost impossible to ever get clearance for a personality profile. Few of us like to read in print the words we have spoken, even when they have been accurately recorded. Rare would be the interviewee who could resist the temptation to tweak a quote here or even revise a whole anecdote. A purist might say that this is the only way to print accurately what the subject thinks and says, but a journalist who has to get a paper out to deadline knows that the result would be bland copy and unacceptable delay.

However, demands for copy-approval are increasingly the norm. In most interviews with celebrities full approval rights must be granted not just for the subbed body copy but also for the headlines, captions, standfirsts, pictures and layouts. Morrish and Bradshaw refer to the practice as a 'creeping disease' which should be resisted if possible as it is 'a serious intrusion' into the affairs of a magazine editor and it 'turns every magazine into vanity publishing' (Morrish and Bradshaw 2012: 147–148). And copy approval is no longer a simple opportunity for the interviewee's team to check for inaccuracies. On the celebrity-dependent glossies it has become an endless and delicate back and forth battle of wills, on the phone or via email, with the editorial team fighting every demand for change. This is not a job for the faint-hearted and is more likely to be tackled by the features editor, entertainments editor or even the top editor.

In other kinds of magazine publishing, the specialist or trade press for example, if an interviewee insists on clearing copy in advance of publication it ought to be possible to insist that the only changes which can be made are points of factual accuracy, not slight alterations in the way something was said for stylistic reasons. Where quotes are obtained on technical subjects, medical issues for example, then it can be a wise safeguard to have the copy read by the expert who is quoted, both for the sake of her professional reputation and for the sake of the reader, who deserves accurate information.

Celebrity interviews as brand management

Whatever style of copy the writer produces, for the celebrity subject the interview is part of a process of establishing or maintaining a myth about themselves as a brand. As often as not journalists want to debunk the myth or at least give what they see as a truer account of what the star is like. So the journalist tries to break down the barriers of hype by using weapons of flattery or charm, while at the same time the interviewee may be trying to charm or flatter the journalist into complying with the myth (Malcolm 1990). One way to control their image is for the stars to do no press interviews at all and for their PR companies to supply copy instead, as Beggars Group did to promote the White Stripes album, *Get Behind Me Satan*, in 2005. The 'interview' was then used by *NME* as its cover story (Glen 2005).

One final point is to ask what this round of interviews and product promotion means to the celebrities who go along with it for professional reasons? There may be some who love the attention, at least to begin with, and many who tire of the process but have to agree to undergo it as a condition of the recording contract or film deal. The difficulty for many celebrities is when they are pursued by journalists even when they have no desire to give interviews. From a journalist's perspective there is an obvious appeal to the idea of tracking down a star and persuading them to give an exclusive interview. Realistically, though, this doesn't often happen. Every potential celebrity-hunter needs to reflect on the purpose of the chase and what the effect of it is on their prey. Megastars, it is argued, benefit so much from their fame that they don't need sympathy from anyone. Does that fame mean they sacrifice the right to a private honeymoon (Zoë Ball and Norman Cook) or a private holiday (most famous attractive women and notably the late Diana, Princess of Wales)? The tension between subjects and writers won't go away for as long as readers continue to buy magazines with a focus on the lives of celebrities. The tight control that celebrities now wield means that formal, set-piece interviews are giving way in some of the women's magazines to shorter, newsier write-arounds built from anonymous insider quotes which make for more exciting copy.

RECOMMENDED READING

Adams, S. with Hicks, W. (2009) 'Interviewing politicians' and 'Interviewing celebrities', in *Interviewing for Journalists*.
Barber, L. (1992) *Mostly Men*.
Barber, L. (1998) 'Life', *The Observer*.
Barber, L. (1999) *Demon Barber*.
Broughton, F. (ed.) (1998) *Time Out Interviews 1968–1998*.
Capote, T. (2002) *A Capote Reader*.
Davies, H. (1994) *Hunting People: Thirty Years of Interviews with the Famous*.
Fallaci, O. (2010) *Interview with History and Power*.
Frith, M. (2008) *The Celeb Diaries: The Sensational Inside Story of the Celebrity Decade*.
Holmes, T. and Nice, L. (2012) 'The rise of celebrity journalism', in *Magazine Journalism*.
Malcolm, J. (1990) *The Journalist and the Murderer*.
Silvester, C. (ed.) (1994) *The Penguin Book of Interviews: An Anthology from 1859 to the Present Day*.
Stafford-Clark, H. (ed.) (2003) *A Life in the Day*.
Wenner, J. and Levy, J. (2007) *Rolling Stone Interviews*.
Wolfe, T. and Johnson, E.W. (eds) (1990 [1973]) *The New Journalism*.

CHAPTER 11

Subediting and production

You don't see many movies in which the hero writes a great standfirst or sensitively cuts down a 1,200-word article to the required 800. Few novels are written about the thrill of the chase for the right headline. Subeditors are the unsung heroes of journalism, and if they are unnoticed by the public, their fate within the magazine office or newsroom can be worse. They are there to blame for everything that goes wrong, yet when they do their job well few reporters or writers will notice. Editors do notice though, because they know how heavily the success of a magazine depends on the quality of the subediting. You can produce a newspaper or magazine entirely from agency copy, but you need subeditors to work that raw material into journalism of the appropriate style and standard for your own publication. The right tone has to be ensured, the interests of the readers taken into account, the presentation made suitable for the publication worked at.

MONITORING STANDARDS

Perhaps here's a clue to why the process is called subediting. In a way the sub (the normal term for subeditor) is deputising for the editor. On a small publication all the things that subs do would be done by the editor. On a large publication the subs ensure that the standards set by the editor are adhered to in the copy.

They do more than that, but essentially their job is to act as the medium between writer and reader by preparing editorial material for printing. When the decision has been taken to use a piece of copy, the subs have to look at it with the eye of a typical reader – to establish that it makes sense and is clear – and with the eye of a professional journalist – to make sure it satisfies editorial criteria. Then they have to work on the presentation of the material and make sure that it finds its way into the final production process.

The point about editorial standards matters. There is plenty of criticism levelled at journalists about how low their standards of accuracy are (Worcester 1998: 47), but the standards of any publication are set by the editor and they depend on resources. It is possible to produce a magazine with no spelling mistakes let alone more serious errors. But that needs an editor who decrees that mistakes are a hanging offence, the employment of reputable writers and subeditors, and staffing levels high enough to allow careful checking and reading of proofs.

So it is not always, or not only, the individual sub or reporter who is to blame when mistakes are made. Everyone who has subbed knows there are reporters who should never be let loose with a notebook, so inaccurate or badly written is their work. As a sub you learn quickly which writers can be trusted with the facts.

It follows that subeditors have to be self-effacing. The glory in journalism goes to the reporter who gets the scoop or nets the elusive celebrity interview. That doesn't mean subediting isn't a fascinating and rewarding job, it just means that its appeal is not obvious to everyone who wants to work in journalism. This can hinder editors from hiring good subs, and most editors say subs are hard to recruit. One reason for this, I suspect, is the exciting image that journalism has in the popular imagination. Many of those who might make excellent subs just don't want to chase fire engines and interview the bereaved or even to deal with ego-filled models on a fashion shoot. What they like is playing with words. They like being in the office. They like messing around with page layout on their computers. They like playing spot the libel. Yet these people are more or less ignored when newcomers are being recruited. There's no denying that subs need to understand what reporters or fashion editors do, but the old idea that the only good news sub is one who has hung out with the hacks is out of date and there's nothing to stop a directly recruited trainee sub from going out as a shadow with a reporter or stylist for a couple of days to find out about their work.

If this makes subediting sound dull, it's not meant to. For many journalists it is a more rewarding activity than gathering stories. And subs often have a lot of power, collectively if not individually. That brings its own rewards and traditionally one of these has been moving up the career ladder to an editorship.

If you work in the editorial office of a magazine you are likely either to be a sub or to have to do quite a bit of subbing whatever your job title might be. Magazines don't employ as many staff as you might expect (see Chapter 3), particularly on the consumer glossies. But they do employ subeditors and, unlike those on newspapers, almost all magazine writers may have to do some subbing at some stage during the production cycle.

THE ROLE OF THE SUBEDITOR

Before going into the minutiae of what subs do, it's worth looking at the general role they play within a magazine office. This role varies according to the size of the staff and in turn depends on the pagination (number of pages), the frequency with which the magazine is published, the proportion of words to pictures, the proportion of staff writers to contributors, and the standards set by the editor.

The people who do most of the subediting on magazines are not always called subs. They may have titles like copy-editor, copy chief, or production editor, or even assistant editor. The commissioning editors (such as features editors, literary editors, or health editors) may also sub or at least do some preliminary subbing on the work they have brought in.

In the days before computers, subeditors would have needed typewriters, dictionaries, type books, pens (or blue pencils), paper, paste, depth scales, set squares and rulers to assist in sizing pictures, and a good head for mental arithmetic. Now they work on computers so instead of all this they need computer skills. Usually this means they know how to use word-processing packages such as Word, design software such as Adobe InDesign and Photoshop if they are involved in the selection and manipulation of pictures. They also need to know how to use the internet and social media as research tools (see Chapter 12).

WHAT SUBS DO

Whoever does it, the subbing function is the same. The copy of a magazine that a reader picks up to read is the result of a series of processes, some of them abstract or intellectual, some of them concrete and involving different sorts of tangible objects. In many respects this sequence is like any other manufacturing production line. The raw materials (the words and pictures) come into the editorial office, are transformed by the editors and then leave the editorial office to be printed before being distributed to the consumer. Increasingly, the processes are almost virtual until the last stage: that is copy, graphics, illustrations and photographs are dealt with in digital form on computers. Even when hard copy is supplied by writers or artists it is likely to be scanned into the computer system.

The stage at which a subeditor gets to see the copy varies. On a small publication the sub, if she's in charge of copy, may also take part in the selection process, effectively to do some copytasting, as it would be known on a newspaper or a news magazine. Otherwise she will be given the copy to work on once those who commissioned it have given their approval. Before this it may have been sent back for clarification or for rewriting. Some subs, especially chief subs, do also take responsibility for chasing copy, which can be an onerous task. However the copy arrives on the desk, this is when the subbing work proper will begin.

On a magazine such as *Vanity Fair* or *The Sunday Times Magazine*, where pictures are a vital element, the photographs or illustrations for the most part will have been commissioned, probably at the same time as the words. The sub may be given the layout with the pictures to work on at about the same time as the copy. More usually the words will be available in advance so that some of the most time-consuming work can be done – reading for clarity, rewriting, checking for legal and factual errors. Then, when the art department has produced a layout, further work on the length and presentation of the copy can take place.

On publications not led by visuals in the same way (the *London Review of Books*, for example) the sub may have to commission some illustrations from photographers or illustrators, or find pictures from the library, the internet, or agencies (see Chapter 14). Or the sub may have pictures supplied with the copy but be responsible for the layout of pages. This is similar to the way newspapers increasingly work, where individual subs often take control of particular pages. In these cases, though, design doesn't mean the same as it does on a visual-led glossy. It means working within a limited range of options laid down by whoever did the overall design of the publication in the first place. In recent years on some publications these style options have been transformed into digital templates which set the story length and picture size in advance. The typefaces will be more or less standard, the headline sizes, the use of rules (lines which separate stories or sections of the paper from one another), how pictures are credited – all the aspects of design that go to make up what is called the 'furniture' of the page – will be pre-ordained. On publications such as these the sub has a part in the design process, if only in the limited sense of deciding which stories go where, how pictures are cropped and so on.

Subs who work on words-focused magazines also need to know how page make-up works. That simply means the mechanisms by which the individual elements find their way onto the page in the right place and at the right length or size.

TYPE MATTERS

There are some terms related to type that subs need to be aware of if they are to understand how and why things are done in a particular way. 'Measure' is used simply to mean the width of a column or line of type. Traditionally it would have been described in units called 'pica ems' or either of those two words alone. Before computers each folio of copy had to be 'marked up' by hand by the sub and given its typesetting requirement as in this example: 9/10 Times Roman across 12 ems. Today the sub would just key in the instruction on the computer. Hard copy also demanded a 'catchline' or 'slugline' which was an identifying word for each story. This had to be written on each folio, as did either 'more', or 'mf' (more follows), or 'ends' on the last folio after the copy. Again, computers have made life easier, although the term catchline is still used as a means of identifying a story in the system.

Measurement of the depth of stories on the page is now done as often as not in millimetres, although at one time picas were the norm. The depth of space allowed between two lines of type is called the leading (for old-technology reasons) and is created because the space in which a letter of type sits needs to be larger than its own measurement. Where an even larger amount of space is allowed (as in nine-point type on ten-point leading) legibility is therefore enhanced. The word 'point' here refers to a measurement of the height of letters. It is rarely up to the sub to make the choice between one typeface and another, and no sub really needs to know the difference between didots and ciceros, breviers and nonpareils. Worth mentioning here, though, is the word 'font', which has come to mean a particular design of typeface such as Helvetica or New York or Roman, regardless of its weight (i.e. whether it is bold or italic). It's quite useful for a subeditor to know the difference between serif and sans serif typefaces. Graphic designers will choose one or the other style of typeface for a variety of reasons. Sans typefaces do tend to look more modern, but they need careful handling – with the wrong leading or used over too dark a tint, for example, they can be more difficult for the eye to read. When type is used over a tint it is called 'reversing out', which means a lighter colour type appears on a darker panel of grey or a coloured tint.

COMPUTERS AS TOOLS

Writers and subs in some offices are entirely responsible for keying in copy (which means a fast, accurate touch-typing speed is essential). Where this is not the case, copy may be scanned in or keyed by typists in the traditional way. Computer systems mean subs can produce pages which are ready to go directly to the plate for printing, eliminating the intermediary process of creating a photographic negative which would then be turned into a printing plate by plate-makers. This system is known as page-to-plate or direct-to-plate printing.

Again from a subeditor's point of view, computers are merely a different set of tools from the ones subs would have used half a generation ago. They don't necessarily mean that headlines are better written, merely that it is much quicker for a sub to play around with type or with picture cropping than it once was.

LIAISON WITH THE ART DEPARTMENT

Where the magazine is picture-led, a vital part of the sub's job will be to liaise with the art department. If a headline space is too small, or a picture is taking up too much space it will have to be discussed, and if there is stalemate the editor will make the final decision. The sub can also prove invaluable to the art editor by spotting problems in the visuals at the proof stage: for example, a photograph of a lunch-table setting in which the bottle of wine being poured by the model still has the cork in it, as it would have had throughout the time the picture was being styled.

SUBBING STEP BY STEP

When things run smoothly the sub will work on the copy in a number of ways. When there is adequate time the copy will get a first read-through, just as if being read by the magazine's reader, and the sub will note any major problems, as well as ideas that might emerge for the story's presentation, if this has not been discussed at an earlier commissioning stage. On a word-led publication the story will be checked for length and the decision of whether to cut on the grounds of the importance of the material will be made. The sub will then scheme the story into the page plan. On picture-led magazines, where the layout has been supplied by the art department, that will almost certainly have been done based on an assessment of the length or a note of what length was commissioned. When it hits the sub's desk the copy will be checked for length.

Copy-editing

Once measured the copy may need cutting by the sub. Occasionally more copy may be needed either to fill the space or to improve the copy, with additional explanations, case studies, or quotes perhaps. Ideally, the writer will be asked to supply additions. At this stage the sub may make notes of ideas about the presentation, such as which material to pull out to run in a box or sidebar, or which lines to use as pull-quotes to break up the text.

The detailed copy-editing now begins. This means reading the piece with care, paying attention to the functional points (clarity and economy of expression, punctuation, grammar, spelling, accuracy, repetitions, legal pitfalls, house style) as well as the meaning of the words and the overall argument. A word here about relying on computer spellchecks. Subs must be aware that spellchecks don't pick up every problem. One obvious example is when a typing error produces a perfectly acceptable word, but one with the wrong meaning: bird instead of bard, for example, which could make a difference to any discussion of Shakespeare's plays. Proper names pose problems too, as one writer discovered when spellchecking a story about a Glasgow woman from the suburb of Bearsden: the computer offered up Bearskin and he didn't notice. The other common problem arises because there are many words which have variant spellings in North America (for example, plough in the UK is plow once it has crossed the Atlantic). A sub's job has always included changing such words to be correct for the country of publication. Spellchecks can be customised to take these words into account and other exceptional words entered – for example, those common to the particular subject matter of the magazine.

The respected writer on any publication will produce copy that requires little change other than that to do with fitting the words into the available space. Yet even good writers should have their work read meticulously, as a careful sub will spot literals (typographical errors) or inconsistencies in the copy that the writer's eye leaps over because the material is so familiar. The less respected writer presents work that is badly written, doesn't make sense, is too long, and contains factual errors or legal risks. Some subs enjoy a tussle with copy like that as they find it rewarding to improve the piece. But most subs are infuriated by badly written copy and feel less inspired to write a good standfirst and headline for it. On some magazines, too, however good the copy is, it may need extensive rewriting to be transformed into the written tone that is part of the publication's identity. Again, this can make the job of subbing more interesting, even if it doesn't always make the magazine more compelling for the reader.

In some publishing houses extensive rewriting is the norm and is not, in fact, entrusted to subeditors. If you look at American magazines such as *Time* and *Newsweek* you'll see that their big stories may carry a list of credits for reporting, research and writing. For example, a piece on the new French President, François Hollande, in the 21 May 2012 UK edition was entitled 'Kiss Austerity Goodbye'. The byline under the standfirst was 'By Bryan Walsh'. At the end of the story three names are credited: Reported by Bruce Crumley/Paris, Joanna Kakissis/Athens and Michael Schuman/Beijing. The reporters put together dossiers of information and quotes which are then turned into full stories by the senior writer, in this case Bryan Walsh. This process may be carried out by senior desk editors at the headquarters of the magazine so a story with global ramifications can be put together using the information filed by reporters from anywhere in the world.

House style

Another important job for the subeditor is to make sure the copy conforms to house style. On the whole this doesn't refer to the tone of voice so much as the rules governing those aspects of punctuation and grammar where a correct writer would have a choice. As far as tone is concerned this is a characteristic of the writing that is unlikely to be laid down in any house-style guide, but to which readers are thought to respond. Magazines for teenagers, for example, have a chatty, light tone and use lots of slang words (snogfest, studmuffin, gorge for gorgeous, totty and so on).

A house style, by contrast, is the set of rules collected together in a book, or more usually now in a computer file, to be used as the reference point and arbitrator on fine points of copy-editing, such as whether Van Gogh should have a capital v; whether King's Cross in London should have an apostrophe; whether Peking should be rewritten as Beijing; whether numbers over ten should be written as a word or in figures; whether news-stand should be hyphenated, or ice-cream or lighthouse; why Thermos should have a capital letter. Any well-organised office will have an up-to-date house style which ought to answer all such queries – some style guides are so well written and useful that they are published online or sold commercially on the grounds that many of these decisions are made daily by people who don't write for journalistic publications at all and yet who might want the help of a respected journalism style book. This turns out to be a fair assumption to judge by the obvious demand from the public when they are published (Cameron 1995: 46). Notable among these are, *The Economist Style Guide* and *Guardian Style* (also available free online and as PDFs). These reflect the material their journalists mainly work with and so in the first example, words to do with finance and economics prevail.

Why have a house style?

The purpose of a house style, in whatever form it is recorded, is to ensure conformity within the magazine of the kinds of points listed above, where doubt would regularly arise. This may seem unnecessary – after all, it's the meanings of the words that count, not how they look on the page. In defence of conformity it is argued that you don't realise how much adherence to a house style contributes to a magazine's image until you look at a publication that doesn't follow one. Variety in the ways of writing numbers or spelling words can become annoying to the reader because it intrudes on the reading process, so this line of argument goes, but without much in the way of supporting evidence. As part of her research for the book *Verbal Hygiene*, Deborah Cameron examined the various style books used by *The Times* during the twentieth century. She notes that *The Times English Style and Usage Guide* tells writers that 'inconsistency in style . . . irritates readers' (Jenkins and Ilson 1992: 5). However, when she asked the editor for evidence for this he was unable to cite any at all (Cameron 1995: 37).

There are, then, those who question the need for house style, arguing that it puts unnecessary and unjustifiable pressure on writers to conform to someone else's way of doing things. A more serious doubt about the arrangement is provoked by a look at the huge number of items that a house style covers and at some of the questionable pronouncements on language use that house styles often make. In her discussion of the politics of style Cameron examines the origins of certain wide-spread notions of what constitutes good or correct writing and notes the arbitrariness of these, many of which are perpetrated in the magazine or newspaper house styles as if they were unarguable truths, not, as they undoubtedly are in some cases, the whims of the editor (Cameron 1995: 62).

One typical example, which may or may not be a whim, is from one edition of *The Economist Style Guide*. It says the word '"relative" is fine as an adjective, but as a noun prefer "relation"', without giving any reason. If you check the meaning of 'relative' in any fairly modern dictionary you find the definition 'a person who is related by blood or marriage'. And yes, there in the style guide for 'hopefully' is the entry 'by all means begin an article hopefully, but never write: "Hopefully, it will be finished by Wednesday". Try: "With luck, if all goes well, it is hoped that. . . ".' Note that this last example breaks a general principle in journalistic writing, which is to be as brief as possible. Note, too, the tone of the instruction: it is typical. The sarcasm carries a presumption of stupidity or at least inadequate education on the part of any writer who might disagree with the style guide's author, even though some of the usages which are being banned (those I've quoted, for example) are part of everyday written and spoken language for many if not most English speakers, and even for those who don't use them carry no risk of misunderstanding when used by others.

From a sub's point of view such detailed regulation can pose problems. It's one thing to turn to your style guide to check whether your publication likes to italicise foreign words. But what would make you think to look up 'relative' or 'hopefully' if you thought they were being used correctly in the first place? The answer must be, apart from campaigning to change it, that if you work for a magazine with such a prescriptive approach to language you must read the style guide carefully and re-read it at regular intervals in an effort to keep the more arbitrary decisions in your head.

Cameron explores some of the implications of the attempts of editors to control the way their staff write. While journalists would argue they are striving towards a neutral, plain language in which to report the news objectively, she argues that what they are actually struggling with is a set of stylistic values which 'are symbolic of moral, social, ideological and political values'. The puzzle, she concludes, is not that writers are prepared to accept so much prescription in what they do – after all, they have their livelihoods to earn – but that they so wholeheartedly embrace the idea of there being prescription in the first place (Cameron 1995: 76–77).

Accuracy

Where it might pay some editors to be far more authoritarian is in the setting of standards of accuracy, another responsibility of the sub. The important thing to understand is that you can't be too accurate: problems arise from not being accurate enough, whether the result is a million-pound libel award or merely an irate reader's letter. In the UK this is certainly something which gives rise to concern and helps to undermine the already tattered reputation of journalists and their publications (Worcester 1998: 47).

This has serious consequences not just because it means journalists have to get used to seeing themselves listed at or near the bottom of any table of the classes of people who can be trusted. That's bad enough, but if readers distrust what journalists offer them then sooner or later it might occur to them not to read journalism at all. It is also likely to mean that they are less willing to help journalists with the quotes or background information that are the lifeblood of journalistic writing. This is not to underestimate the difficulty of getting every fact in a story right, but it is to argue that the decision about how accurate to be is, in the end, one of choice. Most of us can think of reporters who have written grossly inaccurate stories but who are still in work. Editors should think about what message this sends to the other journalists working on the same paper, and even to readers.

The American tradition

We could look across the Atlantic to a completely different tradition of accuracy. Anyone who has written for an American publication will have tales to tell about the breed of journalists called fact-checkers and the diligence with which they do their jobs. If a writer mentions a river in Africa, the fact-checker will look it up in an atlas – online version nowadays, of course. If a writer quotes Sunderland University lecturer Jenny McKay on student welfare issues, the fact-checker will call to check I really said what I said, to check how to spell both parts of my name, to check that I teach at Sunderland University. *Reader's Digest* is a magazine that prides itself on the accuracy of everything it publishes, saying that its 100 million readers worldwide deserve to know that what they read is true and with good reason. A story about a woman who is learning to hang glide is much more interesting if her age is 80, rather than the 30 that a typing error cuts it to. Accuracy is a courtesy: as a writer you are asking readers to give you their time and attention, so the least you can do is produce informative or entertaining copy of the highest standard. At its most serious, inaccuracy can detract from the value of a story, can cause a great deal of personal anguish to the subject of the story, or can land journalists and editors in court.

It's hard to imagine a British publication coming anywhere close to the exacting, time-consuming standards that are the norm in the US. James Thurber writes in his biography of Harold Ross, editor of *The New Yorker* in the 1930s and 1940s:

> Having a manuscript under Ross's scrutiny was like putting your car in the hands of a skilled mechanic . . . When you first gazed, appalled, upon an uncorrected proof of one of your stories or articles, each margin had a thicket of queries and complaints – one writer got a hundred and forty-four on one profile . . . His 'Who he?' became famous not only in the office but outside [and is a joke to this day in the UK magazine *Private Eye*].
>
> (Thurber 1984: 70)

Little slips in copy could drive Ross mad, wrote Thurber: 'A couple, instead of a coupe, found in a ditch; a hippy in place of a happy bride; a ship's captain who collapsed on the bride, instead of the bridge, during a storm at sea.'

The UK approach

Mistakes like these are not always the reporter's fault, they can slip in during the keying-in process – or they could in Ross's day. Nowadays, with computer technology, there ought to be less scope for error if fewer versions of a story have to be typed out. The thoroughness of US fact-checkers can irritate reporters in the UK, probably most of all the ones who do a careful reporting job in the first place (Barber 1998). But it can be salutary for British journalists to encounter this kind of thoroughness, even if it can also seem like a complete waste of time, or worse if it means the style of a piece is ruined by a sub who cuts insensitively because a fact can't be checked.

If those amusing slips of the typing finger quoted by Thurber don't amount to journalistic disaster, there are plenty of examples of inaccuracies which do. There are two brothers who are footballers, and one is charged with fraud. Let's draw a veil over the name of the publication which carried a picture of the wrong brother with the story. All right, you might say, you can't really blame a sub for not knowing there were two brothers because he knew nothing about football. Not really his fault. This won't do as an excuse though, because the name of the brother was correct in the copy and as soon as the photo with its caption carrying a different name reached the sub, his sharp subeditor's eye should have spotted that the two names were different, that something was amiss, and that appropriate checks would have to be made.

I don't want to underestimate the problem of accuracy though. It can be difficult to get everything right in a story, even if working conditions are ideal; obviously for reporters in the thick of a running story and working against a deadline, conditions are rarely ideal. Facts become slightly distorted and then slightly more distorted when the next person works on the story, and a chain rather like a game of Chinese whispers results, sometimes leaving a magazine's editor with a red face. The name of the murdered toddler James Bulger is one example. He never was known as Jamie, but reporters for all kinds of media have persisted in using this name. Given that it is difficult to get things consistently right (we'll ignore unscrupulous journalists who make things up), it is surprising that more publications don't follow the lead of *The Guardian* which, to the dismay of some reporters, appointed a readers' editor to look at complaints about accuracy, to oversee the daily publication of corrections as soon as possible, and to write a regular weekly column of comment about the process. The serious purpose behind the appointment of a readers' editor is a willingness to recognise that the gathering and production of copy by journalists is not a foolproof operation and that if mistakes are acknowledged it goes some way to mitigating the offence (Bromley and Stephenson 1998). *The Guardian* has turned its readers' editor's daily and weekly pronouncements into a cottage industry by publishing anthologies under the title *Corrections and Clarifications* of the most important or amusing mistakes, as well as informative short essays about journalism practice by Ian Mayes, the first readers' editor. Any would-be subeditor should read these as they provide excellent examples of what can go wrong between copy submission and final publication.

Help with checking the facts

There are other aids to the subeditor when it comes to accuracy. In addition to the house-style guide a sub ought to have access to specialist dictionaries designed for publishers which cover much of the same ground: *The Oxford Dictionary for Writers and Editors* and *The Penguin Dictionary for Writers and Editors* (Bryson

1994) are two good ones. As well as answering queries for the writer, as suggested above, these books are useful all-purpose reference books. Bryson, for example, tells us that 'gorgheggio' is a musical term for a trill and that whereas Gordonstoun is a school in the Grampian region of Scotland, the similar sounding town in Grampian has the spelling Gordonstown.

There should also be a wide range of reference sources whether in online or book form. It would be impossible to give here a comprehensive list as it so much depends on the subject matter of the magazine. *Jane's All the World's Aircraft* would be essential for the subs working on a magazine about aircraft, for example. *Crockford's* for the *Church Times* or perhaps even *Country Life.* The latest edition of *Vacher's Parliamentary Companion* for any publication that deals with government. Wikipedia nowadays is the first stop people often make in pursuit of information. If you do use this resource, remember how easy it is to be given the wrong information, as anyone has access to it and hoaxes are easy to perpetrate. However, that doesn't invalidate Wikipedia as a starting point for the checking process as it can direct you to more reliable sources.

Standards of accuracy vary

For the freelance sub one of the most difficult things to learn in a new office relates to the point about standards. On some magazines a sub would be expected to check most facts, but on others it will be assumed that the reporter knows what she is doing and so her work will not need much scrutiny. The time allocated for work on a particular story or layout ought to reflect the care which is meant to go into a story, and a sub who is new to an office needs to establish what is wanted. Most publications keep a detailed record of each story and who worked on it and made which changes. This means if a mistake does occur the guilty writer or sub can be traced.

So far I've perhaps implied that subs are saints. Not all of them are. They can be guilty of injecting mistakes into copy, particularly when rewriting or cutting. They often alter words unnecessarily, make typing errors or may misunderstand the original material. This isn't always serious and we'll assume the mistakes are never made with malicious intent, but for a writer who has taken great care over the words it is justifiably frustrating to find changes have been made for no good reason. Worst is when copy is mauled about by an insensitive sub, usually in the interests of making it conform to the 'tone' of the magazine as a whole. To find your copy filled with clichés, clumsy grammar and factual errors, yet still carrying your name, is one of the most disheartening moments of a writer's working life. It does happen and some freelances have been known to say they can't bear to read the published versions of their copy for fear of what has been done to it.

Once the story has been read and the facts checked, the sub must ensure that the story is not breaking guidelines such as those laid down by the Press Complaints Commission (or whatever eventually replaces it) and does not leave the editor liable to a court appearance. There are several ways in which copy might be risky in this way, the most obvious being if it is libellous, if it breaches copyright, or the Official Secrets Acts, or if it is in contempt of court (for explanations see Chapter 18). The sub is a publication's vital first line of defence. Even if no one else on a small staff has any understanding of the legal pitfalls, the sub must have. This doesn't mean subs have to have a law degree or even a detailed knowledge of cases and precedents, as the sub is most unlikely to take the final decision about whether to publish something that might be unsafe legally. But the sub is the person, sometimes the only person, who will read the copy with enough care and attention to notice a risk. All subs should know exactly what might be problematic and should know exactly who to refer the question to and who is the back-up if that person is not available. Legal decisions may have to be taken instantly, and if the editor is away from her desk, someone else senior must take responsibility.

One of the quirks of the way entry to journalism in the UK works is that magazines are more likely to employ people with no prior training and don't necessarily offer any to them immediately. So, whereas most recruits to newspapers will bring with them, or soon have, enough elementary legal training at least to make them alert to where the danger areas lie, journalists on magazines may not have this. It may be that a fashion editor on *Elle* doesn't need to know much about contempt of court, but she certainly ought to know about copyright, even if it's just for the day when she decides to use a few song lyrics scattered across the page as typographical decoration. A further problem is that magazines use copy from a wide range of freelances, many of whom, especially in the lifestyle and consumer sections of the market, do not have any legal training at all. This makes the sub's vigilance even more important.

Copy preparation

Once all these bigger tasks have been sorted out the sub has to tackle the more technical aspects of copy preparation. Capital letters have to be put in consistently and in any words that are trade names (Thermos, Hoover, Velcro). Small capitals (or small caps) have to be indicated where these are preferred, words put in italics, consistency checked for, repetitions weeded out, paragraph indents inserted along with devices for emphasis such as bullet points (blobs) or dropped capitals. The use of quotation marks has to be harmonised. The list is long and the priorities not the same for all publications. The sub has to become familiar with all the conventions used by a publisher or publication and make sure the copy conforms to it.

Copy presentation

Then comes the more creative part of the job. Starting with picture-led publications, I've already noted that on these the sub works closely with the art department to achieve the most successful union between words, layout and illustrations. Headlines, standfirsts (or sells) and captions have to be written to fit the available space and the photographer's or illustrator's credit included. If the story is an important one a cover line about it may be needed. If this is the case it could be worth drafting ideas while work is being done on the story. Cover lines will inevitably be rewritten when the cover design is being looked at, but it helps to sketch out ideas at the subediting stage so that there is some material to work with. The same goes for the words on the contents page. An additional factor is the need for coherence between those three elements in the magazine: readers are understandably irritated when an enticing cover line bears no relation to anything on the contents page, leaving readers to search through the whole magazine for the thing that attracted them to it in the first place. If the story is not big enough to be displayed on the cover it still needs to be clear from the description in the contents list what it is about and where it is to be found.

Headlines

There's no need to define a headline. In news copy, whether in magazines or newspapers, headlines are meant to draw the reader's attention to the story and say succinctly what it's about. At the tabloid end of the newspaper market headlines can be so jokey as to be almost incomprehensible except to regular readers. On picture-led magazines, at least for the fashion, beauty and home interest pages, the job of a headline is less clear, although it is meant to encapsulate the mood of the pages or 'story'. Stylists, art directors and magazine staff use the word story even for a fashion shoot which carries few words except to list the prices of the clothes and the shops that stock them. By 'story' here they mean some connecting theme around which the shoot has been devised. It might be 'Ballerina Bride' for an edition of *Brides & Setting Up Home* which features wedding dresses in the style of tutus; or 'Evergreen' on a fashion story featuring green-coloured clothes – this provides an excuse for puns about the environment and about envy all in one standfirst. Turn to the contents page and you get another pun 'Evergreen: fashion activists go for green pieces'.

If you are a sub working on this kind of material for the consumer press you'll have to get the hang of what's needed: puns, alliteration, rhymes and jaunty rhythms are much appreciated, although it is hard to convey to someone outside this world exactly how much time may be spent in brainstorming by an editorial team to come up with titles such as 'Seas the moment' for an article about cruises. It is also not easy to convince outsiders that editors on such magazines may demand that the sub or chief sub puts up at least three possible standfirsts and headings for consideration by the senior editorial team before a decision can be taken.

If the purpose of the publication is to publish written journalism which happens to have illustrations, then the headline does not need to strain so hard for effect, although puns and alliteration do inevitably have their place, at least in the UK, however tiresome this might be for readers or for the subs. The usual guidelines for what makes a good heading apply to this kind of story. A headline should be informative within the constraints set by taste, legality and layout. Sometimes these constraints are so unrealistic as to make the headline writer's job into a kind of verbal torture as she wrestles to find words that will mean something and not bust – the technical term for a headline too long for the allotted space.

Apart from the restrictions of word length, subs also have to consider house style on questions such as whether each word should start with a capital or whether the whole headline should be capitalised. On the whole in the UK caps are avoided except for the first word, but in the US, in *Time* magazine for example, all-cap headlines are the norm for big stories and for smaller ones a capital is used for each significant word: 'A Broken Window of Opportunity'.

The other considerations are the shapes made by the lines and how these relate to the sense of what is being written. If there are three decks, say, then a pyramid one way up or the other is not usually acceptable. So Figure 11.1 would be acceptable, whereas Figure 11.2 would not. A second reason that Figure 11.2 would not do is that the last word in the second line should be closer to the next word in order to make the sense as clear as possible. You wouldn't put 'Mr' at the end of a line and 'Blobby' on the next, or 'San' alone without its 'Francisco', or any other words which are closely linked in sense. Nor should a line end with a preposition. However many decks there are, the principle to follow is, more or less, to be ragged in a balanced way; that applies whether the headlines range left or right or are centred, so Figures 11.3, 11.4, 11.5 and 11.6 are acceptable.

This is a
three-deck
headline

FIGURE 11.1

This
is a three
deck headline

FIGURE 11.2

Explanation time. Copy is said to be ranged left/ragged right when the left-hand margin is even and the right one is, well, ragged (Figures 11.1–11.4). Ranged right/ragged left is the other way round (Figure 11.5). The word 'flush' is an alternative for 'range'. Centred is where both margins are ragged (Figure 11.6) and justified type means that both margins are straight, as in the main text for this chapter. (These styles can be produced by a click of the mouse as they appear at the top of the computer screen.) These terms are used for all kinds of type, whether in the text, the captions, the standfirsts, or crossheads and pull-quotes.

> *And this
> here
> is a four-deck
> headline*

FIGURE 11.3

> *And
> this here
> is a four-deck
> headline*

FIGURE 11.4

> **This
> type is
> set as
> range right**

FIGURE 11.5

> *And
> this type
> is
> centred*

FIGURE 11.6

Other than that, many of the things that make a good headline also make good journalistic writing. Ideally a headline should contain an active verb to give the impression of action and, if appropriate, it should describe concrete things rather than abstractions, people not inanimate objects. It should be easily understood at first glance by the kind of people who are expected to read the magazine. Once again this means hard rules can't be laid down for all magazines about what works. What's right for *Prima* ('10 easy projects for a rainy weekend', 'When dizziness is a danger sign', 'Make your home seem twice as big', March 1999), would not be right for *GQ* ('Knob freaks', 'Hidden pleasures', 'Sex Life. Pork and Ride', March 1999), or for *B* ('75% of bridegrooms try it on with me', 'My father is a rapist and Mum is one of his victims', March 1999), or *The Scottish Field* ('The Keeper's Year', February 1999).

In many cases the headlines in a picture-led magazine depend on either a subsidiary heading (known as a strapline and usually running across the top of the page) or a standfirst, to explain fully what the piece is about. One example from *Time* is 'Couture Culture' as a headline, accompanied by 'When designers emphasize workmanship over theatrics, high fashion's best clients think money's no object' (1 February 1999). Or in *Scottish Field*, the headline 'Family Talents' could be about any number of families but the short standfirst which follows explains: 'Everyone

Illustration

Body copy

Crosshead

Caption

Picture credit

Headline

Standfirst/ Sell

Byline

Drop cap

Pull-quote

FIGURE 11.7 Layout designed by Lee Hall

has heard of Robert Louis Stevenson but few are aware that some of Scotland's most famous lighthouses and well-known harbours owe their existence to the Stevenson family.'

Verbal signposts

The headlines and straplines are acting as so-called 'entry points' to the text. If you look at the sample spread of a magazine (Figure 11.7) you'll see that there are others. The thinking is that when readers turn to a page they don't necessarily read in the order you might expect: headline, standfirst, text, caption and so on. What their eyes do is jump about the page and so it may well be that a picture caption is the thing which catches the eye or it may be one of the pull-quotes. Any of these verbal signposts, therefore, must work at attracting the reader's attention enough to make him stop and then perhaps read from the start of the copy. It is normal practice to ensure that no word is used in more than one of these verbal signposts.

The other words, then, which subeditors regularly use and which need some explanation are the standfirst, caption and credit, crosshead, pull-quote, dropped capital, sidebar, widow, end symbol and page turn. Here I take them in turn.

Standfirsts

The standfirst (or 'sell' as it is sometimes known) is the paragraph which introduces an article. It is not usually written by the reporter but by the subeditor, along with the headline and captions. A standfirst will normally include, written in the third person, the byline (or name) of the reporter. If the pictures are an important part of the spread, if they were specially commissioned for example, then there may well be a credit here too for the photographer or illustrator. Failing that, there is likely to be a picture credit in small type (about six or seven point) somewhere else on the page, often in the margin and running at an angle to the main text. These small credits may even be for the picture agency or library that supplied the pictures if these are stock shots. The standfirst differs from the body copy in that it is set in a larger type that may be bolder or in a different typeface from the main text. It is also likely to be set in a different measure (width of a line of text) and to vary in terms of justification. So, if the body copy is justified, the standfirst is likely to be centred or ranged to the left or right. In magazines where the words are of prime importance, features headlines may be more independent and work without standfirsts. Or these magazines may copy some newspapers by having standfirsts on their features but not their news pages.

Guidance for writing good standfirsts is similar to that for headlines and for all good journalistic writing. The more newsy the magazine the more important it is for standfirsts to seem as up to date as possible, perhaps by referring to a recent event or by referring to the future, typically by asking questions about what will happen next. For example: 'The Golden Age. Could Europe and China's fracking forays remake global energy?' (*Time*, 21 May 2012).

As with headlines, there is likely to be a tight restriction on the length of each line and on the overall shape that the lines produce. The guidelines here are the same as for headings and can mean that what seems like a relatively simple task – to write a paragraph of introduction to a feature – can take longer than you'd expect as the line breaks have to be manoeuvred to fall at just the right places.

Captions

The next thing is to write the picture captions. These are the words that relate to individual pictures to give information of differing kinds about them. What this involves varies greatly between publications, as well as between stories. On picture-led magazines the space and shape of the captions will be determined by the art editors, which leaves no choice for the subeditor but can create problems when the space is not adequate.

Starting with a straightforward piece of reportage with commissioned photos, the captions must draw into the story a reader who is not immediately enticed by the headline. The captions must explain what a picture shows without merely describing what is in it. A good caption should somehow add to the information the page has to offer, not merely repeat what is in the text. For some picture spreads there will be a caption to go with each picture, but on others a single caption may have to carry the information for more than one illustration. The important thing, then, is to make clear which picture is being referred to. Words like 'above', or 'clockwise from left', or 'centre' are used, perhaps enclosed in brackets, or using a different weight for the typeface. Where this is done the sub has to keep a close eye on any changes that may be made to the layout at the last minute, in case these directions become wrong.

Captions which carry information about the merchandise featured in fashion, beauty and lifestyle spreads have to be written with immaculate accuracy because readers use the information and will be put out if they discover it is incorrect. This applies to prices, sizes, shops and availability. Large companies such as Condé Nast, which produce a lot of this kind of material, have merchandise departments responsible for all the checking of detail, but it is up to the sub to present the information as accessibly as possible.

In newsier publications the captions are likely to be brief and functional. A typical way of doing them, where photos are usually just head shots or pictures of products, is to run one-line captions which start with the name of the featured person or publication, followed by a colon and then a word or phrase taken from the story.

There is one danger area to watch out for. Where library pictures are used to illustrate news features about subjects such as drug or alcohol abuse, prostitution, child abuse, or anything vaguely criminal or distasteful, care must be taken not to imply that those who appear in an innocent photo are involved in the questionable activity. If you're subbing a feature about parents who have abused their children you can't just use a stock picture of any family unless you have the image manipulated so there is no danger of innocent people being branded as child abusers. One possibility is to commission a picture using photographic models and to make absolutely clear in the caption that the people in the picture are models. Alternatively an artist could be commissioned to illustrate the story.

Crossheads

The more text there is on a page the more likely it is that the page designer will want to see the text broken up to try to help the reader's eye move across the page without tiring of too much grey. One way to do this is by inserting what are effectively small headlines, or crossheads. These can also serve the function of stretching out a piece of text to take up more space in a layout. Crossheads are usually in a bolder typeface than the text and, as with the standfirst, are likely to be set in a different way. They run across just one column of type: the thinking here is that if they ran across two or more at once the reader's eye might be misled into jumping back up the page to the next column of type. For the same reason a picture or illustration should not be run across two columns unless it is at the top or the bottom of those columns or unless it does not take up the full width of the columns and has type ranged around it at either side.

What crossheads contain is, yet again, a matter of house style. Sometimes it is just one word or a couple of words lifted from the following paragraph or two. It does not lift words from the preceding copy and so the careful sub will have to watch that last minute changes to the layout for whatever reason do not affect what is in a crosshead or indeed its position on the page. Across any given page or spread the aim is to balance visually the position of text-breakers such as crossheads and pull-quotes.

Pull-quotes

Another popular method of breaking up grey text is the pull-quote. This is a quotation from the text set in such a way as to stand out from the body copy, much like a crosshead or standfirst. Sometimes a pull-quote is emphasised with the use of rules above and below. A pull-quote should make sense on its own as well as intriguing readers and encouraging them to move into the text. Like crossheads, pull-quotes should always be set across one column of type only, should balance across the page or spread and should relate to text which is yet to come, although not the text which comes immediately afterwards. The additional complication for the sub who is selecting quotes to use in this way is that, like standfirsts and headlines, a pleasing shape has to be created by the lines and the sense of the words must not be impeded by awkward line breaks. Lastly, a pull-quote should conform to the text and if the decision is taken to omit a phrase that is in the text this should be clearly indicated by the use of ellipsis (dots as a substitute for text, three dots being the maximum in any journalistic copy).

Dropped capitals

Another device regularly used to break up the page is the dropped capital letter or 'drop cap'. It means a letter in a larger, bolder and sometimes different typeface set so that it drops down through the first three or four lines of the text, which is then adjusted to range round it. The designer (whether subeditor or art editor) will decide whether these are to be used and whether just for the first letter of a piece or as a way of breaking up the text at other points, probably with at least one line of white space above it. From the subs' point of view there are two possible complications with drop caps. The first is if the sentence which is meant to start with a drop cap begins with a quotation, which would cause a typographical problem: a huge letter preceded by quotation marks in the same size as the body copy will look silly, but equally these can't be enlarged or it puts the typographical balance of the sentence out. The answer is not to start a feature with a quote and to rewrite any opening sentence in the middle of the text where a drop cap is to be used if it starts with a quote. The second consideration is that any given letter should appear as a drop cap only once across a spread.

Sidebars and boxes

In addition to the main text of an article, many features carry what are called sidebars or boxes that carry information not otherwise included in the copy. They may be set in a different typeface or measure and are often set against a tinted background. It may be factual or statistical information relating to the subject of the article, or it may be a case study of some sort. This copy must also be prepared by the sub and checked to make sure it agrees with, but does not repeat, the other information on the page.

Widows

On magazines which allow generous time for the copy preparation stage and which are not designed to look like newspapers there is some further tinkering with the copy to do. This used to be done at the page-proof stage, but with computerised layouts can just as easily be done on screen. Not all editors or chief subs bother much about this but they do on publications which aim for the highest production standards.

This tinkering is to do with line-breaks and the way in which copy flows from one column to another. There are certain guidelines which are thought to enhance the look of the copy as well as its readability. The most widely cared about are 'widows', which occur where a paragraph ends with a line containing one short word or part of a word. When this happens copy may be slightly rewritten to extend the last line to stretch more than half way across the width of the column. Or it may be slightly cut to move the paragraph ending back by one line. Computer technology has made another solution quicker and easier. It's called kerning and means the adjustment of the amount of white space between letters and words. Computers quietly do it all the time, but it is possible to override what they choose to do in order to squash up a few letters or to spread them out. One of the hallmarks of amateur desktop publishing, however, is the overzealous use of this technique without the benefit of a designer's eye being applied to the finished lines of copy. Lines which are too generously or too tightly spaced can seem to jump out of the page at the reader, drawing attention to the wrong part of the copy. The same visual problem arises accidentally with what are called 'rivers' of white space, which appear by chance in a column of type thanks to the positioning of word breaks.

A widow is most problematic if it falls at the beginning or end of a column, immediately before an illustration, or at the end of a page. In these cases the rewriting must create at least a full line with which to start the next section of copy or an awkward gap will be left at the top of the next column. The same principle will apply if a short line occurs in the original copy at the top of a column. The aim is always to achieve a harmonious look to the page. If you bear in mind that graphic designers think of copy in terms of blocks of text, it's clear why they don't want the shape of those blocks marred by having incomplete lines at the top or bottom of rectangles. A word of caution here for the sub: whenever copy is rewritten or cut there's an opportunity for mistakes to creep in. That is why not all publications take so seriously this tidying up of the look of the text.

End symbols and page turns

By the time all this work has been done on a page, there remain a few details to check. The sub must make sure that appropriate picture credits have been included (see 'Captions') and that at the end of a spread there is either an end symbol or an indication of where to turn to (called a turn arrow). The end symbol may be no more than a black bullet or blob. Many publications, however, have a specially designed symbol that somehow reflects the title: *Ms.* has a black blob with '*Ms.*' in white type inside it.

For some publications there is no need to indicate a page turn because no article is allowed to run beyond a double-page spread. Others allow text to turn only onto the next page and so it is obvious from the punctuation and the sense of the story that no conclusion has been reached. It is important where this arrangement prevails for the sub to make sure that the punctuation or sense couldn't be misinterpreted – if a full stop fell at the end of a page, for example. If there is any confusion some rewriting may be necessary to carry the sentence over onto the next page. In *Prima*, which also turns only onto the succeeding page, there is nevertheless a little arrow-shaped box instructing the reader to 'please turn the page'. The more accident-prone arrangement arises where copy flows from one spread to another far away at the back of the book (as magazines are called in the trade). The risks are obvious. Thorough checking of page-turn instructions must be done at the last stage of the magazine's preparation as late alterations to the flatplan play havoc with the turned copy (i.e. the copy which is sent to the back and is known simply as the turn). It has even been known for a turn to have to be fitted in at the front of the book when late advertising appeared which had to be placed in a specified section. In some magazines all the short, newsy or diary items are interspersed with advertisements at the front and back of the magazine. Somewhere in the middle there is an ad-free zone referred to as a 'features well', where for several pages you simply find a long flow of editorial copy. The advantage of this for the editorial department is clear. It means interesting features copy or well-designed, visually striking pages can be allowed to flow from one spread to the next without the awkward interruption of adverts.

There is a further important check to make. If a publication uses an identifying symbol or tag-line to distinguish its various sections then the sub needs to make sure that it hasn't been forgotten and, more crucial, that the right one has been included on the page.

Proofs

Eventually there will be proofs of the copy to look at. Proof-reading can be done on screen, but some subs and editors still prefer to look at a printed version as this is closer to what the readers will be seeing. This can make it easier to spot mistakes and the very fact of reading the copy in a format different from the one in which it was subbed is another safeguard. Whether there is time will depend on the lead time (preparation time) for the magazine, staffing levels and so on. Proof-reading used to be done not only by subs but by professional proof-readers and the story goes that they would read a text backwards so that the sense of what they read did not distract them from the words and punctuation. I've never actually met anyone who worked this way, but it is true that while you do need at least one reading of a proof for sense, you also need one where the sense does not carry your eye across typographical mistakes. On an ideal subs' desk the proof would go not only to the sub who handled the pages originally, but also to at least one other, who had never seen the copy before. It's amazing what a fresh eye can discover in the way of nonsense or missing apostrophes.

Proofs used to be marked up according to a standard set of signs which, in theory at least, didn't vary between publishing houses and printers. (They accord with British Standard 5261.) These are still used wherever hard copy is being dealt with.

Page proofs are the next stage on from what used to be called galley proofs. Galley proofs are of the text only and would not show page or column breaks or any design elements. Indeed, they can be produced before any thought has been devoted to layout. Page proofs show all the elements of a page, the stories, the position of illustrations and all the other aspects of presentation discussed in this chapter. At this stage the problem of overmatter (the technical term for too much copy) is likely to emerge. With computerised setting and page make-up this is much less likely to happen. If it does and yet does not warrant rewriting of the text or alteration of the layout then the overmatter can either be 'killed', which means dropped altogether, or it can be 'held over', to be kept for use on another page or even another edition of the publication.

Whether tackled on screen or as photocopies, proofs must be scrutinised for any lack of consistency or unintended incongruity: 'high-flyers' in the headline but 'high fliers' all through the text, without the hyphen and with an 'i' rather than a 'y'. After the corrections have been made, subsequent proofs are called 'revises' or 'revise proofs'.

Continuity

Page checking also has to be done with an eye to the rest of the magazine, once it is ready. Do the cover lines and entries in the contents page match each other? Are the page numbers accurate in the contents list and on the spreads themselves? Are the turns okay? The only way to be certain about any of these things is to check them at each stage.

Covers

The covers of most magazines, even of those designed to look like newspapers, contain several kinds of copy. There will be the publication's date, edition and logo (or titlepiece or masthead) and its barcode, the familiar black-and-white device which, when scanned by a computer, gives the International Standard Serial Number (ISSN). There will also almost always be some means of promoting the contents of the magazine, whether in a series of short paragraphs with pictures above the logo, as is now common on newspapers and adopted by newsy periodicals such as *Press Gazette*, or in the form of what are known as cover lines. Most people refer to the logo as the masthead, although there are still those who maintain that the masthead is only the box in which is listed the administrative information about the magazine such as staff, phone numbers and name and address of the publishing company (Morrish and Bradshaw 2012: 259). This is also sometimes called a 'flannel panel', which demonstrates that some of the terms used within publishing are not universal. Whether the box containing the administrative information is a flannel panel or a masthead, the chief sub will need to make sure it is kept up to date as staff leave or change job titles.

Cover lines are the phrases or even single words telling the reader what the magazine has to offer. Some random examples are 'Modern manners. Should you ever just "drop in"?' (*The Lady*, 20 April 2012); 'Banking on hunger. How speculators moved into food' (*New Internationalist*, November 2011). For a glossy magazine that is expected to sell largely on the visual strength of its cover (see Chapter 13) the cover lines are so important as to be a subject of much discussion once the cover image has been chosen. The final words may be the result of a long, heated editorial meeting to which the sub or chief sub might have brought a selection of suggestions for each component of the magazine, that are then debated by editors, deputy editors, marketing people and publishers.

Apart from cover lines, some magazines – if they are perfect bound and therefore have a thick spine – will have little mottoes or jokey phrases, or even more cover lines relating to content printed on those spines. Again at random: *Condé Nast Traveller* goes for the straightforward informative magazine title plus 'Marseille. Costa Rica. Hong Kong. Resorts to relax in' followed at the foot of the spine by 'British Edition, June 1998, 009'; *Marie Claire* has that same basic information and then trumpets itself with the words 'The most imitated magazine in the world' (May 1998); *Harpers and Queen*, with more wit, used to print 'The non-drip glossy' on its spine.

On larger publications, where the subbing is done by a team, all the checks that are more to do with the mechanics of the whole magazine than with specific pages or copy are likely to be the responsibility of the chief sub, but on many magazines, particularly monthlies, there will be only one sub (or at least one staff sub) and so the responsibility falls to one person. She will have to check every last detail on the cover and all the other pages where there is editorial matter, as well as the page numbers and the headers or footers which are put on all the pages of some magazines, presumably to remind readers which magazine they are reading. This can be daunting, particularly to a sub who arrives at a magazine with newspaper experience on a big subs' table where the individual's work is always checked by more senior staff.

Copy flow

The chief subeditor, or whoever takes on that function, has to rule over the complicated series of decisions, processes and deadlines which go into the preparation of a magazine for printing. Take deadlines. Even daily newspapers have a variety of deadlines for the different pages. Magazines with large paginations and longish lead times will have much greater differences between page or section deadline times, sometimes as much as weeks. The work that individual copy or layouts require will vary in complexity and this will all be taken into account when the production schedule is drawn up. This document lists deadlines for all pages and types of copy, for the various types of proof to be corrected, and for the final sending of the magazine to be printed, whether that is an in-house operation or one that takes place elsewhere. On magazines with long lead times it is usual for the editorial work being done on any given day in the office to span several issues.

As a result a clear system is essential for the flow of copy and visual material around the office from writer or commissioning editor to the subbing, picture and art departments, to the lawyers if necessary and to anyone else (the editor, for example) who might want to have a look at copy or layouts before they go to press. This may be conceived as a series of clearly labelled 'baskets', each holding copy and layouts with a note of their own internal office history. At the last stage before printing, the initials of the most senior staffer responsible for pages or copy would be written on the final page proof; this initialising process is known as signing off. As the various stages of the production schedule are reached a dummy copy of the magazine (or its electronic equivalent), known as the book, fills up with printouts of the pages, so that whoever is in charge of progress chasing knows exactly what the latest stage is for each page.

In the computerised office, files of paper are not (or should not be much) moved from desk to desk. Instead, this flow of material is managed electronically, even if old-technology words such as 'basket' may be used to identify the files. Again, there needs to be a clear route for the flow of material however it is managed. A sub should know exactly what this is and what procedures at the computer keyboard are required to keep the flow in motion.

On magazines the last stage in this flow, as the final deadline approaches, tends to be more fraught than on newspapers, perhaps because it does not occur so often. Even weekly papers or periodicals have a more relaxed day or two each week, and on monthlies, although there is unlikely to be a day when little has to be done, there is certainly time to breathe and think ahead a little rather than just focus on getting the next page ready. Press day, then, on any periodical is busy and anxious until that moment when the publication has 'gone to bed', when it is in the hands of the printers and no more changes can be made.

Last minute hitches

Even at this stage – though only rarely – problems can arise in the shape of court injunctions or the death of the superstar whose interview took months to arrange and whose portrait makes such a striking cover. What publishers do in these circumstances depends on how far into the printing process the magazine is and how embarrassing it would be to run the story. Pages are not all printed at once, so it is sometimes possible to pull the copy, or some of it, and draw the reader's attention to what has happened. If the relevant article is short it can sometimes be pulled out altogether and other copy inserted, such as a house ad (an advertisement for the magazine or another from the same publishing house). Super-efficient organisations might have files of timeless copy prepared for emergency use.

OVER TO THE PRINTER

For most publishing houses the material to be printed is sent as digital files in PDF or TIFF/IT format (Whittaker 2008: 146). What happens when these reach the printer is the topic for a different book. It is helpful to know enough about it, though, to understand how this affects all the earlier stages in the editorial process, and to be able to think creatively about what can be achieved within the constraints of budget, time and staff. A sizeable publishing company will have a team of production experts and print buyers to advise editorial staff and to take decisions, along with the publisher, about how to make production budgets achieve as much as possible.

As we have seen, the work of writers, photographers and illustrators is transformed by the editorial team, who also assemble it into layouts and instructions for the printer. Yet even when the presses start to roll, the magazine is still an abstract notion and will be brought fully to life only when the task of binding is complete. Only then is the product a tangible object waiting to be picked up and held. Only then is the collection of ideas and digital instructions a paper magazine.

So far in this chapter the various aspects of this preparatory work have been outlined. Now let's consider briefly the way in which the different elements of a magazine are united to create the finished product for the readers.

PRODUCTION PROCESSES

Assembling the flatplan

At the heart of the editorial production process is the magazine's flatplan. This is a kind of map of the magazine, with a square to represent each page. It enables the editorial team to see what is to appear on any given page and therefore how the sequence of articles and advertisements will run. The job of creating this document is called flatplanning and is a collaborative effort between advertising director and editor.

Advertising constraints

At the flatplanning meeting there will already be two lists of constraints drawn up. First, the advertising director will have a list of advertisements that have already been sold (or nearly sold) for the issue and what positions have therefore been guaranteed to advertisers. The flatplan squares will be filled in accordingly. When the advertising team sell space their job is not just a matter of persuading companies to pay for pages and half pages. Advertisers regard some positions in a magazine more highly than others and so will pay higher rates for those spaces. The obvious example is the back cover, which gives the advertisement greater visibility than an inside page. Other prime slots include the inside front cover and the first available right-hand page. In fact, any right-hand page is thought to be better than pretty much any left-hand one, as a reader's eye is more likely to be drawn to it when a spread is opened up.

The flatplan also has to record whether the back or front cover, or occasionally an inside page, is to include what's known as a gatefold. This is where the width of the page is extended but folded back in on itself to fit the rest of the magazine. Sometimes there is more than one fold. Usually a gatefold is provided at the request of an advertiser, but occasionally it can be used for editorial material.

Advertisers also like their material to be 'facing matter'. 'Matter' here simply means editorial material and 'facing' simply means opposite. It's probably obvious why advertisers prefer to be surrounded by editorial – it means the readers are more likely to pause on the page. In addition, advertisers may list other stipulations when they book space. Make-up companies may insist that their adverts are set among the beauty pages, record companies will almost certainly want to be positioned near the music reviews and so on. No real surprises or particularly unreasonable demands there but, as Gloria Steinem found, not all requests are so easy to accommodate in the flatplan. If all advertisers had views about the content of features material near their ads it could prove impossible to get the publication out: food product ads which must be within food editorial but not within six pages of another food ad; engagement ring ads which mustn't be anywhere near stories that ask fundamental questions about the nature of romance (see Chapter 15 and Steinem 1994).

How much space a magazine devotes to advertising varies considerably between publications and can even vary a little between issues of the same publication. The relative number of pages is called the advertising–editorial ratio (or ad/ed ratio). On business publications this is often around 60:40, while on consumer magazines it is likely to be the other way round at 40:60. As it is impossible to be sure how much space will be sold in any given issue, the ratio that is agreed by the publisher is usually set as an average over a number of issues. This means a bad month for ad revenue does not pull down the overall pagination of the magazine so much that it begins to seem too thin to its readers. Nor does an issue with a lot of advertising disappoint regular readers who expect a generous helping of editorial.

Editorial constraints

The second list of constraints relates to the editorial material. Almost every magazine has regular columns and features (often termed 'regulars') that readers are accustomed to finding in the same place in every issue. The contents page is one example. The editorial team's wish-list for positions is much the same as that of the advertisers. Editors prefer right-hand pages, at least for the start of articles or for single-page articles, and they prefer editorial material to be surrounded by other editorial material. Neither side will ever get everything it wants and compromise is necessary, although publishers are apt to remind editors that it is the advertisers who pay the staffing and publication bills.

There are other flatplanning considerations. Most editors take care to ensure that there is a 'flow' to the magazine, by which they mean a logical, balanced and pleasing progression for the readers as they move from one item to the next. In a general-interest magazine this might mean making sure that articles which do not have much pictorial interest are interspersed with those which do. Editorial matter shouldn't clash either with other editorial or with the adverts it is near. To make up an example: the kind of clash that could be problematic is a full-page, colour advertisement for vodka running opposite a harrowing account of a celebrity's struggle against alcohol addiction.

There is no guarantee that readers start to read a magazine at the beginning and then work neatly through the pages in order. Many people start at the back and work forward, or else they use the contents list to jump straight to articles which interest them. Nevertheless, editors do give these issues of flow and balance due concern because it is within their control and getting it right reflects their own professionalism.

The production schedule

Another factor at the flatplanning stage is the production schedule. This is a list of deadlines for the various pages and sections of the magazine. Magazines are printed in what are called sections or formes; each of these is one sheet of paper printed on both sides which will eventually be folded and bound into the magazine. A section can cover up to 64 pages, according to the size of the magazine's pages. Any number of pages that can be multiplied by four, eight or 16 can be printed as one section. So all the pages to be printed on one sheet, even though they may not be from the same part of the final bound copy of the magazine, will comprise one section for the purpose of printing. What goes into an individual section is determined by what is called the 'imposition'. This is the allocation of pages to the magazine's sections that ensures that the individual pages will appear in the correct order once they are printed and bound together.

Each section of a magazine is likely to have a different set of dates for 'copy in' or 'closing', for layouts, for the various proof stages and for the various print processes. The bigger the magazine, the more deadlines it has.

To establish a production schedule in the first place is the work of the editor, production manager, printer and also the publisher, as the decisions have cost implications. A late closing page, for example, might be desirable in a weekly news magazine even if it incurs extra printing costs. To set the various dates the team effectively works backwards from the publication date, deciding how long each stage in the production and editorial process will take and then setting a deadline for each stage. It is then the job of senior staff to ensure deadlines are not missed.

Any production schedule shows how tightly interlinked the various deadlines are: if copy is late it may miss its slot for being subbed or for the layout to be done. Sending material late to be printed means the time allocated for it may have been wasted and the next job may be in place. Printers, whether in-house or outside contractors, can often make up for lost time, but they will charge for doing so because the work is likely to involve overtime and because machines and staff were perhaps idle as they waited for the late material. Every missed deadline has an implication for the flow of work and therefore for costs and ultimately profitability in the case of a commercial magazines.

When decisions are being taken about where editorial or advertisements are to be placed on the flatplan, the relevant deadlines have to be taken into account, so that everything is ready at the right time and a regular flow of work is ensured both through the editorial office and at the printer.

All these competing considerations make the process of establishing a flatplan into the kind of logic puzzle found in IQ tests. The only difference is that with flatplanning some of the constraints are, of necessity, slightly flexible, depending on the importance of last-minute changes either from advertisers or from the editorial team. When adverts fail to materialise, extra copy may be needed or copy may be dropped if the decision is taken to cut pagination. This only makes the process of flatplanning more complicated. Once the essential items are established in the flatplan, however, it only remains for the editor to allocate the rest of the editorial material to the various pages that remain. Copies of the flatplan (whether paper or virtual) will then be distributed to the subbing, production and art departments.

Once the flatplan is established and the information married up with the production schedule the editorial work gets under way.

Colour

Where colour is concerned the last-stage proofs are likely to be called Cromalins, the name reflecting the printing process by which they are produced. On publications with high production values Cromalins receive careful scrutiny as they give an accurate representation of the actual colours as they will appear in the magazine, as well as showing whether the colours are correctly 'in register'.

Register refers to the success with which the areas of printed colour fit into the correct boundaries. Colour printing involves four colours of ink (cyan, magenta, yellow and black) which are applied separately in succession. If there is a slight misalignment then the individual colours will not be properly in place on the final version and the picture will be spoiled by blurred edges where all the differing coloured portions meet. In these circumstances the printing is said to be out of register.

Every production decision has a cost implication. The quality of the ink used and of the paper on which the magazine is printed are good examples. The differing weights of paper and how glossy it is will affect the success with which colour can be printed. The paper used by, say, consumer monthlies such as *GQ* or *Harper's Bazaar* is expensive, but helps to establish the brand image of the magazines and is an essential support for the high-quality artwork which is part of the attraction of those publications. By contrast, colour reproduction of graphic material in newspapers or newspaper colour supplements which do not use high-quality paper can look unacceptably smudgy.

Not all magazines carry content that demands sophisticated use of colour, and some make effective use of what is known as 'spot colour'. This is where one colour of ink in addition to black is used, either throughout a whole issue or on the pages printed together as one section. It doesn't compete with full colour for sophistication, but on a lower-budget publication or one that is primarily about words, spot colour can bring some welcome visual variety.

Binding

As far as the finished magazine product is concerned there are other decisions which affect the look and feel of it, and which are unlikely to be taken by the editorial staff alone. It is useful to have some idea of what influences these decisions. Take binding, for example. The main distinction here is between publications which are saddle-stitched and those which are perfect bound. Saddle-stitching is where pages are simply folded at the seam and then stapled. This is the common method for thinner magazines such as *Prima*, *Take a Break*, *The Spectator*, *Time* and those periodicals, like *Campaign*, that are designed to look like newspapers.

Perfect binding, the other common technique, produces a thicker, harder spine more like that of books and is used for magazines with higher paginations and high production values which probably include the use of thicker paper. This method uses glue to bind together the various printed sections, which are folded so that the pages of one section fall consecutively, rather than, as with saddle-stitched pages, appearing in opposite halves of the book. Examples of perfect-bound magazines are *Vogue*, *FHM*, *Bliss*, *Cosmopolitan* and *Good Housekeeping*.

Printing

The choice about how to print a magazine will be made by the editor, publisher and print buyer. It is really between offset litho or gravure printing, each being appropriate for particular kinds of work. Once the magazine is printed the pages must be folded into the right sections, bound and trimmed. Then all that remains is for them to be bundled and sent on their way to the distributors, wholesalers, newsagents and readers.

RECOMMENDED READING

Click, J.W. and Baird, R.N. (1994) *Magazine Editing and Production*.

The Economist (2012) *Economist Style Guide 2012*, 10th edition.

Evans, H. (2000) *Essential English for Journalists, Editors and Writers*.

Evans, H. (1973) *Editing and Design: A Five-Volume Manual of English, Typography and Layout*.

Frost, C. (2012) 'Production processes' and 'Typography', in *Designing for Newspapers and Magazines*.

Garfield, S. (2011) *Just My Type: A Book About Fonts*.

Hicks, W. and Holmes, T. (2002) *Subediting for Journalists*.

Holmes, T. and Mottershead, G. (2013, forthcoming) *Subediting and Production for Journalists: Print, Digital and Social*.

Mayes, I. (2000) *Corrections and Clarifications*.

Morrish, J. and Bradshaw, P. (2012) 'Managing production', in *Magazine Editing: In Print and Online*.

Ritter, R. (ed.) (2000) *The Oxford Dictionary for Writers and Editors*.

Whittaker, J. (2008) *Magazine Production*.

Websites

The Economist style guide: www.economist.com/styleguide/introduction

Guide to fonts include search facility: www.myfonts.com

The Guardian style guide: www.guardian.co.uk/styleguide

Proof marks: www.interactivetraining.co.uk/proofreading-symbols.html

CHAPTER 12

Magazines in the digital world

Tim Holmes

Lindsay Nicholson could see something wasn't right. The woman she was watching struggled to navigate the online version of *Good Housekeeping*; Nicholson, as editor of the magazine, was concerned. With more readers using mobile devices like iPads and smartphones to access the digital versions of print titles, the process had to be as smooth as possible. Nicholson could see that getting around *Good Housekeeping* on an iPhone was not as straightforward as it should be.

So she went back to the office and invented a new magazine.

Good Ideas was launched in April 2012 as an app-first, print-second magazine. That is to say, it was designed to be read on a tablet, not in print. The magazine was still in the mould of *Good Housekeeping* but its pages were much less busy than the parent magazine's, the articles shorter; it used screen-friendly typefaces and built-in interactivity took readers from the contents pages to the features and from the features to advertisers' websites.

As Nicholson told *Press Gazette*:

> It's part of the 'What If' idea. *Good Housekeeping* was launched 90 years ago in 1922 and we thought: 'What if we had launched it now?' It is an experiment – whatever happens we are really interested. We know so much about what works in print, but hardly anything about that in digital.
>
> (http://bit.ly/mhbgoodideas)

It seems astonishing that the editor of a respected magazine can admit to knowing next to nothing about what works in a digital edition, but this is not a lacuna in Lindsay Nicholson's personal knowledge – she is simply acknowledging a truth that most publishers making the transition between print and digital try to hide: nobody knows what works.

To refine that a little, there is a developing body of knowledge about what seems to work from a technical point of view, and there are some emerging rules for individual journalists to follow, but there is no denying the fact that when it comes to the future, everyone is navigating by the most rudimentary maps.

A BRIEF HISTORY OF MAGAZINES IN THE DIGITAL WORLD

The media have had the best part of 20 years to get to grips with digital journalism – even longer if we go back to the BBC's unsuccessful videotex service of 1969. By 1993 the world wide web had become established enough for media to recognise its potential as a medium of distribution. Magazines were among the earliest of adopters when *Forbes* and *Time* launched online editions, joined a year later by *Wired* magazine, the BBC, the *Daily Telegraph* and the *Financial Times*.

It was 1995 when the boom began in earnest and became global – *The Guardian* (UK), *Le Monde* (France), *Die Welt* (Germany), the *Washington Post* (USA), *Asahi Shimbum* (Japan) and the *Jerusalem Post* (Israel) were just a few of the newspapers to launch websites; CBS, CNN and ABC began to supplement their broadcast material with online additions; *GQ* (Condé Nast) and ZDNet (Ziff-Davis) continued the transubstantiation from print while *Salon* and *Slate* established a new format when they appeared as online-only magazines. After that, the deluge – but no agreement about how to deliver the packages: some publishers opted for the 'enclosed garden' approach of AOL's paid-for subscription service, while others risked the wide-open spaces of the free internet.

Then, as now (mid-2012), no one was sure where the money would come from or how it would come; then, as now, opinions and predictions ranged from subscription models to single copy purchases to advertising revenue. Then, as now, publishers overstated profitability and understated costs. But if much has stayed the same, even more has evolved; the online publishing industry has been through a greater number of changes in 20 years than print managed in the last 100 – changes to technologies of production, transmission, reception and consumption; changes to the skillsets of journalists creating content; changes in reader expectations and demands.

It appears that the original, almost utopian, argument was that because all content would be delivered in a digital stream, creating a common toolset, it would all somehow be made more convergent. This has proved to be false business logic so far. As Herman and McChesney pointed out back in 1997: 'The global media and communication firms in the larger "info-communication" sector act as much out of fear of the unknown as from coherent visions of what a converging communication market might look like in ten or twenty years' (Herman and McChesney 1997: 108).

As far as magazines are concerned, the convergent market has looked confusing for a long time. Read the following quotes and guess what they describe:

> Circulation figures are low to miniscule and the ad pages are almost non-existent . . . the combination of text, graphics, full-motion video, audio and animation . . . 'It's a big educational problem . . . we've had to explain it in terms of existing media and that doesn't quite work because we're creating a new medium' . . . they needed to develop a new kind of publishing system that allows editors, not programmers, to produce multimedia content quickly.
>
> (http://nyti.ms/mhbcdrom)

Can you tell what it is? A CD-ROM magazine – that is, a magazine published on a CD. In 1994, when the *New York Times* published this article on the medium it was quite the happening thing, even though the first title to be published this way, *NautilusCD*, had appeared in 1989. Almost exactly the same things could be written now – indeed, have been written recently – about app-based magazines.

Does this mean the magazine industry is hopeless? Without a clue as to what to do? No it does not – publishers large and small have been able to harness the potential of digital creativity to superb effect. There are examples of beautifully made, inventive, attractive magazines that exist as nothing but strings of zeros and ones, whether those binary digits appear on a CD-ROM or on an iPad.

Even before the CD-ROM, magazines used digital technology to increase circulation. In 1985 Chris Anderson began sticking cassette tapes on the cover of his recently launched title *Amstrad Action*, increased the price and doubled the sales. The tape was analogue of course, but encoded in the ferrous ribbon were instructions for software that could be uploaded to an Amstrad. The success of this move, born out of desperation to increase circulation figures, laid the foundations of Future Publishing – and Anderson's globe-spanning series of TED conferences devoted to 'ideas worth spreading' from the worlds of technology, entertainment and design (www.ted.com).

So rather than an inability or unwillingness to keep up, the biggest problem for magazines has been that the physical expression of technology keeps changing, and each change is not only like starting all over again, it brings in its wake new challenges for modes of production, methods of distribution and means of making money.

Even before the internet had been tamed by Tim Berners-Lee's development of the world wide web as a common communication protocol, magazines were exploring the possibilities offered by global networking. Computing magazines were among the first to offer their readers a foothold in cyberspace via bulletin boards, the services on which users with the relevant expertise could post comments and play games, while some general-interest titles teamed up with private 'walled garden' networks such as Compuserve and AOL to offer an extended range of content.

Once the world wide web had become the dominant protocol it became far easier for publishers, and even individuals, to create websites, but there were a number of restrictive factors. The most important was literally a restriction – narrow bandwidth and slow communication speeds meant that it was usually a very frustrating experience for readers to download multimedia content: the modems and telephone lines through which all the bits and bytes flowed simply could not handle the large files required for video or even fancy graphics.

Nevertheless, from the late-1990s onwards it became increasingly common for magazines to have companion websites, even if there was no common agreement about what they should be used for – some saw them as a place where long features could be dumped (no restrictions on space), others as repositories for unused images from photoshoots. Since those early days (all of 20 years ago!), the uses of magazine websites have become more standardised, as discussed below.

However, no sooner did magazine publishers get to grips with the web than technology changed again. First, the restrictions mentioned above began to disappear: broadband internet connections were rolled out across the UK, either down re-engineered copper telephone lines or through fibre-optic cable channels. Websites could become richer in media and publishers responded by boosting audio and video content; magazine publishers began to build dedicated studios in which to create multimedia content – and journalists previously wedded to print learned to shoot, edit and present video.

Focus magazine – the popular science title – provides an excellent example of how this happened. *Focus* was published by BBC Worldwide's specialist magazine division; based in Bristol, away from the corporate mothership and in a city known for its radical popular culture, the editorial team felt free to experiment and was encouraged to do so by the management. When they wanted to film pop science experiments they blagged a camera, learned how to shoot and edit, and uploaded the results. When they wanted to add podcast discussions of scientific topics they blagged a digital recorder, learned how to script and deliver spoken content and uploaded the results. When sister magazine *The Sky At Night* wanted to add stunning backdrops to their vodcasts (video podcasts) they bought a couple of yards of green material from Bristol market, rigged up a green-screen and digitally back-projected footage from NASA, the American space agency.

The Bristol outpost also broke new ground for the BBC by setting up websites using Drupal software to create content management systems. This was yet another widespread technological change for magazines to accommodate. The first websites had to be constructed page by page using software such as DreamWeaver, a process that required relatively high-level technical skills to achieve good (and consistent) results. New packages like Drupal and Joomla allowed magazines to set up sites that had a standardised look, to which content could be added simply, quickly and directly by the editorial team. Wordpress, the popular blogging tool, rapidly developed a similar capability and many content management systems now use it as a basis. Apart from anything else, this means that any journalist who has ever blogged will be familiar with the interface.

At the same time as broadband was becoming widely available, mobile telephony began to develop in earnest; both handsets and transmission services became more capable, eventually evolving into smartphones capable of accessing the internet and playing multimedia content. This created yet another niche that magazines had to fill – versions of their websites suited to mobile consumption.

Finally (for the moment), Apple created yet another node in the matrix of consumption when it launched the iPad. Neither computer nor phone, the iPad's native operating system supported apps – and did not support Flash, the software that powered a huge amount of online video. The vacuum of the app universe was initially filled with games, but magazine publishers soon saw the need to occupy this new space and began to create apps for their titles. However, as with the early websites there have been varying approaches, partly dictated by theoretical understandings of the medium and partly by software functionality.

Although magazines are still exploring how best to occupy, and make money from, the digital space, there are three main manifestations – the purely digital magazine, the electronic adjunct and the magazine-like community.

The purely digital magazine (i-mag)

This is still the smallest fraction of the triad, despite the apparent financial advantage that being able to publish with no paper or printing costs offers. A small number of online magazines have achieved some kind of stability and an ever-changing roster of launches from established publishers and independent outfits. At one end of the spectrum are what might be called conventional-magazines-online and at the other end are a panoply of indy projects.

Prime examples of the former are *Salon.com* and *Slate.com*, both launched in 1996. Even these two occupy different corners of the market, with *Salon* proudly independent and *Slate* kept afloat for many years by Microsoft before being sold in December 2004 to the *Washington Post* when the newspaper was looking to expand and diversify its online readership.

Salon and *Slate* sit squarely in the classic American news magazine mould typified by *Time*. To get an idea of the range of indy mags at the other end of the scale, spend a few minutes browsing issuu.com – a free online magazine upload-and-publish service that hosts hundreds, if not thousands, of titles. Some are well-known magazines that come into the adjunct category (see below), but any given index page will show never-before-seen publications – and not just in English either. Scribd.com also hosts uploaded magazines but has more of a focus on individual documents and books. Because both are free services, they provide a natural home for the edgier, more experimental magazines that cannot afford – or do not want – to use Zinio, Ceros, Olive or one of the other commercial digitising operations.

The range of i-mags that are more or less conventional products but which use an unconventional means of delivery and distribution has diminished over recent years, after the vision of online advertising revenue proved something of a mirage. Both *mykindaplace.com* and *monkeyslum.com*, websites aimed at teenage girls and boys, respectively, that claimed large readerships, were bought by satellite telly provider BSkyB and then shut down. NatMags (now Hearst Magazines UK) took a bold step forward by creating *jellyfish.com* as an online magazine for teenage girls in March 2007, then backtracked by closing it in August of the same year, when no sustainable business model could be discerned.

Dennis Publishing launched *Monkey* (no relation to *monkeyslum*) in 2006 as an online lads' mag and followed it with *iGizmo* (gadgets) and *iMotor* (cars). *Monkey* made it from website to an iPad app for a while but was eventually incorporated into *kontraband.com*; *iGizmo* can still be downloaded from iTunes and the Apple Newsstand; *iMotor* was totalled in 2010.

Publishers have not fallen over themselves to establish stand-alone app-based magazines but, true to type, Richard Branson was among the pioneers. In 2010 he launched *Project*, an iPad-only title that had been developed by some heavyweight experts, including career magazine man Anthony Noguera. Get a taste of it at www.projectmag.com. Coming at the idea from a different angle was *The Atavist* (www.atavist.com), which publishes not so much a magazine as a discrete series of very (or extremely) long magazine-style features enhanced with 'video, audiobooks, additional layers of information and a host of other features'.

Felix Dennis, founder of the eponymous publishing company, was once heard to dismiss printed magazines as 'hieroglyphics smeared on trees' that would be consigned to history by the digital revolution. That hasn't yet come about – as Dennis has found to both his cost and his profit – and it seems unlikely that digital magazines will entirely supersede printed ones, at least not for some time. Just as CD-ROMs turned out to be best used as cover mounts, rather than publishing substrate, so current thinking among mainstream magazines seems to be that online is best used as a marketing adjunct.

The digital adjunct

With the exception of a few small-scale indies still in love with print, it is unthinkable that a new magazine would be launched without digital adjuncts – website, app, Facebook page, Twitter account.

Back in 1997 the 'website' was a one-size-fits-all solution to a magazine's digital requirements, mainly because that's all there was. Now, thanks to that ever-shifting physical expression of technology, it is so much more complicated than that. Take the UK edition of *Wired* as an example. Naturally, there is a website (www.wired.co.uk) and on that website are:

- news – updated constantly, just like a newspaper;
- features – taken from the latest print issue (but not until digital subscribers have already had their copies);
- videos – lots of them, covering lots of topics;
- podcasts – audio updates from Planet *Wired*; and
- much more, including news of *Wired*-related events, a sign-up for weekly newsletters and an unmissable subscription offer.

There is also an iPad app, via which individual issues of the title can be purchased, and an iPhone app, which is news-focused. *Wired* has a corporate Twitter account (@WiredUK), mainly containing links to editorial content, but several of its staff (for example, @olivia_solon) and contributors (for example, @benhammersley) have accounts in their own names that allow readers to follow them and extend their relationship with the magazine and its personnel. (The development of semi-personal Twitter accounts is discussed below.) Finally, *Wired* has a Facebook page on which editorial content can be posted and with which readers can interact. At the news:rewired 2012 conference Nate Lanxon, editor of wired.co.uk, revealed that material giving readers a peek behind the scenes – goofing around at photoshoots and so on – worked best on Facebook. As a result, he decided 'that our Facebook page was about driving *Wired* to fans and not the other way around' (http://bit.ly/mhblanxon).

Thus, depending on the particular flavour, digital adjuncts are used to

- provide a taste of current content;
- augment the print edition with multimedia;
- encourage subscription;
- facilitate the purchase of a single issue to read on a portable device; and
- act as a community hub and build interaction with the readers.

That final element of adjunct sites, community hub provision, goes to the heart of a key characteristic of the magazine format. For her study of Canadian woman's magazine *Chatelaine*, Valerie Korinek was given access to the magazine's archives, including correspondence, published and unpublished, from the readers. She found 'many of the women's comments suggested that magazines, or discussion about magazines, fostered a sense of identity or membership in a community' (Korinek 2000: 77).

This is not exactly a new proposition, but Korinek reached this conclusion not from a theoretical standpoint but because she was able to draw on the readers' own evidence. For *Chatelaine*'s audience, communication with the hub relied on the postal service and was a many-to-one experience: each individual reader was communicating with a corporate entity (or its representative, the editor) and there was little chance of direct peer-to-peer communication.

Digital communications have changed that forever; in the various ways they are used by magazines they allow, indeed encourage, instant peer-to-peer conversation and threaded debates about the magazine generally, a particular aspect of its contents, or any topic at all which tickles the fancy of a contributor. Similarly, email or Twitter addresses given at the end of features or opinion pieces allow readers to correspond directly with the writer, turning the communications process into much more of a two-way channel.

From a publisher's perspective, digital publishing allows instant and accurate measurement of the success or failure of everything, from an individual article to a complete issue. There are many commercial services that can track:

- visitors to a site (and where they come from);
- the number of page views;
- which content gets the most visits;
- time on site per visit;
- which ads or other referents are driving the most visitors to the site;
- effectiveness of a marketing campaign;

but Google Analytics offers a free and simple DIY option that levels the playing field between corporate and indy publishers.

The magazine-like community

When is a magazine not a magazine? When it is *iVillage.com*, perhaps. *iVillage* began life in 1999 as a site that aggregated content from magazines owned by the Hearst Corporation of America, and as these include *Cosmopolitan*, *Good Housekeeping*, *Redbook* and *Marie Claire*, the range and quality of material was not a problem. As the name suggests, however, the intention was more ambitious than just repurposing magazine editorial. *iVillage* was intended to become a community site which was an adjunct to the magazines but which also supported itself both editorially and commercially. This it achieved rapidly, catching the rising wave of internet awareness among women.

In December 2000 *iVillage* and Tesco joined forces to launch a UK version of the site. Two-and-a-half years later Tesco bought out the American site's 50 per cent share to become sole owner, then in 2004 sold the operation back to the Americans. Tesco.com's CEO Laura Wade-Gery explained to *New Media Age*: 'It's a very different sort of product to the other services that we're embarking on. In my mind, we stand for providing services and products that you buy, which is slightly different to the world of providing information' (Howell 2005).

iVillage may not have offered enough advertising revenue or cross-promotional opportunities for Tesco, but NBC, the American broadcaster, took a different view, buying the entire *iVillage* operation for $600 million in March 2006. NBC boss Bob Wright told Andrew Edgecliffe-Johnson of the *Financial Times* that iVillage and the 15 million users it attracted every month would become the cornerstone of NBC's digital strategy (http://on.ft.com/mhbnbc).

Since then, *iVillage.com* claims to have doubled its readership: '*iVillage* is the largest content-driven community for women online reaching 30+ million unique visitors per month (comScore)' (http://bit.ly/mhbivusa); the UK version claims: '*iVillage UK* has a monthly audience of 3,496,759 and 35,124,109 million monthly page views – and continues to grow' (http://bit.ly/mhbivuk).

But is *iVillage* a magazine? It shares many of a magazine's defining characteristics. Magazines have a specific role to fulfil within the ecology of media forms: as David Abrahamson (1996a: 1). puts it: 'It has long been the unique function of magazines, rather than newspapers or the broadcast media, to bring high-value interpretive information to specifically defined yet national audiences.'

In his book *Magazine-Made America*, Abrahamson offers a further useful definition in his study of post-war periodicals: 'specific information in a specific form that can be expected to appeal to a definable segment of readers' (Abrahamson 1996b: 28), locating this within the commercial context of 'delivering' those readers to 'a group of manufacturers or distributors with the means and willingness to advertise their products and services' to them.

All of the above apply to *iVillage*, but there is more. One of the strongest characteristics of the magazine form is the bond it causes to be forged between producer and consumer. Studies of the magazine, whether undertaken from an academic perspective (Ballaster *et al.*, 1991; Beetham 1996; Ferguson 1983; Hermes 1995; Holmes and Nice 2012) or a more commercial perspective (Barrell and Braithwaite 1979; Consterdine 2002; Mott 1930; PPA 2000) stress the trusting relationship between the magazine and its readers, as well as the way in which this bond creates a sense of community fostered by the publisher or producer.

So is *iVillage* really a community? Again, the answer appears to be yes. Both social and cultural studies have realised that:

> Communities do not have to be solitary groups of densely knit neighbors but could also exist as social networks of kin, friends and workmates who do not necessarily live in the same neighborhoods . . . This conceptual revolution moved from defining community in terms of space – neighborhoods – to defining it in terms of social networks.
>
> (Wellman and Gulia 1999: 169)

Wellman and Gulia study the characteristics and effects of different types of communities in the material world and online, covering many points directly germane to a site like *iVillage*, concluding that:

> Pundits worry that virtual community may not truly be community. These worriers are confusing the pastoralist myth of community for the reality. Community ties are already geographically dispersed, sparsely knit, connected heavily by tele-communications (phone and fax), and specialized in content . . . Just as the Net supports neighborhood-like group communities of densely knit ties, it also supports personal communities, wherever in social or geographical space these ties are located and however sparsely knit they might be.
>
> (Wellman and Gulia 1999: 187)

Furthermore, *iVillage* has editorial content partly generated by its community, but also written by an editorial team of named writers. There are clearly people at work collating and subediting material contributed by community members. In one sense this makes it the most magazine-like proposition possible – a massive realm of material generated directly by the interests of the audience, which is then fed back to that audience in a subtly mediated form.

This idea has not gone unnoticed among other magazine publishers. In 2007 IPC launched www.goodtoknow.co.uk, an aggregation of content from brands such as *Woman's Weekly*, *Woman*, *Woman's Own* and *Essentials*, which clearly owes a strong conceptual debt to *iVillage*. Similarly, Future Publishing has launched aggregator sites like www.techradar.com, www.bikeradar.com and others that aim to reinforce immediately relevant editorial with substantial community interaction.

BLOGS, TWEETS AND LIKES

If *iVillage* lies at the corporate end of the scale of virtual communities, at the other end is 'blogistan' or the 'blogosphere', the sector of cyberspace inhabited by the individual creators and maintainers of weblogs.

It is included here not just because of its magazine-like characteristic of spreading information to special interest groups, but also because magazine journalists are increasingly expected to blog as part of their job – indeed most employers with first-job opportunities will expect applicants to be blogging already. It is not uncommon for magazines and the individuals who work on them to have blogs as part of the expanding mix of content that encourages communication and interaction with readers.

Blogging was the communications phenomenon of the early years of the new millennium. Much was written about it, including a lot of nonsense, but some key points have survived to become common wisdom:

- blogs vary in quality and reliability, so a blog associated with a magazine must become a trusted source;

- blogs still have power and speed as vectors of information and misinformation;

- many large media concerns have made forays into the territory to annexe some space for themselves;

- established journalists and media practitioners write blogs, sometimes to give a personal perspective on their professional duties;

- blogs can provide access to eyewitness material that reporters from outside can't get at.

This democratisation of communication led Ian Hargreaves of Cardiff University to argue that 'in a democracy everybody is a journalist'[1] and at one point the blogosphere was undoubtedly the most advanced means of democratic production, as Peter Preston noted after the tsunami on 26 December 2004:

> 'Bloggers beat conventional media,' said the *Times of India*. The BBC relied on bloggers from right round the Indian Ocean for much of its early reporting. *The Guardian*, like some other papers, ran pages of web testimony. Your readers and viewers were also your correspondents. Your ability to be in touch was digital as well as conventional. That is a quantum shift.
>
> (http://bit.ly/mhbpreston)

Since then there have been two further quantum shifts. Facebook became a global forum for first personal and then corporate interaction; many magazines have Facebook pages for readers to add to their friend lists and 'like'. Then Twitter emerged as a 140-character, multipurpose communication system – multipurpose because it has proved equally suited to yakking about cats, reporting gunfire as the 2008 Mumbai terrorist attacks were in progress, spreading information about protests against the 2009 elections in Iran, or helping to organise the events now known as the Arab Spring.

Twitter has become increasingly important to magazines, and they use it in a number of ways:

- general promotion of a title – done poorly this is probably the least successful use, but done well it can enhance a title's community and feeds into the next category;

- disseminating content – tweeting links to news items of immediate interest or longer features that have been published in a new issue;

- personal communication – if a magazine is very small, very specialist, or hyperlocalised, the editor and staff may literally be exchanging tweets with readers they know in person;

- semi-personal or semi-professional communication – this is where journalists associated with particular titles use Twitter to give readers behind-the-scenes titbits about the magazine (for example, sharing details of a photoshoot or red-carpet event), and also insights into certain aspects of their personal lives (for example, problems on the commute or holiday plans).

To take women's magazines as an example, many editors now run Twitter accounts that identify them and their positions; among the best known and most active are Jo Elvin of *Glamour* (@jo_elvin), Sam Baker of *Red* (@SamAtRedmag), Victoria White of *Company* (@companyedvic), Mandie Gower of *Zest* (@ZestEdMandie), Jane Bruton of *Grazia* (@janeGRAZIA), Louise Court of *Cosmopolitan* (@LouiseCosmoEd) and Lorraine Candy of *Elle* (@LorraineELLE). These accounts can attract massive numbers of followers – Jo Elvin, who uses it really well, has 53,565 – and publishers believe this has huge potential benefits because readers may feel much closer to the editor as each one is in direct personal communication with her; the publishers get promotion that is immediate and relevant.

Used in these ways, Twitter is another tool that can feed directly into the matrix of relationships that exist between a magazine and its readers. Lorraine Candy expanded on this at the 2012 Professional Publishers Association conference, as *Brand Republic* reported:

> The key to the success of using social media in this way, Candy said, is by 'not giving any content away'. Instead, content should drive readers back to the Elle brand, she said, pointing out the live cover-shoot tweets that are being used for archive purposes on the magazine's website . . . She added Twitter can be a crucial tool for journalists, as long as journalists 'always adhere to the mantra that content is king'. She said publications failed on Twitter when they were too bland or tried to sell things, which readers could see through.
>
> (http://bit.ly/mhbbrand)

THE ESSENTIAL SKILLS OF DIGITAL MAGAZINE JOURNALISM

So far this chapter has mapped the landscape of digital magazines. What follows is a more practical look at what it will mean for those involved in magazine journalism.

The good news is that digital journalism needs the same basic skills and knowledge as print. The job still involves finding things out and telling people about them, so digital magazine journalists need the full range of research skills, a facility with words, a good grasp of visuals and the ability to put them together so that stories can be communicated effectively. Also essential is a grasp of media law and methodical archiving of sourced material in case a story comes under legal scrutiny.

Beyond those basics a usefully expanded skill set would include the following.

Online writing and curation

Writing for digital publication is very much the same as writing for print, with a couple of additions. One set of initials gets bandied around a lot – SEO, standing for search engine optimisation, the process that makes a website or web page more visible to search engines and thus brings in more visitors. SEO involves thinking about how readers search for information – the words they search for, the actual search terms or keywords typed into search engines, and which search engines are preferred by their targeted audience. Appropriate words and phrases can then be used in headlines and stories.

Optimising a website may involve more than just editing its content; HTML and other coding may be amended to increase its relevance to specific keywords and to remove barriers to the indexing activity of search engines.

Another common online journalism technique is liveblogging, the name given to a continually updated blog post that provides rolling textual coverage of an ongoing event – a political debate or a judicial inquiry, for example. Although this seems like something better suited to newspapers, magazine websites – particularly B2B titles that have a strong news agenda or tech magazines that want to give their readers blow-by-blow accounts of conferences or launches – find it invaluable.

Liveblogs often combine original reporting with comments made on other sources (tweets from other journalists or commentators; breaking news stories in other media), and in this form incorporate important elements of *editorial curation* – another digital catchphrase popularised by Clay Shirky (you can watch a video of Shirky explaining this concept at http://bit.ly/mhbshirky). One of the most popular editorial curation services is Storify (www.storify.com), which the magazine trade body PPA put to use in reporting the 2012 PPA conference (see http://bit.ly/mhbppa and note the way delegates capture speaker insights):

> 'Everyone is a reporter, the edit is what we own,' says Lorraine Candy of *Elle*. Too right. #Ppaconf

was just one curation, from the twitterstream of Jessica Evans (@jazzy_jess).

Online search skills

Finding data is an everyday occurrence for most journalists. Entering a simple word or phrase into a search box will throw up hundreds of pages to trawl through, so it is worth knowing how to use advanced search techniques, as explained by many authors, including Gilster (1996), Reddick and King (1997), McGuire *et al.* (2002), Keeble (1998), Sherman (2005) and Djurup (2010). Or, indeed, you can search online for advice on how to search online – and how to use search engines other than Google. Up-to-date information on using the internet as a research tool can be found on the site maintained by John Morrish, whose www.journolist.com carries an enormous quantity of information for the digital journalist.

InDesign or QuarkXPress

Desktop publishing (DTP) was among the first digital tools to impact on magazines. A basic ability to use one or other of the main packages, or convert as necessary, is a given. Not all journalists will be making arty spreads, but many are expected to complete templated pages.

Photoshop

As with DTP, the ability to re-size and sharpen digital photographs is widely expected. If you can do convincing cutouts and use layers creatively, so much the better. Magazine journalists should learn to take and process photos anyway – it's good for visual creativity and even better for reporting from events.

Blogging – and by extension content management systems

The importance of blogging has already been noted. Getting started is as easy as signing up to Blogger.com or Wordpress.com. Use basic editorial skills to define a topic, target a specific readership and develop both voice and expertise. Best results come with regular blogging and learning to use analytics (Google offers a comprehensive service) to see what works and what doesn't. This can mean the type of content that readers like but reader numbers can be affected by many other factors – did your post get picked up by an aggregator, did you tweet it out, did it get retweeted?

Twitter

Magazines thrive on community and Twitter is all about forming, developing and nurturing communities. There is no standard set of rules about how to use Twitter 'professionally'; the best way to learn is to follow magazines or their editors and observe what they do. Here are a few suggestions:

- *NME*: @NME, 295,000+ followers
- *Grazia Daily*: @grazia_live, 110,000+ followers
- *BBC Good Food*: @bbcgoodfood, 56,300+ followers
- Heather Brooke, freelance: @newsbrooke, 13,200+ followers
- David Rowan, *Wired UK*: @iRowan, 11,800+ followers
- Lara O'Reilly, *Marketing Week*: @larakiara, 2,500+ followers.

Facebook

As with Twitter, there is no great secret to using Facebook as a magazine journalist. Find magazines that have their own pages (there are loads – pick some you like and some you don't) and look at what they do. Here are a few suggestions in different categories:

- low-key indy: *Oh Comely*, 7,000+ likes
- high-profile indy: *Vice*, 607,000+ likes
- glossy women's: *Glamour*, 86,000+ likes (the US version has 795,000+)
- specialist: *Trail*, 5,400+ likes
- biggest number I could find: *Cosmo* (US), 1,750,479 likes

Experiment with your own page, check your analytics to see what gets the biggest hits and learn from experience. No one has the definitive set of rules.

Video

It is becoming more common for magazine journalists to be asked to do some kind of video test during interviews, particularly for B2B titles (many of which are moving from print to digital). Thus it is a very good idea to learn how to shoot, edit and present video. Fortunately cameras have never been cheaper or better and iMovie or Adobe Premiere are relatively simple to learn. Presenting is an art to be practised and critiqued over and over again, but it can be done.

Audio and podcasting

The same goes for audio and its scripted and performed cousin, podcasting. Journalists record interviews as a matter of course; if professional editing software is not available, audacity (http://audacity.sourceforge.net) offers freeware that does an excellent job. A good podcast will be like a directed, but not stilted, conversation between opinionated and knowledgeable experts.

Computer-assisted reporting

Computer-assisted reporting (CAR) is one specialised digital journalism skill not everyone will have. It is generally taken to mean a form of investigative reporting that accesses and analyses data via various forms of software. This side of the craft is covered well in Philip Meyer's (2002) book *Precision Journalism: A Reporter's Introduction to Social Science Methods*. In its purest form data journalism like this involves downloading spreadsheets and crunching their numbers in multiple ways. For example, take *The Guardian*'s 'Reading the riots' series, analysing 2011's summer riots. It is a superb example of what can be achieved with data journalism (http://bit.ly/mhbriots). For a more magazine-style take, have a look at *Delayed Gratification*'s infographics vault (http://bit.ly/mhb-dginfo).

Finally, don't forget you have a camera, video camera, audio recorder, and transmission system in your pocket – your smartphone. Learn how to use it.

THE FUTURE FOR MAGAZINES IN THE DIGITAL WORLD

As we move into the second decade of the new millennium, the world of publishing has had to endure a lot of bad news: the maggoty mess brought to light by the Leveson Inquiry, the closure of more than 200 local and regional newspapers, once-popular magazines falling into desuetude, an overall reduction in print advertising revenue that is not being balanced by growth in digital revenue.

Despite this, surprisingly few magazines have (at the time of writing) actually closed or been folded. As seen earlier in this chapter, there is still a lot of activity in the digital realm – websites, iPad apps, mobile platforms, social media communities – and plenty of publishers to huff and puff about growing numbers of page views, news-stand sales, subscriptions and online advertising.

But, writing in the *Huffington Post*, media analyst Colin Morrison seemed to blow away the froth and tell us how it is: 'Few magazine and newspaper publishers are generating sustainable profits from digital activity' (http://huff.to/mhbmorrison). Unpromising as this seems, Morrison still saw signs of hope and he is not alone in remaining optimistic about the survival of certain types of magazine. Titles likely to flourish in the future include:

- small, mainly indy, magazines that do a great job of serving a narrow but deep niche, especially if they can develop targeted distribution/subscription systems;
- freemium specialist magazines like *ShortList*, *Stylist* and *Sport*, which exist outside the normal distribution system and thus have much greater control over production costs;
- international magazine brands that have global propositions – *Top Gear*, *Cosmopolitan* and *Elle* are just a few of the titles that are published in multiple countries;
- customer magazines that combine strong editorial with electronic retail opportunities – Morrison's word for this is 'mediatailing';
- hyperlocal magazines that serve tightly defined geographical areas – there are already examples of this in the *Port Talbot Magnet* (www.lnpt.org) and *PitsnPots* (www.pitsnpots.co.uk).

Another way to try to identify magazines that have a future is to apply the General Theory of Magazines that I have proposed elsewhere (Holmes and Nice 2012). The theory isolates the essential characteristics of magazine-ness and detaches titles from specific substrates and formats of publishing, analogue or digital; by doing so it allows analysis and application of the underlying principles. The theory states:

1   magazines always target a precisely defined group of readers;
2   magazines base their content on the expressed and perceived needs, desires, hopes and fears of that defined group;
3   magazines develop a bond of trust with their readerships;
4   magazines foster community-like interactions between themselves and their readers, and among readers;
5   magazines can respond quickly and flexibly to changes in the readership and changes in the wider society.

To this can be added Colin Morrison's clear and useful definition of a trio of attributes that every successful digital magazine must possess. He calls them the Three Cs:

1   Content. User loyalty will be secured by original information (including self-generated content) that is targeted, creative and accessible.
2   Community. Users need to have a sense of belonging, 'ownership', and participation. Think Facebook, LinkedIn, ASOS, Net-a-Porter and Twitter.
3   Commerce. Product sales and services will be the essential engine of profitable media. Media = retail and retail = media. Think Net-a-Porter.

(http://huff.to/mhbmorrison)

Lindsay Nicholson would undoubtedly recognise the need for all of the foregoing in her magazine *Good Housekeeping*. The guardian of one of the magazine industry's most enduring titles in the UK, she is nevertheless aware that a grand legacy is no guarantee of future performance, which leads us back to where we started: 'It is an experiment.'

NOTE

1   Ian Hargreaves, lecture to journalism students at Cardiff University, 7 January 1999.

RECOMMENDED READING

Abrahamson, D. (1996a) 'The bright new-media future for magazines', *Magazine Matter*.

Abrahamson, D. (1996b) *Magazine-Made America: The Cultural Transformation of the Postwar Periodical*.

Bradshaw, P. and Rohumaa, L. (2011) *The Online Journalism Handbook: Skills to Survive and Thrive in the Digital Age*.

Brooke, H. (2011) *The Revolution will be Digitised: Dispatches from the Information War*.

Djurup, R. (2010) *Your Guide to Google Web Search: How to Find the Information You Need on the Internet*.

Gilster, P. (1996) *Finding It on the Internet: The Internet Navigator's Guide to Search Tools and Techniques*.

Herman, E.S. and McChesney, R.W. (1997) *The Global Media: The New Missionaries of Corporate Capitalism*.

Holmes, T. (ed) (2008) *Mapping the Magazine: Comparative Studies in Magazine Journalism*.

Holmes, T. and Nice, L. (2012) *Magazine Journalism*.

Holmes, T., *et al.* (2012) *The 21st Century Journalism Handbook*.

Korinek, V. (2000) *Roughing It in the Suburbs: Reading 'Chatelaine' Magazine in the Fifties and Sixties*.

McGuire, M., Stilborne, L., McAdams, M. and Hyatt L. (2002) *The Internet Handbook for Writers, Researchers and Journalists*.

Meyer, P. (2002) *Precision Journalism: A Reporter's Introduction to Social Science Methods*, 4th edition.

Naughton, J. (2012) *From Gutenberg to Zuckerberg: What You Really Need to Know About the Internet*.

Negroponte, N. (1996) *Being Digital*.

Reddick, R. and King, E. (1997) *The Online Journalist: Using the Internet and Other Electronic Media*.

Sherman, C. (2005) *Google Power: Unleash the Full Power of Google*.

Wellman, B. and Gulia, M. (1999) 'Virtual communities as communities: net surfers don't ride alone', in *Communities in Cyberspace*.

Whittaker, J. (2007) *Web Production for Writers and Journalists*, 2nd edition.

Website

www.bbc.co.uk/academy/collegeofjournalism/how-to/how-to-use-social-media/social-media-an-introduction

CHAPTER 13

Magazine design

Tim Holmes

Many journalists think of words as the starting point of magazines. But they're wrong. All magazines, whether delivered in print or electronically, start as a series of blank spaces waiting to be filled – think of a particular title and you are likely to think not just of words but also images (see Chapter 14). The way these elements combine within a specific visual context – along with other factors such as typefaces, headlines and captions – comprises the magazine's design.

The word 'design' is used in many different contexts and some would argue that consumers now routinely expect well-designed products: 'Design is the greatest factor in modern life. In every home, in shop windows and in every street Beauty is making a profound appeal. Things of Beauty are now the commonplaces of life.' These words could be attributed to any number of people who currently think about, write about and actually do design, but they come from Vincent Steer's book *Printing Design and Layout*, a training manual published in the 1930s:

> Let no printer remain under the delusion that the 'man in the street' cannot tell the difference between designed printing and printing that merely happens, he says. [It] will not be long before every buyer of printing insists that the work he gives to the printer shall also be well designed and beautifully printed.
>
> (Steer, no date: 11)

WHY MAGAZINE JOURNALISTS NEED TO KNOW ABOUT DESIGN

Many things have changed since Steer wrote those words, not least the introduction of computers into publishing houses in the late 1970s and early 1980s. This changed the production of magazines and newspapers forever. Journalists are expected to set type and make up pages, so now it is rare to see a journalism job advertisement that does not call for desktop publishing (DTP) skills and the ability to use online publishing software. The craft of printing still requires specialised skills and equipment, but typesetting can now be done by anyone with a computer – even the most basic machine running standard word-processing software comes with an enormous library of typefaces. Page design and make-up has changed from a job done on the compositor's worktable with paper, scalpel and glue to one completed within the confines of a journalist's computer, very probably an Apple Mac running either InDesign (the current industry standard) or QuarkXPress (the previous industry standard).

Even though magazine journalists are not usually expected to undertake the whole design process from initial concept to final delivery – most titles can still draw on specialised production and design staff – they are increasingly expected to be able to tweak pages (by fitting copy, for example) or complete a layout to the designer's brief.

But the demand for technical ability is only one reason why magazine journalists need to understand page design. Any writer hoping to progress beyond an entry-level job is now expected to be able to visualise the way their work will look on the page. Matt Swaine, then in charge of editorial training at Bauer Consumer Media, made this point at the Periodical Training Council's 2010 Academics & Industry Forum:

> Good writers need to be able to visualise exactly what a feature is going to look like . . . They need to get their ideas across to designers. They need to write with a clear visual end result that they are working towards . . . The ability to visualise features generates stronger features, that have visual impact and it seriously speeds up the creative process.

Similarly, anyone aiming for the heights of a top editorship must know how to work effectively with an art editor; print magazines that reach the peak of creativity invariably have an editor and art editor who understand and complement one another.

Magazines delivered electronically, however, are still evolving (see Chapter 12) and designing for digital platforms is a whole new field. Journalists who lived through the DTP revolution may recognise some of the stages, but increasingly magazine journalists will be expected to have digital skills. Understanding how to post to a blog will furnish most of what you need to know about uploading material to a content management system; being able to tweak the HTML coding to change the look or make a picture fit better will give you an edge.

WHAT IS GOOD DESIGN?

Readers expect their magazines to look appealing, but to explain exactly what constitutes good design is difficult because it is so subjective. This point was made by Ruari McLean, whose book *Magazine Design* is still one of the best introductions to the topic. He writes that when he uses the phrase 'good design' what he actually means is 'This pleases me, and I hope it pleases you', that 'what is "good design" in one particular context may not be "good design" in another' (McLean 1969: 3).

This means designers may disagree profoundly about what counts as 'good'. For Neville Brody, one of the best-known graphic designers and typographers of the late twentieth century, even the idea of 'pleasing' is too limiting. Brody was responsible for the distinctive look of style magazine *The Face* from 1981 to 1986, where 'his work . . . questioned the traditional structure of magazines design'. For him there was no question of seeing design as mere problem solving, to do that is 'to please rather than to invent', in the sense of satisfying expectations rather than communicating with the reader in an emotive way (Wozencroft 1988: 96, 10).

Brody's work for *The Face* has been credited with the 'reinvention of magazine language', the reflection of a new sensibility, one underpinned by the notion that to give the public what it wants is merely to give it what it is used to (Wozencroft 1988: 94–95). One of the interesting things for Brody about magazine design is the three-dimensional nature of the space that has to be worked with:

> Magazines are 3D items in space and time – there's a connection between page 5 and pages 56 and 57, a continuum. A magazine doesn't have to divide up space on a page like a newspaper, and the information it carries has more time to make connections between the different ideas that might be present. Why be inhibited by the edge of the page?
>
> (Wozencroft 1988: 96)

This comparison with newspapers was made in the 1980s, before it was common for newspapers to be sold with quite so many sections as they are now. Newspaper designers were, in any case, aware of the influence on the reading public of Brody and those designers who plunged into his wake, as well as of the changing expectations of readers. No surprise, then, that newspapers made efforts to modernise and enliven the way they looked. When *The Guardian* launched its revised design on 19 April 1999, the move was considered important enough to be recorded in a panel at the foot of the front page. This, in turn, directed readers to more detail about the changes, and the reasons for them. Tellingly, the story was headed 'Design to create pages people want to read', and one of the key quotes came from the paper's design director, Simon Esterson, who noted: '[W]e are in a situation where magazines are very well produced. Newspapers have to try to keep up with the standards set by magazines' (Glaister 1999).

WHAT IS 'DESIGN'?

At its simplest magazine design is the way in which words and images and the physical elements such as paper and binding work together. It is also much more than that, as the following example of a relaunch makes clear. *Motor Cycle News* hit the news-stands in a new guise on 14 April 1999. Although there was no reference to this on the cover, the editor took space on page two to explain the changes, which went well beyond a different typeface or two. Emap Active, publishers of the weekly, had decided it was no longer serving its readers effectively. As industry magazine *Press Gazette* explained: '*Motor Cycle News* has relaunched and moved more upmarket to cater for bikers who are becoming "more intelligent"' (Addicott 1999). Introducing the new look, editor Adam Duckworth told his readers, 'What I hope you'll notice is an *MCN* that's different in style, attitude and content.'

Leaving aside the attitude and the content (which are also of great importance), the most obvious change was the look of the weekly. The typeface for headlines and cover lines had changed from a brashly tabloid square-cut sans serif to a sans with chiselled ascenders, taking the look away from the *Sun* and into the little-mapped territory of a tabloid magazine (or 'magloid', a phrase that seems to have been coined when Emap relaunched another of its stalwart performers, *Garden News*, a few months later). The headlines themselves changed from upper case to upper and lower in a smaller point size, both changes giving the pages a less frantic look. The body face was clearer, allowing more white to show on the page which, in turn, gave a more spacious feel. (For an explanation of these terms, see the Glossary.)

Thus, the magazine's intention to move up-market was indicated by the look of the pages. Without reading a word, most potential readers would have been able to tell that something had happened and to interpret what it meant. Visual images have great power, and consumers learn to read and decode them immediately, including those consumers who don't have the analytical vocabulary to explain why. There is no absolute or universal reason why a woman's weekly magazine like *Chat* should have pages filled to bursting with short, bitty items and be spattered with bright colours. A convention could just as easily have evolved which meant big pictures and white space were the norm for C2DE readers and lively, information- and story-packed pages were the rule for their wealthier AB cousins. (These terms are explained in Chapter 15.)

VISUAL LITERACY

This understanding of visual conventions is what we mean by visual literacy. Most of our information about the outside world comes through our eyes; hearing, touch, smell and taste are all subordinate to sight in our culture. As a result, we are surrounded by images. Newspapers, books, television, films and advertising all play with images, to varying degrees and for varying purposes.

That's one key reason design is important to a magazine – it communicates the values and aspirations of a title before the potential consumer has read a word. However, it does not follow that 'design' necessarily means a highly creative arrangement of shapes on the page. As Ruari McLean notes: 'Magazine design cannot . . . be generalized; it is always a specific problem. Each publication has its own problems, its own aims, its own conditions and limitations' (McLean 1969: 1). Publications whose purpose is merely to impart factual information to a busy reader (financial newsletters, for example) may be best served by a straightforward arrangement of headlines and text. Readers don't have the time or inclination (such a layout implies) to bother with superfluous decoration when there is money to be made; what they are paying for is hard information, and that's what they should get. Nevertheless, there are different ways of achieving this look, and financiers are less likely to be impressed by an amateurish production that looks like a parish magazine than by one which features good typography in an unobtrusive but clear layout.

Those same readers, however, probably have interests outside their working lives. They may read a yachting magazine, for example, and when they pick it up they would not feel well served if it looked as plain as a newsletter. The sailing section in any newsagent shows that in magazines such as *Yachting Monthly* and *Yachting World* lavish photography and glossy paper are the norm, and usually these are accompanied by a high standard of page design.

As Neville Brody put it:

> At the root of it, design is a language just as French and German are languages. Whilst some people are able to understand design fluently, there are those who just use phrase-books. They don't understand the words they are using, but the phrase meets their need.
>
> (Wozencroft 1988: 10)

Brody was making the distinction as a comment on design practice, in the sense that the less innovative designers are the phrase-book wielders. But for those whose job is not to design but to work creatively with designers the phrase-book approach is perhaps a positive thing. Better anyway than those old-school journalists who sometimes make the mistake of thinking design is something separate from the prose that they so lovingly craft. A few have a more entrenched attitude and rate visual presentation as unimportant. Click and Baird attribute some of this to what they characterise as:

> the excesses of 'screaming graphics' that made some magazines almost impossible to read in the 1960s . . . [the] de-emphasis of content by some designers to the point where they seem to be designing for the sake of design alone also presents some difficulty.
>
> (Click and Baird 1990: 211–212)

Designers and writers do sometimes hold contrary opinions about the importance of words, and that can lead to trouble. Andy Cowles worked as a designer on magazines ranging from *Your Horse* to *Rolling Stone* before becoming editorial development director of IPC Media. In his view, 'designers are their own worst enemies because they don't learn how to write. They can empower themselves by getting a facility with the written word and learning to appreciate the power of one word as against another.'[1] This idea echoes one put forward by Colin McHenry, formerly group art director of Centaur Publications, who encouraged fledgling designers to develop a range of skills, including 'the ability to interpret a manuscript. You need to be able to read it, understand it and get some visual ideas from it' (McHenry, quoted in Swann 1991: 132).

COVERS

Nowhere in a magazine is the interaction of words and pictures more important than on the front cover. The cover has to do two key jobs for a magazine: 'It has to sell the general concept of the publication as well as to reflect, through its design, the intellectual level of the editorial content' (Swann 1991: 133). Other commentators suggest it has more personal than intellectual functions: 'It is the magazine's face . . . Like a person's face it is the primary indicator of a personality' (Click and Baird 1990: 98).

What's more, the cover has to do this more or less instantaneously, in an environment where there are shelves bearing hundreds of titles, including all the competing rivals in a given field. If it's doing its job really well the cover will tempt readers away from those rivals too, as John Morrish notes: 'The fundamental thing is for the cover to sell the issue, both to your regular readers . . . and to other people's readers, who might be looking for a change' (Morrish and Bradshaw 2012: 184).

This chapter can't attempt a comprehensive discussion of cover design (although some of the books recommended at the end of this chapter do). There are, however, certain guidelines relevant to all magazines sold on the news-stand rather than by subscription. Remember that about one-third of all decisions to buy a magazine are made on the spur of the moment in a shop, and readers take, on average, between two and three minutes to choose from the hundreds of titles in front of them; the average time spent by a potential purchaser on appraising each women's magazine cover is three seconds.[2] According to research carried out for the PPA, the cover is a publisher's main method of enticing shoppers to buy and every other cover in the shop is trying to do the same thing.[3]

Guidelines for cover design

- Put the emphasis on the top left-hand side of the cover as that is what will show on the newsagent's shelf whether it is stacked horizontally or vertically.

- Use a strong image, though not necessarily a photograph; sometimes a dramatic typographic concept can work well.

- Make sure the logo (also called the masthead) is clearly identifiable. This doesn't mean the whole thing has to be visible, but enough of its distinctive lettering should be there to make it clear to readers what they are looking at.

- Make sure cover lines are legible from two to three metres away. Some publishers refer to this as the floor test. If you throw a magazine on the carpet you should be able to read the cover lines without bending down.

- Promise a clear benefit to the reader.

- Offer something for beginners or new readers.

- Create strong links from the cover to the contents page and from the contents page to the content. Readers are irritated if the fascinating story heralded on the cover is impossible to find in the contents list, perhaps because it is given a different title.

- Deliver everything you promise.

- Plan the cover as early as possible and spend as much time on it as you can. Publishers and editors have even experimented with deciding a cover first and then commissioning the features to go with it. It's even been said some editors think up the cover lines first and then order the features.[4]

These guidelines do not apply to news-based publications that choose to look rather like newspapers, adopting some of the conventions of newspaper design such as using blocks of type on the front page. *Campaign*, the trade magazine for the advertising industry, is one example, although it is printed on glossy paper rather than newsprint. There are some signs now that this fashion may be changing. *Media Week* – before it closed its print version in November 2009 and became online only – moved from a cover full of news stories to a full-colour conceptual approach with just one strong image. Such a shift is never a guarantee of success, however. The newsprint tabloid music weekly *Melody Maker* turned into a glossy A4 magazine format in October 1999. By the end of 2000 it had been merged with its stable-mate *NME*.

Titles that are largely sold by subscription or reach the reader as part of a weekend newspaper package have the freedom to be more adventurous in their designs as the cover is not necessarily the selling point, although it still has to do the job of tempting the reader to open the magazine. Depending on the target readership the covers of newspaper supplement magazines may be much simpler, with perhaps just a picture and one or two words to draw attention to the cover story. Readers will be getting the magazine anyway, they don't make a purchasing choice based on the magazine's cover lines and that gives the designer greater freedom to concentrate on the visual aspects of the design.

Writing good cover lines is a craft in its own right. There is a temptation to try out clever wordplay, as in some headlines, but in Morrish's view this should be resisted:

> They are there to tempt the reader, to intrigue and invite closer scrutiny. They should be positive and enthusiastic . . . Above all they need to be short, colloquial and absolutely straightforward . . . Readers should be able to glance at the line and understand what it means. They shouldn't have to puzzle it out.
>
> (Morrish and Bradshaw 2012: 189)

A further point is that, generally speaking, the more down-market a title is, the more words and individual pictures there will be on the cover to the extent that magazines like *Chat* or *Take a Break* can seem to some eyes to be a visual mess.

Whatever kinds of covers are under discussion, a designer who recognises the importance of the verbal elements that contribute to the success of a cover is more likely to be able to influence the outcome. So too is a writer who appreciates the principles of good design and has at least an inkling of the ways in which designers are trained to think. IPC's Andy Cowles is not the only person who believes that 'the best editors are those who understand a visual language', the ones who, if not fluent in the language of design, perhaps, at least carry the phrase-book.

LOOKING FOR THE READER

Peter Booth, whose expertise as a designer helped the successful relaunch of many magazines, puts neither writer, photographer, nor designer at the heart of the matter. 'You have to think of it from the reader's point of view,' he says. 'It can be very easy to get into a particular way of writing, or for an editor to expect to see a feature presented in a certain way, but the full impact must be considered. Maybe the reader sees it or would like to see it in a different way. It's important to think about that.'

He also believes the designer has a responsibility to introduce new ideas to those whose primary language is not visual:

> I like to get people to look at different designs and see what it 'says' to them. This is quite easy to do now. Experimental layouts can be created quickly and the process can be seen immediately on screen. It is important for journalists and editors to develop visual awareness. Writers have tended to think only of the words, although it has changed since the days when an editor would just hand over a package of words and pictures and say 'fit that'. Then the possibility of changing the words around to make a better overall design was never even considered.

Peter Comely, another experienced magazine designer, agrees but thinks that people can learn to appreciate the visual for themselves: 'You can train yourself to become aware of how things look in magazines and on TV or in films. Design has become so important in everything we see or buy.' Attention to detail is key for him and he thinks too many journalists overlook lines of type out of alignment, or a missing 'end blob' at the finish of a story. On the other hand, he has also worked on titles that:

> [have] had very little design input in the past, so the editorial staff are just appreciative of anything I do to make it look better. But one thing which is really important is forward planning and an organised work style. It's vital to think of the feature and the magazine as a whole, and that's much more difficult, if not impossible, when you're constantly working right on the deadline and in a rush.
>
> (personal communication, Peter Comely)

What, then, can a word-loving magazine journalist, adept at headlines, standfirsts, captions and copy, do to improve on an underdeveloped visual awareness? Some guidance is essential if only to ensure that you're thinking about the right things and asking the right questions. Talk to art editors and graphic designers about why they make the decisions they do. Read some of the books listed at the end of this chapter, all the time trying to learn about the visual conventions that magazines follow or, in some cases, deliberately try to challenge and flout.

This still doesn't explain how to 'do' design, and in any case, as Ruari McLean was experienced enough to acknowledge: 'what the public will buy can be guessed, but cannot be predicted, any more than the winner of the 2.30' (McLean 1969: 5). Nevertheless, one of the best ways to begin understanding the process of magazine design is by breaking down a page into its various elements and considering why each is important.

PAPER QUALITY

Paper is, literally, the basis on which everything else rests (the 'substrate'). But what kind of paper? The weights, grades and finishes are legion. Should it be glossy, matt or like newsprint? Thick or thin? More or less white? (If you think all white paper is 'white', you haven't been looking closely enough.) Some of these decisions will be limited by the budget; paper can be the single biggest item of expenditure for any magazine. Other choices will be determined by the type of publication. Glossy stock might not suit a news magazine that runs long stories – the reflections make it harder for the eye to read – but may be essential for a fashion title whose main purpose is to show high-quality photographs. In addition to practical considerations, the look and feel of paper carries its own message to potential readers; thin and flimsy signifies low quality, thick and glossy signifies luxury – there is a whole branch of science devoted to this, known as haptics.

PAPER SIZE

It's not just the quality of paper that counts, size is another variable. Magazines are produced in a variety of formats, each with their own strengths, limitations and significance. A large page, such as in *Vogue*, allows the use of larger pictures; a small one, as in *Glamour*, allows the magazine to be slipped into a pocket or handbag but limits the kinds and shapes of illustrations. Paper size will also determine the number and width of columns that can be used on a page. The more columns there are, the more possibilities are open to the designer to combine widths for either text or pictures, thus adding to the variety of shapes in a layout. Think also of what different numbers of columns signify – four on an A4 page indicate 'news', while a single column of text floating in a sea of white space on a double-page spread is something else entirely – an arty feature perhaps.

THE GRID

Like the city of New York, magazine pages are designed on a grid system, a skeleton plan that allows consistent placing of page elements such as columns, page numbers, running heads and repeated rules. The word 'grid' is used in two ways: first, to describe the abstract pattern to the placing of columns, etc.; and second, as the physical thing with which a designer works – paper in old technology, a computer screen for most designers now. Web pages are also designed on a grid. Devising the grid is probably the single most important stage in determining how a magazine will look, and some commentators give it a heavy weight of significance. In a study of *Elle Decoration*, Barbara Usherwood cites Robert Craig, an American design historian, in support of the grid's symbolic importance. Craig, she says, 'stresses the semiotic connotations of quality associated with use of the grid: "professionalism, concern with detail, carefulness, thoughtfulness, exactitude"' (Usherwood 1997: 186).

TYPE

Type is a complex area of design and the study of it – typography – is a fascinating discipline in itself that can be traced back to the fifteenth century. Most journalists don't need to know the fine detail, but all journalists should familiarise themselves with some basic points.

The style(s) of type selected for any given magazine will be subject to many variables. Legibility is important and at the simplest this means a title aimed at young or old readers will need larger type than one intended for teenagers. There are thousands of typefaces to choose from, with new ones being introduced all the time, but to make a beginning you need understand only that there are two main forms – serif and sans serif. A serif typeface has pointed embellishments finishing off the strokes of letters which make the shape; a sans serif face does not, as these examples show:

TIMES IS A SERIF FACE   Times is a serif face

HELVETICA IS A SANS SERIF FACE   Helvetica is a sans serif face

Most designers agree that large blocks of copy are easier to read if set in a serif face. Sans serif, on the other hand, is effective for headlines or for shorter blocks of copy that need to be distinct.

Another print design axiom is that type is easier to read if set in lower case (small letters; capitals are referred to as upper case). This is because when we read we do so by recognising the shapes of words, rather than by spelling them out letter by letter. Lower case typesetting makes much more recognisable shapes and so is less tiring on the eye.

The width of a piece of typesetting is also crucial, which is why the width of columns must be decided in conjunction with a suitable size and form of typeface. Columns should ideally contain between 50 and 70 characters (these include letters, spaces and punctuation marks). Any more and it becomes increasingly difficult for the eye to follow; any less and words become broken up and the spacing may go awry. Other variables include the justification (alignment of line endings and beginnings) and leading (pronounced *ledding*: the space between lines); both of these have a great impact on the legibility and the overall look of the page. (For more information see Chapter 11).

LAYOUT

At its simplest, layout design could be characterised as determining the dynamic relationships between various elements on the page – type (both greyish text and blacker headlines), photographs or illustrations (whether colour or mono) and the colour of the paper itself. By arranging these elements in various shapes and juxtaposing them so that, for example, a horizontal form is balanced or challenged by a vertical form, a designer can create pages that look attractive and interesting. Ronald Walker suggests a further exercise to demonstrate the importance of these basics: 'Note the interaction, study how balance has been achieved, pay particular attention to the white space, cut up pages and rearrange them, see how a simple change of position of one element can transform a design' (Walker 1992: 30).

Before cutting up those pages, try to analyse how your eyes move over the page. Most people tend to start in the upper left corner, then move right and down; the typical movement is often represented as a Z-shape. This can give a clue as to where the most important element of the page or spread might go. There are no rules about what that 'important element' is – it could be a photograph, a headline, a block of text, or even white space. The key is to decide the hierarchy of importance of the different elements, and then use them appropriately. Always remember, though, that rules are often broken, and just as 'good writers don't always use only simple declarative sentences . . . good magazine designers don't always put the starting element in the upper left' (Click and Baird 1990: 216).

The use of white space as a positive design element is nothing new. Russian designer Alexey Brodovitch began to devise 'new rules of page composition organised around three elements – text, photography and white space' for *Harper's Bazaar* in the 1930s (Bauret 1999). Vincent Steer's manual for typographers states that a successful trainee will be able to combine the technical skills of a printer with artistic sense. Among the former are 'the principles of type selection and the methods of distinguishing one type from another', while the latter include 'the basic laws of design and the best way to train the mind to visualise; the use of white space and the disposition of margins' (Steer, no date: 12).

COLOUR

The choice of colours for paper and ink can affect more than the straightforward look of a page – like all other design choices they carry additional significance. Christmas issues of women's magazines, for example, often have covers with lots of red on darker backgrounds than in spring, when pastel colours reflect the freshness of the season. The connotations here go beyond what looks good on the page in a particular month: the red brings with it the cheery mood of Christmas celebrations; the pastels connote unfurling leaves and primroses. These are broad generalisations and ones that might make a brave art editor, anxious for a publication to stand out on the news-stand, think of adopting the unconventional approach. It all depends on the publisher's interpretation of the psychology of potential readers: would more readers be put off a publication that stood out from the throng than would be attracted to it in the first place by its being more noticeable?

From a technical point of view, it is worth knowing that 'normal' colour is achieved through a four-stage printing process, as part of which the image is separated into shades of magenta (process red), cyan (process blue), yellow and black. These shades are then recombined as the paper passes through the four stands of a colour printing press; look at a four-colour image through a magnifying glass and you will see the dots that make up the image. This works because of a mix of physics and perception. The way that 'in printing, nearly all colours can be obtained by mixing yellow, magenta and cyan inks in their correct proportions', is explained in Alastair Campbell's designer's handbook; following this, the brain interprets the mix of fine dots which we see through the magnifier as a solid image (Campbell 1985: 88).

Occasionally a designer will want to use a special colour that cannot be achieved through the four-colour process. Gold or silver, for example, can't be made truly this way, nor can true fluorescent oranges or yellows. In these instances the designer will specify a fifth colour – at extra cost, of course.

CONCLUSIONS

Vincent Steer, in summarising what he saw as the primary truths of design back in the 1930s, truths that still influence today's designers like Peter Comely, wrote: 'To become a qualified typographer only requires patience and study . . . In short, the key to complete mastership of the art of Printing Design and Layout lies in attention to detail' (Steer, no date: 12). That was only partly true 60 years ago and it will still be partly true whenever you happen to read this. Such a functional view omits the creativity of the best designers, the willingness of a Neville Brody to challenge the accepted ways of working, the accepted visual tools. It also overlooks the wider significance of graphic design. According to designer and editor Jon Wozencroft, 'design is a . . . great deal more pervasive than is suggested by its primary function of preparing artwork for the printer, or even blueprints for an architect' (Wozencroft 1988: 159). Since almost everything we see is mediated in some way by conscious design decisions, the designers of consumer magazines may wield considerable influence over readers and, as a consequence, over the visual choices (in clothes, home decoration, etc.) those readers make in their own lives.

NOTES

1   Andy Cowles, conference on design and communication at the Business Design Centre, London, 2 February 1999.
2   Figure from Yolanda Green, Capital City Communications, 1999.
3   'Magazine Retailing: Beyond 2000' published by the PPA, November 1998.
4   Among them Andy Cowles, Ian Birch of Emap Elan, and Nick Gibbs of Future Publishing.

RECOMMENDED READING

Bauret, G. (1999) *Alexey Brodovitch*.
Campbell, A. (1995) *The Designer's Handbook*.
Click, J.W. and Baird, R.N. (1990) *Magazine Editing and Production*, 6th edition.
Daly, C.P., *et al.* (1996) *The Magazine Publishing Industry*.
Frost, C. (2012) *Designing for Newspapers and Magazines*, 2nd edition.
Garfield, S. (2011) *Just My Type: A Book About Fonts*.
Glaister, D. (1999) 'Design to create pages people want to read', *The Guardian*.
Hebdige, D. (1988) 'The bottom line on Planet One: squaring up to *The Face*', in *Hiding in the Light*.

Holmes, T. and Nice, L. (2012) *Magazine Journalism*.
Johnson, S. and Prijatel, P. (2006) *The Magazine from Cover to Cover*, 2nd edition.
Klanten, R. and Ehmann, S. (2010) *Turning Pages: Editorial Design for Print Media*.
Losowsky, A. (2007) *We Love Magazines*.
McLean, R. (1969) *Magazine Design*.
Morrish, J. and Bradshaw, P. (2012) *Magazine Editing: In Print and Online*.
Nava, M., Blake, A., MacRury, I. and Richards, B. (eds) (1997) *Buy this Book: Studies in Advertising and Consumption*.
Steinberg, S.H., revised by Trevitt, J. (1996) *Five Hundred Years of Printing*.
Taylor, S. (2006) *100 Years of Magazine Covers*.
Usherwood, B. (1997) 'Transnational publishing: the case of *Elle Decoration*', in *Buy This Book: Studies in Advertising and Consumption*.
Walker, R. (1992) *Magazine Design: A Hands-on Guide*.
Wenner, J. (2006) *'Rolling Stone' 1,000 Covers: A History of the Most Influential Magazine in Pop Culture*.
Wozencroft, J. (1988) *The Graphic Language of Neville Brody*.

Websites

www.coverjunkie.com
www.designishistory.com/design/editorial-design
www.magforum.com
http://linefeed.me
http://magculture.com/blog
www.losowsky.com/magtastic
www.vogue.co.uk/magazine/archive

CHAPTER 14

Magazine illustration and picture editing

Tom Ang with Phil Cullen

For many magazine readers the photographs and illustrations are one of the main reasons for buying the publication. This may not be welcome news to writers and obviously doesn't hold good for all publications, especially those which concentrate on information and news. But for periodicals as diverse as *National Geographic*, *BBC Wildlife*, *Vogue*, *Homes & Gardens*, *Classic Cars*, *Country Life*, *Men's Health*, *Time*, *Glamour, Take a Break* and *Kerrang!*, the pleasure readers get from their purchase is as much to do with looking as reading. Readers want to indulge themselves by lingering over photographs of the highest quality. This gaze is one reason magazines still thrive even in this era of digital media. You can pause over, cut out, pin up or keep images from magazines in ways with which television and the internet can't quite compete.

News periodicals such as *Paris Match*, *Time*, *Newsweek* and *Stern* owe much of their appeal to the quality of the photographs, although here the purpose is to offer an additional, complementary and often more emotive and dramatic dimension to the coverage of current affairs and news. The heyday of using photographs in this way was in the middle of the twentieth century, when magazines such as *Life* in the US and *Picture Post* in the UK flourished by providing photojournalism which sought to entertain as well as inform. This style of photographic essay, although seeing a resurgence online, has lost much of its prevalence in print. Still photographs of news events can be more evocative, more informative and infinitely more shocking, or funny, than video footage, again because the viewer controls the length and quality of time devoted to them.

The distinction between what counts as an illustration and what as a photograph is increasingly fuzzy. In any case, the word illustration can be used in two rather different ways, both relevant to this chapter. In the context of a magazine it most often means a kind of artwork (drawing, watercolour, computer graphic, map, cartoon). But the word can also be used in a more general sense to cover any pictorial material that accompanies a text. In this sense it includes photographs, but for the purpose of this chapter it will be used mainly in the former sense.

Just as photojournalism in print was nudged aside by television news, so were illustrations by artists nudged aside by the arrival of photography. There are still illustrations to be found in many magazines and newspapers. These may take the form of cartoons, line portraits and caricatures, drawings of people or places featured in the text, or artworks created to relate to a text by capturing a mood or the essence of an argument. Fashion drawing, which was once the only way to show readers what the chic were wearing, has all but disappeared from women's magazines even though it is still occasionally used to great effect.

There is another type of image, which often involves the amalgamation of both photography and illustration – this is called collage by some picture editors, composite or photomontage by others. In its traditional meaning collage refers to any picture made from scraps of paper, bits of photographs, fabric or other odds and ends pasted together. It has also come to mean pictures assembled from a variety of sources and is now commonly applied to digital images. As digital technology has made the alteration of photographs easier, it has become more common to make substantial changes to the images that the photographer originally saw through the lens.

Minor changes to photographs in the sense of retouching are nothing new, of course, and big publishers had dedicated staff whose job was to eradicate facial hair or enhance the breast curves of fashion models by using a very fine paintbrush on the original negative, slide or print. Digital technology has made the process quicker, cheaper and much easier, and it can provide far more radical changes. Heads can be placed on bodies that don't belong to them, frowns replaced with smiles, Asian car workers converted into Caucasians. Naturally, this kind of treatment is controversial. Readers may complain that they expect photographs to show only what is 'real' in the sense of what the photographer could actually have seen on one occasion through the lens. Photographers, too, can reasonably find fault with a process that alters their work while keeping their byline. (There are also implications for copyright and moral rights when this happens.) One way of avoiding controversy is to credit any photograph which has been substantially changed as a digitally enhanced or manipulated picture, particularly if it is not clear from the image on the page that anything has been altered.

PHOTOGRAPHY OR ARTWORK? WHO DECIDES?

The decision about which kind of illustrative material to use will be made in different ways on each magazine, depending on the size of its staff and its policy on visual material. Journalists working on smaller magazines might even be expected to undertake some of their own picture research, editing and commissioning.

On a few periodicals, particularly those which look more like newspapers and place most editorial emphasis on print, the subs will decide whether to commission artwork or photographs or whether to find existing pictures from the publication's own library, through an agency or from a photographer's own stock of images.

On most magazines, however, the choice is likely to be made by the art or picture editor. On a largish magazine the picture editor may well be responsible for commissioning or finding photographs at the request of the art department, while the art editor will commission his or her own illustrations. Some magazines will have staff whose whole job and professional expertise is searching for pictures. Depending on the kind of magazine, the picture editor may be in a position to suggest features ideas, perhaps on the basis of photographs submitted by photographers who show their portfolios in the hope of attracting commissions.

It should be clear that, whatever the set-up on a publication, the picture editor and art editor work in collaboration, even if not always in close harmony. Like all editorial staff they need to have negotiating, selling and diplomatic skills to resolve differences of opinion – a thick skin helps too, for those times when other members of the team are not convinced by the vision of one individual. It will usually be the art editor who is responsible for the overall look of a spread and for the appearance of the whole magazine. The picture editor is part of the interdependent team which supplies the raw materials.

When photographs are to be shot specially for the magazine, it's likely several staff will contribute to the creation of the concept and then to its execution. Typically this might mean the editor, the fashion editor, the art editor and the picture editor, along with their junior staff. Where the story is a more journalistic one, such as the coverage of a news event, then the commissioning editors will need to be involved. Ideally, for big stories, the photographer and writer will work on the story together, but sometimes one part is supplied before the other can be commissioned. From a photographer's point of view a rare but welcome event is to be commissioned to produce a photo-feature where the photography is pre-eminent and will be accompanied on the page by the barest of captions. Specialist photography magazines such as the *British Journal of Photography* (UK) or travel titles such as *Geo* (published in 20 countries) and *National Geographic* do this. Some of the weekend newspaper colour magazines still carry this kind of story.

Before we look in more detail at the factors which influence picture selection, it's worth being aware of the distinction, as designer Ruari McLean puts it, between informative illustration and decorative art. Clearly an ideal example of the former would also be the latter, but he was making the point with reference to *Reader's Digest*, where illustrative material has to earn its place by enhancing the reader's interest or understanding (McLean 1969: 340). On other publications illustrations can be used in a slightly less integrated, less demanding way, perhaps as a tool of the layout artist who wants to break up blocks of text on the page. Sometimes the pictures may be the dominant element, while the words take second place.

Whichever approach is adopted, the task of the picture editor (and/or art editor) is to get the best possible illustrative material into the publication. There will be constraints of budget, time, and the availability of artists, photographers or agency pictures. What follows is intended to give journalists on magazines an elementary understanding of that process. This will be useful for anyone who works in magazines, but of particular importance to writers and editors on smaller publications who may take on some picture-editing responsibilities, including picture research.

PHOTOGRAPHS OR ILLUSTRATIONS?

As we have seen, the distinction between photographs and illustrations is becoming more blurred. A good example here would be a photograph that is digitally manipulated to look as if it had been painted in water-colour. Is it then an illustration or a photo?

There are other, technical, ways in which the distinction between photographs and illustrations has been eroded. It used to be that photographs would have been supplied to the picture or art desks as prints, negatives or transparencies, while illustrations would have arrived as finished artwork on paper or board. Now either is more likely to be supplied in digital form and will arrive at the magazine on a DVD, CD or flash drive, be sent by email or be downloaded direct from a website. This change means that the artist or photographer is responsible for ensuring that the digital file is in a form suitable for the magazine. This may mean more than just the correct file format, and could include detail such as image size, resolution and even the definition of colour space to ensure the file is compatible with the publisher's colour management system. Artists and photographers are now expected to carry out many of the functions that would formerly have been the job of pre-press technicians.

There is another important change brought about by technology. The traditional model of magazine production described the process as a chain of contributions and interventions through design and pre-press production to printing press and then to distribution. This model, which was always somewhat simplistic, is now out of date. Before digital technologies much of the material that went into the making of a magazine could physically be in only one place at a time. A print of a photo could not be simultaneously on the editor's desk and in front of the caption-writer unless, unusually, there were multiple copies. Digitisation of the pre-production processes means that the photo or drawing can now be worked on by several people at once. And this is a further reason for the blurring of boundaries between the work undertaken by different staff members. The subeditor will now be expected to undertake design, the picture editor to write captions and the art director to specify picture formats.

THE PROCESS OF PICTURE EDITING

Picture editing is, essentially, the process by which photographs and illustrations are created, selected and assembled from a variety of sources. It's helpful to think of it as taking place in four steps. First is the formulation of aims; second, the sourcing of pictures, which may be done by commissioning original photography or illustration, or from existing picture or art collections; third, the images gathered must be edited and assembled or organised ready for the fourth step, which is preparing the images for production. (It is these last two steps which are now becoming a single step.) A brief outline of each step follows.

Aims

There are usually two sets of aims for the picture editor. There is the specific project (the individual layout or sequence of spreads) and there is also the overall purpose of the publication or even the publisher. So, for example, the aims of an up-market fashion magazine such as *Harper's Bazaar* are clearly different from those of a trade publication such as *Media Week*. A publisher such as Condé Nast with a stable of glossy monthlies will not have the same corporate aims as the publisher of the radical monthly *New Internationalist.* These aims, although they may not be explicit, can influence picture-editing policies. At a simple level a company might, for reasons of corporate PR, wish to distance itself from anything controversial: this could affect the choice of photographer in fashion shoots, the kind of 'story' which is portrayed, whether the models can be photographed with their breasts bared. What is at issue here is the ethos or ideological background to the publication. This has general implications for all staff, including the picture editor. For some companies, budgets must be adhered to even at the cost of editorial quality. For another publication the most important thing is to publish the best innovative work at whatever cost.

Sourcing

Whatever the picture-using environment, a great deal of a picture editor's skill and effort is knowing how to get hold of the required images. If pictures are to be sourced from libraries and agencies, a picture editor must be able to find the best as quickly and cheaply as possible. Specialist publications may have staff picture researchers, but a general-interest magazine may hire a picture researcher for one feature if the research for the topic is specialised. If images are to be commissioned, a picture editor, often working with the art director, has to select the right photographer or illustrator for the job. To do this well the picture editor needs a network of contacts and experience of working with a range of photographers, as well as an awareness of the contemporary art scene.

One cause of confusion over sourcing is the availability of tens of billions of images on the internet. Digital technology has progressed so far and so fast that copyright legislation, and understanding of the law, seems to struggle to keep up with developments in the dissemination of digital images. The most important point to remember is that, by default, all images are automatically protected by copyright at the moment they are created, and this copyright protection lasts until 70 years after the death of their creator. There are hundreds of online picture libraries and agencies, some of which offer images for free usage, some of which require payment. There are also many photo-sharing sites such as Flickr and Photobucket, where millions of images are available for use without payment but many more are not. There are almost always, however, terms and conditions attached even to 'free to use' images. One of the most widely recognised and useful standards for negotiating the minefield of usage agreements is the Creative Commons licence, but these are available in six different categories, each of which has its own specific terms and conditions.

It is vital to ensure that the correct permissions are obtained from the copyright holder of an image before any decision is made to use that image for publication. It is also worth bearing in mind that, most of the time, you tend to get what you pay for.

Assembly

The selection of a small number of photographs and illustrations from a choice of possibly hundreds is what most people think is a picture editor's job. Many people think it is a job they themselves would be able to do and indeed anyone with basic visual literacy could probably pick out the one good photograph from an offering of otherwise mediocre work. However, it takes experience and confidence to be able to spot the gem whose brilliance is revealed only when used imaginatively in a layout. Like talent scouts in search of future stars, good picture editors have the ability to spot potential. They also know how to watch the budget.

It should be clear that a picture desk must be well organised and have an efficient, logical workflow to handle both digital and analogue images. A typical picture desk can handle tens of thousands of pictures each year from dozens of different sources. It must be able to deal with everything from 100 digital images of the latest celebrity happening, to a set of transparencies from a sought-after photographer, to a unique and treasured print of someone's great grandparents. A well-run desk needs to maintain tight control over its picture resources, to sort and store these ready for use, to make sure that caption information is supplied and not mislaid, and to return pictures promptly to their sources when necessary. Where these housekeeping points are neglected problems will always arise.

An additional task has arisen thanks to the growing practice for publishers of magazines and newspapers which commission photographs to negotiate (or wrest) the rights to allow them to re-use or sell on the pictures they have bought. This means that picture desks also operate as picture agencies.

Production

Once they have been selected, photographs and illustrations must be fitted into the production cycle. They will need tagging with caption information and other data and then they may need to be retouched before they can be worked on by layout artists. Even digital images from professional sources may need colour correction and cropping. Part of a picture editor's responsibility is to ensure that photographs and illustrations are of good enough technical quality for the publication.

COMMISSIONING ILLUSTRATIVE MATERIAL

When presented with a story idea to illustrate, the picture desk has to decide which would be more appropriate – photography or illustrative artwork. There are several factors which influence the choice.

First, to commission an artwork or caricature may be just as expensive as commissioning a photograph – although it depends on the fees charged by individuals. Typography used in a decorative way may be the cheapest alternative, but calligraphy or specially designed type is more expensive.

Second, artwork can be done without reference to a real subject or by using photographs as reference points, whereas a photograph needs the sitter to be available if it is a portrait. Other subjects may have to be shot on location, which raises costs and takes longer.

Third, there is the risk that commissioning photographs or illustrations can go wrong, most usually if the brief has been misunderstood. If the subject of a portrait changes her mind, the photographer would be left with nothing while an artist might still be able to produce something usable.

Fourth, setting up a photographic shoot can take a lot of time, whereas a good cartoonist or artist can run up an illustration in ten minutes or less. Last, artwork is particularly effective if a story does not need an illustration that shows an actual scene or person, but is instead used to invoke a mood or give a visual interpretation of an argument or concept.

Once the choice has been made, the picture or art editors need to be clear about a number of points. They must decide what it is essential to include in the image and distinguish that from what it would be good, but not essential, to cover. They must establish the deadlines and a budget for the photography itself, travel and subsistence, materials and research. Reproduction rights must also be agreed.

There are also organisational points which need to be checked. Do all production staff know the timetable for the delivery of images and their processing for publication? Have all possible (and improbable) permits, visas and permissions been cleared? Is there any back-up in case of disaster? Is there any way in which the photographer or illustrator might cause problems for the reputation of the magazine by their behaviour, beliefs, personal habits or dress? Is the commission in writing, and does this include all the negotiated agreements?

The art of commissioning well, and this is true for writers as well as artists and photographers, is to be as informative as possible about what is wanted and which, if any, of the stipulations may be regarded with a degree of flexibility. Those who commission visual material must be sure that what they are asking is manageable, making clear the required level of quality, the key facts of the story and how images will relate to them. They should also discuss what might go wrong. An artist should have clear instructions about size and format. A photographer may need guidance about image quality and format or other technical matters.

SELECTING THE RIGHT PICTURES

Once the pictures have reached the picture desk the best must be chosen for publication. For artwork this is usually simple enough: because it can be specified with more precision than photography it is usual for just one piece of artwork to be submitted. If the art director doesn't like it then it might have to be altered or done again, but there is unlikely to be anything comparable to the photo selection process. Here, from the dozens or hundreds of images provided, a tiny number have to be chosen. Artistic considerations are important here, but there are several technical considerations for photographs too.

Every magazine has its own standards for image submission. Even now, many high-end glossies still prefer to work from original slides rather than digital files, and might commission a photographer who still works with traditional materials. Some publications will only accept digital camera RAW files, while others are happy to work with TIFF or even JPEG images. Edgier, youth-oriented or low-budget periodicals might well make a feature of mobile-phone photography, the toy-camera aesthetic or, often, both.

Whatever the magazine's technical specification for images, however, it is important that pictures are clearly identified with the name of the photographer or agency, date, location, title of the event and names of subjects; with digital photographs, this information can be preserved within the metadata of the image file so that it is part of the picture package. A model release form will often be required when a person is the main subject of a photograph, but this depends upon several factors, including the intended use of the image and the age of the models. It is acceptable to depict people who happen to form part of the image but who are not its main subject, such as passers-by or faces in a crowd.

The picture edit

Most discussions of picture editing start here. But by the time this stage is reached much of the hard work has already been done and, if it has been done thoroughly, the edit hardly feels like work at all. When asked how they choose the best photograph from a selection of good ones, most picture editors will shrug their shoulders. One attempt at a definition of a great photograph is that it possesses the three qualities of resonance, history and revelation. We'll look at these in turn.

First, resonance. This is used to mean a visually emotive quality that emerges from the structure and composition of the photograph but which could not be predicted from the contributing components. Resonance arises when the photographer organises the material in a way that suits both the subject of the photograph and what is being said about the subject. It is a partnership between composition and content and gives a photograph a lasting impact on the mind. Next, history. A great photograph acquires a historic dimension when it comes to represent a significant event. It may have importance as a historical record, whether as evidence or because it somehow captures the mood of a moment. Finally, revelation. A great photograph is in some way revelatory. Its content lifts it out of the ordinary by offering new insight.

Non-technical factors in picture selection

In addition to the technical factors outlined above, several other, non-technical, considerations influence picture editors.

Subjective response

Picture editing is a subjective process. Technical decisions are, in a sense, objective, as certain requirements have to be met, but a picture editor still has to decide which technical standards to apply. There are certain responses to photographs that are held to be more or less universal – for example, response of nausea to a photograph of the victims of a massacre. More usually, though, tastes, cultural background and life experience shape the viewer's responses to an image. Experienced picture editors (and photographers) know this. Here are some examples.

Narrative

The dictum that a picture is worth a thousand words carries the implication that photographs can be used to tell stories, and when photojournalism was in its prime, photographs were expected, almost literally, to tell a story, with only the barest of prompting from a caption or text. Today the preference continues to be for photographs that tell a story. However, for a picture to do this it almost always needs some support from text: words can be used to increase a picture's narrative strength. It's also true that a strong picture may take the text's story in a different direction from the copy. The strongest picture from a shoot in a war zone may, for example, show people with big smiles. If the reporter was concentrating on the country's misery then a different picture would have to be chosen or additional copy written to take account of the happy faces.

Expression

One quality in a photograph that usually needs no textual support is the expression on a person's face. Choosing the right expression may be hard because the camera catches in one instant a person's constantly changing expression. This may then be used to represent the whole of a complex character: yet one smile cheaply won for the camera may mask years of suffering.

The choice of expression is an uneasy balance between two considerations. On the one hand a picture editor will try to find the shot with the facial expression that seems in some sense most 'true' to the person. On the other, an expression, any expression, is assumed to be true if the camera has caught it. What matters is that the photograph shows the expression that best fits the story.

When judging facial expressions picture editors will look at various factors. The eye nearest the viewer should normally be in focus as this mimics what we do naturally: when we look at a face we focus on the eye nearest our face. Catch-lights (or specular highlights, the reflected image of the light source) in the eye give animation to the face. The mouth is also important, as it is the part of a face that people normally look at after the eyes. If the hands are in view they can be evocative – gripping each other tightly gives away an underlying tension. Portraits may show more than head and shoulders; the body's posture and the position of other parts of the body will contribute to the image by the information they offer. The way that a subject is lit also shapes the viewer's interpretation.

Eroticism

Eroticism has long been used as an ingredient in the production of art and photography. It means that a photograph or illustration which may produce a sexual response is likely to be preferred over one that will not.

Exoticism

A photograph showing something exotic – that is, having a strange, bizarre or unusual attraction or allure – is likely to catch the eye of a picture editor. This may seem obvious, but less obvious is the way culture and context determine what is considered exotic. Pursuit of the exotic can thus cause cross-cultural problems. A feature for a European magazine about tropical rain-forest dwellers may show the semi-naked bodies of nearly-nude tribes-people going about their daily lives. For many European readers such photographs would be acceptable as an accurate record of how people dress in a distant country, but for readers from that distant country the pictures might be seen as degrading. Different cultural responses have to be taken into account by picture editors, especially by those working for magazines with an international distribution which, given how widespread the presence of magazine brands now is on the internet, is most magazines to some extent.

Composition

A photograph's composition is the arrangement of its parts in relation to each other and to the whole. Many photographers think that to be clever or innovative is the sure way to a picture editor's heart. Not at all. For most published pictures unusual styles of composition are not wanted and conventional ones, as outlined below, are preferred.

Elements of composition

Orientation or 'format'. This refers to which way the longer axis of a rectangular image runs. The vertical or portrait orientation places the long axis vertically and the horizontal or landscape orientation has the long axis running horizontally. Picture orientation or format is essentially a way to crop or cut down the roughly circular image of normal vision into a practical shape. In practice, landscape format pictures are much more common even though almost all books and magazines are vertical in format. This has implications when pictures are commissioned for a cover or a full page.

Lines. Horizontal lines (such as the sea's horizon) and vertical lines (such as the sides of tall buildings) can influence the image. On the whole, horizontals and verticals should be parallel to the sides of the picture.

Symmetry. An image exhibits symmetry if half of it is mirrored in the other half. This property is important in picture composition: viewers often respond well to bilateral symmetry, which is where the image is divided into two main mirror images of each other. Perfect symmetry tends to make a picture look and feel static and weighed down, although this can be used to good effect in landscape and architectural photography.

Thirds. Pictures in which the centre of interest lies about one-third or two-thirds along the main axis often appear balanced and well composed.

Apparent depth. Because they represent a three-dimensional world, photographs always contain three-dimensional information. This is, of course, more apparent in some pictures than in others as a sense of depth or receding distance. The effect is achieved in a variety of ways.

- Scalar perspective. The further away from the viewer an object is, the smaller it appears. This is particularly true for objects such as the human body, or parts of it, which are so familiar that the viewer's interpretation of the image scale is almost automatic. One effective compositional technique is to place an object very close to the camera with the next nearest object much further away.

- Converging parallels. This is a special case of scalar perspective where the distance between the lines appears to decrease as the image scale gets smaller.

- Depth of field. This usually works in conjunction with the above scalars as they help interpret the variations in image sharpness. Otherwise, it is difficult to know whether an object that appears out of focus is in front of or behind the plane of good focus. A shallow depth of field can increase the apparent sense of depth as the background falls out of focus rapidly.

- Overlap. An object can overlap and cover up part of another only if it is the one nearer to the viewer, and this is another way to show receding distance.

Apparent movement

Visual clues and cues about movement not only suggest depth in a photograph, but also bring vitality to the image. Visual clues include blurring and multiple images. Blurring is caused by the image being 'spread' over the film like butter: it can apply to either the main subject which moves against a static background, or the background which is blurred against a sharp image of the subject. Stroboscopic flash or multiple exposures create multiple images that display some of the steps making up a movement. Visual cues to movement are graphic elements that suggest, rather than depict, movement. A winding road suggests movement through a landscape, as do symbols such as arrowheads or speed flashes. In general, pictures with a sense of movement in them are preferred to those without.

Colourfulness

Photographs full of bright colours attract attention. As always, what works best depends on the intended use. Consideration has to be given to the effect a photograph's colours will have on the design of the page as a whole, in relation both to other photographs and to the use of coloured type. One colourful shot can unbalance the page, especially if black and white illustrations are also being used nearby. The use of coloured type on a page can be effective: the type's colour can be matched to a colour in the photograph or be chosen to complement or contrast with it.

Croppability

A croppable picture is one that can lose parts of its side, top or bottom edges to improve the way it fits into a given space. Croppability improves the versatility of a shot. Empty areas around the main subject may appear to be wasted within the composition but, looked at from the demands of a page layout, such areas are valuable. Pictures may also be cropped for reasons other than fit, usually to improve their impact by focusing on one area of the image while losing other distracting parts of it.

Other factors

Depending on how a picture is to be used, the following factors may also need to be taken into account during the edit.

Markers of date or time

Almost any element in a photograph has the potential to give away the date or time the photograph was taken. Here are some of the most common clues.

The date of a picture may be revealed by the clothes, for example. Fashions easily give away era, as do faces, make-up, hairstyles, beards, even facial features. Advertising posters, cars, buildings, street furniture such as streetlamps, traffic lights, bollards and bus stops, and any publications such as newspapers, magazines and books that are in view. The technical quality of the image may also suggest an approximate date.

Time or season may be apparent from the state of deciduous trees and flowering plants, or the coats or plumage of animals and birds. Sunlight and shadows or stars can also be clues as to time.

Markers of locality

Much travel and landscape photography is an attempt to capture the *genius loci* (or spirit of the place), be it a village square, the copse of a wood or a concrete townscape. Locality markers in photographs may be used as clues about where the picture was taken, making captions less necessary. For example, a photograph of a green valley with sheep grazing could be taken in many parts of the world. To indicate where it was taken it needs a locality marker such as a European church spire or an Asian yurt.

Effective locality markers include styles of architecture, dress, artefacts, transport, facial features, well-known topographic features such as Mount Fuji, well-known man-made features such as Angkor Wat, or natural features such as animals and vegetation.

Locality markers may have to represent an entire country or even become iconic shorthand for it: the Eiffel Tower stands for Paris or France, for example.

Identifiable people

Publishing a photograph of identifiable people (other than those who have agreed) can cause problems depending on three things: the use to which the photographs are put, the content and tone of captions, and the circumstances in which the photograph is taken. There may also be issues of privacy. Or there may be legal problems over libel or model releases (these are the documents signed by the subjects of a photograph to give permission for the picture to be used). Let's take these in turn.

Usage. Photographs can be used in a variety of ways to tell different kinds of stories. In the context of news and current affairs there are fewer problems, although picture editors must watch out for images showing identifiable people who are doing illegal things or even just things they may not want publicly displayed. The further from news you move towards news features and features pages in general, the more care is required. Pictures are more likely to be used as general illustrations of a phenomenon rather than a specific event. They are also more likely to be drawn from a library. A classic mistake here would be to illustrate an article about drug abuse among teenagers with a stock shot of identifiable teenagers in the street. They would have just cause for complaint because of the defamatory implication that they were drug-users.

Captions. Factual captions cause, or have the potential to cause, fewer problems than opinionated or critical captions. The difference is plain: 'Mother with her four children' has less potential for offence than the objectionable 'Evil temptress playing with children'. While 'Prostitute goes shopping with her family' may well be factually accurate, a picture editor would need sound reasons to offer this as caption material to the subeditors. (One reason might be that the picture was taken specially for a feature on the family life of prostitutes and the subject had agreed to be interviewed and photographed in this role.)

Circumstances of photography. There are photographs that capture a person's private moment as an incidental feature of a street scene. These are less likely to cause trouble for a picture editor than a snatched shot of a celebrity who is trying to retain some privacy. This is partly because the unknown individual may not mind or, if he does, will soon realise there is nothing much to be done if a picture appears without his permission. Unwilling photographic subjects have tried to use the UK's Data Protection Act as a kind of privacy law, but the Information Commissioner's Office has confirmed that it is not illegal to take photographs in the street without the subject's consent. In the UK, at least, celebrities in public places are not specially protected from the unwanted attention of photographers – although the Press Complaints Commission guidelines give some indication to photographers about what is regarded as acceptable (as will whatever body replaces it). The picture editor's job, in consultation with the editor and possibly the publisher, must be to weigh up three things: the public interest, respect for the privacy of the person depicted, whether famous or not, and the need to maintain or boost circulation figures (see Chapter 18 on privacy.)

Where ordinary people are concerned it is common for standards of intrusion into grief to become more permissive as the distance between the event and the place of publication is increased. So, for example, picture editors of British newspapers might refrain from using a harrowing close-up picture of a mother grieving over a child killed in a railway accident in Birmingham. But they would not think twice about using a similar picture of a mother who has lost her child in a ferry accident in Bangladesh (Galtung and Ruge 1981; Taylor 1991).

Sequencing

Pictures work with their context – in a page layout or an exhibition – but they also work with each other. Photographs in a picture essay, for example, may be printed in a sequence that assumes the reader will look at them in order. So a country doctor's working day might be dramatised by the picture layout to enable the reader to re-create the sequence of events.

Censorship

While a picture editor may be expected to know the censorship laws in his own country, photographs that are taken in foreign countries or perhaps by foreign photographers may bring problems, as the laws about privacy and decency or the censorship policy differ between countries. As publications and publishing houses become increasingly international, with multinational syndication of photographs becoming the norm, so picture users and distributors are safest if they restrict their material to stay within the most stringent censorship laws found in their distribution area.

National security

In almost every country it is illegal to publish photographs that threaten national security, although what is construed as a threat varies. Even in the comparatively liberal-minded West censorship may be tight.

CONCLUSION

It remains only to emphasise that the way a magazine looks is vital to the way in which it attracts readers. The overall design, the layout of individual pages and the illustrative material such as drawings or photographs all play their parts. Magazine readers seek different things from a magazine, but they can tell from the look of it whether one is right for them to buy or to read.

RECOMMENDED READING

Ang, T. (2000) *Picture Editing*, 2nd edition.
Ang, T. (2010) *The Complete Photographer*.
Evans, H. (1978) *Pictures on a Page*.
Frost, C. (2012) 'Using pictures', in *Designing for Newspapers and Magazines*.
Fulton, M. (1988) *Eyes of Time: Photojournalism in America*.
Galtung, J. and Ruge, M. (1981) 'Structuring and selecting news', in *The Manufacture of News: Deviance, Social Problems and the Mass Media*.
Giles, V. and Hodgson, F. (1990) *Creative Newspaper Design*.

Irby, K. (2001) 'Magazine covers: photojournalism or illustration', Poynter Institute.
Jaeger, A.-C. (2010) *Image Makers, Image Takers*.
Keaney, M. (2010) *Fashion and Advertising: The World's Top Photographers' Workshops*.
McLean, R. (1969) *Magazine Design*.
McNally, J. (2008) *The Moment it Clicks*.
Meggs, P.B. (1989) *Type & Image*.
Michalos, C. (2003) *The Law of Photography and Digital Images*
Ritchin, F. (1990) *In Our Own Image*.
Taylor, J. (1991) *War Photography*.
Taylor, J. (1998) *Body Horror*.
Wright, T. (2004) *The Photography Handbook*.

Websites

BBC Picture Editor's Blog: www.bbc.co.uk/news/correspondents/philcoomes
British Association of Picture Libraries and Agencies: www.bapla.org.uk
British Institute of Professional Photographers: www.bipp.com
British Journal of Photography: www.bjp-online.com
Creative Commons: http://creativecommons.org
New York Times Photography Blog: http://lens.blogs.nytimes.com/
Picture Research Association: www.picture-research.org.uk

CHAPTER 15

The business of magazine publishing

Until recently magazine journalism students didn't have to pay much attention to the business aspects of periodical publishing, and this was perhaps a fair reflection of how things were in many editorial offices. One good reason for this was the understandable desire on the part of journalists to retain their independence, something they felt might be compromised if they got too involved with what many see as the slightly grubby world of advertising revenue.

In reality such independence begins to be compromised the minute a reporter accepts her first freebie, whether it's lunch with the PR for an electronics company or a bottle of champagne delivered to the desk by a make-up company; the minute she agrees to write an advertorial feature or to include in a fashion spread a dress from a big advertiser rather than one from a new designer. The impulse to independence is a worthy one and many writers would prefer not to think about the financial aspects of their publication, especially if that means being pressurised to give a positive mention to a product in the editorial pages to clinch an advertising deal. Apart from the personal conscience of the journalist, the credibility of the magazine can be damaged if readers begin to suspect there is too close a liaison between advertisers and journalists. Credibility is particularly important in the B2B sector of magazine publishing, but consumer magazines, too, as we shall see, pride themselves on the trust their readers place in what they publish.

Yet nowadays editorial recruits to magazines are encouraged to have some understanding of how magazine publishing works, if for no other reason than that they need to know where the jobs are, what these might involve, and by what business model their livelihood is supported. If you don't know what B2B or contract publishing mean, and if you think newsletters are what the vicar sends out once each month, then you'll be missing out on a huge range of titles which might employ you. Whereas newspapers tend to be openly visible to the world on the news-stands, there is a majority of periodical titles that hardly appear in public at all except when readers subscribe to them. In the UK there are getting on for 9,000 periodical titles, of which almost 3,200 are consumer publications and the remainder are categorised as B2B, professional or learned academic journals. A further reason for the importance of some understanding of the publishing business is that advertisers have had, and continue to have, greater influence on what gets featured in magazines than they do in newspapers (Clark 1988: 345). This is not to say that advertisers have no influence over newspapers, as can be seen in almost every local weekly or, more seriously, in the way described by Blake Fleetwood in *Washington Monthly*. He notes widespread changes in the US which mean 'editorial, advertising, circulation and promotion are all co-ordinated around the goal of marketing a product. Instead of worrying about whether this is a good story, editors ask whether the proposed story will connect with the reader's lifestyle' (Fleetwood 1999). His examples bear out the findings of commentators such as Curran and Seaton, who argue that the power publishers ascribe to advertisers means the advertisers are 'a *de facto* licensing authority' (Curran and Seaton 1997: 34). (For a fuller discussion of the political economy of publishing and other mass media, see Herman and Chomsky 1988; Schudson 1984.)

A final reason for looking at the business background is that any new magazine journalist will be exhorted to have the reader and the reader's expectations clearly in mind when writing a story. The people who think they have the clearest idea about these things tend to be those whose job involves money: they are the ones who have to convince advertisers that the product is reaching those readers in substantial enough numbers to make it worth their while booking space. In order to convince advertisers they have to do detailed research into who is buying (in the case of consumer magazines), why they are buying and, of course, what they might want to buy that an advertiser might want to sell. Sometimes the advertising salespeople or the publisher have rather blinkered views based on the generalisations put together by market researchers, but these can be useful pointers to what the readership wants – *can be*, but as any serious businessman knows, the only dependable information concerns what the public has actually bought. You can't predict for sure what they will buy in the future.

It's probably obvious what advertising salespeople do. They sell space in magazines to advertisers and the revenue they raise goes a long way to covering the costs of publication and providing profits. The job of a publisher (the individual with this as a job title rather than the publishing house) is slightly less clear to the outside world, partly because it varies between publications. It is possible for a journalist to work on a magazine for years and never meet the publisher, even though some of her decisions will be relayed to the editorial office, probably through the editor, and probably suggesting ways to save money. The publisher is the controller of the purse strings, not necessarily on a day-to-day basis but certainly in general.

She is likely to be senior to the editor in the management hierarchy and ideally is the point of contact (and perhaps even arbitrator) between advertising director and editor. In small companies, the publisher is often the proprietor too. In large companies there might be several publishers, each taking charge of a group of magazines, perhaps ones with the same field of interest – the equestrian titles at IPC for example.

CONSUMER PUBLICATIONS

What most people immediately think about when magazines are mentioned are consumer publications, that is the ones that give readers information, advice and entertainment which relate to the time when they are not at work. This wasn't quite an accurate definition in the days when magazines for housewives were regarded as the trade press for those who worked at home (Garvey 1996), but if 'leisure interest' can encompass the field of home interest, whether for full-time housewife or weekend-only homemaker, then it's a useful enough definition. Under the 'consumer' umbrella would come all those titles related to hobbies or special interests such as cars (*Classic Cars*, *Top Gear Magazine*), boats (*Canoe and Kayak*), fish (*Koi Carp Magazine*), riding (*Horse and Hound*), pets (*Catworld*), sport (*Shoot!*, *Cycling Weekly*) and embroidery (*Cross Stitcher*). What links all these publications is that they carry adverts that aim to encourage readers to buy something, whether it's forks for a mountain bike or the latest in scuba-diving equipment. Where titles are not clearly about one activity or interest they are likely to be about lifestyle: most of these are for women and girls, but since the early 1990s several new ones have been aimed, initially with spectacular success (*FHM*, *Loaded*, *Front*, *GQ*, *Nuts*, *Zoo*), at the men's market. Winship points out that for all the talk of 'options' for women that surrounded the launch of *Options* magazine (now defunct), the only real choice 'the magazine offers are, first and foremost, between one set of goods and another' (Winship 1987: 39). What Cynthia White asked in her study of women's magazines in the 1970s – how far they 'support acquisition as a primary goal in life, thereby relegating other possible goals' – is still pertinent today for all lifestyle magazines (White 1977: 63). That's the point of them and whether you regard that as a strength or as a weakness probably depends on whether you are an advertiser or a reader and, possibly, how green-tinged are your political views.

BUSINESS-TO-BUSINESS PUBLICATIONS

The B2B (or trade or professional) press refers to all those publications whose aim (in addition to making money) is not to provide general news to a wide audience, but to provide news in a limited field to a tightly targeted audience. Some of these publications look like newspapers (although usually printed on glossier, heavier paper) but can nevertheless be classed as periodicals. In these publications display ads tend to be for jobs, while classified ads tend to be placed by those seeking jobs. In a typical issue there might also be adverts publicising awards or announcing new services. Display adverts are bigger and more strikingly laid out, usually with some graphic design element, and with rules to separate them. Classified ads are the small ones that are laid out in columns, grouped together by subject.

Range of trade publications

The number and range of these publications is enormous, whichever indicator you choose to use – over 5,000 is a fair estimate in 2012. Some of the titles you might not have heard of unless you know someone in a particular industry. These include: *Campaign* (for the advertising professionals), *British Dairying*, *Convenience Store*, *Insurance Age*, *Drapers*, *Trucking* and *Nursing Times*.

While subscriptions account for about one-quarter of the trade press circulation, most of these publications are circulated free of charge on what is called a 'controlled circulation' basis. This means readers qualify to be sent a copy under whatever terms the publisher establishes: so, to make up an example, if a publisher decided that politics lecturers had enough in common and were likely to have enough spare cash to make them attractive targets to advertisers, then *Politics Lecturer Monthly* might be launched and sent free to all politics academics in the UK, a list of whom could be compiled by contacting politics departments in universities, by advertising, by buying access to the mailing lists of other companies such as, in this case, academic bookshops. The great selling point to advertisers of controlled circulation publications is that the readership is precisely targeted. There should be no 'wastage' (people who get to see a publication but for whom a particular advert is of no relevance). An advert in *Farmers Weekly* about chicken-feed will be of interest to some readers only – the ones who keep poultry – whereas everyone who reads *Poultry International* would be a likely target for chicken-feed information. Which would turn out to be the more cost-effective publication for an advertiser would depend on additional factors, however, such as cost of the advert, total circulation of the magazines, their penetration into the target market, how well established the magazines are, and what reputation they have among farmers. Publishers and advertisers refer to this indicator as the cost per thousand (or CPM, with the M standing for 1,000 in Latin): the figure relates to the cost of reaching with an advert 1,000 buyers, readers or viewers of a magazine or website.

Circulation and readership

Circulation figures differ from readership figures because any given copy of a magazine will almost certainly have more than one reader. Indices for this are drawn up by publishers so that they can tell you how much bigger the readership is than the circulation. For example, *Vogue* sells around 210,000 copies each month, but the estimated readership is 1,237,000, meaning that roughly five people see each copy. For *Private Eye* the circulation is 228,112 with 788,000 readers, so roughly three readers per copy. For *Radio Times* the circulation is 925,000 and there are 2,230,000 readers, just over double the number of readers compared with purchasers. (All figures from ABC and NRS in early 2012.) If the difference between the two figures is small it may indicate that a magazine isn't popular or else that it is so sought after readers feel they must have their own copies. This question is no doubt the subject of intensive research in circulation and marketing departments. A study of these figures is instructive in many ways. Women will not be surprised to note that whereas women's magazines get their own womanly categories, magazines which are quite clearly aimed at a male readership, such as *Loaded*, *FHM*, *Men's Health* and *Esquire*, are categorised as 'general' by the National Readership Survey.

Penetration

Another term that needs explanation is penetration, which refers to the percentage of potential target readers who actually buy the publication. So if half of all mothers in the UK bought a made-up title called *Mothers' Weekly*, then its penetration would be described as 50 per cent. Clearly a controlled circulation trade or B2B magazine should be able to get close to 100 per cent penetration, give or take those recent newcomers to the particular trade who are not yet on the mailing list.

Contract, customer publishing

A further category is contract or customer publishing, now often associated with the label content marketing. This is where a company or an organisation pays a publishing house to produce content for a publication or other appropriate media (such as e-zines, email, mobile apps, video) on its behalf. Sometimes these are in-house magazines for distribution to the staff or customers of a large company, or they may be provided by an airline to all passengers in their seats. Redwood Publishing is such a publisher and it produces magazines for a wide range of high-street names such as Boots, Barclays and Marks & Spencer. How far these publications resemble what (perhaps optimistically) might be called the editorial objectivity of consumer magazines depends largely on what the contractors wish, as they are paying the bills. Some of them have genuinely interesting editorial that doesn't exclusively connect with the company's products; others are little more than vehicles by which a company extends methods of advertising and marketing.

Many contract publishers do not publish their own titles but some companies that are well known for their consumer titles also produce content under contract to other companies. Condé Nast Contract Publishing is one example. As well as the familiar Condé Nast magazines such as *Vogue*, *GQ* and *Glamour* the contract publishing wing produces content for Ferrari, Selfridges and the Mandarin Oriental Hotel Group, among others.

Contract publishing is a relatively new undertaking, having begun in the 1980s. Yet by early 2012 five out of the top seven UK consumer magazines by circulation were content marketing brands – *Tesco Magazine*, *Asda Magazine*, *The National Trust Magazine*, *Tesco Real Food* and *Morrisons Magazine.*

In-house journals

In-house journals for big companies or other organisations may of course be produced and published in-house and not involve a contract publishing house. Whether this is the case is likely to depend on the size of the company and whether it can afford to have a team of journalists working to high enough standards. International companies which have an in-house publications team can provide their huge staffs with well-written, glossy publications which fulfil some of the function of all in-house magazines – that of keeping staff informed about company news and developments. At their best these can be promising places to start a career, the better companies offering far better salaries and more opportunities to travel than a new journalist might encounter on an ordinary trade or consumer magazine. On the other hand, it does mean that everything you write for the first couple of years is, effectively, a kind of puff for the company. At their worst these publications may be produced at well below professional standard and the promotion of the company is the only noticeable characteristic.

The alternative and independent press

In addition there are increasing numbers of niche magazines, often with low circulations, which don't fit into the usual business models of magazine publishing. They may have sponsors or subscribers (the US magazine *MS* is an example of the latter) as financial backers or they may be produced by people who simply have a passion for the subject matter and are not looking to make a profit. Distribution, which would traditionally have been the most serious problem faced by such a publication, is made easier by the way small orders can be handled on the internet. (Examples can be found at magculture.com and stackmagazines.com).

There are, too, many magazines which are effectively produced by amateurs or at least by people who don't expect to make any kind of living from their efforts. The most publicised sort are the pop and football fanzines, which nowadays usually look sharper than they used to thanks to computer technology, but which only 20 years ago might have been produced with a typewriter and a photocopier. There have also always been literary and political publications produced for the sake of the subject rather than for profit. Broadly, this area of publishing may be referred to as the alternative press, but it is a label that describes a huge variety of publishing enterprises and there is no simple definition, as Chris Atton demonstrates in his essay 'A reassessment of the alternative press' (Atton 1999). The fruits of these alternative publishing labours, which now are often called 'zines, may be distributed in a variety of ways: by an individual with a carrier bag; by post; or they may depend on subscriptions or even just donations from supporters. Increasingly, of course, they are produced and published online as well as or instead of in print.

Then there is *The Big Issue*, which can't really be called alternative, in that its circulation figure throughout the UK of 105,000 puts it well out of the usual alternative press bracket. Its distribution system is well known – copies are made available to homeless people who keep the profit when they sell them on to customers in the street.

Newspaper supplements

One of the huge changes in magazine publishing over the past five decades is how much this kind of material has become a regular part of what newspapers do. *The Sunday Times* launched its colour magazine in 1962 and since then there is hardly a Sunday or a Saturday newspaper that hasn't followed suit. And this trend is not confined to the parts of newspapers that so obviously look like other consumer magazines. As Brian Braithwaite points out: 'Newspapers, particularly the tabloids, are increasingly becoming magazines, not only in their day-to-day features, but with their Saturday and Sunday supplements' (Braithwaite 1995: 158). He's referring to the enormous expansion in the number of pages all newspapers devote to copy that is not hard news. Some are dismissive of this material, saying it is 'too soft', but it can be of just as much interest and importance as any news story. This expansion has been led, it is true, by the trawl for advertising revenue.

We have already seen that however much influence advertisers have over what gets published, that influence is greater in consumer magazines than in newspapers (Clark 1988: 345). Curiously, though, readers are thought not to develop such intimate dependence on the magazines that come with newspapers as they do with lifestyle ones they buy from choice (Consterdine 1997; 2002). For magazine publishers this finding lends strength to their sales pitch to advertisers. At its worst this can mean that newspaper magazine supplements look like little more than shopping catalogues. In his book *My Trade* Andrew Marr is critical of the way so much journalism has now been taken over by shopping to the extent that this now represents 'the biggest new area of mass reporting' (Marr 2004: 106).

This aspect of magazine publishing is now commonplace: information about where to buy the goods featured in editorial fashion and home pages gradually crept into women's magazines (Winship 1987: 40). For a long time some kind of photographic set has been created through which the stylists tell in pictures a 'story' such as grunge chic, where all the featured clothes look like they're being worn by vagabonds. But in many magazines this process has now been pushed to the extent that there are always several pages where what is on offer are small pictures of the goods alone (the garments, handbags, tableware or even guns) with captions bearing the price and stockist. And the now defunct *PS*, launched in February 2000, featured only goods that could be ordered from home. The main difference between this and a catalogue designed for home shoppers was that the magazine's merchandise came from a variety of suppliers instead of just the one company. The logical progression here is for the magazines to sell and promote goods in their own right. Newspapers have begun to follow suit. Is there perhaps cause for concern from readers when papers and magazines become retailers of what they also review, as several publications now are, *The Spectator* being one example?

THE COMMERCE OF PUBLISHING

To return, now, to the business of publishing magazines for commercial gain, there are some aspects which it is essential for newcomers, whether to trade or consumer magazines, to know about.

Revenue

It is often forgotten by readers that the cover price of a consumer magazine does not cover the cost of publishing it, let alone provide a profit. That's why the adverts are there; one way of looking at this, popular with advertisers and publishers for obvious reasons, is to see the advertising as a subsidy of the editorial material. The alternative to advertising, they argue, would be government subsidy, with all the dangers of censorship and control that this would carry. (They ignore, of course, the shaping of editorial content that goes on to please advertisers.) Another possible alternative is to charge the reader the full cost of the publication. From the perspective of journalists and readers the picture is not quite so rosy as advertisers suggest, because advertisers are not a neutral force. Their power and influence over editorial is enormous and inevitably how they choose to use it does not necessarily serve the best interests of anyone other than themselves.

Leaving that discussion aside for the moment, let's look at some figures. The proportion of the revenue of a magazine that comes from sales as opposed to its advertising differs between titles and also between sectors of the market. Consumer magazines get roughly 38 per cent of their income from advertisers and 62 per cent from sales. (Braithwaite pointed out that if readers were bearing the full cost it would mean a doubling of the cover price in the case of *Cosmopolitan*, of which he was publisher (Winship 1987: 38).) Business and professional magazines by contrast take 82 per cent from advertising and 18 per cent from circulation (PPA 2000). This is because, as we have seen, much of the B2B sector's output is distributed free. According to the PPA, the financial characteristics of the sector are that revenues are growing and magazine publishing houses are highly profitable. It is also evident that a successful entrance to the publishing business can now be made far more cheaply as computer technology has led to a reduction in production costs (PPA 1999: 10).

For publications that are sold, the cover price is important. It should be low enough to ensure that target readers are not deterred and high enough to bring in maximum profit or to contribute to the branding of the magazine as a luxury product. This may, in itself, be a selling point. The price therefore has to reflect not only what the market will bear, but also the cost of the direct competition. It's often assumed that the higher the circulation the better, but this is not quite the case. For expensive glossy magazines the number of readers is less important than their quality, or at least their spending power. If as an advertiser your aim is to market an expensive perfume or brand of watch then you don't need to reach a lot of people who can't afford those things, what you need is to reach the few people who can. When *Vogue*'s founder, Condé Nast, said in 1909 he was creating the magazine as a lure for certain advertisers, it was then a relatively new way of thinking about magazine advertising (Clark 1988: 321). It seems familiar enough now, though, when the job of a publisher has changed from selling products to those who might want to buy, into selling potential buyers to the advertising industry (Clark 1988: 377). Any sceptic who is in doubt about how far along this road lifestyle magazine publishing has travelled needs only to look at what publishers and advertisers say about the industry when talking among themselves: 'The magazine environment delivers a reader in the right frame of mind to be receptive to advertising' (Consterdine 1997: 6). This phrase, 'delivers the reader', is a constant refrain in any discussion of the commercial aspects of magazine publishing and for new journalists has a chilling ring to it. Whereas they thought their job was going to be the delivery of exciting editorial to eager readers who might glance at an advert as they make their way through the magazine from one article to the next, the reality is that with many publications it is the readers who are being delivered to the advertisers.

Identifying the reader

One effect of this is that there has grown up a whole industry based on identifying who readers are and who they might be. You won't work for long in magazines without hearing readers referred to as predominantly ABC1s or C2DEs or some other combination of letters and numbers. What this refers to is the market research categorisation of the population according to their social and economic status. The gradings were devised by Research Services Ltd in 1946. There is no point in quoting the actual income levels 60 years later, but the rough distinctions looked like this:

> Grade A is the highest level of income.
>
> Grade B is the next level down.
>
> Grade C is split into two to distinguish socially between sets of workers who earn roughly the same money but do different kinds of work. C1s are the non-manual (clerical) workers. C2s are the skilled manual workers.
>
> Grade Ds are unskilled manual workers.
>
> Grade Es are those on low incomes who are retired or unemployed.

From Condé Nast's point of view only the As were needed, and possibly a few aspirational or wealthy Bs. He did not need or want to attract the rest of the population. This would have affected, and still affects, the kind of advertising a publication might accept. Just as the highest number of readers is not always the goal for a publisher, neither is the highest number of adverts. If you flick through a copy of *Vogue* today it is clear not only that the ads would be of little interest to those on low or even middle incomes, but that the ads themselves are a contribution to the lavish feel of the magazine's editorial. A cheap, badly drawn, or unappealing advert could detract from the overall look of the magazine. A publication can regulate the number of adverts by charging more as it's the revenue total that matters, not the number of pages bought.

The A to E categorisation is regularly used by advertising departments when persuading advertisers to buy space and is also a useful shorthand way for the editorial staff to think of their readers. For both, of course, there are other considerations in any readership profile. Age is perhaps the most obvious, gender another. Geographic location may be another. A great deal of knowledge can be amassed about a given readership. Take this example from the media pack for *More!* The core age for readers is 18–34 and the mean age is 27. They live for the weekend, are obsessed with men and with shopping, and are said to spend an average of 42 minutes reading each issue.

These figures are arrived at by various organisations. One is the National Readership Survey, which collects and publishes statistics about readerships for the benefit of newspapers and magazines. One of its indices is the OTS or 'opportunities to see' score, which measures the number of readers who will read some part of the title during its currency. Another organisation is the Audit Bureau of Circulations, an independent organisation which measures and monitors the circulation of magazines and newspapers in the UK to give what's known as an ABC figure. It publishes its figures every six months and the results can produce dismay or elation depending on how they compare with the previous figure. At *FHM* a leap in circulation of 217.6 per cent in the second half of 1996 was a cause for great celebration at Emap. Much less rejoicing at the same magazine's new publisher, Bauer Media, when the second half of 2011 figure was released, showing that circulation had plummeted to 140,716, a fall of 20.6 per cent. The ABC now also publishes separate ABCe figures to indicate how many visitors a website has had.

To complement the NRS and ABC figures the Quality of Reading Survey was launched in 1998 by the PPA, among others, to get at even more data, such as how long individual readers spend reading a particular magazine, how many times they open the magazine at a particular page (this gives a PEX or 'page exposure' score) and where they get their magazines from. Companies also spend small fortunes on market research specific to their own titles. For journalists this can sometimes lead to the disheartening experience of an editorial meeting where the magazine is looked through page by page with statistics about reader interest and reader satisfaction attached to each article. All of this kind of research has its place in the business of publishing, but most journalists treat it with some scepticism because its accuracy, given the modest size of the research base, can't be counted on.

A further point to note about revenue, as you hand over your £3.90 for a copy of *Elle*, is that only about half of that money will make its way back to the publisher. The other half goes on distribution, to the wholesalers, and the retailers. This explains why publishers are so keen to get readers to take out subscriptions and why they are prepared to offer sizeable inducements in the shape of discounts or gifts. The fortnightly magazine *Private Eye*, to take one example, costs £1.50 per issue, which would work out at £39 for the 26 issues in a year: a subscription is therefore a bargain to the reader at £28. A further advantage for the publisher is that a subscription guarantees that income over the year, even during the weeks when a casual news-stand purchaser might forget to buy or be away on holiday. This makes financial planning more secure. Against this has to be set the cost of postage and of advertising for subscribers. For this reason in the US, which traditionally sees a much higher proportion of consumer magazines sold by subscription, there is now a move towards increasing news-stand sales.

Distribution

The method of distribution is something that can never be far from the magazine editor's mind as it has a bearing on the presentation of the publications. At its most obvious a magazine which depends on news-stand sales must have as eye-catching a cover as possible and its cover lines (the words describing the content) must be intriguing. If, on the other hand, a publication arrives unasked for and unpaid for as a controlled circulation magazine that everyone in a particular industry must read, then the designer is under less pressure as there is no immediate competition for the reader's attention at a point of sale. A news-stand magazine designer must also assume that when the title fights for attention on the shelf, only the left-hand side of the cover will be visible as other magazines will usually be placed in front, concealing the right-hand side (see Chapter 13).

In fact, the subject of distribution is enough to bring publishers close to exasperation (and probably distributors too). One reason is that the traditional shops which supplied us with our magazines, the confectioners, tobacconists and newsagents (or CTNs as they are known), have seen their business drawn away by new kinds of retailers such as supermarkets, convenience food stores, garages and so on. Publishers may find these new outlets unwilling to carry the range of magazines that the CTNs once did, and this adversely affects specialist publications with smaller circulations. Yet the market is fragmenting as more titles are launched at smaller target markets, putting additional pressure on the space available for display in any shop of whatever kind.

Furthermore, in magazine publishing the so-called supply chain is more complex than it is for newspapers. First there is the publisher. Then there is the distributor. This may be the equivalent of an in-house circulation department (direct distribution).

Or it may be through a separate distribution division in which the large publishers have a shareholding (for example, The National Magazine Company and Condé Nast Publications through Comag). Lastly there are the companies that are paid by publishers to do the distributing for them.

The next stage in the journey of magazine to reader is through the wholesaler. This area, like distribution, is increasingly dominated by huge companies such as Menzies and W.H. Smith. The wholesalers are the ones who take orders from and deliver to the retail outlets and can decide what to stock. As they increase in size, efforts to keep costs down and profits up are made by cutting the number of depots from which deliveries are made. This introduces economies of scale but the fear is that it mitigates against the kind of personal touch that enables retailers to cater for quirky, specialist markets.

Subscription sales, which could provide one solution and are certainly growing, are nevertheless hampered by the increasing costs of postage. Competition for readers is fierce, because although more people are reading magazines than a few years ago, 'the consumer is much less brand loyal and is buying from a pool of titles rather than a limited shortlist' according to PPA research (PPA 1998: 10). This reader gets the nickname 'repertoire buyer', one of whose characteristics is that he buys on impulse. Irritating, that, for publishers who used to be able to depend on a number of devoted fans for a particular title. The loyal buyers of a magazine are called 'solus' readers in the industry.

One strategy the publishers of monthly magazines use to secure the money of the repertoire buyer is to get into the newsagent first. It used to be normal to buy an April edition, say, in the last four or five days of the preceding month, that is, March. But these dates have gradually crept forward so that the April edition of most consumer magazines is actually on sale throughout March and some are on the news-stands in the last week of February.

Promotions and cover mounts

In other attempts to counteract this fickleness, or grab the attention of the impulsive buyer, many publishers now seem to offer promotional free gifts (or cover mounts). At one end of the quality scale a magazine like *Time* offers inducements to subscribe such as a watch with the word Time in the *Time* magazine logo on it, or travel luggage or electronic personal organisers. Some magazines offer tokens that could be exchanged for goods. The advantage of tokens is that they induce people to buy and then more copies have to be bought for the reader to save enough tokens. One edition of the now defunct *Smash Hits* had tokens, little card pictures of popstars to cut out and keep, a free CD holder and a packet of hot chocolate powder, all held in place with a plastic bag. This arrangement is called 'bagging' and is necessary when the free gifts are of awkward shape or are so desirable that they might otherwise be ripped off in the newsagent's shop by dishonest customers, desperate to own yet another bright pink, inflatable picture-frame. Another possible reason to bag is if raunchy material is on offer. So the edition of *More!* with its separate booklet entitled 'Men unzipped. Find out what's inside their minds and their trousers', was carefully bagged to stop girls peeking without buying.

The drawback to bagging a magazine is that it may deter new readers who can't flick through to get an idea of what's inside. One advantage (to the publisher at least, although I'm not sure they would put it like this) is that the reader can't examine too closely the gift on offer.

Gifts can range from the practical and appropriate – a CD with *Classical Music*, nail varnish for a teenage girls' magazine – to the awkward – a trowel stuck to the cover of a gardening magazine which was so heavy that it pulled the copies off the news-stand onto the floor. There's no doubt that one-off purchases are made as a result of these inducements, particularly if they really do have some value, such as paperback books offered by women's magazines at holiday time. For some magazines, such as computing and classical or dance music titles, a gift is more or less essential now. There is considerable doubt in the trade about whether they have any lasting effect on circulation, although editors and publishers seem to believe that if there is a beneficial effect from cover mounts it relates to sampling. That is, gifts may induce readers to pick up a magazine they have not bought before. But Marie O'Riordan, a former publishing director at Emap and editor of *Marie Claire*, has spoken of the danger of readers becoming immune to 'gifting', and Margaret Hefferman, publishing director of *Big!* and *Smash Hits*, has said she thinks 'the promotional gift war is detracting from the real issue . . . the content on the inside of the magazine' (*Press Gazette* 19 February 1999: 7; 21 August 1998: 6). These views were echoed vehemently by Mandi Norwood when she was editor-in-chief of *Cosmopolitan*: 'I absolutely loathe it that I have to be involved in discussions about scented candles' (J. Gibson 1999: 7). She has a point. Everyone likes to get something for nothing, but publishers would go out of business if they really provided that, so many promotional gifts are useless as well as tacky and are likely to attract only those buyers who are devoted collectors of kitsch. Worthless to the reader as so many cover mounts are, their estimated cost to the industry in 2001 was £30 million (Morrish 2003: 175).

Prizes

One further way publishers try to attract readers is with prizes in competitions although, again, no one seems convinced of their value as circulation builders, even if they may contribute to the satisfaction that a reader gets from the magazine. Competitions do, however, have a further value as they can assist publishers in their search for data about readers.

Brand extension

For almost as long as there have been magazines there have been ways for publishers to make money out of their products other than merely from advertising and sales. The technical name for much of this is 'brand extension' and that can mean selling through the pages of the publication anything from T-shirts to expensive leather desk diaries bearing the magazine's logo. What it typically means, in the trade press, is the organisation of exhibitions or conferences based on the subject matter of the publication. It might mean the publishing of directories or books in a particular field; *The Economist Style Guide*, the *Time Out Guide to London*, and the Annual *Music Week Directory* are examples. In these cases new content is being used to build on the core brand. There are also a growing number of websites and apps and other services that relate to magazines (see Chapter 12). Consumer titles also organise events to promote the brand and even make a profit. Literary lunches are held by *The Lady* and dinners or debates by *The Spectator.* (Newspapers are heavily involved too: *The Guardian* now organises and charges substantial fees for a range of educational events for readers who want to develop as writers.) Perhaps the most spectacular example of this kind of brand extension is the establishment in 2013 of the Condé Nast College in London, which will offer the *Vogue* Fashion Foundation Certificate, a ten-week course costing £6,600, and the year-long Diploma costing £19,560. If the fees for these courses are too high then there is always the *Vogue* festival day, launched in April 2012 as an opportunity for readers to hear and see models, designers and *Vogue* staffers: fee £150 for the day.

In the current highly competitive marketplace, brand extension can no longer be regarded as a source of a little extra money to be earned from a small, peripheral sideline, but rather a key source of revenue. Events such as exhibitions, seminars and awards activities clearly need the brand name of the magazine to attract custom, but if they work well they feed into the identity of the brand. When Mandi Norwood took on the new title of editor-in-chief of *Cosmopolitan* she revealed to an interviewer that only about 60 per cent of her time would be spent on editorial activities, the rest being brand extension work (J. Gibson 1999). And in a report for the PPA, Peter Dear noted that brand extension was 'already big business for most consumer magazine publishers and that they were becoming . . . increasingly reliant on brand extension enterprises in their revenue mix' (Dear 2000: 32).

None of this is surprising, especially as so many of the big media companies are keen to have interests in more than one medium. The BBC is best known for its radio and television products, but through its publishing arm BBC Worldwide (now licensed to Immediate Media) it built up several successful publications including *Radio Times*, *BBC Wildlife* and *BBC Gardener's World*. And not all of its magazines were directly related to individual programmes. *Family Life*, although it folded, was an attempt to produce a general-interest lifestyle magazine without relying on such a connection. And Bauer Media, in addition to its 80 UK magazine brands, has thriving radio, TV, online and digital businesses.

Brand extension clearly works in two directions. On the one hand it is a way of offering additional goods or services to readers for which they pay like any other customer, but which fosters the idea that reading a magazine is like being a member of a club. On the other hand it works as a promotional tool for the magazine itself. New readers may be attracted after they attend an exhibition organised by a publisher or when they purchase a trade directory, or these things may just help towards a general raising of public awareness. Like any licensing agreement this kind of brand extension needs careful monitoring: editors should try to keep control over the name that is such a valuable asset in the marketplace and perhaps try to stick to the kind of merchandise that reflects the expertise and subject matter of the publication. There is no doubt publishers are moving into these areas of business 'with increasing vigour – but often some trepidation' and that the limited amount of research done into these activities shows that it works best when the core brand of the magazine is strong (Dear 2000: 5). Or, as publishers like to put it, 'when content is king'.

Promotion

Promotion of a magazine title or brand is something in which senior editorial staff often have to be closely involved. It can mean being interviewed by the broadcast media about either the magazine or its field of special interest. So, for example, the editor of *Jane's Defence Weekly* is likely to be invited by radio and television current affairs programmes to comment on stories about the arms industry. And the staff of *Flight International* were in demand to comment after the World Trade Center in New York was attacked in 2001. Or it can mean making sure a magazine is constantly getting publicity – ideally good, positive publicity but sometimes more controversial publicity too, just so long as the paper is being talked about.

The importance placed on this kind of work by publishers is shown by the citation for Alexandra Shulman, editor of UK *Vogue*, when she won the accolade of magazine editor of the year from the PPA. She was praised most for being 'a clever and imaginative editor who gets her title talked about . . . with almost every issue containing at least one story which has been picked up by the other media'. Getting a title talked about can, however, backfire as James Brown found when the March 1999 issue of *GQ* hit the news-stands. Its article '200 most stylish men of the 20th century' included the Nazis, to the understandable outrage of right-thinking people, including the Anti-Nazi League (*GQ* March 1999: 56). Brown resigned.

ADVERTISING

Back in 1900 newspaper proprietor Lord Northcliffe could seriously advise his staff on the *Daily Mail* 'Don't go out after your advertisers. Wait for them to come to you' (Clark 1988: 322). Any newspaper or magazine publisher which took that view today would soon close down. During a century the competition for advertising revenue has intensified so that aggressive sales teams are now dedicated to the task and have the full array of market research tools at their disposal when trying to work out ways to clinch a deal. Advertising directors are now responsible for bringing in the vast sums of money (or revenue), which the editor is then responsible for spending.

Delivering the reader

In a journalists' utopia that would be all there was to it: the revenue would be spent by the editor on whatever she chose to fill her magazine with. In the real world, however, and in the absence of a multi-millionaire sponsor with no agenda and a bulging bank account, the editor has to spend the revenue in such a way that the advertising director will be able to raise as much revenue as possible. This is the part of the job that many journalists would prefer to ignore, although unless they lead a cushioned existence on a very successful magazine, they ignore it at their peril. If they work for a commercial organisation of any sort their job is not really, or not exclusively, about producing accurate analysis or perfect prose on whatever topic takes their fancy; their job, at least in the eyes of the publisher, is to 'deliver' readers so that the advertisers will flock to buy space and pay handsomely for getting it. This in turn will deliver profit for the benefit of shareholders or proprietors.

Keeping a distance

This may seem an extreme view but it's a realistic one. No wonder the question of magazines and money arouses strong feelings. Susan Young, as editor of a monthly business magazine among others, said: 'The advertising department is the most important part of my company' and magazine publisher Eve Pollard has said the most important thing she learned when she moved into that role from newspapers was 'Be nice to advertisers' (Morgan 2000). In his book *Magazine Editing*, John Morrish acknowledges that the relationship between the editor and the advertising department can be a vexed one: 'A certain distance is desirable if the independence and integrity of the editorial department is to be maintained,' he says. He goes on to describe what causes the vexation. Advertisers spend a lot of money with magazine publishers and are therefore inclined to expect favours, particularly if, as advertising salespeople like to imply, they have influence over editorial. This should be resisted, says Morrish, while acknowledging that 'few editors will pass through their careers without at some point or other receiving a threat of the removal of advertising for some slight, whether real or imagined' (Morrish 1996: 94; 2003: 103). And Jeremy Seabrook notes that it's not only favours, it's the right of approval over 'provocative' editorial material (Seabrook 2000: 108).

An editor, then, is faced with the task of satisfying two sets of customers, whereas in many industries one is seen as quite enough. An editor has to attract readers as well as advertisers because, on the whole, you can't have one group without the other. This shouldn't necessarily cause any conflict: a good consumer or trade magazine that has found its target market should also be able to attract advertising.

Conflicts of interest

But things are not that simple, as American journalist Gloria Steinem explains in her account of her days as editor of *Ms.* magazine in the US. She makes an important point that Morrish evades, which is that the demands of advertisers cast a pall over the editorial staff on consumer magazines. Advertisements can be attracted by a magazine provided its journalists are producing editorial that supports the idea of consuming more goods and provided its target audience has money to spend. At its most shameless this means inserting favourable comment about the actual product into editorial copy. More subtle, in fact so subtle as to be the norm, so subtle as to attract little academic or press comment, is when the editorial team provides the kind of context which Steinem calls 'supportive editorial atmosphere or complementary copy'. What this means is that to attract shampoo adverts a magazine has to publish articles about hair care; to attract adverts for cookers or food products, there have to be articles about the cooking and preparation of food (although not, usually, about the adverse aspects of this such as food poisoning or the conditions in which battery hens live). As Steinem argued repeatedly with potential advertisers, there is something daft about this. Someone who is on the lookout for a new brand of mascara won't be deterred from reading an advert for one just because it is placed next to an article about people who choose not to wear make-up at all, or even one about education policy. Unfortunately the advertisers she met didn't see this point: no recipes in *Ms.* magazine meant no adverts for food. 'It isn't just a little content that's designed to attract ads; it's almost all of it', she comments (Steinem 1994: 131), although, according to a leading specialist in consumer research, Joseph Smith, 'there is no persuasive evidence that the editorial context of an ad matters' (Steinem 1994: 152). In fact, in Steinem's view, the opposite is true: 'The greatest factor in determining an ad's effectiveness is the credibility and independence of its surroundings' (Steinem 1994: 165), and she cites research from the *Journal of Advertising Research*, which concluded 'the higher the rating of editorial believability, the higher the rating of the advertisement' (Steinem 1994: 152).

Editorial mentions

Some of the ways in which advertisers influence editorial copy are explicit – for example, agreements to take out a series of expensive ads if good editorial coverage is given to a particular product, perhaps not even the one that is being advertised. Where this is a product that might have been mentioned anyway perhaps there is no harm done, but the line, in most editorial offices, is not that clearly drawn. Which clothes will be featured in a fashion spread is a good example. Of course fashion directors say they have complete autonomy, but if you study carefully the featured clothes and compare them with the advertisers you will notice that the same names recur. Richard Shortway, then publisher of American *Vogue*, was frank about the link between editorial and advertising: 'The cold, hard facts of magazine publishing mean that those who advertise get editorial coverage' (Clark 1988: 338). This point is illustrated in almost any edition of any consumer magazine.

Betraying the trust of readers

One reason that this matters is the confidence which readers place in the guidance offered by magazines. Research commissioned by the PPA concluded that readers enjoy a strong relationship with a favoured magazine and that a bond of trust grows up between reader and magazine. 'This creates a particularly powerful and trusting relationship' (Consterdine 1997: 5; 2002). Teenage girls buy spot-creams they have read about in *Bliss*, teenage boys buy bike equipment they have read about in *Dirt* magazine, parents buy toys they have read about in *Practical Parenting* magazine. They do this because magazines catch them in the right mood. This effect is described with engaging honesty by one advertiser as being that the quality of trust in the relationship between reader and editor creates 'an aperture or opening to the reader's mind and heart . . . through which we advertisers can establish communication' (Consterdine 1997: 40). If what was in magazines were not influential then advertisers would not bother booking space. A mutual understanding is required. Even if the commercial pressure on editorial staff is not overt, the evidence for it is nevertheless there.

Consider, for example, how many years it took for most women's magazines to introduce any kind of health warning into their reporting about sunbathing. Long after reputable research linking sunbathing to increased rates of skin cancer had been published and absorbed by readers of serious newspapers, magazines for women and girls were (and are) undiminished in their admiration for a golden tan. It's as if they couldn't risk the loss of advertisement revenue from sun-cream manufacturers. Now, of course, sun-creams are sold as a way of avoiding the harmful effects of the rays, but as any dermatologist would tell you, the best advice about exposure to the sun is simply to avoid it by staying in the shade. But if everyone did that then an industry would collapse and lifestyle magazines would suffer a loss of revenue, so the serious questions are not much raised in magazines which depend on this kind of advertising.

Meeting the demands of advertisers

Yet it's not just in this way, which some might argue is fairly innocuous, that advertisers try to exert control. They want a supportive environment in the positive sense, but they may also want a right of veto, and this obviously can have a more negative effect. Here are one or two of Steinem's examples: she quotes the insertion orders which accompany agreements to place adverts in particular publications: cleaning products should be adjacent to editorial about children; a diamond company selling engagement rings insists that its ads are well separated from 'hard news or anti-love/romance themed editorial' (Steinem 1994: 156). (She points out that this kind of demand poses unrealistic logistical problems at the flatplanning stage, quite apart from the ethical ones for editors.) At one level this can seem funny, trivial almost, but there's a serious side to it. How many lifestyle titles find space for controversial (other than sexually explicit), challenging articles or reportage? Some do on some occasions, but most don't.

This means that many potential topics of interest to readers are squeezed out of the pages of consumer magazines. In spite of the label, many of them contain little material that calls particular products or services into question. (*Good Housekeeping*, it's worth noting, does not fall into this category – its Good Housekeeping Institute seal of approval is earned after very thorough testing of products.) Fashion coverage is, by and large, reduced to stylish photographs and captions, and the absurdity of some of what appears on the catwalks is accepted unquestioningly. Rarely is there any interesting analysis of the designs, let alone the political economy or the history of fashion. The absurdity or even on occasion the offensiveness of what appears on the fashion pages is offered so solemnly to readers it would seem that some editors have failed at birth to pick up the usual allocation of critical faculties.

Steinem describes the sense of liberation she felt as an editor when she took the decision to stop taking adverts altogether. It wasn't just that the magazine didn't have pages of irrelevant material to detract from the editorial. It was the fact that the advertisers could no longer bring other sorts of pressure to bear. She had found them very conservative so that they would, for example, be unwilling to advertise cars in a feminist magazine, even though she could demonstrate how many millions of dollars a year were being spent by her women readers on cars. It has to be said, though, that her liberation was partly made possible by the fact that in the US there is a higher proportion of magazines sold by subscription than at the news-stand. For a while, even so, it looked as if the future of *Ms.* was in doubt unless it began to take ads again, but in mid-1999 its re-launch was announced after new backers had been found.

Steinem's account is instructive because many magazine editors are unwilling to admit publicly how far the demands of advertisers influence what they publish. An exception is Sey Chassler, who was editor-in-chief of *Redbook* for several years.

> Most of the pressure came in the form of direct product mentions . . . We got threats from the big guys . . . blackmail threats. Advertisers want to know two things 'What are you going to charge me? What else are you going to do for me?'
>
> (Steinem 1994: 161)

More recently, the novels *Streetsmart* by Nicholas Coleridge, Condé Nast UK's managing director, and *Front Row* by the *Daily Telegraph*'s fashion editor, Lisa Armstrong, illustrate how these relations work.

Some editors will deny that they ever meet the advertising people in their company, saying there is an invisible wall between the two. In some cases this may be true, but in reality it probably shows the extent to which the editor in question has subconsciously absorbed what it is that advertisers are looking for. There are a few exceptional magazines, which survive financially because they have a loyal readership or proprietor, but on the whole these are the ones with a more serious intent.

Some editors contend that their readers are highly sophisticated and won't be taken in by advertising. Anecdotal evidence is against this. Most women, for example, think the make-up credits on fashion photos mean that the products credited have been used to create the look. Yet most often the faces are made up by the make-up artist using her own palettes and then the PR from a company (obviously one which spends a lot on advertising in the magazine) comes in to look at the picture and suggest which products by her company could have been used to achieve the same effect.

Steinem's research showed that while readers do care about the influence of advertisers 'most of them were not aware of advertising's control over the words and images around it'. And Consterdine's research for the PPA bears this out. He notes that readers of consumer magazines are likely to feel a strong affiliation with their chosen title and that the stronger this is 'the higher the level of endorsement that the advertising receives' by virtue of appearing in that particular publication. This endorsement is even stronger for 'advertorial' or the 'advertisement features', which are discussed briefly below.

Encouraging consumption

Yet this, in the end, is why there are so many magazines which encourage readers to spend more money (whether on hair-care products, vacuum cleaners, nose-hair trimmers, personal pension plans, nappies, wallpaper or cars), and why there are so few which are devoted to an alternative. Put simply, this is why there are consumer magazines but almost no anti-consumer ones. (*Which?* is not anti-consumer, although it fulfils an alternative function by genuinely testing and researching the performance of goods and by not being beholden to advertising for survival.) That's understandable enough, although not good for those who want to read intelligent, unpartisan debate or reportage in magazine form.

This is partly offset by the increase in the number of supplements and magazines that newspapers push out, but the territory is not quite the same perhaps because the community of interest among the readers of a given newspaper is so much less defined. Less understandable, perhaps, is that the lifestyle consumer magazines don't allow more space for the discussion of ideas or for general reporting on issues. The truth is that where lifestyle magazines are concerned the aim is to 'create a desire for products, instruct in the use of products, and make products a crucial part of gaining social approval'. In the case of women's magazines this often means catching a man and pleasing him (Steinem 1994: 154).

Advertorials

There is another aspect of magazine advertising which causes journalists and many readers more heartache than any other, and that is what is called, particularly by those who frown on the practice, 'advertorials', or more euphemistically, 'special features'. These are pages for which an advertiser pays, as with any advertisement, but which are designed and written in the same style as the magazine's editorial, often by the magazine's editorial staff or freelances working to the same standards. They are, in Consterdine's words, 'a halfway stage between editorial pages and normal display advertisements. Readers can be very interested in and learn from advertisement features' (Consterdine 1997: 53). But they can also be misled – as research conducted for the PPA shows. 'Advertisement features ("advertorials") . . . are understood by readers as being under the joint control of the editor and the advertiser, and consequently there is a strong implied endorsement by the magazine' (Consterdine 2002: 7). This is a point that is echoed in guidance to PR professionals. They are told that the implied endorsement from a magazine (whose style and format are embodied in the advertorial) gives 'greater credibility to the products they are advertising, by explaining them in apparently objective terms through a third party, the journalist' (Harrison, quoted in Theaker 2004: 10).

It follows that however necessary the business-minded may argue advertorials are, they can't deny the point that advertorials are pretty close to being an attempt to fool readers into thinking that they are reading objective editorial matter and that the goods featured in the advertorial enjoy some kind of endorsement from the magazine.

The endorsement matters because, as we have seen, readers of lifestyle magazines, at least, regard their regular magazine as a trusted and loyal friend. This is not just surmise. Consterdine notes the touching naivety of readers, although as his report is for the industry he doesn't put it quite like that: 'There is a strong implied endorsement by the magazine' was the finding of a survey for the National Magazine Company, and 1996 research for IPC showed that readers 'assume the editor has been involved in the selection of the product shown in the advertisement feature, and this implies researching the products and choosing the one that's best for readers'. The closer the match between editorial style and the advertorial style, the stronger the endorsement (Consterdine 1997: 54).

Even if we're prepared to believe that most reputable magazines would not enter into an advertorial agreement with a company whose products were thought to be faulty or fraudulent, there is nevertheless huge influence being exercised over what subjects and what themes readers get to read about. Simply put, if American Express gets endorsement by association from advertorials in glamorous Condé Nast magazines, the service provided by other companies is not available for serious comparison unless they want to spend equally huge budgets on buying an equivalent endorsement. An objective assessment by the magazine's editorial team of the relative merits of different types of plastic money is unlikely to be offered. It is perhaps too strong to say that readers are being duped but, in the words of Consterdine: 'the magazine's own brand values feed into the advertorial, and they in turn feed into the readers' perception of the product' (Consterdine 1997: 54). Industry guidelines say these advertorials are meant to carry a kind of health warning (or perhaps more appropriately a truth warning) clearly on the page to indicate an 'advertising feature' or 'special advertisement feature'. In practice they don't always carry this and even if they do it's not at all certain that readers recognise the implications of it unless they've worked in newspapers or magazines.

Advertorials can cause problems for journalists if the writer does not want to work on material that might compromise his integrity as an objective reporter. Some publishers always use freelances for advertorials while others pay their staff extra for working on them and bylines are not used. Either way the practice of pretending to readers that advertisements represent objective editorial recommendations is ultimately damaging to the magazine's integrity and therefore to its value as a brand. The PPA does issue its members with a set of guidelines to cover the preparation and use of advertorials, but these are not always observed (Morrish 2003: 105–107). Morrish also draws attention to the B2B press and the way that publications which concentrate on the promotion of new products are increasingly wont to ask companies to pay for the additional cost of using photographs in colour rather than black and white. Again, there are guidelines as to the way these should be labelled.

Ad-get features

Closely allied to the advertorials are what some publishing houses call ad-get features, and others call special sections or special supplements. For these a theme or topic is proposed as a basis for the advertising department to sell space. At its least dubious this might involve *The Times Higher Education Supplement* alerting book publishers to the dates on which it is going to carry features and reviews on a particular topic – such as cultural studies – and inviting them to advertise in that week's issue in the knowledge that those working in the cultural studies field are more likely to buy the paper that week, but with the advertisers having no say at all in which books get reviewed or what features are written around them. The reason I say this is less dubious is that here the topic is one which would be covered anyway by the paper. Things get slightly murkier when topics are chosen only because they are likely to bring in advertising rather than on their own merit. And murkier still when the editorial which accompanies the ads is altered or even written from scratch to include favourable mentions for the advertisers as is so commonly done in weekly and regional newspapers.

Matters of taste

One further problem that advertisements can sometimes cause is if they are offensive to readers, perhaps by being too sexually explicit or showing images of violence or blasphemy. If this happens readers can complain to the Advertising Standards Authority.

The appeal of advertising

In this discussion of advertising I have so far ignored most of the positive aspects of this way of funding magazine publishing. Publishers certainly believe that readers like to look at ads and that these are seen as an essential part of the whole product. 'Relevant advertising is valued by readers, and is consumed with interest', writes Consterdine in his report for the industry on how advertising works, although informal anecdotal evidence is less positive. Either way, almost half of the pages in the average weekly or monthly consumer magazine consist of advertising. This ratio of roughly 40:60 is known in the trade as the ad/ed ratio. In B2B publishing the ratio of advertising to editorial is roughly the reverse.

Where advertising is viewed positively is when it contributes another dimension to the strengths of the editorial. A good example is *Vogue*, which is devoted largely to fashion coverage and has high production values for all its photography. It insists on the same from its advertisers and so a four-page advertising spread from Armani, say, brings to the reader yet more glamorous, high-quality fashion pictures than the editorial budget alone could justify. At a humbler level the adverts in lots of magazines, such as hi-fi or sports titles, serve a useful basic purpose for readers who are aiming to buy equipment, say, and want ideas to help them with sourcing: if you buy a house for the first time and have no idea where to buy furniture or fittings, then the classified ads can be of help; with hobby magazines the adverts quite definitely provide a service to readers in suggesting where to shop.

For readers and journalists, whether they like to make use of ads or question their influence (or most likely do both), the unmistakable fact is that if advertising revenue dries up then staff are sacked and the magazine disappears, along with its related websites, apps and brand extensions. As Clark notes, the relationship between magazine and advertiser is symbiotic – no advertising means no magazine, just as no magazine means no advertising message delivered to readers (or indeed readers delivered to advertisers). Ellen Gruber Garvey shows that the tension between advertising and editorial emerged early in the history of the mass-market magazines as vehicles for consumer culture. By the early twentieth century, a question emerged: 'Was the reader accepting an unwanted pile of ads in exchange for a lowered price for the literary matter of the magazine? Or was the reader being bribed by entertainment to read ads?' (Garvey 1996: 169).

What does give rise to legitimate concern is not so much that advertisers exert some influence on editorial, but how strong that influence is allowed to become. As Vincent P. Norris wrote: 'The role of the publisher has changed from seller of a product to consumers, to gatherer of consumers for advertisers . . . The role of the reader changes from sovereign consumer to advertiser bait' (Clark 1988: 377). And the role of the journalist in these circumstances is little more than the hook on which to hang the bait, unless they work for publications where the content is the prime purpose of publication.

RECOMMENDED READING

Armstrong, L. (1998) *Front Row*.

Braithwaite, B. (1998) 'Magazines: the bulging bookstores' in *The Media: An Introduction*.

Brierley, S. (2003) *The Advertising Handbook*.

Clark, E. (1998) *The Want Makers*.

Coleridge, N. (1999) *Streetsmart*.

Consterdine, G. (2002) 'How magazine advertising works IV'.

Daly, C.P., Henry, P. and Ryder E. (1997) *The Magazine Publishing Industry*.

Garvey, E.G. (1996) *The Adman in the Parlor: Magazines and the Gendering of Consumer Culture, 1880s to 1910s*.

Holmes, T.A. (2012) 'The political economy of magazines', in Holmes, T. and Nice, L., *Magazine Journalism*.

Marr, A. (2004) *My Trade: A Short History of British Journalism*.

Morgan, J. (2000) '"There is money out there", Pollard tells launch hopefuls', *Press Gazette*.

Morrish, J. and Bradshaw, P. (2012) *Magazine Editing: In Print and Online*, chs 1, 4.

Packard, V. (1981) *The Hidden Persuaders*.

Reed, D. (1997) *The Popular Magazine in Britain and the United States 1880–1960*.

Schudson, M. (1984) *Advertising, the Uneasy Persuasion: Its Dubious Impact on American Society*.

Seabrook, J. (2000) *Nobrow: The Culture of Marketing, The Marketing of Culture*.

Steinem, G. (1994) 'Sex, lies, and advertising', in *Moving Beyond Words*.

Theaker, A. (2004) *The Public Relations Handbook*.

Turner, E.S. (1965) *The Shocking History of Advertising*.

Websites

Adbusters magazine: www.adbusters.org.uk

Audit Bureau of Circulations: www.abc.org.uk

BRAD (British Rates and Data directory): www.brad.co.uk

International Federation of the Periodical Press: www.fipp.com

www.magforum.com

http://magculture.com

MediaGuardian: http://media.guardian.co.uk

Ms.: www.msmagazine.com

National Readership Survey: www.nrs.co.uk

Professional Publishers Association: www.ppa.co.uk and www.ppa.co.uk/magnify for an account of how advertisers think.

Press Gazette: www.pressgazette.co.uk

UK Association of Online Publishers: www.ukaop.org.uk

CHAPTER 16

The magazine industry

The magazine industry is increasingly dominated by large companies. Not surprising, perhaps, but it's not long since the arrival of new computer technology brought with it the hope that it would become so cheap and easy to produce magazines that anyone would be able to do it. For some this meant a real possibility that a new democratised magazine publishing industry would open up its arms to smaller, minority interests. It hasn't happened quite like that. It is now more expensive than ever to launch a magazine brand, although a company such as Future Publishing demonstrates how quickly a new commercial publisher can, in just a few years, become one of the UK's largest companies. Fanzines and alternative magazines are launched and survive, as they always have, because someone cares passionately enough to work for nothing. Subscribers buy them in spite of the paper quality because the subject matter is of interest. But there has been no burgeoning of a half-alternative or non-commercial press (Atton 1999), the success of *The Big Issue* being a notable exception.

The main players in the UK in addition to Future Publishing are, in the consumer market, IPC, Hearst (National Magazine Company), Condé Nast, D.C. Thomson, Bauer Media, Dennis and Immediate, which incorporates the former BBC Worldwide. In business publishing some of the biggest names are Reed Business Information, Redwood, United Business Media, Haymarket, Incisive and William Reed.

In early 2012 there were signs of optimism among publishers, even though global world economic conditions were in a perilous state. There are, of course, fears about the flight of advertising revenue in general to the internet, but magazine brands are very often part of the internet too, as they increasingly appear across a range of media platforms including mobile phone, iPad and tablet. And they are often global in a way that few newspapers can be. International cross-border activity continues to flourish. *Vogue* was launched in India in 2007; *Glamour* started a Brazilian edition in March 2012, and *Women's Health* arrived from the US in the same month. These factors may help to explain why the mood among magazine publishers is less gloomy than that of those who publish newspapers. The Professional Publishers Association noted that circulation figures for the second half of 2011 showed that demand for magazines in print was stable and the total average net circulation was only slightly lower than the same period the previous year, down 1.4 per cent (*Magazine World* Q1.2012). Not many newspaper proprietors could report anything so positive.

Even in troubled times there have been successful launches in the UK. *ShortList* is a free weekly lifestyle magazine for men launched in 2007 by Mike Soutar, who had been editorial director at IPC Media as well as editor of *FHM* in the UK. It represented a break from the topshelf and lads' mag traditions of providing salacious and largely sexist content, and had soon established a circulation of more than 500,000. A magazine for women, *Stylist*, then followed. In April 2012 Bauer Media launched *LandScape*, a seasonal lifestyle magazine for women. It's a more straightforward version of a consumer magazine format, but demonstrates that there are still creative ideas and people willing to back them in the magazine publishing world.

CHANGES IN THE MARKET

There are, of course, other kinds of activity in the market. Some titles close or are sold off as their strength declines. *Loaded* is a good example. Launched in 1994, its circulation was around 450,000 within five years, but IPC sold it in 2010 and by 2012 circulation was down below 35,000. In 2011 BBC Worldwide, the successful commercial arm of the BBC, sold off or licensed several publications now collected together in Immediate Media, although in this case it wasn't to do with declining circulations but with political arguments about what activities are appropriate for a public service broadcaster. In 2008 Emap sold its consumer and trade titles to Bauer Media, now Europe's largest publisher of magazines. The Hearst Corporation, as Hearst Magazines UK (formerly National Magazine Company), publisher of such titles as *Cosmopolitan*, *Good Housekeeping* and *Esquire*, moved to acquire Lagardère in 2011, thus taking on *Elle* and making it responsible for 25 titles in the UK, not to mention an ever-growing international portfolio.

All of these changes involve companies which, whatever their size, understand that closely targeting the reader is essential, and those involved in the business side of magazines often refer to this ability as being one of the industry's strengths. Publishers like to say there is a magazine for everyone – whatever an individual's interests or workplace needs. A survey of any large news-stand suggests this must be true, so varied and so many are the titles on offer. But there is one statistic that is absent from the upbeat industry annual surveys: about half of the UK's women never read a women's magazine. This point is made by Brian Braithwaite, who worked for many years as a publisher of women's magazines for National Magazine Company. His view is that what is on offer to readers – women readers at any rate – is not as diverse as it could be. He criticises publishers for duplication: 'Too many titles are devoid of originality or innovation . . . The future has to lie with innovation, not parrot publishing' (Braithwaite 1995: 158). He argues that the leaders in any given sector (*Hello!*, *Marie Claire*, *Cosmopolitan*) were mould-breakers in their time, but that publishers now seem to be more willing to produce copies of what works than to break new ground. His criticisms still hold good and have been echoed by commentators who worry that where an idea (celebrity gossip, most embarrassing moments, explicit sexual material) is seen to be successful in mainstream consumer magazines, the material is then allowed to take over the editorial pages almost to the exclusion of anything else. One example is the extent to which sex is used as bait for readers, even readers who are not yet out of childhood.

SECRETS OF SUCCESS

What, then, are the secrets of success? Editors and many publishers believe that a good magazine depends on the vision of a strong editor: 'We need big editors with big ideas,' says Braithwaite, and he gives as examples what he calls the superstars Tina Brown and Helen Gurley Brown (no relation), a list that might be expanded to include Ian Hislop of *Private Eye*, Anna Wintour of American *Vogue* and any number of others. Good 'editorial technicians' are needed too, but these are not enough to ensure success. The point here is part of a recurring debate in the consumer magazine world: how far should a magazine be designed around the findings of market researchers and focus groups to fill a 'gap in the market' and how far should a magazine be launched because someone has a good idea which will generate its own market even if potential readers did not realise in advance that they wanted such a publication.

Sometimes a myth grows up around this sort of issue. The magazine *Loaded* enjoyed spectacular success after its launch in 1994, and sure enough the copycat publications came rolling off the presses soon afterwards. Tim Southwell, who was originally its deputy editor and became editor in 1998, recounts that the idea was a brilliant hunch on the part of launch editor James Brown while he and a couple of friends were on a wild football bender in Barcelona (Southwell 1998: 2). No amount of asking boys of 18 what they wanted in the way of a glossy monthly magazine could have come up with the idea as it finally emerged from IPC.

However, it's only fair to say that publishers had already noticed there was a gap in the market for magazines aimed at young men. Alan Lewis, who became editor-in-chief of *Loaded*, had worked on several of IPC's music titles and was on the lookout for ideas for a men's title. In Southwell's account of the first two years of *Loaded*'s life, Lewis is quoted as saying:

> If I'm totally honest the whole idea of us starting a men's magazine was ad-driven . . . *GQ*, *Arena* and *Esquire* had been around for a while but they weren't at the top of anyone's list of important cultural happenings. Nonetheless, they were steady and contained loads of ads that we [at IPC] weren't getting – clothes, fragrance, booze, cars etc.
>
> (Southwell 1998: 16)

His point is echoed by IPC publishing director Robert Tame: 'IPC had had a feeling that there's a fairly good advertising market there. But you can't go to it just because there's a market there, you've got to go to it with a proposition' (Southwell 1998: 35). This may well be the secret of the initial success of *Loaded* – the coincidence of a good market-driven proposition with a strong, original journalistic idea. That would certainly bear out Braithwaite's point about diversity and perhaps explain some of the deaths in the women's magazine market, where a failure to provide anything new or with which to maintain a differentiated identity can lead to a title being killed off with little ceremony and could well account for the pretty dismal set of circulation figures seen by women's magazines in the late 1990s.

The reality is, though, that consumer magazine publishing is a volatile industry. The popularity of *Loaded* has slipped away, yet this doesn't necessarily mean that the title was a failure, merely that it was a creature of its time, the mid 1990s, the moment when it was launched and became successful. So while it is correct to note that some magazines die because they probably should never have been born, others die because they have reached the end of their natural life.

From a publisher's point of view births and deaths can be expensive. In early 1999 IPC spent at least £2.5 million on the launch of a new title for men aged between 24 and 35, called *Later*. In 2004 IPC and Emap spent around £8 million each to promote their respective new weekly magazines for young men, *Nuts* and *Zoo Weekly*, and in March 2005 Condé Nast spent £17 million on the launch of a women's magazine *Easy Living*. As Braithwaite notes, 'there are rich rewards to be made if the publisher gets it right or alarming losses if a new launch misses the target' (Braithwaite 1995: 156). He gives the salutary example of *Riva*, launched into the women's weekly market in 1988 with an investment of £3.5 million. Within six weeks it was closed. Similarly, *Sorted*, aimed at teenage boys, was born in late 2003 and killed off within a few months. *Later* never caught on either. No wonder Braithwaite describes the magazine industry as paranoid.

What he doesn't explore in his discussion of the consumer magazine industry is what helps to drive the lack of diversity – the power of the advertisers. Many commentators have noted that the dependence of publishers on advertising gives business interests ultimate control over what gets published (see Chapter 15). It's easy to imagine magazines for women (and indeed men or children) which

PROFILE

Robin Hodge, independent publisher

Robin Hodge is in the rare position of being an independent publisher. In 1985 he was one of the founders of *The List*, the monthly (originally fortnightly) events guide for Edinburgh and Glasgow. It's still going strong in spite of competition from other entertainment publications. So strong, in fact, that it's now in the process of diversifying into other media, just like its bigger rival publishing companies. It's part of the group that in 1999 invested in Beat 106, a radio station in Scotland, and there are electronic online projects under way. It publishes a range of books and its website has won many awards for the strength of its content, design and navigability.

Looking ahead, exploring possibilities for expansion and development, is all part of Hodge's role as publisher. Otherwise the work revolves around money and organisation. 'My job is to co-ordinate activity and make sure the different elements of what we do hold together well,' he says.

> I have to ensure that each issue is published on time, that it's a comprehensive and reliable guide to what's going on, that the features are written and designed to as high a standard as possible, that the advertising sales effort is thorough and professional, that the copies are distributed promptly and efficiently to the shops and that the bills are paid.

To begin with, though, back in 1985, being publisher meant also taking responsibility for all those things that no one else wanted to do. 'With money so scarce it was easier to find people to write and design than to sell advertising space or drive the delivery van,' says Hodge. Gradually as the business built up he was able to bring in more staff so that by the early 1990s he was able to take on the role of editor as well as publisher.

The editorial side of journalism is what had originally attracted him. As a student of politics and economics at Durham University in the mid 1970s he was editor of the fortnightly student newspaper. 'The student press was much more political then than it is now. It was such fun working with friends and tackling issues that concerned us that I thought it would be great if I could earn a living that way,' says Hodge.

Many of his friends thought so too and also became journalists, most of them foreign correspondents because, as Hodge recalls, 'the other routes into mainstream journalism at that time were limited and quite frustrating.' Those were the days when news reporters had to serve at least two years

PROFILE

on provincial papers learning to write in a very formulaic style. 'It was difficult to get the chance, at a young age, to write about a subject that interested you. You had to become a hack.'

That didn't appeal to Hodge so he found himself working for the Edinburgh book publisher Canongate, doing every kind of task – advertising, sales, publicity, production, editing. Eventually, in the early 1980s, he became a director of the company.

Next came *The List*, the idea of a group of friends who wanted to stay in Scotland if that didn't mean sacrificing interesting careers. 'We thought that there was a need for a publication that focused on all that was happening in Glasgow and Edinburgh and on the new creative talent that was beginning to emerge. We thought by publishing a magazine we could both get the jobs we wanted and help encourage growth and development in the arts in Scotland.'

At the time they were 'very naive' about the practicalities of launching a magazine, and assumed 'that the world would rush out to buy it'. They were sure they would be rich and successful in no time, so much so that they didn't even get round to preparing a proper business plan. 'We thought that kind of stuff was dull,' says Hodge. Nor was there a dummy issue.

They managed to sell 4,000 copies of the first issue. The trouble was, that meant tipping the other 11,000 they'd printed into a skip. Hopes that circulation would grow fast were unfounded: sales even went down as the initial interest provoked by a launch fell away.

Other problems soon emerged. 'It was a real struggle to publish on time as we were overambitious about what it was feasible to research and write in the available time,' Hodge admits. 'We often missed our printer's deadlines and were late getting the magazine into the shops. This didn't help with circulation – a guide to events that happened yesterday is obviously not a must-have purchase.'

> We assumed advertising revenue would come rolling in and that we would be able to choose to publish what we liked best. The reality is that any new publication takes a long time to be successful as advertisers like to wait until they are sure it has a well-established readership before booking into a new title. There is only a limited amount of revenue about.

In time, circulation did begin to grow slowly and steadily so that after 25 years, it was between 18,000 and 25,000, depending on the time of year. 'It's still a challenge to make each issue as strong as possible,' says

Hodge. 'We're competing with countless glossies who have deep pockets, high-quality printing presses and easy access to celebrity interviews. We have to fight our corner with much more limited resources.'

As publisher he has to worry about the increasing competition in the entertainment and lifestyle fields from magazines and from the newspaper magazine supplements. One source of satisfaction for Hodge, however, is to see the number of successful writers and editors on other publications who started out at *The List*. 'The magazine has helped launch the careers of many talented writers and editors, which is something I'm proud of.' And the magazine now employs around 25 staff, with around 30 regular freelance contributors.

Hodge is pleased that *The List* has managed to retain its independence. 'With so much of the media controlled by huge corporate conglomerates with vast resources it can be quite uncomfortable at times and we have to dodge and weave occasionally to survive. We are fortunate to be in control of what we do.'

Interview by Mark Robertson

would look different and have a different agenda or tone from the ones which prevail. Occasionally such magazines emerge onto the news-stands and some survive for several years: *Spare Rib* lived for 14 years, longer than many a more commercial magazine; the glossy women's magazine *Working Woman* lasted for about a year in the mid-1980s and one reason for its failure, undoubtedly, was the conservatism of advertisers. Now with the internet making it possible to publish ideas and images cheaply and instantly to the tiniest and indeed the largest of markets, you might expect print titles to be pushed out of the running. There are signs, though, that things are not quite so simple. Brands that start as digital are finding out that print also has an appeal and are extending into it: style.com is one example; the print version, *Moshi Magazine*, of the online children's game Moshi Monsters is another.

THE FUTURE

From a commercial point of view today, however, there is plenty to worry about, but as consumers spend less on newspapers they seem to spend more on magazine brands. Research is telling advertising agencies that whatever they spend on television advertising will produce even better results if campaigns are linked with magazines, partly because (research again) readers are in a more receptive frame of mind than viewers: they are more likely to concentrate on their magazine, whereas television viewers are notoriously likely to be doing other things too (Consterdine 1997; 2002). These findings emphasise the extent to which the various media now intertwine: with neat reciprocity three out of the eight best-selling consumer maga- zines in the UK in July to December 2011 were television listings titles, between them selling more than 3.48 million copies weekly.

Futurologists suggest that the number and diversity of titles will continue to grow as social trends create the right conditions for such growth (Consterdine 1997: 9). When they make this kind of prediction the Henley Centre stargazers are drawing attention to a number of things. What they call the growth in the 'knowledge society' will, they say, entail an increasing demand for information. The 'continuing frag- mentation of social identities', particularly among the young, presumably means they will want a wider range of magazines as badges of and guides to those social identities. There is a reference, too, to the 'polarisation between income groups and consequent increase in the diversity of lifestyles, needs and aspirations'. (Not every reader will share this rose-tinted vision which seems to mean that as the rich get richer and the poor get poorer everyone will need ever more consumer mag- azines. Good news for publishers perhaps, but not for the rest of humanity.) The Henley Centre's report, *Media Futures*, also refers to the demand for specialist titles from the babyboomers as they move into retirement. It's not clear whether this means specialist in the sense of having editorial specifically about growing old or whether there are leisure and lifestyle issues that are of such unique concern to the greying babyboomers that they will want to read whole publications devoted to their coverage. (Incidentally, the tenth best-selling magazine in the UK, *Saga*, is aimed exactly at that grey market). Lastly, the 'continued expansion and frag- mentation of leisure interests across society as a whole' was cited as a further provoker of more, and more diverse, titles (Consterdine 1997: 9), although of course since he conducted his research the internet has provided increasing scope for the publication of diverse content.

Brand extension

What is not in doubt is that there have been recent developments in the way that magazines earn money or 'develop revenue streams'. Many magazine publishers, especially in the B2B sector, now use a publication's title as a brand name on the strength of which to set up exhibitions, conferences, directories, databases, direct mail, electronic and social media publishing operations, as well as ways to sell branded goods (see Chapter 15). Even as far back as 2003 fewer than half of the leading consumer magazine publishers thought of themselves as just consumer magazine publishers. The predictions were for an evolution from magazine publishers to multimedia publishers and communicators which would represent an 'important and significant shift for the industry' (Dear 2000: 20). The predictions turned out to be true, and not just for consumer magazines. The B2B publishers embraced the idea readily. One example is Jane's Information Group, which was originally known for its coverage of the arms industry in *Jane's Defence Weekly*. In recent years it has developed as an information gathering and analysis service used by clients throughout the world.

The international dimension

Another marked trend in magazine publishing is towards globalisation as companies move across national borders to expand their operations even in straitened financial times. 'Cross-border publishing is as vibrant as ever', wrote Chris Llewellyn, president and CEO of FIPP, the International Federation of Magazine Publishers, in *Magazine World* in late 2011. At a time when other companies are reining in their activities, global launch activity was up 14 per cent year on year in late 2011. One reason for what *Magazine World* calls 'this golden age of cross-border activity', is that it is 'relatively easy to do': the other main reason is that 'it can be very profitable' (*Magazine World* Q4.2011: 3, 15). This can mean a variety of things. It is not a new trend, merely one that has speeded up in recent years as publishing houses grow and become part of multinational conglomerates, and as many industries, wherever they are based, have increasingly looked abroad for new or expanding markets.

At its simplest it means that a publisher with a successful magazine in the US, say, will launch versions of its magazine in other countries. Condé Nast did this when it brought *Vogue* to the UK in 1916, followed by other titles such as *Brides*. Bauer Media Group publishes more than 300 magazines in 15 countries. *Cosmopolitan* began life with Hearst magazines in the US in the late 1960s, came to the UK in the early 1970s. By 2012 it was being published in more than 100 countries, in 63 international editions and in 32 languages. In the reverse direction, Gruner+Jahr set up G&J of the UK to bring *Best* and *Prima* over from their base in Germany. (The UK company was then bought by The National Magazine Company in 2000, and this is now part of the Hearst Corporation.)

When companies look abroad, they can do it in a variety of ways. Condé Nast has a British branch to look after its British titles (*Vogue*, *Tatler*, *GQ*, *Condé Nast Traveller*, *House and Garden*, *Vanity Fair* and *Brides*). Big multinational companies can own outright magazines in a number of countries. Future Publishing bought Italy's biggest publisher of computer and videogames magazines in the spring of 1999. Even small companies can operate across national boundaries. *Hello!* magazine is published by a small family firm in Spain which built on the success of the original *¡Hola!* by launching in Britain. Sometimes companies from one country license companies in other countries to produce versions of the parent title. (This is commonly the route for publications in the vast, booming market in China.) One advantage of this system is thought to be that it ensures the characteristics of the local market will not be forgotten when editorial content is being prepared.

Increasingly, however, companies are entering into partnership agreements with foreign companies. In some cases this is because the legislation in the new country demands partnership with local industry if it is to allow a foreign company in. In Brazil, for example, foreign ownership in a new company can only account for a maximum of 20 per cent of the value. It took many months of negotiation for *Vogue* to be allowed entry to India as part of Condé Nast UK rather than as a licensing deal, the more usual route for magazines moving from abroad into the Indian market.

This can mean job opportunities abroad for UK journalists. When Attic Futura decided to take its teenage title *Sugar* to Germany, it sent along a British journalist as editor. Kevin Hand, then chief executive of Emap, said he hoped staff would be able to benefit from international expansion: 'My dream is that you can start working anywhere in England and then be able to move around two or three countries' (*Press Gazette*, 16 October 1998). In 1998 Emap began developing a new international division to work on recent purchases in Australia, Singapore and Malaysia, where it was investing somewhere between £600 million and £800 million. It was, in any case, already a truly international company – one-fifth of its 5,000 staff being based abroad (*Fact File 1998*, Emap). By 2004 it was producing versions of *FHM* in 27 countries and had agreements for three more signed. In August 2005 it launched a Spanish edition of *Zoo*. And in 2008 its titles became part of Bauer Media. Chris Llewellyn, managing director of Emap International in 2005, said that advertisers like the 'consistency of brand values throughout the world' which a magazine with international editions can offer. Readers benefit too, he says, because the expense of editorial and pictures which might be too high for a magazine published in one or two countries alone, can become affordable if spread across a much bigger global circulation.[1]

Companies moving into foreign markets have to remember that national and local tastes differ and this is likely to mean a substantial number of local staff should be recruited. Thomaz Souto Corrêa of Editora Abril in Brazil made this point to American editors: 'Magazine brands are not Coca-Cola, the same product, the same formula around the planet. Rather they are a creative mixture of ideas presented in an original way to a specific audience' (*Magazine World*, December 1998: 2). The local publisher's job is to 'adjust and recreate the brand's formula to the wants, needs and desires of the local reader'. Anyone who doubts this has to do no more than compare Condé Nast's American and British magazines for brides. The styling of the fashion pages (too many tacky tuxedos for British tastes), the tone in which the copy is written, even the kind of topics that are covered have clear differences. For *FHM* in Hungary, Emap learned to leave out copy about car maintenance that would be appropriate for the magazine in the UK, because the subject is comprehensively taught in Hungarian schools.

It's not just the consumer magazines that are moving into global markets. A title such as Bloomberg's *Business Week* has been active internationally for many years (*Magazine World*, July 1998: 10). Commentator Charles McCullagh of DeSilva and Phillips in New York says B2B publishers 'go global for the same reason consumer publishers do: to increase revenue, to remain competitive, to satisfy advertisers, to strengthen and protect a brand, to improve a domestic edition and to gain market share'. He notes that the speed of development is very fast indeed: 'Countries that were not on most publishers' radars in 1994, now have become potentially lucrative markets', giving the examples of Russia, China and Argentina. His point about speed was echoed by Eric Verdon-Roe of Haymarket at the annual conference of the PPA in May 2004, who says the move of UK publishers into international markets is welcomed by those customers abroad who admire our publications (PPA conference 2004). Haymarket in 2012 has 127 magazine licences and publishes magazines in 29 languages in 42 territories. One key difference, however, between the B2B press and consumer titles is that there are not that many subject areas in the B2B sector, other than finance, oil, gas, telecommunications and computers, that are truly international. Here it is technology, not lifestyle, which leads the editorial way.

CONCLUSION

While it might not, in 2012, yet be time for full-blown optimism in the international magazine publishing market, there is a feeling that magazines have the power to withstand troubled times so long as they regard themselves as brands that encompass a wide range of multimedia platforms and extensions to their activities. The B2B sector's recovery is likely to be slower, but publishers in this area are effectively following the lead from advertisers into other media and activities, where their knowledge of product information, industry news and data is valued. It is true that in many developed countries magazine readerships are about as high as they're likely to go. The reasons are to do with the demands on the time of individual readers. The new media may tempt readers away and tempt publishers to broaden their activities, but print on paper nevertheless looks set to retain its attraction for readers and advertisers in the foreseeable future. If publishers are justified in their firm belief about the loyalty of readers to brands, then there is nothing to fear and much to be gained from the digital world, especially if that world includes apps and mobile phones. Indeed, a survey by Deloitte in 2012 in the UK found that '88 per cent of magazine readers . . . still prefer to consume articles via print and 35 per cent subscribed to at least one printed magazine' (Hooper 2012).

One thing that might give them pause for thought, however, is a much less discussed threat to circulation figures. As more people begin to think about the environmental consequences of the mass consumption of magazines and newspapers, will they decide to cut down the number of copies they buy? Publisher Felix Dennis drew attention to this problem in 2004. Some consumers will no doubt decide that it's one thing to use up trees in order to produce information we need, but quite another to use them up in order to promote new brands of lipstick or to prop up the sagging careers of minor popstars. Publishers can't do much about this other than hope that most readers don't care too much about the environment. What little publishers can do is demonstrated by the Recycle Now icon carried by some UK titles since late 2004. The icon is meant to remind readers to recycle their magazines. The PPA also runs an annual Environment forum to facilitate discussion between representatives from politics, business and magazine publishing. Such environmental goodwill is, however, likely to be lost on serious Greens as they will probably not be interested in buying consumer magazines in the first place.

NOTE

1   Lecture at Stirling Media Research Institute, November 2004.

RECOMMENDED READING

Braithwaite, B. (1998) 'Magazines: the bulging bookstores', in *The Media: An Introduction*.
Dennis, F. (2004) 'The Four Horsemen of the Apocalypse', *British Journalism Review*.
The Economist (2012, June 9) 'Non-news is good news'.
Holmes, T. and Nice, L. (2012) 'The political economy of magazines' in *Magazine Journalism*.
Johnson, S. and Prijatel, P. (2006) *The Magazine from Cover to Cover*, 2nd edition.
Magazine World (2011) 'A licence to print money'.
Morrish, J. and Bradshaw, P. (2012) *Magazine Editing: In Print and Online*, chs 1, 4.
Reed, D. (1997) *The Popular Magazine in Britain and the United States 1880–1960*.

Websites

American Society of Magazine Editors: www.magazine.org/asme
British Society of Magazine Editors: www.bsme.com
International Federation of the Periodical Press: www.fipp.com
www.magforum.com
http://magculture.com/blog
Magazine World: www.fipp.com/Default.aspx?PageIndex=2508
Guardian Media: www.guardian.co.uk/media
Professional Publishers Association: www.ppa.co.uk; www.ppamarketing.net
Press Gazette: www.pressgazette.co.uk

CHAPTER 17

Issues of conduct

The American reporter Janet Malcolm argues persuasively that journalists behave with treachery towards their sources. For her it's inherent in the nature of the encounter between someone who is seeking information and someone who is willing to give it, because the interests of journalist and subject rarely coincide except in the simplest of publicity transactions – and those are unlikely to be the stuff of interesting journalism. Malcolm (2004: 3) suggests in her book *The Journalist and the Murderer* that journalists try to 'justify their treachery in various ways according to their temperaments. The more pompous talk about freedom of speech and "the public's right to know"; the least talented talk about Art; the seemliest murmur about earning a living.' It's true that questions about what is acceptable behaviour for a journalist are rarely to be answered simply. And what makes this perplexing for a beginner is that there is no clear answer to the question 'How far can I go?' in pursuit of a story or a quote: is it ever acceptable to break the law, or a code of conduct, or merely to break the bounds of good taste? What if your employer asks you to do any of those things? Do you have the right to refuse? This chapter looks at these questions, and some of the issues related to them.

Anyone who doubted there was a problem about how some journalists behave, in the UK at least, now has to explain away the evidence put before the Leveson Inquiry into the role of the press and police in the phone-hacking scandal. Journalists were revealed to have behaved in ways that many would find hard to credit – unless they had read the book *Flat Earth News* by *Guardian* reporter Nick Davies in which he outlines many of the discreditable practices that some powerful newspaper industry people tried to dismiss as exaggerated. Tapping the phones of celebrities, politicians or victims of murder and terrorism was revealed, as were many other kinds of harassment. While magazines have not been heavily implicated (at the time of writing) the weekly glossies do carry stories and pictures that bear the hallmark of questionable activity.

Yet it's fair to say that public perceptions of journalism have long been unfavourable, a finding that opinion polls have demonstrated in their measures of how low journalists are rated in terms of honesty and trustworthiness (Kellner 1991; Worcester 1998). The common reaction of journalists used to be to laugh this off, but the problem is now recognised as serious. Ian Jack, former editor of *The Independent on Sunday* and *Granta* magazine, who now writes a column for *The Guardian*, argues that while reporters have never had much social status in Britain, things have got much worse (Jack 1998: vi). He attributes the decline to the way journalism has become part of the entertainment industry and to the cost cutting which is characteristic of a competitive market. Andrew Marr, broadcaster and former political editor of the BBC, agrees that there are serious problems with British journalism and even before Leveson suggested that these should be talked about more openly. He thinks the underlying problem is one of trust both because reporters get things wrong and because journalists are so reluctant to apologise when they do. For him 'the problem is less direct lying than slimy misrepresentation' and it means that it is sources and victims in particular who are most likely to regard journalists as untrustworthy (Marr 2004: 379). One worry is that if the readers don't trust journalists then they may choose to withdraw their co-operation from reporters and may even stop reading journalism altogether. In *Flat Earth News* Davies entitles a chapter 'The Dark Arts', to give a flavour of what to expect when he outlines the activities that were being sanctioned by the editors and publishers of some newspapers.

There is further evidence of a problem: the existence of more than one code of conduct attempting to define what is acceptable behaviour. The codes from the Press Complaints Commission, the National Union of Journalists and the Teenage Magazine Arbitration Panel, while not identical, are intended to rein in the worst excesses of behaviour. They also give clues about what journalists get up to. If journalists always behaved well then there would be no need for such codes. But journalistic endeavour is too varied to simplify into a universal statement of proper conduct of journalists. Some journalists are engaged in preserving the democratic process, in seeking out fraud, or in describing social realities. Others are engaged in promoting or undermining the careers of celebrities or in helping to create a market for blue mascara. So although there are ethical questions about how journalism is produced, these are not the same for all journalists.

It may be that journalists on consumer or trade magazines are not faced with the same doubts about their behaviour as those who work in hard news. It is noticeable that most of the more extreme examples of questionable practice from journalists do seem to revolve around the news agenda, although increasingly this includes the mundane daily doings of celebrities. Nevertheless, many magazine journalists write news and all magazine journalists should be aware of what some of the ethical issues are. News brings its own pressures to do with deadlines, speed of work, competition between both reporters and publications and, it has to be said, the machismo style of many newsrooms. But some of the more down-market women's weekly celebrity-filled magazines definitely require journalists and photographers to be intrusive, while some of the magazines aimed at young men are notorious for filling their pages with salacious and misogynist content.

So any journalists who are prepared to think in terms of morals may find their work threatens to compromise their beliefs. This is why it's important for beginner journalists to reflect on the implications of what they've chosen to do, even if traditionally young reporters were told that if they spent any time worrying about morals they'd never write any stories. This used to be a common position but was always a weak one for two reasons. First, journalists have an impact, good or bad, on the lives of their readers. Readers of magazines, in particular, trust what they are told in their favourite publications. People who feature in stories may have their lives ruined as a result, whether by intention or by accident. The pressure group MediaWise (formerly Presswise) was set up by 'victims of media abuse' and documents such cases, including several of mistaken identity, that have left the lives of ordinary citizens in tatters. As Belsey and Chadwick note, 'if harms can be measured on a scale of distress, some cases of invasion of privacy may cause more distress than certain kinds of injury to health' (Belsey and Chadwick 1992: 9).

Second, some journalists lay claim to the high moral ground in defending behaviour (sneaked tapes or photos of people in bed together) that most of us would be ashamed to admit. When 'journalists' do this kind of thing they set themselves up as moral guardians. They decide what is acceptable behaviour for the rest of us: if we stray for a second, and are even slightly famous, then the wrath of the tabloids will be upon us.

COMPROMISING POSITIONS

Many journalists do, of course, have high ethical standards. For some that is one reason for becoming a journalist in the first place. They talk of democracy, accountability in public life, of honesty and truth, of making the world a better place. They look at their skills and talents and realise that writing for a good magazine or newspaper is the best way for them to make a living while making a contribution to the good of society. The talented, the fortunate or those who don't need much money to live on, may well be able to pursue a career without ever compromising their ideals. It is true, though, that for others compromises may have to be made.

The extremes are well known and can be read about in the account of *The Sun* newspaper and tabloid culture given by Chippindale and Horrie (1999), by Davies in *Flat Earth News*, and now in the Leveson Inquiry documentation. At the tabloid end of the scale it seems there are no lower levels to which to stoop. Hacking phones and rummaging through the dustbins of politicians are two examples.

Doorstepping celebrities whose husbands are spending the night with a mistress is another. The merciless deception and hounding of staff and patients in hospitals where the famous lie dying is yet another, memorably described by Alan Bennett in his account of the last illness of his friend Russell Harty, the television personality: 'Now as he fought for his life in St James's Hospital one newspaper rented a flat opposite and had a long lens trained on the window of his ward' (Bennett 1994: 50). A less extreme example and perhaps more typical behaviour was when the cleric due to marry a moderately famous couple who wanted their wedding to be private was phoned by a reporter seeking the location by pretending to be a relative of the groom.

There are reporters who would refuse to do some of these things and might try to get out of others. But almost any reporter can expect to be asked to do some things that would raise the eyebrows of the ordinary citizen. Why, for example, do journalists assume they have the right to ask to interview people who have recently suffered a tragic bereavement or been victims of a crime? The better sort of news editor will argue that his staff have every right to ask for an interview, but should not persist if asked to go away. Other news editors will insist that reporters keep on asking and that they try to get pictures too. The journalists' case is that people often want to talk when they are in a state of shock, they want to share their emotions and their memories of the dead person. To which the devil's advocate might respond: are journalists the best people to talk to in these circumstances? Do people really benefit from sharing their raw emotions with the reporters and readers of *The Daily Mail*? Their aim, if they are any good as reporters, is not to soothe a troubled soul but to extract the most exciting story. (For a more positive view of this staple of journalistic practice see Duncan and Newton 2010).

Janet Malcolm suggests that the journalist is 'a kind of confidence man, preying on people's vanity, ignorance, or loneliness, gaining their trust and betraying them without remorse' (Malcolm 2004: 3). Her observations about the transaction between reporters and reported are more usually made by outsiders, but Malcolm is an experienced and successful journalist so she can't be lightly dismissed. While public figures may be able to look after themselves, for the ordinary journalist working with ordinary folk, there often is, or ought to be, what Malcolm calls a moral impasse: 'The wisest know that the best they can do . . . is still not good enough. The not so wise, in their accustomed manner, choose to believe there is no problem' (Malcolm 2004: 162).

This reflects the approach of much traditional journalism training in the UK, which for many years did not formally recognise the need for journalists to worry about whether their behaviour was morally acceptable. Then, in universities at least, it became normal to have some kind of debate. This doesn't mean reporters who study journalism at university are any less willing to be reliable staff for their editors, it merely means that they have thought through some of the issues before they hit the streets. This can be invaluable, whichever end of the moral spectrum they veer towards. And in 2012, with the detailed examination of journalistic wrongdoing by the Leveson Inquiry, the ethical values of those who work in the print media are now under intense public scrutiny.

Student journalists, at any rate, are encouraged to think about how they might behave in terms of 'moral dilemmas' and 'ethical questions'. This is somewhat disingenuous, as to some extent the ethical dilemmas are sorted out before you become a journalist. You choose journalism over advertising or PR because you are more interested in truth than deception, but recognising there might be times when you have to do things to people that you would not want to have done to yourself. It is for this reason I would suggest that momentous phrases like 'moral dilemma' are occasionally used by journalists when they mean merely that their conscience is pricking them. A dilemma implies that you might make either of two choices. In most cases journalists know which choice they are going to make (thanks to their training, their commitment to an employer, or their fear of getting fired), so there is no dilemma, just an awareness that they are behaving badly when they relentlessly pursue a bereaved parent for no serious purpose, or when they make up a quote, or lie about who they are.

PRETENCE

The question of pretence often arises and it illustrates the usefulness, or otherwise, of codes of conduct. Undercover reporting means pretending to be someone you are not. It may be harmless enough: pretending to be a tennis fan in order to write a piece of reportage about Wimbledon or dressing like a beggar for a month to report on what it's like to be poor. It may seem to be the only way to get at important matters of public concern. By working undercover as a trainee policeman Mark Daly was able to report for the BBC on the racist views of some policemen. By getting work in care homes Panorama reporters were able to expose the mistreatment of residents.

The justification for working undercover falters when the journalist pretends to be someone else in order to access information that is trivial or prurient. If you pretend to be a junior hospital doctor in order to get into the ward to read the case notes of a celebrity, then you have entered a dubious moral realm. This is not the same kind of journalism as that which exposes the mistreatment of patients.

The current PCC code of practice offers guidance, but there is vagueness too. Take point 10: 'Engaging in misrepresentation or subterfuge can generally be justified only in the public interest and then only when the material cannot be obtained by other means.' In the case of the tennis example, what harm could be done by misrepresentation? And in the case of Mark Daly's report about the police, much that is positively good is likely to be the result as it prompted the police to try to change the behaviour and attitudes of its officers (Press Complaints Commission Editors' Code of Conduct 2004: point 10). It's the word 'generally' in the clause that seems to provide the freedom. Does it mean most of the time, or most journalists, or most publications? Is it okay to use subterfuge sometimes but not often and, if so, how often is acceptable? What is the definition of public interest which provides the protection? This, we learn, includes 'Preventing the public from being misled by an action or statement of an individual or organisation'. For most circumstances, where wicked deeds are suspected, that may be adequate, but what about the popstar who merely wants to pretend he's on holiday when in fact he's at a drying-out clinic?

What about journalists who attempt to set people up to commit crimes they might not otherwise have committed, the so-called 'stings'. That's a kind of subterfuge. Journalists might argue that the police do this all the time, but what they forget is that broadly speaking the police have a mandate from the rest of us to keep the peace and tackle crime in society. Journalists do not. Do they have a right to frame someone, particularly someone who is not in his own right a public figure but merely the teenage son of one (Greenslade 2005)?

Another kind of pretence is more widespread. It is where a journalist interviews several people and then draws together the quotes to make it appear as if the words came from one person whose name is invented. As a practice this doesn't worry all journalists, provided the quotes were genuine in the first place, but I'm not sure that readers feel so relaxed about what is, after all, a deception. The PCC code says nothing about this practice.

What about the feature writer who simply invents quotes to fill the available slot in a story. This is done by some lifestyle magazines even when the people they are quoting in a vox pop are photographed and their pictures appear right next to the 'quotes' the reporter has created.

CHILDREN

Currently the PCC does offer guidance about the treatment of children by journalists, but again these are imprecise and inequitable. How old is a child? Why should 17-year-olds at school attract more protection than those who are not? Why is parental consent required for interviews or photographs of the under-16s only if the journalist is seeking information about a child's welfare (Press Complaints Commission Editors' Code of Conduct 2004: point 6)? If young people should be free to complete their time at school 'without unnecessary intrusion' what would constitute 'necessary' intrusion?

CODES OF CONDUCT

One unarguable benefit of the existence of the codes is that journalists who are asked to do things they feel uneasy about can try quoting the codes as a reason for refusing. Some journalists even have the PCC guidelines written into their contracts of employment. For them the code can be a useful protection from rogue editors. For other staffers, though, and for freelances, the guidelines are open to interpretation by editors and may indeed be ignored. If a journalist wants to question what he is being asked to do (persist unreasonably in trying to get interviews with eyewitnesses, for example) then he often risks his livelihood. What both the NUJ and the PCC codes depend on is the notion that the end (exposure of a villain) can sometimes justify the means (breaking into his private office) that would otherwise be questionable. (At the time of writing the PCC is in a 'transitional phase', waiting for a new regulatory body to be set up in the wake of the Leveson Inquiry.)

JOURNALISTS AS MORAL ARBITERS

The problems with the ends–means argument are, first, that some journalists take this to mean that they are free to break the law or at least behave badly so long as *they* think they have a good reason. Second, this implies, yet again, that they are in some way licensed to act as moral and almost legal guardians for society. Not everyone would see that as necessarily a bad idea and there is a way in which the public humiliation that the press can provide is distantly related to the public humiliation sinners used to get in church when their sins were denounced from the pulpit. The problem here lies in the assumptions which underlie some of the activities of journalists. If their role as moral arbiters (ferreting out fraudsters, paedophiles, drug-dealers and so on) were more openly acknowledged, then perhaps a more rigorous selection and training would be recommended. Perhaps more consistency would then emerge in their thinking. It isn't logical to look at media output as if it all comes from one source, but if you allow yourself to do that for a moment there are some contradictions. To read the tabloid press (and the broadsheets which hang on the coat-tails of the tabloids) you'd think that extramarital sexual encounters were only for deviants, that one-night stands were beyond the pale and that oral sex was the province of the prostitute. Meanwhile, in another part of the media forest, there are several lifestyle magazines for women and men, girls and boys which fill their pages with advice about how to have as much sex as possible. Another topical example: many newspapers are so fierce in their condemnation of paedophiles that they publish photographs and names to help parents know who their children should avoid. Meanwhile, other 'journalists' on magazines for young teenage girls publish photographs that would delight the average paedophile and are encouraging behaviour that can only make young women more vulnerable (McKay 1999).

PRIVACY

Then there is the awkward question of privacy. How far should journalists be allowed to intrude into the lives of those they want to write about? Should there be a distinction between public figures and private individuals and, if so, how do you distinguish between the two? The tension here is the old one about freedom: when does my freedom to act impose on your liberty to act? In journalism terms this tension is between, on the one hand, those who want reporters to have the freedom to research and write stories as part of the underpinning of the democratic process, even if this means some intrusion into private lives and, on the other hand, those who feel that an individual has the right to a private life and that even his professional life should be scrutinised only in the most restrained way. In a serious investigation a reporter can't be sure she has a story until, perhaps, the invasion of privacy has taken place. Getting proof may be the point of the doorstepping or the long-lens photography from an adjacent building. Where serious misdemeanours are revealed in this way there is little public outcry.

The cases which cause outrage, and which could, in the end, lead to stringent curbs being put on the press, may be ones where no criminal activity is discovered or even suspected: why should a woman, however famous, not be free to exercise in her gym without secret cameras taking pictures of her? Why should a footballer not be free to use the services of a call girl if he wants to, without this being revealed in the press? Why should magazines have the right to publish photographs of film stars having bad-hair days and wearing awful shorts? Why should the newly married Countess of Wessex find 11-year-old pictures of herself frolicking on the beach being used to boost the circulation of a tabloid newspaper, *The Sun*? The impotence of the old PCC was only highlighted by the fact that an apology was forced from the paper in this case, probably because she was a member of the royal family; others who are damaged by the press may get nothing, especially as they have to weigh up the probability that the damaging material will be reproduced while their complaint is being considered.

The tale of Diana, Princess of Wales is well enough known, and although photographers have been exonerated from causing her death, almost the most chilling story to emerge from the tragic events in Paris in 1997 was the hour-by-hour account of the last three days of her life published in *The Sunday Times.* It revealed the extent to which she was a prisoner of her fame and good looks, hunted and haunted by journalists who made their living by the pursuit. One of the justifications journalists offered for their mercilessness is that she courted the press herself on some occasions, but it would have been surprising if she hadn't, and would have taken almost superhuman restraint, given that the press were already writing about her every twitch. Diana is the best example of someone who suffered at the unscrupulous hands of the rat-pack, as the more extreme reporters are nicknamed, one irony being that as she was happy to oblige the camera, there wasn't even any real excuse for intrusion. Put simply, hers was an image exploited for financial gain by publishers all over the world. This is what happens to many public figures for no other reason than profit. Even journalists who don't hunt their prey like paparazzi should not forget they are implicated if they work on, or edit, magazines that buy the pictures and the copy from agencies.

In a case involving Diana's brother, Earl Spencer, the PCC found that just because you choose to invite one set of reporters to write about and photograph your house, it does not mean that another set of reporters can freely hide in the bushes outside a clinic to take unauthorised pictures of another family member who is ill. Yet journalists frequently argue that anyone who is in any way in the public eye has, effectively, forfeited their right and that of their family to freedom from intrusion. The trouble with this argument is that it could mean that in the long run there will be a shortage of people willing to shoulder the burden of public office. Maybe it has also meant, in the past, that potentially good reporters have been deterred from journalism as a career because of the unpalatable things they might be asked to do.

The whole issue of the regulation of privacy moved into the spotlight in 2011 with the revelations about the behaviour of 'reporters' and those in the pay of the some of News International's British titles as well as other newspapers. Criminal activity of various kinds, including the tapping of phones, has been investigated. Whatever body replaces the discredited PCC will be tasked with monitoring and regulating issues of privacy, among many other things.

One further way in which privacy can be an issue for journalists relates to the reporting of societies or individuals outside the audience for whom the stories are written. Foreign correspondents and journalists who undertake any kind of immersion reporting may encounter serious issues about informed consent. The speed of international communications makes it almost impossible to assume that the subjects of close observation won't be in a position to see the finished written product as once would have been the case. The best-known recent example of a clash of interests between the writer and the subject is that of Åsne Seierstad's book-length reportage, *The Bookseller of Kabul* (McKay 2012).

HYPOCRISY

Journalists often defend some of the more questionable things they do as being part of a crusade against hypocrisy, yet seem unable to look with candour at their own behaviour. There may be journalists who have never claimed a pound more on expenses than they actually spent, or who have never had too much to drink or been near a drug. Some, but not most. Hypocrisy is probably as prevalent in editorial offices as it is everywhere else. Minor human weaknesses are exaggerated by journalists to the point of destroying lives, while systematic wickedness goes unreported, as John Pilger and many others have demonstrated (Pilger 1998).

In the news press (especially, but by no means exclusively, the tabloids) and in a wide range of consumer periodicals, the apparent prurience of the British is exploited as an excuse to print sexually titillating material which will boost circulations. A good example of hypocrisy creeping in is with magazines for young teenage girls. Editors of these use arguments about sex education and empowerment to justify their generous use of sexually explicit material. No one doubts that some of this is informative, but that doesn't explain the extent of it or the contextual tone it creates. When being frank, editors will admit that it's all about sales (McKay 1998) and it would be interesting to see whether the publishers' public devotion to the good causes of education and empowerment would survive were these shown to push sales down rather than up.

The lifestyle sector's obsession with sex (whether explicitly, in articles about sex, or implicitly, in articles about other topics which in turn depend on a particular attitude to sex) has been good for sales even if it has attracted some adverse comment. Most of this has been focused on magazines for adolescent girls, because it seems to be more acceptable to question material aimed at a youthful and therefore more vulnerable audience. (Women, also, are thought to need more protection than men in this respect.) Arguments about the way sex is used in magazines for grown-ups naturally stumble at the question 'Why shouldn't a 28-year-old read what she wants to read?' The diet of diets, dubious health advice, sex, fashion and celebrity tittle-tattle that typifies many magazines for women may attract condemnation but there's not much to be done about it unless you have the resources to set up a new magazine with richer content. A recent example of a title in this market which does offer refreshing and fascinating content is *Oh Comely*, launched in 2010 by Adeline Media.

One line of 'post-modernist feminist' argument is that it doesn't much matter what's in magazines for women because of what academic commentator Joke Hermes calls 'the fallacy of meaningfulness'. By this she suggests that the pleasure women get from reading magazines is transitory and forgettable (Hermes 1995: 143). Critics of the general content of consumer lifestyle magazines, whether for men or women, might take comfort in the hope she's right; her arguments are echoed by Angela McRobbie, who suggests 'girls and women are now "knowing" enough to recognize how they are persuaded to consume' (McRobbie 1996: 189). The difficulty with these arguments from the academy is that the research done for publishers finds exactly the opposite to be the case. It shows that readers build up strong feelings of trust in their magazines (Consterdine 1997: 16), something that could happen only if they believed and remembered what they read.

When feminists criticise the magazines aimed at younger men for their adolescent blokishness (at best) and unreconstructed misogyny (at worst), they know that the soaraway circulation success is all the justification publishers and journalists need. In the case of sexually explicit editorial for men no attempt is made to justify its inclusion in terms of health education. Lads are free to dream about what they'd do to the unclad glamour girls in their favourite magazines, without having to wade through endless articles about thrush or STDs first. (This is an observation, not an endorsement.) In a notable development, by 2011 the circulations of magazines aimed at young men were in freefall. *Loaded* had slipped to below 35,000 in 2011 from a former peak of 350,000 in 2000. Its former editor, Martin Daubney, has spoken publicly of feeling 'ashamed' of the title he edited with such success, and that he feels regret because he believes that magazines like *Loaded* 'did give young men a "taste" for soft porn that led to "darker desires"' that the internet can feed. For him, a 'dream job' had become a 'moral nightmare' and he resigned in 2010. *Loaded* has been sold twice and is now owned by a producer of 'adult films' (Daubney 2012).

One further way journalists may demonstrate hypocrisy is in relation to payment not to contributors but to the ordinary people who have stories to tell, eyewitness accounts to give or even expert explanations and comments to share. The PCC guidelines say that criminals or witnesses in criminal trials should not benefit financially from those circumstances. No need to question that, but journalists often express their disdain for the idea that others should be paid for their time and efforts. Perhaps their approach is the necessary corollary of the altruistic, high-minded seeker-after-objective-truth model of news reporting, but it overlooks the fact that even this sort of journalism is nevertheless a commodity and that ordinary eyewitnesses or commentators provide journalists with their raw material. Some of the women's magazines recognise this and have no hesitation in paying people modest sums to tell their stories of tragedy overcome. Yet 'chequebook journalism' gets a bad name when huge sums of money are handed over.

In respect of payment, the position of *Hello!* and *OK!*, the good-news gossip magazines, is more open. They pay generously those who agree to feature in their pages, especially for exclusive access to an event such as a wedding or the first picture of a new baby. Tensions can nevertheless arise as was shown by the protracted legal battle between these two publications about the right to use pictures of the wedding of Catherine Zeta Jones and Michael Douglas.

NEWS VALUES

Many of these examples imply that questionable journalism arises only out of exploiting the innocent or at least the naive, but there are sins of omission too, and these often raise basic questions about news values. When reporters get wind of stories they don't pursue because of the embarrassment these might cause to their contacts, their government, or even their friends, they are undoubtedly behaving in a questionable way. Stories may lie unpursued because they don't fit the picture of reality that a particular publication supports.

Ian Jack, among many others, is worried, as we have seen. He says 'the craft of what the late Martha Gellhorn called "serious, careful, honest journalism" has entered its own small crisis'. He sees a trend away from reportage towards pages dominated by frivolous journalism with its emphasis on showbusiness and its pathological fear of 'the spectre of the reader's boredom' (Jack 1998: vii). Photographer Christopher Shewen gave a typical example in *New Internationalist*:

> On the same day in May 1998 two things happened. Geri Halliwell quit the Spice Girls and war broke out between Ethiopia and Eritrea. One story got full front-page coverage in Britain, the other a few meagre words buried in the deadground of a couple of broadsheets. The career change of a transient pop star cuts more media ice than half-a-million troops squaring up for the biggest current land war, between two of the poorest countries on earth. This is called the 'cuddliness factor' – spice is cuddly, a major war in Africa is not.
>
> (Shewen 1999)

His criticisms of daily press news values could be made more strongly of a range of magazines except those, like *New Internationalist*, which are devoted to coverage of the poorer countries of the world. You won't read much about social or political issues at home or abroad in the average lifestyle magazine, and for many readers that is the point of reading them; they provide a kind of escape from everyday concerns. Shewen's point, like Jack's, is that the news agenda is being trivialised. Whether you call it the process of 'dumbing down' or the rise of 'infotainment', there is no denying that gossip about celebrities, however minor their names, however speculative the story, does seem to occupy a growing amount of space not just in those magazines devoted to it (*Hello!*, *OK!*) but also in publications that might be expected to carry other items as well, or even instead.

Perhaps celebrity tittle-tattle is more tedious than it is harmful. The *Hello!* approach is usually innocent enough: if you buy the magazine for the story of a footballer's wedding you can probably assume the words and pictures haven't been acquired in an underhand way. Compare this with publications at the rougher end of the trade, where the slightest incident in a star's life (arriving too late to be served at a restaurant in the case of one) is twisted out of all recognition into an account of a sex-crazed couple driving miles through the Scottish night in the hope of buying oysters (Ronson 1999). This kind of story is probably no more than irritating to a star who has grown used to being treated in this way, but it is of no justifiable interest to readers, especially if it isn't even true. Sociologist Todd Gitlin, in an edition of *Brill's Content* devoted to a debate about gossip, cites the more serious case of actress Jean Seberg, who eventually killed herself after a story appeared suggesting the baby she was carrying was not her husband's. It was, in fact, his. She had a breakdown and lost the baby before committing suicide.

An extreme example perhaps. There obviously is space and demand for light stories, but Gitlin argues that the problem lies in the way 'the gluttonous media' is unwilling to draw boundaries. Gossip has been allowed to spill out of demarcated gossip columns: 'With news annexed to the entertainment business, tabloid logic rules, gossip isn't left in its place . . . Gossip displaces news. Gossip unbounded has grown into a national – make that global – game of Trivial Pursuit' (Gitlin 1999). Journalist Pete Hamill agrees, citing the whole 'salacious soap opera' of the Monica Lewinsky story as an example which puts journalists to shame (Hamill 1998: 15). He condemns the way the mass media devote so much time and space to celebrities.

He even identifies a sub-genre as 'necrojournalism – the journalism of dead, or near-dead, celebrities' of which Diana, Princess of Wales is the greatest ever example, with Marilyn Monroe a close second.

In defence of her trade the successful American gossip writer Liz Smith says 'gossip is one of the great luxuries of a democracy. It is the tawdry jewel in the crown of free speech. You don't read gossip columns in dictatorships.' She may be right, but you could not hope for a better example of the pomposity to which Janet Malcolm draws attention. In any case, against Smith I would argue that dictatorships are often founded on, and maintained by, the wide and malicious circulation of half-truths and outright lies. With her other defence – that she's made an enormous amount of money out of gossip and 'it beats being a news reporter by a country mile' – she is surely closer to the truth (Smith 1999).

If too much frivolity in journalism really is a problem, then it is nowhere more so than in the lifestyle magazines created around specific themes as a way of attracting well-defined kinds of readers and 'delivering' them to advertisers. Anyone who wants to work for this kind of magazine should think in advance about the general context within which all her work will be set. A general reporter on a newspaper will cover a range of subjects, which means that even if one causes a frisson of distaste she'll be onto the next story before the day is out. In magazines it's different. The same subject matter, treated in roughly the same way, constantly recurs. Could a radically green environmentalist work for a magazine company most of whose profits derive from adverts for cars? Could someone with strong religious beliefs work for the magazines for women which portray as a norm a way of life they find offensive? Could a feminist bear to work for *Nuts* or a vegetarian for *Poultry International*? Once Martin Daubney became a father, he could no longer work for *Loaded* magazine because of its content.

Equally, anyone who wants to work in consumer lifestyle magazines needs to think through her approach to sexually explicit copy. So explicit is some of what is produced for adolescent teenage girls that publishers have also been forced to discover that although sex sells, it also offends. In 1996, to try to convince the world that they are not as irresponsible as concerned parents and politicians began to suspect, the PPA helped to set up the Teenage Magazine Arbitration Panel (TMAP) as a response to public criticism of the content of magazines like *Sugar* and *Bliss*. The TMAP drew up guidelines for publishers, although there is nothing much to act as a deterrent either in the guidelines or in the sanctions available for the TMAP to use against offending editors (McKay 1999).

If that's not a problem (which for most journalists it wouldn't be), is there a difficulty in working for a publisher whose mainstream magazines aimed at men move beyond the merely erotic into the realms of sado-masochistic cruelty and violence towards women?

Journalists have to earn a living, a fact they remember whenever they're asked to do something they would rather not do, whether it is on grounds of taste or conscience. For most there is no difficulty, or they wouldn't be in the job in the first place, but a problem of conscience is no less acute for being a small, private one rather than a large, public one. It would probably be true to say that many journalists with strong moral convictions of whatever sort aspire to starting their own magazines or to working on magazines published by organisations whose work they support: magazines, that is, which have a purpose beyond encouraging readers to spend their cash.

There are two further aspects of the work of magazine journalists that regularly cause a heart-search, if not anything quite so strong as a moral dilemma. The first is peculiar to the specialist magazine reporter, the second is the more widespread problem of the freebie.

SPECIALIST REPORTING

A specialist reporter is one who concentrates his writing in a particular field (or 'beat', the US term) such as football or the environment, or beauty or crime or pensions. Many magazines are devoted to specialist fields of interest and so there are many journalists on trade papers who spend most of their time writing about a small group of companies or activities, and who therefore get to know a relatively small group of people as contacts or sources of stories and quotes. The potential for conflicts of interest is easy to see. Contacts are useful assistants until the day arrives when the reporter has to write a negative story about the contact's company or organisation. That's when the contact can put pressure on to have a story left out or, at the very least, can decide to offer no help in the future. See Tunstall (1971) for a full discussion of specialist reporting.

FREEBIES

The difficulty raised by the culture of freebies so prevalent in the UK is also one of reciprocity, as I have outlined elsewhere in this book (Chapter 15). It may not always be so crude as an offer of certain goods in exchange for editorial coverage, but it comes close, even if the general effect is more cumulative. A literary editor, say, may look with particular favour on authors from a publishing house that always sends any books requested, even from the back catalogue, and which provides expensive lunches at regular intervals. This probably wouldn't ensure a good review, but it might be enough to ensure that a review appears. Cosmetics companies can't guarantee that a product will be given prominent editorial mention just because they choose to launch it with a three-day, all-expenses-paid trip to Barbados, but such generosity is unlikely to harm the relationship it has with the beauty editors who go along. This kind of exchange may seem innocent enough, but it can easily blur the edges of impartial journalism, as a few British editors have realised. (In some countries the offer of gifts, hospitality or inducements to journalists is simply not acceptable.) On a few publications reporters are not allowed to accept hospitality and their employer pays their way if they review holidays or theatre or opera.

One obvious thing that can make freebies a little (if not very) corrupting, particularly for reporters working in the more glamorous fields such as fashion, music or motor industries, is the discrepancy between their own incomes and those of the people they are surrounded by as part of their job. Anyone who is living on an ordinary reporter's salary is likely to warm to designers who make sure they always have respectably expensive clothes or cars to borrow, or who enable the reporters to eat, drink and travel in ways they could not otherwise afford. In her account of taking up the editorship of *The Lady*, Rachel Johnson expresses her amazement at how there seemed to have been 'a total gravy-train when it comes to travel' on the magazine. Hacks would 'file a slavishly positive piece' after the free travel, hospitality and sightseeing. And, says Johnson, 'I had to run it, in order to fulfil our side of the equation: if your hack has freebie, your paper then is honour-bound to puff her holiday. It's deeply corrupt, but that's how it works', adding that these free trips had been used 'like MPs' expenses – in lieu of income' (Johnson 2011: 47–48). A similar point was made by the anonymous fashion journalist who wrote about the freebie culture she is part of: 'This is our dirty little secret,' she says, describing the stuff she had been sent over the previous fortnight, worth more than £3,000 (handbags, camera, £900 laptop sleeve and so on). 'We supplement our lower-than-you'd-think wages with thousands of pounds worth of free stuff,' she wrote, prompted by the fear that the new Bribery Act might soon put paid to this kind of largesse (quoted in Pugh 2011).

At the time of writing, publishers and editorial staff are waiting to see how far the Bribery Act 2010 might affect this aspect of their work. (Guidance is offered through the PPA website.) The regulatory bodies, curiously, have little to say about the exchange of gifts, the PCC confining itself to guidance for financial journalists who are enjoined not to make private use of information they acquire in confidence as part of their job. Some editorial contracts, though, do tackle this issue. *The Guardian*'s editorial code, for example, notes that any gift worth over £50 should be returned or entered into the staff raffle for charity.

FASHION JOURNALISM

One way in which fashion journalism has increasingly come to the attention of the public is in relation to the use of very thin or very young, possibly unacceptably exploited, models for photoshoots, a problem that stems from the fashion industry, on which the journalists base their material. (See Edwards-Jones and Anonymous, 2006, for a fictionalised account of the fashion world based on extensive immersion reporting and interviewing.) It's not only a question of whether photographic models are being driven unreasonably to keep their weight under control, but also of the effect on readers who are constantly faced with images of impossibly slim women whose shapes may have been tampered with through the miracle of Photoshop software. Fashion magazines don't often ask questions of doubtful practices in the industry and the tendency is simply to go along with what they find and to promote it. However, there is now some recognition that an ethical stance should be taken, at least in relation to models, and so the 19 editors of the various editions of *Vogue* have introduced a Health Initiative through which they pledge 'to be ambassadors for the message of healthy body image' (*Vogue*, UK edition June 2012).

CONCLUSIONS

In this chapter I have tried to show how journalists on magazines may be faced with issues of conscience as they go about their work. Some of these relate to the context in which their writing appears and the editorial concept of the publication for which they work. Others reflect a journalist's individual beliefs and practice. The more spectacular lapses from human decency are more common among hard-news reporters and may sometimes occur without malice, being rather the result of thoughtlessness, mistaken identity, or just the constraints under which journalists work. There are various codes of practice which offer guidance to reporters and these can provide support for journalists, as well as restricting how they operate. It seems to be true, however, that when publications breach guidelines such as the Editors' Code the punishment doesn't reflect the magnitude or the effect of the crime and when journalists breach the guidelines they still seem to keep their jobs. As one agency reporter put it: 'Perhaps the best protection a reporter has if asked to do something really crass by an editor is the knowledge that he can lie to the news-desk just as much as he can lie to the public.' I'm not advocating that reporters lie to their editors, but merely recalling the wisdom of Mrs Do-as-you-would-be-done-by.

The intense competition for readers and the rivalry between journalists perhaps make it inevitable that stories will sometimes be bent or invented. But the more often this happens the less worthy of respect will be magazines and newspapers, television and radio journalism. As Todd Gitlin puts it: 'A press that infantilizes its public forfeits that public's respect, or deserves to' (Gitlin 1999). Whether the fallout from the evidence offered to the Leveson Inquiry will result in a further loss of respect for journalists in the UK or more serious sanctions can only be speculated on at the time of writing.

The reason any of this matters is that good journalism matters. As a society we need reporters to be asking questions on our behalf, to be describing events and situations on our behalf as well, of course, as to be entertaining us. That's why it gives cause for concern to see journalists being so justifiably vilified, often over the reporting of trivia, and at the same time being bound by restrictions (see Chapters 5 and 18) when it comes to reporting the things that really do matter.

RECOMMENDED READING

Allan, S. (2005) (ed.) *Journalism: Critical Issues*.

Baggini, J. (2002) *Making Sense: Philosophy Behind the Headlines*.

Beales, I. (2009) *Editors' Codebook*, 2nd edition.

Bradford, J. (2013, forthcoming) *Fashion Journalism*.

Brill's Content, May 1999 edition.

Chippindale, P. and Horrie, C. (1999) *Stick It Up Your Punter!*

Curran, J. and Seaton, J. (2003) *Power Without Responsibility*, 6th edition.

Davies, N. (2008) *Flat Earth News*.

Duncan, S. and Newton, J. (2010) 'How do you feel? Preparing novice reporters
    for the death knock,' *Journalism Practice*.

Edwards-Jones, I. and Anonymous (2006) *Fashion Babylon*.

Ethical Space: The International Journal of Communication Ethics.

Frost, C. (2011) *Journalism Ethics and Regulation*, 3rd edition.

Frost, C. (2012) 'Publishing ethics' in *Designing for Newspapers and Magazines*,
    2nd edition.

Hamill, P. (1998) *News is a Verb: Journalism at the End of the Twentieth Century*.

Harcup, T. (2007) *The Ethical Journalist*.

Johnson, R. (2011) *A Diary of The Lady: My First Year and a Half as Editor*.

Knightley, P. (2000) *The First Casualty: The War Correspondent as Hero and Myth-
    maker from the Crimea to Kosovo*.

Kovach, B. and Rosenstiel, T. (2003) *The Elements of Journalism: What
    Newspeople Should Know and the Public Should Expect*.

McKay, J. (2012) 'Åsne Seierstad and *The Bookseller of Kabul*', in *Global Literary
    Journalism: Exploring the Journalistic Imagination*.

Malcolm, J. (2004) *The Journalist and the Murderer*.

Marr, A. (2004) *My Trade: A Short History of British Journalism*.

Marsh, D.R. and Hodsdon, A. (2010) *Guardian Style*.

Morrish, J. and Bradshaw, P. (2012) 'Where the buck stops', in *Magazine Editing:
    In Print and Online*.

Pilger, J. (1998) *Hidden Agendas*.

Tunstall, J. (1971) *Journalists at Work*.

Whyte, J. (2003) *Bad Thoughts: A Guide to Clear Thinking*.

Websites

BBC College: www.bbc.co.uk/journalism/ethics-and-values

British Journalism Review: www.bjr.org.uk

Campaign for Press and Broadcasting Freedom: www.cpbf.org.uk

Institute of Communication Ethics: www.communicationethics.net

Leveson Inquiry: www.levesoninquiry.org.uk

MediaGuardian: http://media.guardian.co.uk

The MediaWise Trust: www.mediawise.org.uk

National Union of Journalists: www.nuj.org.uk

Professional Publishers Association (PPA): www.ppa.co.uk/resources/Legal

Press Complaints Commission: www.pcc.org.uk (in a transitional phase as of
    2012)

Teenage Magazine Arbitration Panel: www.ppa.co.uk/tmap

CHAPTER 18

The magazine journalist and the law

Carole Watson with Anthony Richards and Linda Ventry (Scots law)

Journalists who don't have a strong working knowledge of the law as it affects the media pose a real danger to their publications. Just because magazine journalists may not be covering the criminal courts daily or exposing wrongdoing through major investigations, as would be expected of a newspaper reporter, this does not mean they won't face potentially expensive defamation or privacy actions at some point in their careers.

Further, many human-interest features favoured by consumer magazines may require a strong understanding of the criminal and civil courts – for instance, can you fully identify a rape victim who wants to tell her story in a women's monthly glossy? Can you write about a soap star who is facing trial for assault? And what about describing an individual's health issues, such as an eating disorder or a problem with alcohol? How about the divorce of a millionaire footballer?

Knowing the basics of anonymity, libel, copyright and defamation should ensure that alarm bells ring when a writer is researching his story and then writing it up, and will help him avoid running into costly legal problems such as being accused of invasion of privacy or libel.

Subeditors, too, must also know their law. They are the last line of defence in the magazine production process. Any transgressions which get past them may prove costly. Subs must carefully examine every piece of copy with an eye for legal problems and raise queries with writers in any case of doubt.

The writer, in turn, needs to look carefully at the copy once it has been subbed to ensure that the sub has not introduced any errors which were not there originally or changed its meaning while cutting it to length.

Many decisions on questions of law affecting the media (sometimes, whether a story should be published at all if there are doubts about its legal safety) have to be taken hurriedly by senior editorial staff as the magazine nears deadline. A final publish-or-not decision is unlikely to fall to the subeditor or writer alone, but would be referred up through the chief sub to the editor, or even the publisher, sometimes with advice sought from in-house or freelance legal experts.

Magazines have traditionally been produced on paper, and the internet has signalled a revolution. Many magazines now appear online, either as electronic versions of the printed magazine, or as one that is created for the digital world only. But the same basic legal principles apply to material transmitted through the internet, and to the publication of material downloaded from the internet, as apply to material obtained from any other source and published through any other medium.

So which aspects of the law affect magazine journalists? First, let's cover where the law comes from.

SOURCES OF ENGLISH LAW

Statutes (Acts of Parliament) will have passed their various stages through each House of Parliament and received the Royal Assent – nowadays a mere formality. Except for the overriding authority of legislative acts of the European Union and decisions of the European Court, they are of supreme authority and binding on the courts. Statutes may or may not apply to Scotland or Northern Ireland. Some statutes (or some sections of a statute) may not come into effect until an appropriate statutory instrument (see below) has been passed.

Delegated legislation. This is made by a subsidiary body under power delegated in a statute.

- *Statutory Instruments* contain regulations put before Parliament by a government minister.
- *Orders in Council* tend to consist largely of constitutional matters put forward by the Privy Council. Few are likely to affect the work of journalists.
- *By-laws*. Local authorities and certain other bodies have power to make local laws within specific authority.

Laws of the European Union. Membership of the European Union requires UK courts to observe European treaties and decisions of the European Court, and to apply EU legislation (regulations and directives) even if it conflicts with statutes:

- *Regulations* apply generally throughout member states. They are immediately binding.
- *Directives*, too, are binding, but the mode of implementation is left to the member states themselves.

Judicial precedent. Decisions on legal points by judges of the superior courts create precedents which must be followed by inferior courts when dealing with similar cases.

Decisions of the European Court of Human Rights. As a signatory to the European Convention on Human Rights, the UK has for long been bound to give effect to this Court's decisions, which have thus been an indirect source of law. Since the relevant provisions of the Human Rights Act 1998 came into effect in October 2000, the provisions of the Convention have been enforceable in UK courts. Of most interest to journalists are the conflicting Articles 8 (right to privacy) and 10 (right to freedom of expression).

CIVIL AND CRIMINAL LAW

Criminal law is concerned with wrongs against the sovereign: anything from speeding to murder. Civil law is concerned simply with disputes between citizens, perhaps to obtain compensation (called 'damages') for injuries suffered in a road accident, or an order (called an 'injunction') to restrain one person from, for example, assaulting or pestering another or, another common example, to get a divorce.

A person may find himself in trouble with both the civil and criminal law over the same incident. A motorist who causes an accident may be both prosecuted in a criminal court for careless driving and sued for damages in a civil court for any injury which he caused to the other driver.

THE CRIMINAL COURTS

Magistrates' courts

Virtually every criminal case starts life in a magistrates' court, where three types of case are heard.

Summary offences

Cases which must be tried by magistrates. They are generally the least serious.

Either-way offences

Cases which may be tried by magistrates. They may, alternatively, be tried by a jury in the Crown Court. If the accused intends to plead 'not guilty' he may choose that his case is tried by jury. Otherwise it will be tried by the magistrates unless they decline to hear it because of its apparent seriousness. Theft, burglary and indecent assault are three examples of either-way offences.

Where a person appears before magistrates accused of an either-way offence, and is convicted, the magistrates will sentence him unless they feel that he deserves greater punishment than they have power to impose. In that case they will send him to the Crown Court to be sentenced.

Indictable-only offences

These are cases which cannot be tried by magistrates. Because of their seriousness they can be tried only in the Crown Court. Murder, rape and robbery are three examples. Such cases are transferred directly to the Crown Court, the magistrates having no jurisdiction to decide otherwise. Their jurisdiction is limited to questions of bail and legal aid.

Committal proceedings

If the offence is indictable-only, the magistrates, as stated above, must transfer it to the Crown Court, where the accused will come first before a judge in a preliminary hearing.

If it is an either-way offence and the accused has opted for trial by jury (or the magistrates have refused to hear it) the magistrates sit as 'examining justices' to decide whether the prosecution case is strong enough to warrant trial in the Crown Court. They will not hear oral evidence, but will base their decision on written statements by prosecution and defence witnesses, and arguments advanced by lawyers for the two sides.

In some cases (called 'paper committals') the accused will have consented through his lawyers to the case being sent to the Crown Court for trial, and will indicate which of the prosecution witnesses he requires to be present. In such a case the magistrates will not study the witness statements. The prosecution may require some cases to be transferred to the Crown Court. These are cases alleging serious fraud, or sexual or cruelty offences against children.

Appeals

A person who is convicted before magistrates may have his case re-heard by a judge sitting with magistrates in the Crown Court. That court's decision is final on any question of fact. If the Crown Court upholds the conviction, it may impose any sentence which the magistrates could have imposed.

If the accused wishes to argue that he was wrongly convicted by the magistrates in law (that is, he does not dispute the facts but argues that, on those facts, he was not guilty of the offence charged) he can appeal to the High Court (the Queen's Bench Divisional Court) 'by way of case stated'. The magistrates set out in a 'stated case' the facts of the case and how they applied the law.

This procedure is open to the prosecution as well as the defence. So a person who has been acquitted by magistrates on a legal point may later be convicted by decision of the High Court. If the legal point is one of general public importance either party may, if leave is granted, take the case to the Supreme Court (formerly to the House of Lords).

Magistrates

Most benches of magistrates, when trying a case, consist of at least two (more commonly three) magistrates. Most are not legally qualified, and are unpaid except for travel and subsistence. They are advised on legal points by a legal adviser. Some courts, especially in large cities, are presided over by district judges (previously called stipendiary magistrates). These are experienced barristers or solicitors who sit as professional magistrates. They are paid a salary and sit alone to try cases.

The Crown Court

The main Crown Courts such as Old Bailey in London and in most major towns and cities across England and Wales try the most serious cases, such as murder, before the more senior judges (usually High Court judges). Others, presided over by circuit judges, recorders or assistant recorders, try lesser offences. The cases will have been committed to the Crown Court by magistrates' courts.

If the accused pleads not guilty he will be tried by a jury. If he pleads not guilty to some counts but guilty to others, a reporter must make no reference to the pleas of guilty while the trial on the other charges is proceeding. As in the magistrates' court, the accused cannot be found guilty unless the prosecution proves him to be so, beyond reasonable doubt. It will call witnesses, each of whom will be examined in chief (the prosecution 'counsel', or barrister, will ask them questions aimed at proving the guilt of the accused). The witnesses can then be cross-examined – counsel for the defence (or a suitably qualified solicitor) will put questions aimed at shaking the credibility of the witnesses' evidence. Finally they may be re-examined – prosecuting counsel will put questions to deal with points raised in the cross-examination. The defence witnesses will be similarly questioned. Then the respective lawyers will address the jury, and finally the judge will give his 'summing up' of the case. He will explain the functions of judge and jury, the relevant law and what has to be proved. He must always explain that it is for the prosecution to prove its case and that proof must be beyond all reasonable doubt. If the jury cannot reach a unanimous verdict then a majority verdict, with no more than two dissentients, may be accepted.

If the accused is found guilty the judge will proceed to sentence.

Appeals

A person convicted in the Crown Court may appeal against his conviction or sentence, or both, to the Court of Appeal (Criminal Division). His appeal will be heard by three senior judges. On an important legal point either the prosecution or the defence may, if leave is granted, appeal to the Supreme Court (formerly to the House of Lords).

THE MAIN DIFFERENCES BETWEEN ENGLISH AND SCOTS LAW

The civil courts

In Scots civil actions, for 'claimant' read 'pursuer' and for 'defendant' read 'defender'.

Scotland is divided into six sheriffdoms, each of which is further divided into sheriff court districts. Each sheriff court district has its own sheriff court – roughly the equivalent of a county court. An appeal from a sheriff court lies to the 'sheriff principal' (though for certain small claims, appeal lies only on a point of law) and beyond that to the Inner House of the Court of Session – and ultimately, with leave, to the Supreme Court of the United Kingdom.

A major civil action will come before the Outer House of the Court of Session and will be heard by a Lord Ordinary. The Inner House of the Court of Session hears appeals against decisions of the Lord Ordinary, and also against those of inferior courts. The Inner House has two Divisions – the First presided over by the Lord President, and the Second presided over by the Lord Justice Clerk. (A Lord Ordinary may seek the guidance of the Inner House before deciding a case.)

In defamation, Scotland draws no distinction between libel and slander. Scots law draws much from Roman law rather than from the English common law. Roman law looked to injury to the feelings rather than to the reputation, and Scots courts will take account of convicium (invective or abuse), especially when deciding questions of malice. However, for the pursuer there are strict rules of pleading, especially when an innuendo is relied upon.

The criminal courts

Scotland's approximate equivalents of the magistrates' courts are the Justice of the Peace courts. As in England and Wales, these may be staffed by lay or professional magistrates. The sheriff courts (see above as to their civil jurisdiction) deal with crimes of a more serious nature, while the most serious offences are tried by the High Court of Justiciary. (Note that whereas the High Court in England and Wales is the highest first-instance civil court, the High Court in Scotland is the highest criminal court.) The High Court is presided over by judges of the Court of

Session. Unlike in civil courts, there is no appeal to the Supreme Court of the United Kingdom.

Children who are adjudged to require 'protection, guidance, treatment or control' (and this includes offenders) are referred to a Children's Panel, to be arranged by a local officer called a 'Reporter'. Only by leave of the Lord Advocate (roughly the Scots equivalent of the Attorney-General) may court proceedings be instituted against children – and only in the Sheriff Court or the High Court.

The Procurator Fiscal is a public officer, similar in many respects to a District Attorney in the US. He directs the inquiry into an alleged offence, and also decides whether to prosecute, and, if so, what mode of procedure to adopt. He may choose either the solemn procedure or the summary procedure, depending on the gravity of the alleged offence.

In the solemn procedure, carrying more severe maximum penalties, the trial is before a judge and a jury of 15, the verdict being by a simple majority. The summary procedure involves a hearing before a judge alone.

Fatal accident inquiries

Fatal accident inquiries (FAIs) are roughly the equivalent of English inquests. Such an inquiry may be held if it appears that a death may have been sudden, suspicious or unexplained, or if the circumstances give rise to serious public concern.

CIVIL COURTS IN ENGLAND AND WALES

Magistrates' courts

Magistrates exercise civil jurisdiction in hearing matrimonial and allied cases in the Family Proceedings Court – separations of spouses, custody and maintenance, and paternity orders against men for the support of children whom they have fathered.

County courts

Most county court cases involve claims for money owed or for damages for injury resulting from civil wrongs, usually road or industrial accidents. Whether such cases are tried in the county court or the High Court will depend usually on the amount of money likely to be involved, but sometimes on the complexity of the case.

All divorce petitions are issued in county courts. Most are undefended. Defended cases may be transferred to the High Court.

County courts deal also with property and tenancy disputes, equity cases (trust funds, for example) and, within financial limits, wills and intestacies. Some have jurisdiction in bankruptcy. County court actions for relatively small sums are usually heard in arbitration, a more informal procedure, in private, where costs are not normally awarded. Larger county court cases will be heard by a circuit judge, others (mostly in private) by a district judge.

The High Court

The High Court consists of three divisions whose jurisdiction is, to a great extent, similar to that of the county courts, but on a larger scale. Some areas of jurisdiction are, however, exclusive to the High Court.

The **Queen's Bench Division** has unlimited jurisdiction in contract and for civil wrongs, often awarding huge damages in cases such as medical negligence and libel. It also exercises a general supervisory jurisdiction over other courts and tribunals and it deals with cases of contempt of court, usually referred by the Attorney General, arising from media reports of court proceedings.

The **Chancery Division** deals in the main with cases not involving money damages – those dealing with property rights, tax law, probate, trust funds, intellectual property, business associations and non-pecuniary remedies such as injunctions. This is, in many cases, to prevent publication in cases involving allegedly confidential information.

The **Family Division** hears some defended divorce petitions, though these nowadays are rare. Since the Family Law Act 1996 much time is devoted to questions arising from that Act in relation to mediation before divorce, parental responsibility, custody and maintenance, and domestic violence. Much of the business is in chambers (that is, in private) but a judge may sit in open court to give his ruling on a point of law, or to seek the co-operation of the press and broadcasters to help to trace a child who has been snatched in a 'tug of love'. This division also hears appeals against decisions by magistrates in family proceedings courts.

Appeals

An unsuccessful party in the county court or the High Court may appeal to the Court of Appeal (Civil Division). From there the unsuccessful party may, if leave is granted, appeal on a legal point to the Supreme Court.

Coroners' courts

Nearly all cases in these courts are inquiries into deaths where there may be some doubt as to whether the cause was natural. The inquest is held to determine the identity of the deceased, and how, where and when he died. If it can be shown that the inquest was not fairly conducted, a High Court order can be obtained – on a 'judicial review' – to quash the verdict and arrange a fresh inquest before a different coroner. Inquests are also held, rarely, to decide whether ancient gold or silver, which has been buried or hidden, is to be classified as 'treasure' and therefore belongs to the Crown.

Tribunals

Numerous tribunals decide various rights to benefits, etc. The tribunals most commonly covered by journalists are employment tribunals which deal with, among other matters, cases of unfair dismissal, redundancy and discrimination at work on grounds of race or sex.

Admission to courts

All courts must admit the public unless they have power to exclude them. A court cannot exclude the press and public simply because it thinks that the case before it should not be published, or to spare a person embarrassment. (However, a court may exclude the public, but not the press, when a child is giving evidence in a sex case.)

Members of a court cannot hide their identities from the public. However, any court may exclude both public and press if it considers that justice cannot otherwise be served, or if it has power by statute to exclude the public – for instance, a criminal court trying a case under the Official Secrets Acts, or where a witness might be intimidated. In the latter case, one journalist, representing himself and his colleagues, must be admitted.

In youth courts the press, but not the public, have a right of admission.

In family proceedings the press have a right of admission, but may be excluded during the taking of indecent evidence or when the court is exercising powers under the Children Act 1989 in relation to a child or young person.

Rules of court permit sittings in private, for example when dealing with patents, welfare of children, certain nullity of marriage cases and cases involving persons of unsound mind.

Admission rights to various kinds of tribunal vary. One must look at the appropriate procedural rules for a given tribunal in order to ascertain admission rights. Coroners may exclude the public only for reasons of national security.

The above are examples of where a court may sit *in camera* (that is, in private). Where proceedings are ancillary to a case they may be held in chambers – for instance, preliminary procedural matters relating to a civil action, or such matters as maintenance and custody concerning a divorce. Wardships and bail appeals are also commonly heard in chambers.

Article 6 of the European Convention on Human Rights authorises exclusion of the public and press 'in the interests of morals, public order or national security' in order to protect juveniles, privacy or the interests of justice.

LIBEL

A libel action can be cripplingly expensive and the outcome wildly uncertain. With the introduction of conditional fee agreements (no win, no fee) in 1998, the opportunity of suing for libel, formerly the domain of the very rich, became open to the everyman (and woman) in the street.

Awards of damages can be unpredictable (although a change in the law in 1990 means the Court of Appeal can now lower damages deemed excessive) and the legal costs of libel cases are always enormous. The losing side usually has to pay them, but rarely will the successful party recover all its costs, so a magazine will almost invariably lose out financially even if it wins its case.

Juries' verdicts, too, are unpredictable. Much may depend on how the jury construes the disputed words. The list of unpleasant things which you might write about a person is endless, but implying immorality, dishonesty or financial difficulties are the most common ones that give rise to libel actions.

Mistake is no defence

It is no defence to plead that the defamatory words were published by mistake. The law is concerned with what was in fact published and the meaning which it might convey to a reader, not with what the journalist intended to publish or the meaning which he intended to convey. Nor is it a defence that you are reporting a mere rumour, even if you say that it is untrue: a racing correspondent reported an allegation by punters that a jockey had 'thrown' a race in collusion with bookmakers, adding that the allegation was untrue; nevertheless, damages were awarded.

Innuendos and inferences

Double meanings can be very costly. Often the 'other meaning' can arise through circumstances unknown to the journalist but known to other people. In 1928 the *Daily Mirror* published a picture and caption of a couple who had just announced their 'engagement'. Unknown to the newspaper and the 'fiancée', the man was already married. His wife was awarded damages. In order to marry lawfully, he could not be married already. So people who knew that he and she had lived together would conclude that they must have been cohabiting outside wedlock.

An inference is a meaning which anyone could draw, even without any special knowledge. An example is a case in 1945, when a newspaper reported that a bomb-damaged house belonging to a councillor had been repaired by the local council to a better standard than the house next door, which had been equally damaged but whose owner was not a councillor. This was factually correct, but the newspaper could not prove the likely inference – that the councillor had pulled strings to secure preferential treatment for himself.

Tests for libel

Judges have evolved four tests for deciding whether words are capable of being defamatory, asking whether they tend to do any of the following:

1   Lower the claimant in the estimation of right-thinking members of society generally. Here lies the beauty of trial by jury – jurors are drawn from various walks of life.

2   Expose him to hatred, contempt or ridicule. Many obviously damaging statements will tend to give rise to hatred or contempt. Satirical writers and cartoonists make a living from lampooning prominent people, but good-natured ribbing is one thing; imputing misconduct is quite another.

3   Disparage him in his office, profession, trade or calling. Anything which suggests that a person is incompetent at his job, or has behaved in a manner unbefitting his profession or calling, comes under this heading. When a critic 'pans' an actor's performance, or a sports writer 'slags off' a footballer, clearly the person criticised is disparaged in his profession. If sued, the magazine would almost certainly use 'honest comment' as its defence. Note, however, that merely to state incorrectly that a person has ceased to carry on his profession, perhaps through retirement, does not disparage him in it, even if it may cause him financial loss. It may, however, give rise to malicious falsehood (see p. 303).

4   Cause others to shun or avoid the claimant. If a hypothetical reasonable person would be less inclined to associate with him after reading the words in dispute, this test is satisfied.

'Referring' to the claimant

Defamation is concerned with damage to a person's reputation – that is, what other people think of him. The words of which he complains must therefore be reasonably capable of being understood (if by only a few people or perhaps by only one) to refer to him, or to a small group (for example, a board of directors) to which he belongs. To publish, for instance, that 'all lawyers are thieves' would not enable any lawyer to sue the publication for libel unless there were something in the story which pointed towards him.

When cruel practices in 'a certain factory in the south of Ireland' were alleged it was held that sufficient clues had been included to enable a reader, familiar with southern Ireland, to glean which factory was referred to. And when a woman was stated to have been raped 'by Banbury CID', all ten male officers in Banbury CID recovered damages.

You cannot libel a local authority, but a disparaging story about a council may well reflect on identifiable members or officers.

Referring with insufficient particularity to an offender – 'Harold Newstead, 30-year-old Camberwell man' – was an invitation to all the other Harold Newsteads in Camberwell who were aged about 30 to sue the *Daily Express* for libel. One did!

A work of fiction is usually obviously fictitious, so the portrayal of a 'baddy' in such a work should not normally entail a risk of libel of a namesake. But there have been cases where the character and the namesake have had so much in common that libel proceedings have been threatened, even though the similarity was unintentional. The relevance here for magazines is that they may buy serialisation rights from authors of fiction.

Publication

The defamatory words must have been communicated to at least one person other than the claimant. In media cases there can be no difficulty in proving publication, but some points must be borne in mind.

Every repetition is a fresh publication. Where a story appears in several different publications – as when it is supplied by a press agency – each of those publications can be sued, as can the agency.

There is a common misconception that once a story has been broken it somehow becomes common property and is therefore fair game for everyone. So, for example, if a story is published saying that a politician has been having an affair with a prostitute, the fact that the politician does not appear to have taken or threatened any action against the publication which broke the story does not mean the story is true or safe to publish. He may be wary of taking on a powerful national newspaper because he knows that he would have a costly fight on his hands. However, he may more readily sue a smaller publication because he knows that the high costs of fighting a libel action might persuade the publishers, or their insurers, to settle out of court.

There is a one-year limitation period. A claimant for libel must commence his action within one year of publication, though the court may, in exceptional circumstances, extend this period. So, although a defamatory story may have escaped through lapse of time, a journalist must be careful not to repeat the allegation, otherwise the 12-month period will begin again.

Defences

If the claimant proves that defamatory words referring to him have been published, he is entitled to succeed unless the publication can make good one of the following defences.

Justification

Except where the Rehabilitation of Offenders Act 1974 (see below) applies, it is a complete defence to prove that the words are true. But they must be proved true, on the balance of probabilities, in both substance and fact. A story alleged that a solicitor had trapped a girl 'for sex', when he slapped her bottom but did not have intercourse. The story was true in substance (that he was a lecherous man) but not in fact. Conversely, in the above-mentioned story that alleged that a councillor's house had been repaired by the council to a better standard than his neighbour's, the allegation was true in fact (this was not disputed) but not true in substance, because it implied that the councillor had misused his position on the council.

The publication must prove the truth of any inference created by the words in question (as in the above example) and also any innuendo. We have seen how the *Daily Mirror* reported that a couple had announced their 'engagement'. This was true. But the newspaper could not prove the innuendo: that the woman with whom the man had until recently been living could not be his wife.

The full 'sting' of the words must be proved. Thus, it is dangerous to call a person a 'thief' on the basis of only one conviction for theft. 'Thief' implies that he steals habitually.

If a story consists of more than one allegation and not all are proved to be true, the defence of justification will not fail if, in view of the most serious one which is proved, no real harm is done by the others.

In pleading justification the magazine bears the burden of proof. If the defence depends on the evidence of a star witness, what happens if that witness dies before the case comes to trial? A journalist should always preserve carefully his notebooks and other evidence. But what happens if important exhibits become lost, or the judge rules them to be inadmissible?

The claimant in a libel action is often a celebrity. He or she may captivate the jury, who may regard the press as intrusive and scandal-mongering. Where justification is pleaded unsuccessfully, damages are likely to be all the heavier.

If the publication has disclosed a previous criminal conviction that is now 'spent', the defence of justification will fail if it is shown that the claimant's criminal past was unearthed with malice. The Rehabilitation of Offenders Act 1974 sets out a table of periods after which convictions become 'spent' and cannot be reported.

The main ones are:

- where the offender was fined – five years;
- imprisonment for not more than six months – seven years;
- imprisonment for more than six but not more than 30 months – ten years.

Note that a jail sentence of two and a half years or more, whether immediate or suspended, is never 'spent'.

Privilege

The law accepts that there are occasions when journalists, in reporting matters on which the public have a right to be informed, need protection, provided that they produce fair and accurate reports. One such occasion is in reporting proceedings in courts of any kind in the UK, or in the European Court of Justice or the European Court of Human Rights. Here, the protection is absolute privilege. If the report is fair (not one-sided), accurate and published contemporaneously, there is total protection, regardless of any question of malice. 'Contemporaneously' means as soon as practicable. In the case of, for instance, a monthly magazine, publication may be 'contemporaneous' even though it takes place several weeks later.

If not published contemporaneously the protection is qualified privilege (that is, it is protected if it is fair and accurate and not shown to have been published with malice). Qualified privilege protects also reports of various other kinds of press conferences, gatherings and official statements. These include:

- parliamentary proceedings and parliamentary papers (documents published by order of either House of Parliament, and reports to Parliament);
- proceedings of local councils and their committees, if heard in public;
- tribunals and inquiries, if heard in public;
- public meetings such as bona fide gatherings, lawfully held, to discuss matters of public concern, such as election meetings and residents' association meetings;
- statements for public information by certain official bodies, including local authorities and the police;
- general meetings of public companies;
- findings and orders of bodies regulating professions, such as the General Medical Council, and sport, such as the Football Association.

In all of the above examples (except parliamentary proceedings and papers) the publisher will lose his protection if he does not publish, at the request of a person who has been criticised, a reasonable letter or statement by way of explanation or contradiction, or if he does so in an inadequate manner. Note, though, that this is not an apology. If the story was fair and accurate there is nothing for which to apologise.

The Defamation Act 1996, which provides the above protection, also sets out various kinds of report where no such letter or statement needs to be published. These include fair and accurate reports of proceedings of courts outside the UK, notices issued for public information by judges and court officers anywhere in the world (for example, receiving orders in bankruptcy, and company windings-up) and information from public registries (for example, companies, and births, deaths and marriages).

There is a privilege at common law if the publisher and all the readers have a common interest in the subject matter. If, as in most cases, it is possible for a publication to be read by someone who does not have such an interest, the defence will fail.

The defence of qualified privilege at common law was extended by the House of Lords when a newspaper published allegations against a former head of state of a European country. The House held that qualified privilege at common law could arise in respect of political information where there was a reciprocal duty to publish and receive the information, but dependent on the steps taken to verify the story, the urgency of the matter, the source, and the circumstances of publication, including the timing. The defence did not succeed in this case, but was later used successfully by a newspaper in Leeds. When the MP George Galloway sued the *Daily Telegraph* in 2004 over allegations that he had received money from Saddam Hussein, the defence failed. The judge said that the newspaper did not give Mr Galloway a reasonable chance to respond to the allegations.

Honest comment

Comment appearing in magazines includes editorial columns, writers' columns, reviews of plays, books, sports reports, tests on motor vehicles, and readers' letters. A comment differs from a statement of fact in that a comment cannot be proved to be 'right' or 'wrong'. A reader is able merely to agree or disagree with it.

The law protects the free expression of opinion if it is honestly held and expressed without malice on a matter of public interest.

Spending of public money and provision of public services are essentially matters of public interest. Opinions differ as to whether this extends to the moral indiscretions of public figures, but expressed judicial opinion is that such matters are of 'public interest' if they reflect on the person's suitability to remain in office. But the facts on which the comment is based must be true or privileged. It is not sufficient that the writer believed the facts to be true. A 'privileged' fact would be, for example, a jury's verdict or the findings of an official inquiry.

Editors must be careful when publishing criticisms of a person's actions or words to avoid any suggestion that he had an improper motive for making or speaking them. Damages were awarded when a TV commentator suggested that a referee's decision to send a player off during a Wembley Cup Final was prompted by a desire to get his own name into the Football Association record books.

Malice, in the contexts of both honest comment and qualified privilege, means any deviation from the objective, or any ulterior motive. If an editor wanted a textbook reviewed it would be unwise to give the task to someone who had himself written a book on the same subject.

A criticism may be in harsh terms, although the use of invective or immoderate language may provide evidence of malice, as when critic Nina Myskow wrote of the singer Charlotte Cornwell: 'She can't sing and her bum's too big'. Ms Cornwell was awarded £11,500 damages after the court heard there had been previous bad feeling between the two. (Note that it is permissible to quote the defamatory allegation in a subsequent report of the case, as this is.)

Consent to publication

There is a general legal rule that he who consents to a wrong cannot afterwards complain about it. If a married MP calls a press conference to deny a rumour that he has a secret homosexual lover, he obviously consents to publication of the rumour together with his denial of it. If a damaging allegation is to be published – for example, against a company – it is important to ensure that any consent to publication comes from a person who has authority to speak on the company's behalf.

It is important that there is a categorical consent. A mere 'no comment' will not suffice.

Offer of amends

The Defamation Act 1996 provides that a publisher may make an offer to publish, in an appropriate position, a suitable correction and apology, to pay the complainant's costs and, possibly, to pay a suitable sum by way of damages. If the offer is not accepted the publisher may rely on it as his defence and it will succeed if the court considers that it was adequate. If he does so, he will not be allowed to put forward any other defence. The defence is not available if the publisher knew or believed the words to be defamatory of the claimant and to refer to him.

Corrections and apologies

Here the magazine must tread carefully between being too profuse or inadequate. The correction should remove the full sting of the libel, but do no more. It is easy to escape from one libel and perpetrate another.

Unless published with the consent of the complainant, a correction will not absolve the publication from action for libel, and may well give the complainant more ammunition. It is always best to seek professional legal advice first.

Slander

Defamatory words published in any medium, including radio and TV as well as newspapers and magazines, will give rise to libel, not slander. Slander concerns transitory (usually spoken) words. However, a journalist needs to take care how he phrases his questions, and to whom he addresses them, when investigating a person's alleged misconduct. Otherwise the subject of his investigation could sue for slander.

Malicious falsehood

Much rarer than libel, this consists of an untrue, albeit not defamatory, story of a kind likely to cause financial loss (for example, that a business is to close down). Publication will be deemed to be 'malicious' if the reporter does not check it out before publication.

Contempt of court

A person who is involved in a court case, whether criminal or civil, is entitled to expect that its outcome will not be influenced by prejudicial media stories. When writing about crimes in respect of which court proceedings are in progress, or may shortly be, journalists can be at risk of publishing material which may influence the outcome of a trial. The Attorney General, who in practice institutes virtually all proceedings for this kind of contempt, is concerned to ensure that accused persons who may appear before juries are tried on the basis of the evidence in court, and not on reporters' speculative stories.

Liability for contempt in criminal cases starts when a person is arrested, when a warrant is issued for his arrest, when a summons is issued, or when he is orally charged. At this point proceedings become 'active' under the Contempt of Court Act 1981. Publication after this time of material which creates a 'substantial risk' that court proceedings may be seriously impeded or prejudiced can result in a heavy fine or, rarely, imprisonment. Your intention, as a journalist, in carrying the story is irrelevant, though you have a defence if you can show that, having taken all reasonable care, you had no reason to believe that proceedings were 'active'.

A description, or picture, of the accused in a criminal case may amount to a contempt if a question of identification may arise. Eyewitness quotes may similarly cause a risk of prejudice.

The risk applies until the accused is acquitted or, if he is convicted, until he is sentenced. However, once a jury has given its verdict it is most unlikely that a background story would be likely to influence the judge when passing sentence. When the accused has been sentenced proceedings cease to be active until he lodges notice of appeal, if he does so. But again, as an appeal from the Crown Court will be heard by experienced judges in the Court of Appeal, there can be little risk of serious prejudice here.

Criminal proceedings will also cease to be 'active' if an arrested person is released without charge (but not if he is released on police bail); if the person named in a warrant is not arrested within 12 months; if a charge is ordered not to be proceeded with; if the accused is found to be unfit to plead or to be tried; or if he dies.

It is rare for contempt to arise in respect of civil proceedings, since most civil cases are tried before a judge sitting alone, and the risk of prejudice is therefore minimal. Furthermore, the liberty of the subject is not at stake.

Civil proceedings become 'active' when an action is set down for trial (in the High Court) or a date fixed for the trial (in the county court). They continue to be 'active' until the case is over, or until it is withdrawn or abandoned.

It is not a contempt under the 1981 Act to discuss in good faith a matter of public interest which figures in 'active' proceedings, whether civil or criminal, if the risk of impediment or prejudice to those proceedings is merely incidental to the discussion. There was no contempt in publishing an interview with a woman who was contesting a parliamentary by-election as a pro-life candidate at a time when a doctor was on trial for the alleged 'mercy killing' of a Down's syndrome baby.

Contempt at common law

Even if proceedings, civil or criminal, are not 'active', it is possible to be in contempt of court by publishing a highly prejudicial story with intent to prejudice court proceedings – as when *The Sun* described a doctor as a 'real swine' at a time when the newspaper knew that he was likely soon to be arrested on a charge of rape.

The press frequently criticises court decisions, judges and magistrates, sometimes in harsh terms. A judge once said that justice 'is not a cloistered virtue' and the public have a right to make their comments. You will, however, be in contempt at common law by 'scandalising the court' if you undermine the court's authority, dignity, integrity or impartiality.

RESTRICTIONS ON COURT REPORTING

1925   It became unlawful to take photographs in court for publication, or to take or publish pictures of persons involved in court cases while in the ill-defined 'precincts of the court'.

1926   It was made illegal to publish evidence from a divorce case. One may name the parties and witnesses, report allegations and so on, in respect of which evidence has been given. One may also report points of law and their outcome, and the decision of the court and any observations made in giving it. The same Act made it an offence to publish, in a report of court proceedings, any indecent medical, surgical or physiological details such as might injure public morals.

1933   Special courts (now called youth courts) were set up to deal with cases involving youngsters. The age range now is 10–18. A report from a youth court must not include a juvenile's name, address, school or any other particulars which might identify him, or any still or moving picture of, or including, him. This applies regardless of the capacity in which he appears before the court – even if, for instance, he is a witness. The restrictions can be lifted in the following circumstances:

- By the court or the Home Secretary, in order to avoid injustice to the juvenile concerned.

- In the public interest; for example, if the juvenile is a persistent offender against whom the public should be warned. In such a case the press may submit a request to the magistrates, who must give each side a chance to be heard before making a decision.

- On an application by the Director of Public Prosecutions, if the juvenile is on the run and has been charged with, or convicted of, a sexual or violent offence, or one which, for an adult, carries a sentence of 14 years or more of imprisonment.

1967 Parliament decided that evidence from committal proceedings should not be published, as it might influence jurors who sit at the subsequent trial. The restriction was re-enacted in the Magistrates' Courts Act 1980. Oral evidence is no longer given in these proceedings, but it is unlawful, unless reporting restrictions are lifted, to report anything that is said, or anything else except the names of the court, the magistrates and the lawyers; the names, ages, occupations and addresses of the parties and witnesses; the charge(s) on which the accused appears; the decision to commit him for trial, to which court and on what charge(s); any adjournment; whether he gets legal aid; any arrangements for bail (but not the reasons for refusing it); and whether an application was made for the lifting of restrictions.

The restrictions apply from the first appearance in court of the accused. They will be lifted if he so requests. If he has a co-accused who objects to the lifting, then lifting restrictions may be done only if the magistrates are satisfied that it is in the interests of justice.

1976 It became an offence to identify the alleged victim of a rape offence – such offences now being rape, attempted rape, aiding and abetting, counselling or procuring rape or attempted rape, incitement to rape, conspiracy to rape and burglary with intent to rape.

Once a complaint of a sexual offence is made it is an offence to publish the alleged victim's name, address, identity of school or workplace or a still or moving picture. When an accusation of such an offence is made it is unlawful to publish anything which might enable a member of the public to identify the alleged victim.

The Sexual Offences (Amendment) Act 1992 made similar provision in respect of a long list of other sexual offences, the most frequent being indecent assault and unlawful intercourse. The complainant (that is, the alleged victim) may be female or male. He or she may be identified:

- if the court permits it for the bringing forward of defence witnesses;
- if the court considers that the restriction is a substantial and unreasonable curb on reporting the case and it is in the public interest to lift it;

- if the complainant (only if aged 16 or over) consents in writing to being identified, unless the consent was obtained by pestering him or her;
- if the complainant dies;
- if the complaint of rape is mentioned in criminal proceedings for a non-rape offence, for example if the complainant is charged with wasting police time by making a false allegation of rape.

The restrictions apply, however, to reports of civil proceedings which involve an accusation of a rape offence – for example, where a rape victim sues the alleged rapist.

1980 The restrictions on reporting of committal proceedings (see above) were re-enacted. Reporting of Family Proceedings in magistrates' courts was restricted to the same basic points which apply to reports of divorce.

1989 It became an offence under the Children Act 1989 section 97 to identify a child appearing in a family court in proceedings under that Act, unless the court otherwise directs.

Powers of courts to restrict reports

Juveniles

We have seen that a juvenile appearing before a youth court may not be identified. If he appears in any other court he may be identified unless the court makes an order (a 'section 39' order under the Children and Young Persons Act 1933) which imposes restrictions in similar terms to those of the automatic ban in the youth court. Such an order can be only in respect of a juvenile and the juvenile must be alive. Such orders should not be made automatically and can relate only to proceedings in the court in which they are made.

If a person's identity is protected, whether by a court order or by a statute, a journalist must be careful to avoid 'jigsaw' identification – that is, identification made possible by the clues in the journalist's own story, or by reading that story in conjunction with a story in another magazine or newspaper. When reporting cases where the defendant is accused of an offence against a child who is a relative, journalists have been advised to name the accused but blur the nature of their relationship with the child. Many publications still seem, however, to prefer to report the case anonymously, stating (incorrectly) that the accused 'cannot be named for legal reasons'.

'No names'

A court may, under section 11 of the Contempt of Court Act 1981, prohibit the publication of any 'name or other matter' appearing in a case, most often used in cases of blackmail or those involving state secrets and national security. But such an order cannot be made unless the 'name or other matter' has been held from the public during the proceedings. The High Court has held that such an order should not be used for suppressing details of an accused person in a criminal case.

Postponement

A court may direct that all, or part, of a case before it shall not be reported until some specified future time, if it considers that publication immediately may prejudice the case in question, or any other connected case which is being heard or shortly to be tried. The High Court has ruled that such an order must be no more draconian than necessary.

Where the defence, in a speech in mitigation of sentence, attacks the character of a person not involved in the case, the court may prohibit for 12 months reporting of the allegation if it was not made during the hearing. Such an order may also apply to a speech on behalf of a defendant when magistrates are considering whether or not to commit him to the Crown Court for sentence.

Gathering of information

Until very recently, except in certain limited instances, there has been no legal obligation on public bodies, or indeed on anyone, to give information to the press. The Freedom of Information Act 2000, which came into force on 1 January 2005, gives a right to information. It applies to legislatures in London, Cardiff and Belfast, government departments, health-care bodies, the police and educational bodies.

Scotland has its own Freedom of Information Act which also came into force on 1 January 2005 and is also enforced by a Commissioner.

However, traditions die hard, and the authorities can make use of several loopholes. They can, for example, say that the information is available from another source (section 21); that it is a certified security matter (section 23); that it relates to court proceedings or has been created by a court (section 32); or that it relates to the privileges of either House of Parliament as certified by the Speaker (Commons) or the Clerk of the Parliaments (Lords) (section 34).

Other exemptions include information which would prejudice the prevention or detection of crime; investigations by a wide range of public safety authorities, including the Railway Inspectorate, the Civil Aviation Authority, and local government officers such as trading standards and environmental health officers; or if disclosure of the information would be likely to prejudice the effective conduct of public affairs. It is no doubt on this last ground that most of the rejections of requests will be made.

A person who is dissatisfied with the way his request for information is treated may apply for a ruling by the Information Commissioner or his Scottish equivalent.

A major snag is that the request and the reply must be in writing. This would serve a journalist who is seeking information for a feature to be published in a week or two, but would be of no help to a reporter who is seeking a quote for a story when his publication is about to go to bed. Some authorities may accept communication by fax or email as 'in writing', but others are likely to treat this as an easy way to delay public disclosure of matters they would rather suppress by insisting on using the post. Bodies which don't wish to divulge information are wont to give as a reason that it is protected under the Data Protection Act 1998. In many cases this may be so. In others, however, the information may be freely accessible without reference to any data storage system and the Act is being used as an excuse. The Freedom of Information Act and the Data Protection Act are now both enforced by the Information Commissioner.

Another legal pitfall in the course of obtaining information could turn out to be the Bribery Act of 2010. This makes it a crime (punishable by up to ten years in jail and/or an unlimited fine), to offer a bribe (money or otherwise) for information, particularly to public officials. Whether this would include accepting or offering 'freebies' is as yet untested in court with this new legislation, but note that there is no public interest defence. (For the prevalence of 'freebie' culture in consumer journalism, see Chapter 17.)

So far this chapter has concentrated on the legal restrictions that affect a reporter's work. For a full account of the formal and informal climate of secrecy that prevents journalists from doing their job properly, see Heather Brooke's (2010) informative book *The Silent State*, especially chapters 6 and 7.

COPYRIGHT

Print journalists will be concerned with 'literary and artistic' works. Editorial copy counts as 'literary'. Even compilations such as football league fixture lists come under this heading. 'Artistic' works include photographs, sketches, cartoons and graphics. Copyright lasts for 70 years from the end of the year of the author's death. If the author is not ascertainable, or if the copyright belongs to a corporation (as in the case of most newspaper and magazine articles), copyright runs for 70 years from the end of the year of publication.

A person will infringe copyright if he copies or reproduces a copyright work in any form. A journalist who 'lifts' a story from another publication will no doubt 'rejig' it in the hope of disguising his misdemeanour. He may fail, however, if the original story contains an error that the rewritten version repeats. And, in any event, one can usually recognise one's own story, whatever efforts have been made to disguise it. Don't confuse 'lifting' with 'follow-up'. You can always follow up a rival's story, unearthing your own material. A judge once said that there is no copyright in news, but there may be a copyright in the way in which it is presented.

Ownership of copyright

Copyright in a work belongs to its creator, unless it was produced in the course of an employment. In that event, copyright will belong to the employer unless the author's contract provides otherwise. Where, however, the author of the work is a freelance, he owns the copyright unless he assigns it to the publisher. The writer of a letter to the editor implicitly authorises the publication to which he sends it to publish his letter on one occasion only. Many publications reserve the right to shorten letters. Even where no such right is reserved, the judicial view has been towards a right to shorten unless the writer of the letter has stipulated that it is to be used in full or not at all.

Fair dealing

There are occasions when it is permissible, to a limited extent, to quote from a copyright literary work, or even to reproduce a copyright artistic work, with acknowledgement.

When criticising or reviewing. What would be 'fair dealing' for this purpose has never been judicially quantified. When reviewing a book a critic may quote from it for the purpose of making his point. It may not be so much a question of *how many* words, as *which* words he quotes. If, for instance, in reviewing a thriller, he were to give the game away, this would exceed fair dealing.

Reporting current events. It is permissible to quote from a copyright work where the words relate to a current event – again, within limits. For instance, if a cabinet minister sent a letter of resignation to the Prime Minister, a quotation from the letter setting out his reasons for resigning would be likely to be protected as fair dealing.

Moral rights

The most important right for journalists under this head is the right of a person not to have his name put on work which is not his. One example of a newspaper falling foul of this rule was when one gave a byline to Dorothy Squires for an account of her married life, even though it included a line in small print saying that the story was 'as told' to a reporter.

Commissioned photographic works

Where any photographic work has been produced under a commission since 1989, the copyright belongs to the person commissioned. So a wedding photographer has the copyright in the wedding photographs. The person who commissioned the pictures, however (since such pictures are of a private and domestic nature), has the right not to have them made public without his consent.

When borrowing a photograph one should look for a photographer's stamp on the back. If it is a family-album shot, one is likely to have permission to use it. If it is by a professional photographer no doubt he will want payment. And to use it without his consent will infringe his copyright. Even with his consent one will need also that of the person who commissioned it, if it is of a private and domestic nature. For pictures taken before 1989 copyright belongs to the person who commissioned it.

Spoken words

Copyright in a report of spoken words belongs to the first person to reduce them to writing unless the speaker reserved copyright in his speech before making it. But, as fair dealing permits limited inclusion of copyright material for reporting current events, to this extent a reporter could report the speaker's words despite his reservation of copyright.

Confidentiality

A servant is duty bound not to betray his master's secrets. A spouse is similarly bound. In 1962 the Duchess of Argyll obtained an injunction to stop her ex-husband, the duke, from revealing secrets of their marriage. Sometimes an injunction may be granted against a 'kiss-and-tell' ex-lover. In 1988 a judge refused to strike out an action by a well-known woman, known only as 'T', to stop disclosure of her alleged lesbian relationship with a young woman. Basically, the tests will be as follows:

- Is the material confidential in its nature?
- Would disclosure be likely to damage the legitimate interests of the claimant?
- Was it communicated in breach of confidence?

If the answer to each of these questions is 'yes' an injunction is likely to be granted unless one of the following is the case:

- The public interest in disclosure outweighs the claimant's interest in keeping his information confidential. For instance, a story from a manufacturer's internal memorandum showing that equipment in widespread use in police stations for breath-testing motorists gave erratic results.
- The material in question is 'iniquitous'. For instance, a story, based on correspondence supplied by a former sales manager, stating that laundry companies had formed a liaison to inflate prices.

Often when an aggrieved person obtains a banning order from a judge (sometimes simply to save his own face), the editor learns of it for the first time when it is served on him. The order may later be lifted, either by the judge who granted it or on appeal. But in the meantime the publication will have been prevented from running the story and its potential impact is likely to have been lost.

Journalists' sources

Every journalist has contacts. No journalist worth his salt will betray a contact, even on pain of imprisonment. At present a reporter may be ordered to reveal his source if, in the opinion of the court, such revelation is necessary in the interests of justice, national security or for the prevention of disorder or crime. However, the European Court of Human Rights has ruled that a penalty imposed on Bill Goodwin, a trainee reporter on *The Engineer*, for refusing to reveal his whistleblower source was in breach of Article 10 of the European Convention on Human Rights.

Further, the Editors' Code of Conduct clearly states a journalist has a 'moral obligation' to protect confidential sources.

Privacy

Privacy is a fast-developing area of the law that is likely to affect the next generation of journalists as much as libel does today, with damages awarded as high as those for libel. Many celebrities, public figures, and sports stars have used their Article 8 right of privacy to gain injunctions, and so-called super-injunctions, pre-publication, to prevent damaging stories about their private lives ever seeing the light of day. This would have worked for Manchester United star Ryan Giggs were it not for the power of Twitter and an MP naming him in Parliament with the protection of absolute privilege.

When a story has been published, the redress is to claim damages for privacy through the civil courts. This happened when Max Mosley (the former president of the Fédération Internationale de l'Automobile) won a record £60,000 in privacy damages in 2011 against the now-defunct *News of the World* over a story concerning his private life.

Any court considering an alleged invasion into privacy will consider whether the complainant had a reasonable expectation of privacy and whether there is any public interest in intruding into that privacy. Stories about someone's health will almost certainly be frowned upon. However, as in the case of England footballer Rio Ferdinand, who lost a claim for privacy damages against the *Sunday Mirror*, the public interest in some public figures seen as 'role models' means the media's right to expose hypocrisy outweighs the individual's right to a private life.

Meanwhile, the Editors' Code of Conduct outlaws (among other things) unnecessary reference to a person's religion, sexual orientation and so on, and states that 'everyone is entitled to respect for his or her private and family life, home, health and correspondence'. This does not apply where there is an overriding consideration of public interest.

Journalists who obstruct the highway or footway while 'doorstepping' in pursuit of an interview or photograph could be prosecuted under section 137 of the Highways Act 1980. A person who, while allowed on private premises for a particular purpose, attempts furtively to obtain information or take photographs, could be sued for trespass to land.

The Human Rights Act 1998, incorporating the European Convention on Human Rights into English law, provides (Article 8) a remedy in UK courts for wrongful violation of a person's privacy in relation to his private and family life, his home and correspondence. This, again, is subject to considerations of public interest, and has to be weighed against Article 10, which upholds freedom to receive and impart information, subject to such constraints as 'territorial integrity' and 'national security'.

Official secrets

Since 1911 it has been unlawful to disclose, or attempt to discover, military secrets, and for unauthorised persons to be present for unlawful purposes in prohibited places such as Army and RAF bases and naval dockyards.

Under the Official Secrets Act 1989 it is an offence to make a 'damaging' disclosure. This may relate to the strength and/or disposition of troops, aircraft and naval vessels, their equipment, armaments and capabilities (particularly state-of-the-art equipment), the nature and standard of their training and logistics, and to defence strategies. The Act penalises journalists and their publications, and also Crown servants and government contractors. There is a defence if they can show that they did not know and had no reason to suspect that the disclosure would be 'damaging'.

If in doubt a journalist should seek advice from the secretary to the Defence, Press and Broadcasting Committee. Such advice would be most desirable when reporting, for example, the embarkation of troops, or the departure of aircraft or ships, for an overseas trouble spot, or before publishing a photograph of a crashed military aircraft. The Committee issues 'Defence Advisory Notices' which ask editors to seek the secretary's advice before publishing articles on specified topics.

A 'damaging disclosure' may relate also to the police or prison service, if it is of a kind which may facilitate crime or escapes from custody.

RECOMMENDED READING

Brooke, H. (2007) *Your Right To Know*, 2nd edition.
Brooke, H. (2010) *The Silent State: Secrets, Surveillance and the Myth of British Democracy*.
Caddell, C. and Johnson, H. (2010) *Blackstone's Statutes on Media Law*, 3rd edition.

Crone, T. (2002) *Law and the Media*, 4th edition, Alberstat, P., Cassels, T. and Overs, E. (eds).

Hanna, M. and Dodd, M. (2012) *McNae's Essential Law for Journalists*, 21st edition.

McCormick-Watson, J. (1994) *Essential English Legal System.*

McInnes, R. (2008) *Scots Law for Journalists*, 8th edition

Quinn, F. (2011) *Law for Journalists*, 3rd edition.

Robertson, G. and Nicol, A. (2008) *Media Law*, 5th edition.

Rozenberg, J. (2010) *Privacy and the Press.*

Websites

Acts of Parliament: www.legislation.gov.uk/ukpga

Bar Council: www.barcouncil.org.uk

Court procedure and personnel: www.justice.gov.uk/about/courts.htm

Crown Prosecution Service: www.cps.gov.uk

Data protection: www.ico.gov.uk/for_organisations/data_protection.aspx

Editors' Code of Practice:
www.pcc.org.uk/assets/111/Code_of_Practice_2011_A4.pd

Freedom of Information: www.gov.uk/make-a-freedom-of-information-request/the-freedom-of-information-act

Home Office: www.homeoffice.gov.uk

Judicial system: ybtj.justice.gov.uk

Law updates: www.telegraph.co.uk/news/newstopics/lawreports

Laws: www.legislation.gov.uk

Law Society: www.lawsociety.org.uk/home.law

Media law news: www.guardian.co.uk/media/medialaw

Media law updates: www.holdthefrontpage.co.uk/category/news/law

Press Complaints Commission: www.pcc.org.uk

Scots law: www.scotland.gov.uk/Topics/Justice/legal

Glossary

ABC: the Audit Bureau of Circulations, the independent organisation which audits and publishes the sales figures of newspapers and magazines. The ABCe figure gives the figure for digital editions.

ABC figure: the audited circulation figure for a magazine or newspaper from the *Audit Bureau of Circulations.*

ABCDE: categorisation of the population by market researchers based on their social and economic status: A is high and E is low.

ABCe: See *ABC* (Audit Bureau of Circulations).

ad: *advertisement*.

ad/ed ratio: the ratio of space in a magazine filled by advertising and editorial material, respectively.

ad-get feature: editorial material prepared specifically to attract advertisers.

adjacency: the position of an *advertisement* next to certain editorial material for which publishers can charge higher rates.

advertisement: written or pictorial material which is included in a magazine for payment by the advertiser.

advertisement feature: see *advertorial*.

advertising revenue: money a publication earns from advertisers who buy space on its pages to advertise their products.

advertorial: copy and pictures paid for by advertisers but prepared to look like editorial material. The more formal name is *advertisement feature.*

affinity sales: describes magazines that are on sale in specialist outlets where the magazine's content is related. An art gallery, for example, might stock *Art Monthly* in its shop.

agony column: regular feature in which readers' letters about personal problems are answered. Usually written by an agony aunt, but there are some agony uncles.

angle: the way of approaching a story.

art editor: person who is responsible for the visual aspects of the magazine.

artwork: the illustrative material ready for printing.

ASA: Advertising Standards Authority.

ascenders: the parts of letters such as k, f and d which extend above the basic *x-height* in a *typeface.*

author's corrections: changes made to *copy* by the author once setting has been done.

author's proof: a *proof* sent to the author for correction.

back issues/numbers: issues of a magazine published before the one which is current.

back of the book: pages in a magazine that fall after the *centre spread*.

bad break: a word which has been hyphenated clumsily in order to fit into a given space.

bagging: the practice of enclosing a magazine in a transparent plastic bag. Keeps *cover mounts* safe and prevents browsers from reading before buying.

banner: a *headline* that extends across the whole of a page or spread.

bar code: on a magazine's cover the black and white serial number which can be read by computer.

bastard measure: type that is set to a *measure* that is not standard for a given publication or page.

beat: more commonly used in the US: a journalist's specialist field of interest.

bellyband: an advertising term for a paper *outsert* wrapped round a magazine. In editorial terms – a wide strap designed across the waist of a magazine as a fake *outsert* to promote added value content, particularly a one-off special section.

binding: the way in which pages are united to produce the finished magazine.

bleed (bled off): where the printed matter extends to the edge of the page.

blog: short for weblog, a digital diary usually incorporating the writer's thoughts, opinions and, crucially, links to other websites. Maintaining a blog is blogging and the person who does it is a blogger. Most blogs are updated regularly (often daily) using software that allows people with little computer expertise to upload material.

body copy: the main text.

bold: version of a *typeface* in which the letters appear thicker and darker than in the standard version.

book: another word for the magazine.

box or **box out**: area of type that is surrounded by rules to create a 'box' shape on the layout. Sometimes called a panel.

brand extension: the use of a magazine's title (or brand) by a publisher to expand into other areas of business such as *masthead television*, exhibition organisation, or selling goods as diverse as bedlinen and cheese.

browser: software used to navigate the *world wide web.*

bulks: bulk sales or circulation refers to copies of a publication that are given away free.

business-to-business: the current name for the trade press. Publications which concentrate on work and professional interests rather than leisure and lifestyle.

bust: a *headline* or *standfirst* busts if it is too long for the allocated space.

byline: the name of the writer as it appears with the story.

camera-ready: the elements of a page ready to be photographed for printing.

caps: short for 'capital letters'.

caption: words that accompany a picture or illustration.

CAR: computer-assisted reporting.

catchline: a short word used to identify a story during the editorial process but not printed. Called a slug-line in the US.

centre spread: the middle two facing pages of a magazine. Also called the centre-fold.

centred: type that is set as if from the centre of the column so that the margins on either side of the type are equal in width in any give line. This produces ragged margins in a column of type.

chapel: the name for a branch of the journalists' and printers' trade unions, led by a mother or father of the chapel.

character: an individual letter, number, punctuation mark, symbol or space.

chief sub: the senior *subeditor* who is in charge of the subediting process.

circulation: the number of copies of a magazine issue which are sold or otherwise distributed.

classified advertising: small *advertisements* grouped together on the page or 'classified' by subject matter

cliché: a phrase that has grown dull through overuse.

close/closing: time at which a page or a publication is finally sent to the printers.

close up: instruction to reduce the space between characters, words or lines of space.

CMS: content management system

coated paper: paper that has been treated to give it a glossy finish, suitable for high-quality printing.

collation: the assembly of sheets of paper into the correct order ready to be bound.

colour: printed in colour.

colour correction: the checking of colours at the *proof* stage.

colour piece: descriptive writing as distinct from narrative reporting.

consumer magazines: publications that provide their readers with information and entertainment in relation to their leisure time.

contact sheet: sheet of small photographic prints which are the same size as the negative.

contacts: people who supply journalists with quotes or information. Also refers to small photographic prints as in a contact sheet.

contacts book: address book or computer file in which journalists list their contacts.

contract publisher: a publisher that produces magazines on behalf of organisations which are not themselves in the magazine publishing business but distribute magazines to their customers or employees.

controlled circulation: the system by which a publisher distributes a magazine free to its target audience, usually those who work in a particular field.

copy: words written by journalists for publication.

copy-flow: the movement between staff of copy during the process of editing and production.

copyright: the right to license the use of editorial material. May rest with the author or the publisher.

copytaker: a typist who takes down copy dictated over the telephone by journalists working outside the office.

cover lines: words on the cover of a magazine which indicate what articles can be found inside.

cover mount: a 'free gift' attached to the cover of a magazine.

cover price: price paid by the reader who buys a magazine from a retailer. It is indicated on the cover.

credit: the name of the artist or photographer which accompanies their work on a page. Sometimes called a credit line.

Cromalins: a type of colour proof named after the process by which it is produced.

cropping: to alter the shape or size of a photograph or illustration.

crosshead: a small *headline* that appears in the text as a graphic device and to attract the reader's attention to a story.

CTNs: the trade's name for the traditional shops which sell magazines: the confectioner, tobacconist and newsagents.

customer magazine: magazines supplied by large companies to their customers. Often produced to order by *contract publishers*.

cuttings: editorial matter that has already been published.

cuttings job: a story that is written largely from *cuttings* and without any or much original research.

deadline: time by which something (*copy*, *layout*, *proofs*) is due for delivery.

deck: correctly means a whole *headline* but usually used to mean one line of a headline which is made up of several lines.

delayed drop: an introduction to a story where the most important information is not used first.

descenders: the parts of letters such as g, p and y which extend below the basic *x-height* of a letter.

diary: the list of routine events which will be covered by reporters. Also used to mean a gossip column.

display advertising: *advertisements* in which large type or images are used to attract the reader's attention. To be distinguished from *classified advertising*.

distribution: the means by which a publication reaches its readers.

D-notice: a formal warning from the government to journalists that a subject should not be written about because it might affect the nation's security.

double-page spread: a story or advertisement which takes up two facing pages.

down-market: market research term for readership with lower disposable income and social class.

drop cap: a capital letter in a size larger than the *body copy* type, which is used at the beginning of a story or a section of a story to enhance the look of a page. It drops down into the text below, which is arranged (or 'ranged') around it.

dummy: a small mock-up of the magazine used for reference during the editorial and production processes.

editor: the most senior journalist on a publication. The person responsible for the editorial content.

editorial: material in a magazine generated by journalists and not by advertisers. Can sometimes mean an opinion piece by the editor or editorial staff.

editorial mention: inclusion in editorial material of the name of a product.

e-journalist: a journalist whose work is published electronically. Also a journalist who uses electronic means to conduct research.

embargo: a request not to publish before a specified time. Applies to information released to the press in advance of a public event or announcement.

end blob or **symbol**: characteristic symbol used by a magazine to denote the end of a story.

expenses: out-of-pocket expenses incurred by journalists or photographers while on assignment. Also known as 'exes'.

facing matter: position in a magazine opposite editorial material (or 'matter'), favoured by advertisers.

fanzines or **'zines**: amateur magazines produced out of devotion to the topic (such as a rock group or a football club) rather than with a view to making money.

finishing: the processes such as *binding* which take place after printing.

FIPP: International Federation of the Periodical Press.

fit: to cut copy so that it fits an allocated space exactly.

flannel panel: the place where the magazine gives its address and other contact information as well as the list of staff and the copyright notice. Sometimes also called the *masthead*.

flatplan: the two-dimensional diagram of a magazine used in planning to show what will appear on which page.

flatplanning: the process of producing a *flatplan*.

flush: type that is set so that one margin is even, as in 'flush left', meaning the left margin is straight while the right one is *ragged*.

focus group: group of people brought together by market researchers to discuss a particular topic.

folio: page.

font or **fount**: name given to the range of *characters* in one *typeface*.

four-colour: the printing technique that uses four colours to produce colour pages.

fragmentation: term used to describe the effect on the market of the proliferation of titles in a particular publishing sector.

freebies: gifts or inducements sent to journalists by organisations seeking publicity through *editorial mentions*.

freelance: someone who is self-employed, usually working for a range of publications.

full out: where type is set across the full *measure* (width) of the column.

furniture: the regular features that appear in a magazine. Also used to mean the graphic devices used to indicate differing sections of the magazine or a page.

galley proof: proof of typeset copy which is not yet assigned to a *layout* and so is produced as a single column of type.

gatefold: an extra page which folds out, usually from the cover. Most often used for *advertisements.*

gone to bed: the publication has been sent to the printers and no more changes are possible.

graphics: illustrative material.

grey market: potential readers of magazines who are older than those typically thought of as *consumer magazine* purchasers.

grid: established shape for the design of the pages of a magazine which determines such things as the width of columns and margins.

gutter: the vertical space between columns or between two pages in the same spread.

halftone: a way of representing light and shade by using black dots of differing size.

handout: information supplied as a *press release*.

hard copy: *copy* supplied on paper, either typewritten or handwritten.

headline or heading: words in larger or distinctive type which attract the reader to a story.

hold over: instruction to keep *copy* for use at a later date.

house ad: *advertisement* by a *publisher* in a magazine it owns.

house journal: a publication given to the employees of an organisation bringing them news and information about its activities.

house style: the collection of guidelines about English usage and editorial policy established by a publisher for a publication as a way of ensuring consistency.

i-mag: a magazine-like publication which exists only in digital form. Examples include *Popbitch* (www.popbitch.com) and *The Friday Thing* (www.thefridayproject.co.uk/tft).

imposition: the way pages are arranged for printing so that they will be in the correct order after the folding process.

imprint: the details of the printer and publisher which a publication is legally obliged to include.

indented: line where the type starts a few character spaces in from the margin to which the rest of the column adheres.

in-house: taking place within a publication's own publishing house.

insert: loose sheet or sheets of paper, usually an advertisement, inserted into a magazine after binding.

insertion orders: requests from advertisers about where in a magazine their *advertisements* are to be positioned

internet: a global network of computers which supports several applications including email and the *world wide web*.

intro: usual term for the first paragraph of a news or feature story.

inverted pyramid: describes the typical way in which a news story is written, with the information included in descending order of importance.

ISDN: Integrated Services Digital Network. A means of transmitting editorial material, using an ISDN telephone line.

justified: typeset copy in which both left and right margins are *flush*, i.e. without indentations. Justification is the process by which this is achieved.

kill: to drop a story.

kill-fee: fee paid to a journalist whose story has been commissioned but is not used.

landscape: describes pictures which are wider than they are deep.

layout: the design for a page.

lead: the main story on a page or in a publication. Also, an idea for a story or a tip-off for one.

leading: pronounced 'ledding', this is the space between lines of type, originally achieved by the insertion of bars of metal or leads.

libel: a defamatory statement in permanent form.

line drawing: an illustration that uses lines rather than shaded areas.

lineage: fee paid to a journalist which is assessed on the basis of the number of lines of text used in the publication.

literal: a typographical error. Also known as a *typo*.

liveblogging: a continually updated blog post that provides rolling textual coverage of an ongoing event.

logo: commonly used to describe a magazine's title design as it appears on the cover and any other page or merchandise where it may appear. See *titlepiece*.

loupe: a small magnifying glass held up to the eye through which to view *transparencies*.

lower case: small (not capital) letters.

mark up: to indicate the *typeface*, size and *measure* in which copy is to be set by the printer.

masthead: now a common term for the *titlepiece* or *logo* of a magazine which used to refer only to the place in a magazine, usually near the beginning, where its address and contact information are published as well as the *staff box*. See *flannel panel*.

masthead television: television programmes developed around a magazine brand.

matter: typeset copy or editorial material i.e. not advertising.

measure: the width of a piece of typesetting.

media pack: information prepared by the publisher for advertisers, giving details about a magazine's circulation and readership.

merchandising: information about stockists and prices included in consumer articles.

MF: abbreviation for 'more follows'. MFL means 'more follows later'.

model release: document signed by a photographic model authorising the use of pictures in which he or she appears.

mono(chrome): printed with one colour, usually black.

mug shots: portraits showing head and shoulders only.

NCTJ: National Council for the Training of Journalists.

news agency: an agency that supplies stories and pictures to a wide range of media organisations.

newsletter: *business-to-business* publications with small niche readerships to which they supply specialised information.

niche market: a relatively small group or sector of potential purchasers of a publication, usually with a shared specialist interest.

nose: the beginning of a story or *intro*.

NRS: National Readership Survey.

NUJ: National Union of Journalists.

off the record: words spoken to a journalist which the speaker does not want to have reported or at least attributed to her.

OTS: stands for 'opportunity to see' and is one of the indices used by the *National Readership Survey*. An OTS score measures the number of readers who will read some part of a title during its currency.

outsert: pages that are attached to the outside of the cover of a magazine to carry advertising.

overmatter: typeset material for which there is not enough space on the *layout*.

Ozalid: a type of *proof*.

page proof: a *proof* of the whole page showing text in relation to *layout* and presentational material such as *headline*, *standfirsts*, *captions*.

page rate: the cost of a page of advertising in a magazine. Also used for the amount of money an editor can spend on the editorial content of a page.

page traffic: term used by publishers to describe how well read a page is.

page-to-plate: name for the process of sending copy directly to the printing plate without intermediate stages.

pagination: the number of pages in a magazine.

paparazzi: photographers who take pictures of celebrities without their consent.

par: a paragraph.

passed for press: stage at which authorisation has been given for printing to begin.

PDF: stands for portable document format and is a file format used by Adobe Acrobat.

peg: reason for publishing a story at a particular time.

penetration: describes the proportion of a publication's target *readership* which is reflected in its *circulation* figures.

perfect binding: the *binding* system using glue which creates a hard, squared *spine*. Usually used on thicker magazines printed on good-quality paper.

Pex: an index used by the *QRS* to measure page exposure, or the number of times an individual reader opens an issue of a magazine at a particular page.

photomontage: a picture created from more than one original or heavily *retouched*.

picture byline: a *byline* that includes a photograph of the writer.

picture editor: person who commissions and selects photographs for a publication.

picture-led: publication where the visual material takes priority over the words.

pix: abbreviation for pictures.

plate: the name for the printing plate, whether made of metal or plastic, from which pages will be printed.

point: the unit of measurement used in *typography*. One point is roughly 1/72 of an inch.

position: on a magazine refers to the site where particular elements will be placed. Editorial positions are where editorial material is found. Advertisers pay higher rates for certain special positions such as the back page, *facing matter*, first right-hand page, or even 'first fragrance'.

PPA: Professional Publishers Association, the trade organisation for *publishers.* Formerly the Periodical Publishers Association.

PR: abbreviation for someone who handles public relations for a company or person.

press release: written (or electronic) announcement of news by an organisation.

print run: number of copies printed.

production schedule: the list of times at which various editorial and production processes for a magazine are to be undertaken.

profile: an article that describes a person or, more rarely, an organisation.

progressives: *proofs* pulled at each stage of the colour printing process.

promotion: means other than advertising by which a publication is brought to the attention of the public.

proof: a typeset version of the *copy*, which can be used for checking. As a verb it means to read a proof carefully, checking for mistakes.

proofreader: someone who reads *proofs*.

PTC: Periodicals Training Council, the wing of the *PPA* that has responsibility for training matters and accreditation.

publisher: a company that publishes printed material. Also the name for the person within a magazine publishing company who takes overall responsibility for the commercial aspects of a publication.

pull-quote: a few words taken from the following text and set in a contrasting type to be used as a visual device to break up the text as well as an enticement to read the story.

QRS: stands for Quality of Reading Survey, a source of data for publishers launched in 1998 to complement the *ABC* and *NRS* figures.

ragged: with an uneven margin.

range right/left: type that is *flush* or straight on the right-hand/left-hand side of the column.

rate card: the information for advertisers about the rates a magazine charges for advertising space.

readership: the number of readers of a magazine. Distinct from *circulation*, which is the number of copies sold or otherwise distributed.

register: the alignment of the coloured inks on the printed page. If a page is 'out of register' the pictures and the lines within them look blurred.

regulars: regular columns or features that appear in every edition of a magazine.

repertoire buyers: those readers who don't remain loyal to one publication.

reportage: reporting. May also mean extended feature articles which include descriptive writing.

repro house: place where colour pictures are scanned and married up with *layouts* ready for printing. Also known as a colour house.

retainer: regular payment to a *freelance* to secure a commitment to the publication.

retouch: to enhance the quality of, or otherwise alter, a photograph.

returns: copies of a magazine that are returned unsold to the *publisher* by the retailer.

reversed out: type printed in white on a black or tinted background.

revise: a *proof* to be checked after corrections to a previous proof have been made.

river: white space that forms by chance during setting and which creates a distracting gap running down a column of type.

roman: the standard style of type, as compared with *bold*, in which the letters are thicker, or italic, in which they are finer and sloping.

rough: a 'rough' sketch showing a suggested *layout*.

rule: a line separating columns of type or surrounding illustrations.

saddle-stitching: means of *binding* the pages of a magazine by folding and then stapling.

sale or return (SOR): an arrangement for the publisher to take back copies of a publication which a retailer can't sell.

sales revenue: income derived by publishers from sales of copies of magazines as opposed to income from advertisers.

sans serif: typeface whose letters don't have *serifs*.

scanner: computer equipment that translates *hard copy* or illustrations into digital form.

schedule: collective name for all the *advertisements* a company will place with a magazine over a specified period of time.

scheme: to make a plan of a page *layout*.

section: that part of a magazine which is printed on one sheet of paper before being folded and trimmed and bound into the magazine. Sections can be of any number from four to 64 pages, but must be divisible by four.

sell: paragraph of copy to entice a reader into reading a feature article. Also known as a *standfirst*.

SEO: search engine optimisation

separations: the parts into which a colour picture is separated before printing begins.

serif: the small embellishing strokes at the ends of letters in serif *typefaces*.

shoot: a photographic session.

sidebar: a complementary story or additional material relating to the main text which is placed in a *box* or panel at the side.

sitting: a photographic session or shoot.

slander: a defamatory statement which is spoken.

small caps: capital letters in shape but of the same size as the lower-case letters in a given *typeface*. LIKE THESE.

solus reader: a reader who remains loyal to one publication. (See *repertoire buyers*.)

special feature: another term for *advertisement feature*.

spike: the old word for the metal spike on which unwanted *copy* was stored.

spine: the bound edge of a *perfect-bound* magazine.

splash: the main story on the front page of a news magazine.

spot colour: a colour other than black which can be used throughout a publication or on individual pages.

spread: two pages that face each other.

staff box: the list that appears in a magazine of its staff members and contributors. Often includes the *imprint*.

standfirst: text in type larger than the *body copy* and usually written by *subeditors* which introduces the story to the reader. Also known as a *sell*.

standing artwork: *artwork* which stays the same from one issue to the next.

stet: literally 'let it stand'. Used to indicate that a correction which has been marked should in fact be ignored.

stock: the grade of paper used for a magazine.

strapline: subsidiary *headline* that expands on the main headline and runs above it.

style: abbreviation for *house style*.

style book/sheet: the document in which *house style* is recorded.

stylist: person who organises a photographic session.

subeditor or **sub**: the journalist responsible for checking, editing, *fitting* and presenting the *copy* on the page.

subscriber: reader who pays in advance for a specified number of copies of a publication.

subhead: a subsidiary *headline*.

syndication: selling on to other publications of material used by a magazine or agency.

take back: instruction to take words back to the previous line.

tint: shaded panel over which type can be printed.

titlepiece: the correct name for the name of a magazine as it appears on the cover (although this is regularly called a *masthead* and a *logo*). *Masthead* is often said to be the wrong term but it is now common as in the phrase 'masthead programming'.

TMAP: Teenage Magazine Arbitration Panel. Organisation set up by *publishers* to monitor the material which appears in magazines aimed at girls in their early teens.

TOT: stands for 'triumph over tragedy' and refers to a type of feature article that tells a real-life story in which the subject overcomes difficult personal circumstances.

transparency: a photograph in film form, also known as a tranny.

turn: the term to describe the section of a story that is continued on a page other than the one carrying the majority of the *copy*. Indicated to the reader by an instruction such as 'Turn to page' or what's known as a turn arrow.

typeface: the letters in a given family of type.

typo: a typographical error. Also known as a *literal*.

typography: the craft of using type.

u/lc: short way to write *upper/lower case*.

unjustified: column of typeset copy where one of the margins is uneven.

up-market: market research term for a *readership* with larger disposable income or higher social class. See *down-market*.

upper case: capital letters, e.g. ABC.

upper and lower case: mixture of capital and small letters.

vox pop: stands for *vox populi*, which means voice of the people. A story where the reporter canvasses opinion from ordinary members of the public.

website: a grouping of several pages together from the *world wide web*.

weight: the thickness or boldness of letters in a *typeface*.

white space: area on a page with no words or illustrations.

wholesaler: the intermediary who organises the delivery of publications to retailers.

widow: a line of type at the end of a paragraph which has only one syllable or one short word in it. If it falls at the top or bottom of a column the text may have to be altered to remove it.

WOB: stands for 'white on black' and means where the usual arrangement of black type on a white background is reversed so that white words appear on black. Also known as *reversed out* type.

world wide web: electronic network of computer files.

x-height: the height of the lower-case letter x in any given *typeface*. See *ascenders* and *descenders*.

'zines: see *fanzines*.

Bibliography

BOOKS, JOURNAL ARTICLES AND PAPERS

Abrahamson, D. (1996a) 'The bright new-media future for magazines', in *Magazine Matter*, the Newsletter of the Association for Education in Journalism and Mass Communication, Magazine Division, Summer 1996.

—— (1996b) *Magazine-Made America: The Cultural Transformation of the Postwar Periodical*, Cresskill, NJ: Hampton Press, Inc.

Adams, S. with Hicks, W. (2009) *Interviewing for Journalists*, London: Routledge.

Aitchison, J. and Lewis, D.M. (eds) (2003) *New Media Language*, London: Routledge.

Alden, C. (2004) *Guardian Media Directory 2005*, London: Guardian Books.

Allan, S. (ed.) (2005) *Journalism: Critical Issues*, Maidenhead: Open University Press.

Anderson, P. and Weymouth, A. (1999) *Insulting the Public?: The British PR and the European Union*, London: Longman.

Ang, T. (2000) *Picture Editing*, 2nd edition, Oxford: Focal Press.

—— (2010) *The Complete Photographer*, London: DK Publishing.

Armstrong, L. (1998) *Front Row*, London: Coronet.

Atton, C. (1999) 'A reassessment of the alternative press', *Media, Culture and Society*, 21: 51–76.

Baggini, J. (2002) *Making Sense: Philosophy Behind the Headlines*, Oxford: Oxford University Press.

Bak, J.S. and Reynolds, B. (eds) (2011) *Literary Journalism Across the Globe: Journalistic Traditions and Transnational Influences*, Amherst, MA: University of Massachusetts Press.

Ballaster, R., Beetham, M., Frazer, E. and Hebron, S. (1991) *Women's Worlds: Ideology, Femininity and the Women's Magazine*, London: Macmillan.

Barber, L. (1992) *Mostly Men*, Harmondsworth: Penguin.

—— (1999) *Demon Barber*, London: Viking.

Barrell, J. and Braithwaite, B. (1979) *The Business of Women's Magazines: The Agonies and the Ecstasies*, London: Associated.

Bauret, G. (1999) *Alexey Brodovitch*, New York: Assouline Business Press.

Beales, I. (2009) *The Editors' Codebook*, 2nd edition, London: Newspapers Publishers Association, Periodical Publishers Association.

Beetham, M. (1996) *A Magazine of her Own: Domesticity and Desire in the Woman's Magazine, 1800–1914*, London: Routledge.

Belsey, C. and Chadwick, R. (1992) *Ethical Issues in Journalism*, London and New York: Routledge.

Bennett, A. (1994) *Writing Home*, London: Faber.

Benwell, B. (ed.) (2003) *Masculinity and Men's Lifestyle Magazines*, Oxford: Blackwell Publishing.

Berendt, J. (1994) *Midnight in the Garden of Good and Evil*, London: Chatto & Windus.

Bergner, D. (2005) *Soldiers of Light*, Harmondsworth: Penguin.

Bradford, J. (2013) *Fashion Journalism*, London: Routledge.

Bradshaw, P. and Rohumaa, L. (2011) *The Online Journalism Handbook: Skills to Survive and Thrive in the Digital Age*, Harlow: Longman.

Braithwaite, B. (1995) *Women's Magazines: The First 300 Years*, London: Peter Owen.

—— (1998) 'Magazines: the bulging bookstores', in A. Briggs and P. Cobley (eds) *The Media: An Introduction*, London: Addison Wesley Longman.

Brierley, S. (2003) *The Advertising Handbook*, 2nd edition, London: Routledge.

Bromley, M. and O'Malley, T. (eds) (1997) *A Journalism Reader*, London: Routledge.

Bromley, M. and Stephenson, H. (eds) (1998) *Sex, Lies and Democracy: The Press and the Public*, London and New York: Addison Wesley Longman.

Brooke, H. (2007) *Your Right To Know: A Citizen's Guide to the Freedom of Information Act*, 2nd edition, London: Pluto Press.

—— (2010) *The Silent State: Secrets, Surveillance and the Myth of British Democracy*, London: William Heinemann.

—— (2011) *The Revolution Will be Digitised: Dispatches from the Information War*, London: William Heinemann.

Broughton, F. (ed.) (1998) *Time Out Interviews 1968–1998*, Harmondsworth: Penguin.

Bryson, B. (1994) *The Penguin Dictionary for Writers and Editors*, Harmondsworth: Penguin.

—— (2009a) *Mother Tongue*: *The English Language*, Harmondsworth: Penguin.

—— (2009b) *Troublesome Words*, Harmondsworth: Penguin.

Buchan, J. (1999) 'Inside Iraq', in *Women and Children First, Granta 67*, London: Granta Books.

Butterfield, J. (2008) *Damp Squid: The English Language Laid Bare*, Oxford: Oxford University Press.

Caddell, C. and Johnson, H. (2010) *Blackstone's Statutes on Media Law*, 3rd edition, Oxford: Oxford University Press.

Cameron, D. (1995) *Verbal Hygiene*, London: Routledge.

—— (1996) 'Style policy and style politics: a neglected aspect of the language of the news', *Media, Culture and Society*, 18: 315–33.

—— (2000) *Good to Talk?*, London: Sage.

Campbell, A. (1985) *The Designer's Handbook*, London: Little, Brown.

Capote, T. (2002) *A Capote Reader*, Harmondsworth: Penguin.

Carey, G.V. (1976) *Mind the Stop: A Brief Guide to Punctuation*, Harmondsworth: Penguin.

Carey, J. (ed.) (1987) *The Faber Book of Reportage*, London: Faber.

—— (2003) 'Reportage, literature and willed credulity', in J. Aitchison and D.M. Lewis, *New Media Language*, London: Routledge.

Chippindale, P. and Horrie, C. (1999) *Stick it Up Your Punter! The Uncut Story of The Sun Newspaper*, London: Simon & Schuster.

Clark, E. (1988) *The Want Makers: Lifting the Lid off the World Advertising Industry – How They Make You Want to Buy*, Harmondsworth: Penguin.

Clayton, J. (1994) *Interviewing for Journalists*, London: Piatkus.

Click, J.W. and Baird, R.N. (1990) *Magazine Editing and Production*, 6th edition, Dubuque, IA: W.C. Brown Publishers.

Cohen, S. and Young, J. (eds) (1981 [1973]) *The Manufacture of News: Deviance, Social Problems and the Mass Media*, London: Constable.

Coleridge, N. (1999) *Streetsmart*, London: Orion.

Conboy, M. (2002) *The Press and Popular Culture*, London: Sage.

Consterdine, G. (1997) 'How magazine advertising works II', Research Report, Periodical Publishers Association.

—— (2002) 'How magazine advertising works IV', Research Report, Periodical Publishers Association.

Crewe, B. (2003) *Representing Men: Cultural Production and Producers in the Men's Magazine Market*, Oxford and New York: Berg.

Crone, T. (2002) *Law and the Media*, 4th edition, Alberstat, P., Cassels, T. and Over, E. (eds), Oxford: Focal Press.

Curran, J. and Seaton, J. (1997) *Power Without Responsibility: The Press and Broadcasting in Britain*, 6th edition, London: Routledge.

Curtis, S. and Manser, M. (2006) *Penguin Pocket Writer's Handbook,* Harmondsworth: Penguin.

Daly, C.P., Henry, P., and Ryder, E. (1996) *The Magazine Publishing Industry*, Needham Heights, MA: Allyn & Bacon.

Davies, H. (1994) *Hunting People: Thirty Years of Interviews with the Famous*, Edinburgh: Mainstream Publishing.

—— (1998) *Born 1900: A Human History of the Twentieth Century – For Everyone Who Was There*, London: Little, Brown.

Davies, N. (1997) *Dark Heart*, London: Vintage.

—— (2008) *Flat Earth News,* London: Chatto & Windus.

Dawson Scott, R. (1997) 'Getting noticed: how arts journalists decide what goes on the arts and entertainment pages', unpublished MLitt dissertation, Strathclyde University.

Dear, P. (2000) *Developing Consumer Magazine Brands*, London: Periodical Publishers Association.

Delano, A. and Henningham, J. (1997) *The News Breed: British Journalists in the 1990s*, London: School of Media, London College of Printing and Distributive Trades.

Dennis, F. (2004) 'The Four Horsemen of the Apocalypse', *British Journalism Review*, 3 (15): 45–50.

Department of Culture, Media and Sport (1998) *Creative Industries Mapping Document*.

Didion, J. (1974) *Slouching towards Bethlehem*, London: Penguin.

Dignall, C. (2011) *Can You Eat, Shoot and Leave? (Workbook)*, London: Collins.

Djurup, R. (2010), *Your Guide to Google Web Search: How to Find the Information You Need on the Internet*, Gentofte: Rebidu

Duncan, S. and Newton, J. (2010) 'How do you feel? Preparing novice reporters for the death knock', *Journalism Practice*, 4 (4): 439–53.

The Economist (2012) *The Economist Style Guide*, 10th edition, London: Economist Books.

Edwards-Jones, I. and Anonymous (2006) *Fashion Babylon: From High Fashion to High Street – Looking Up the Skirts of the World's Most Glamorous Industry*, London: Transworld.

Ehrenreich, B. (2002) *Nickel and Dimed, Undercover in Low-wage America*, London: Granta Books.

Eisenhuth, S. and McDonald, W. (eds) (2007) *The Writer's Reader: Understanding Journalism and Non-fiction*, Melbourne: Cambridge University Press.

Evans, H. (1973) *Editing and Design: A Five-Volume Manual of English, Typography and Layout*, London: Heinemann.

—— (1978) *Pictures on a Page*, London: Heinemann.

—— (2000) *Essential English for Journalists, Editors and Writers*, London: Pimlico.

Fallaci, O. (2010) *Interview with History and Power,* New York: Rizzoli.

Ferguson, M. (1983) *Forever Feminine: Women's Magazines and the Cult of Femininity*, London: Heinemann.

Fowler, R. (1991) *Language in the News: Discourse and Ideology in the Press*, London: Routledge.

Frith, M. (2008) *The Celeb Diaries: The Sensational Inside Story of the Celebrity Decade*, London: Ebury Press

Frost, C. (2002) *Reporting for Journalists*, London: Routledge.

—— (2010) *Reporting for Journalists*, 2nd edition, London: Routledge.

—— (2011) *Journalism Ethics and Regulation*, 3rd edition, London: Routledge.

—— (2012) *Designing for Newspapers and Magazines*, 2nd edition, London: Routledge.

Fulton, M. (1988) *Eyes of Time: Photojournalism in America*, New York: New York Graphic Society/Little, Brown.

Galtung, J. and Ruge, M. (1981 [1973]) 'Structuring and selecting news', in S. Cohen and J. Young (eds) *The Manufacture of News: Deviance, Social Problems and the Mass Media*, London: Constable.

Garfield, S. (2011) *Just My Type: A Book About Fonts*, London: Profile Books.

Garvey, E.G. (1996) *The Adman in the Parlor: Magazines and the Gendering of Consumer Culture, 1880s to 1910s*, New York and Oxford: Oxford University Press.

Gellhorn, M. (1989) *The View from the Ground*, London: Granta Books.

Gibson, S.-M. (1999) 'An analysis of the use of language in today's teenage magazines', unpublished MA essay, Napier University, Edinburgh.

Giles, V. and Hodgson, F. (1990) *Creative Newspaper Design*, Oxford: Focal Press.

Gilster, P. (1996) *Finding It on the Internet: The Internet Navigator's Guide to Search Tools and Techniques*, London: John Wiley.

Goldacre, B. (2009) *Bad Science*, London: Harper Perennial

Granta (1998) *The Granta Book of Reportage*, London: Granta Books.

Greer, G. (1999) *The Whole Woman*, London and New York: Doubleday.

Griffiths, D. (ed.) (1992) *The Encyclopaedia of the British Press 1422–1992*, London: Macmillan.

Hamill, P. (1998) *News is a Verb: Journalism at the End of the Twentieth Century*, New York: Ballantine.

Hanna, M. and Dodd, M. (2012) *McNae's Essential Law for Journalists*, 21st edition, Oxford: Oxford University Press.

Harcup, T. (2007) *The Ethical Journalist,* London: Sage.

—— (2009) *Journalism: Principles and Practice*, 2nd edition, London: Sage.

Hebdige, D. (1988) *Hiding in the Light*, London and New York: Comedia/Routledge.

Hennessy, B. (2005) *Writing Feature Articles: A Practical Guide to Methods and Markets*, 4th edition, Oxford: Focal Press.

Herman, E. and Chomsky, N. (1988) *Manufacturing Consent*, New York: Pantheon.

Herman, E.S. and McChesney, R.W. (1997) *The Global Media: The New Missionaries of Corporate Capitalism*, London: Cassell.

Hermes, J. (1995) *Reading Women's Magazines: An Analysis of Everyday Media Use*, Cambridge: Polity Press.

Hicks, W. (2006) *English for Journalists*, 3rd edition, London: Routledge.

Hicks, W. and Holmes, T. (2002) *Subediting for Journalists*, London: Routledge.

Hicks, W., with Adams, S., Gilbert, H. and Holmes, T. (2008) *Writing for Journalists*, London: Routledge.

Holmes, T. (ed.) (2008) *Mapping the Magazine: Comparative Studies in Magazine Journalism*, London: Routledge

Holmes, T. and Mottershead, G. (2013) *Subediting and Production for Journalists: Print, Digital and Social*, London: Routledge.

Holmes, T. and Nice, L. (2012) *Magazine Journalism*, London: Sage.

Holmes, T., Hadwin, S. and Mottershead, G. (2012) *The 21st Century Journalism Handbook*, Harlow: Pearson

Irby, K. (2001) 'Magazine covers: photojournalism or illustration', Poynter Institute. Available online at: http://poynter.org/centerpiece/021601.htm

Jack, I. (1998) 'Introduction', in *The Granta Book of Reportage*, London: Granta Books.

Jaeger, A.-C. (2010) *Image Makers, Image Takers*, London: Thames & Hudson.

Jenkins, S. and Ilson, R. (eds) (1992) *The Times English Style and Usage Guide*, London: Times Books.

Johnson, R. (2011) *A Diary of The Lady*: *My First Year and a Half as Editor*, Harmondsworth: Penguin.

Johnson, S. and Prijatel, P. (2006) *The Magazine from Cover to Cover*, 2nd edition, New York: Oxford University Press.

Junger, S. (1997) *The Perfect Storm: A True Story of Man Against the Sea*, London: Fourth Estate.

Kapuściński, R. (1998) 'The soccer war', in *The Granta Book of Reportage*, London: Granta Books.

Keaney, M. (2010) *Fashion and Advertising: The World's Top Photographers' Workshops*, Hove: Rotovision

Keeble, R. (1998) *The Newspapers Handbook*, London: Routledge.

—— (2001) *Ethics for Journalists*, London: Routledge.

Keeble, R. and Tulloch, J. (2007) *The Journalistic Imagination: Literary Journalists from Defoe to Capote and Carter*, London: Routledge.

—— (eds) (2012) *Global Literary Journalism: Exploring the Journalistic Imagination*, New York: Peter Lang.

Kelsey, L. (2003) *Was It Good For You, Too? 30 Years of 'Cosmopolitan'*, London: Robson Books.

Kidder, T. (1982) *The Soul of a New Machine*, Harmondsworth: Penguin.

Klanten, R. and Ehmann, S. (2010), *Turning Pages: Editorial Design for Print Media*, Berlin: Die Gestalten Verlag.

Knightley, P. (2000) *The First Casualty: The War Correspondent as Hero and Myth-Maker from the Crimea to Kosovo*, London: Prion Books.

Korinek, V. (2000) *Roughing It in the Suburbs: Reading 'Chatelaine' Magazine in the Fifties and Sixties*, Toronto: University of Toronto Press.

Kovach, B. and Rosenstiel, T. (2003) *The Elements of Journalism: What Newspeople Should Know and the Public Should Expect*, London: Guardian Books.

Kroeger, B. (1994) *Nellie Bly: Daredevil, Reporter, Feminist*, New York and Toronto: Random House.

Leverton, M. (2010) *How to Work as a Freelance Journalist*, Oxford: How To Books.

Long, P. (2012) *The History of the NME: High Times and Low Lives at the World's Most Famous Music Magazine*, Stevenage: Portico.

Losowsky, A. (2007) *We Love Magazines*, Berlin: Die Gestalten Verlag.

McCormick-Watson, J. (1994) *Essential English Legal System*, London: Cavendish Publishing.

Macdonald, M. (1995) *Representing Women: Myths of Femininity in the Popular Media*, London: Edward Arnold.

McGuire, M., Stilborne, L., McAdams, M. and Hyatt, L. (2002) *The Internet Handbook for Writers, Researchers and Journalists*, New York: The Guilford Press.

McInnes, R. (2008) *Scots Law for Journalists*, 8th edition, Edinburgh: W. Green & Son.

McKane, A. (2006) *Newswriting*, London: Sage.

McKay, J. (1999) 'Manuals for courtesans', *Critical Quarterly*, 41: 1.

—— (2004/2005) 'The invisible journalists', *Media Education Journal*, 36: 13–15.

—— (2011) 'Reportage in the UK: a hidden genre?', in J. S. Bak and B. Reynolds (eds) *Literary Journalism Across the Globe: Journalistic Traditions and Transnational Influences*, Amherst, MA: University of Massachusetts Press.

—— (2012) 'Åsne Seierstad and *The Bookseller of Kabul*', in R.L. Keeble and J. Tulloch (eds) *Global Literary Journalism: Exploring the Journalistic Imagination*, New York: Peter Lang.

McLean, R. (1969) *Magazine Design*, Oxford: Oxford University Press.

McLoughlin, L. (2000) *The Language of Magazines*, London: Routledge.

McNair, B. (2009 [1996]) *News and Journalism in the UK: A Textbook*, 2nd edition, London and New York: Routledge.

McNally, J. (2008) *The Moment it Clicks*, Berkeley, CA: Peachpit Press.

McPhee, J. (1970) *The Crofter and the Laird*, New York: Farrar, Straus and Giroux.

—— (1989) *The Control of Nature*, New York: The Noonday Press, Farrar, Straus and Giroux.

—— (1991a) *Oranges*, New York: The Noonday Press, Farrar, Straus and Giroux.

—— (1991b) *Looking for a Ship*, New York: The Noonday Press, Farrar, Straus and Giroux.

—— (1991c) *The John McPhee Reader* (ed. William L. Howarth), New York: The Noonday Press, Farrar, Straus and Giroux.

MacQueen, A. (2011) *Private Eye: The First 50 Years – An A–Z*, London: Private Eye Productions.

McRobbie, A. (1996) '*More!* New sexualities in girls' and women's magazines', in J. Curran, D. Morley, and V. Walkerdine (eds) *Cultural Studies and Communications*, London: Arnold.

Malcolm, J. (2004 [1990]) *The Journalist and the Murderer*, New York: Alfred Knopf.

Marr, A. (2004) *My Trade: A Short History of British Journalism*, London: Macmillan.

Marsh, D.R. and Hodsdon, A. (2010) *Guardian Style*, London: Guardian Books.

Mayes, I. (2000) *Corrections and Clarifications*, London: Guardian Newspapers Limited.

Meggs, P.B. (1989) *Type & Image*, New York: Van Nostrand.

Metzler, K. (1986) *Newsgathering*, 2nd edition, Englewood Cliffs, NJ: Prentice-Hall.

Meyer, P. (2002) *Precision Journalism: A Reporter's Introduction to Social Science Methods*, 4th edition, Lanham, MD: Rowman & Littlefield.

Michalos, C. (2003) *The Law of Photography and Digital Images*, London: Sweet and Maxwell.

Michie, D. (1998) *The Invisible Persuaders: How Britain's Spin Doctors Manipulate the Media*, London: Bantam Press.

Mitford, J. (1980) *The Making of a Muckraker*, London: Quartet Books.

Morrish, J. (1996) *Magazine Editing*, London: Routledge/Blueprint.

—— (2003) *Magazine Editing: How to Develop and Manage a Successful Publication*, 2nd edition, London: Routledge.

Morrish, J. and Bradshaw, P. (2012) *Magazine Editing: In Print and Online*, London: Routledge.

Morrison, J. (2011) *Essential Public Affairs for Journalists*, Oxford: Oxford University Press.

Mott, F.L. (1930) *A History of American Magazines 1841–1850*, Cambridge, MA: Harvard University Press.

Naughton, J. (2012) *From Gutenberg to Zuckerberg: What You Really Need to Know About the Internet*, London: Quercus.

Nava, M., Blake, A., MacRury, I. and Richards, B. (eds) (1997) *Buy This Book: Studies in Advertising and Consumption*, London: Routledge.

Negroponte, N. (1996) *Being Digital*, London: Coronet.

Nichols, J. and McChesney, R. (2000) *It's the Media Stupid*, New York: Seven Stories Press.

Oltermann, P. (2009) *How to Write*, London: Guardian Books.

Orwell, G. (1946 [1993]) 'Politics and the English language', in S. Orwell, and I. Angus (eds) *The Collected Essays, Journalism and Letters of George Orwell, Volume IV*, London: Secker.

—— (2003 [1933]) *Down and Out in Paris and London*, Harmondsworth: Penguin.

Packard, V. (1981) *The Hidden Persuaders*, Harmondsworth: Penguin.

Pape, S. and Featherstone, S. (2006) *Feature Writing: A Practical Introduction*, London: Sage.

Parker, T. (1994) *May the Lord in His Mercy be Kind to Belfast*, London: HarperCollins.

Phillips, A. (2006) *Good Writing for Journalists*, London: Sage.

Phillips, D. and Young, P. (2009) *Online Public Relations: A Practical Guide to Developing an Online Strategy in the World of Social Media*, London: Kogan Page.

Pilger, J. (1998) *Hidden Agendas*, London: Vintage/Random House.

—— (ed.) (2004) *Tell Me No Lies: Investigative Journalism and Its Triumphs*, London: Cape.

PPA (1998) *Magazine Retailing: Beyond 2000*, London: PPA.

—— (1999) *Magazine Handbook 1998–1999*, London: PPA.

—— (2000) *Handbook*, London: PPA.

Preston, P. (1999) 'Inaugural Alastair Hetherington lecture', Stirling Media Research Centre, Stirling University.

Quinn, C. (2010) *No Contacts? No Problem! How to Pitch and Sell Your Freelance Feature Writing*, London: Methuen Drama.

Quinn, F. (2011) *Law for Journalists*, 3rd edition, Harlow: Pearson Education Ltd.

Reah, D. (1998) *The Language of Newspapers*, London: Routledge.

Reddick, R. and King, E. (1997) *The Online Journalist: Using the Internet and Other Electronic Media*, Fort Worth, TX: Harcourt Brace College Publishers.

Reed, D. (1997) *The Popular Magazine in Britain and the United States 1880–1960*, London: The British Library.

Ritchin, F. (1990) *In Our Own Image*, New York: Aperture.

Ritter, R. (ed.) (2000) *The Oxford Dictionary for Writers and Editors*, Oxford: Oxford University Press.

Robertson, G. and Nicol, A. (2008) *Media Law,* 5th edition, Harmondsworth: Penguin.

Robinson, M. (1985) 'The Waste Land', in *The Granta Book of Reportage*, London: Granta Books.

Rozenberg, J. (2010) *Privacy and the Press*, Oxford: Oxford University Press.

Rudin, R. and Ibbotson, T. (2002) *An Introduction to Journalism*, Oxford: Focal Press.

Scanlon, P. (ed.) (1977) *Reporting: The Rolling Stone Style*, New York: Anchor Press/Doubleday.

Schlesinger, P. and Tumber, H. (1994) *Reporting Crime*, Oxford: Clarendon Press.

Schudson, M. (1978) *Discovering News*, New York: Basic Books.

—— (1984) *Advertising, the Uneasy Persuasion: Its Dubious Impact on American Society*, New York: Basic Books.

—— (1995) 'Question authority: a history of the news interview', in *The Power of News*, Cambridge, MA and London: Harvard University Press.

Seabrook, J. (2000) *Nobrow: The Culture of Marketing, the Marketing of Culture*, London: Methuen.

Seierstad, Å. (2003) *The Bookseller of Kabul*, London: Virago.

—— (2004) *101 Days in Baghdad*, London: Virago.

Sherman, C. (2005) *Google Power: Unleash the Full Power of Google*, New York: McGraw-Hill Osborne

Silvester, C. (ed.) (1994 [1993]) *The Penguin Book of Interviews: An Anthology from 1859 to the Present Day*, London: Viking.

—— (1998) *The Penguin Book of Columnists*, London: Routledge.

Sims, N. (ed.) (1984) *The Literary Journalists: The New Art of Personal Reportage*, New York: Ballantine.

Smith, A. (1979) *The Newspaper: An International History*, London: Thames & Hudson.

Smith, M. and Kollock, P. (1999) *Communities in Cyberspace*, London: Routledge.

Sobel, D. (1996) *Longitude*, London: Fourth Estate.

Southwell, T. (1998) *Getting Away With It: The Inside Story of Loaded*, London: Ebury Press.

Stafford-Clark, H. (ed.) (2003) *A Life in the Day*, London: Times Books.

Steer, V. (no date) *Printing Design and Layout*, London: Virtue.

Steinberg, S.H. (revised by J. Trevitt) (1996) *Five Hundred Years of Printing*, Harmondsworth: Penguin.

Steinem, G. (1994) 'Sex, lies, and advertising', in *Moving Beyond Words*, London: Bloomsbury.

—— (1995 [1963]) 'I was a Playboy bunny', in *Outrageous Acts and Everyday Rebellions*, 2nd edition, New York: Henry Holt.

Strunk, W. and White, E.B. (2008) *The Elements of Style*, Harlow: Longman.

Swann, A. (1991) *Graphic Design School*, London: Quarto.

Talese, G. and Lounsberry, B. (2000 [1996]) *The Literature of Reality*, Harlow: Longman.

Taylor, J. (1991) *War Photography*, London: Routledge.

—— (1998) *Body Horror*, London: Routledge.

Taylor, S. (2006) *100 Years of Magazine Covers*, London: Black Dog Publishing.

Terkel, S. (2007) *Coming of Age: The Story of Our Century by Those Who've Lived It*, New York: The New Press.

Theaker, A. (2011 [2004]) *The Public Relations Handbook*, 4th edition, London: Routledge.

Thompson, D. (2008) *Counter-knowledge: How We Surrendered to Conspiracy Theories, Quack Medicine, Bogus Science and Fake History*, London: Atlantic Books.

Thurber, J. (1984) *The Years with Ross*, London: HarperCollins.

Tomalin, N. (1966 [1990]) 'The General goes zapping Charlie Cong', in T. Wolfe and E.W. Johnson (eds) *The New Journalism*, London: Picador.

—— (1969 [1997]) 'Stop the press I want to get on', in M. Bromley and T. O'Malley (eds) *A Journalism Reader*, London: Routledge.

Truss, L. (2009) *Eats, Shoots and Leaves*, London: Fourth Estate.

Tunstall, J. (1971) *Journalists at Work*, London: Constable.

Turner, E.S. (1965) *The Shocking History of Advertising*, Harmondsworth: Penguin.

Turner, J. (1998) 'Powerful information: reporting national and local government', in R. Keeble (ed.) *The Newspapers Handbook*, 2nd edition, London: Routledge.

Usherwood, B. (1997) 'Transnational publishing: the case of *Elle Decoration*', in M. Nava, A. Blake, I. MacRury and B. Richards (eds) *Buy This Book: Studies in Advertising and Consumption*, London: Routledge.

Venolia, J. (2001) *Write Right! A Desktop Digest of Punctuation, Grammar, and Style*, 4th edition, Berkeley, CA: Ten Speed Press.

Walker, R. (1992) *Magazine Design: A Hands-on Guide*, London: PIRA International.

Wallraff, G. (1985) *The Lowest of the Low*, London: Methuen.

Waterhouse, K. (1991) *English our English (and How to Sing It)*, London: Viking.

Weisberger, L. (2003) *The Devil Wears Prada*, London: HarperCollins.

Wellman, B. and Gulia, M. (1999) 'Virtual communities as communities: net surfers don't ride alone', in M. Smith and P. Kollock (eds) *Communities in Cyberspace*, London: Routledge.

Wenner, J. (2006) *'Rolling Stone' 1,000 Covers: A History of the Most Influential Magazine in Pop Culture*, New York: Harry N. Abrams

Wenner, J. and Levy, J. (2007) *Rolling Stone Interviews*, Boston, MA: Back Bay Books.

Wesker, A. (1977) *Journey into Journalism*, London: Writers and Readers Cooperative.

Whale, J. (1999) *Put it in Writing*, London: Orion.

Wheen, F. (2004) *How Mumbo-Jumbo Conquered the World: A Short History of Modern Delusions*, London: Harper Perennial.

Wheeler, S. (2009) *Feature Writing for Journalists*, London: Sage.

White, C. (1969) *Women's Magazines 1693–1968*, London: Michael Joseph.

—— (1977) *The Women's Periodical Press 1946–1976: Report for the Royal Commission on the Press*, London: HMSO.

Whittaker, J. (2007) *Web Production for Writers and Journalists*, 2nd edition, London: Routledge.

—— (2008) *Magazine Production*, London: Routledge.

—— (2009) *Producing for Web 2.0: A Student Guide*, 3rd edition, London: Routledge.

Whyte, J (2003) *Bad Thoughts: A Guide to Clear Thinking*, London: Corvo.

Winship, J. (1987) *Inside Women's Magazines*, London: Pandora.

Wolf, N. (1991) *The Beauty Myth*, London: Vintage.

Wolfe, T. and Johnson, E.W. (eds) (1990 [1973]) *The New Journalism*, London: Picador.

Worcester, R.M. (1998) 'Demographics and values: what the British public reads and what it thinks of its newspapers', in M. Bromley and H. Stephenson (eds) *Sex, Lies and Democracy: The Press and the Public*, London and New York: Addison Wesley Longman.

Wozencroft, J. (1988) *The Graphic Language of Neville Brody*, London: Thames & Hudson.

Wright, T. (2004) *The Photography Handbook*, London: Routledge.

The Writers' and Artists' Yearbook, 2013 (2012) London: Bloomsbury.

Zeldin, T. (1998) *Conversation*, London: The Harvill Press.

ARTICLES

Addicott, R. (1999) 'MCN goes upmarket', *Press Gazette*, 16 April: 4.

Barber, L. (1998) 'Life', *The Observer*, 8 November: 9.

Bauret, G. (1999) 'From Russia with love', *The Guardian 'Weekend'*, 10 April: 33.

Daubney, M. (2012) 'The lads' mag I edited turned a generation on to porn: and now I'm a father I bitterly regret it – A remarkable confession from the longest-serving editor of *Loaded*.' Available online at: www.dailymail.co.uk/news/article-2156593/The-lads-mag-I-edited-turned-generation-porn–Im-father-I-bitterly-regret-A-remarkable-confession-longest-serving-editor-Loaded.html#ixzz1z53zFuBM (accessed 28 June 2012).

Duckworth, A. (1999) 'The start of something great', *Motor Cycle News*, 14 April: 2.

Dunn, S. (2008) 'Would you be better off hiring an accountant?' *The Guardian*. Available online at: www.guardian.co.uk/money/2008/jun/14/consumeraffairs.tax (accessed 16 September 2012).

The Economist (2012) 'Non-news is good news', 9 June.

Evans, H. (1999) 'Freedom of information: why Britain must learn from America', *Guardian Media*, 31 May: 4.

Fleetwood, B. (1999) *The Guardian* 'Editor' section, 17 September.

Gibson, J. (1999) 'She's sticking with sex', *Guardian Media*, 1 February: 6–7.

Gitlin, T. (1999) 'Why gossip can be hazardous', *Brill's Content*, May: 109.

Glaister, D. (1999) 'Design to create pages people want to read', *The Guardian*, 19 April: 6. Available online at: www.guardian.co.uk/uk/1999/apr/19/danglaister?INTCMP=SRCH

Glen, A. (2005) 'PRs set up camp with festivals', *Music Week*, 30 July: 15.

Greenslade, R. (2004) 'We have sailed through a perfect storm', *MediaGuardian*, 6 December: 3.

—— (2005) 'The story behind the Straw splash', *MediaGuardian*, 21 March: 10.

Hitchens, C. (2006) 'Oriana Fallaci and the art of the interview', *Vanity Fair*, December. Available online at: www.vanityfair.com/politics/features/2006/12/hitchens200612 (accessed 29 June 2012).

Hooper, M. (2012) 'Who says print is dead', *The Guardian*. Available online at: www.guardian.co.uk/media/2012/jun/03/who-says-print-is-dead/print (accessed 7 June 2012).

Howell, N. (2005) 'Delivering the goods', *New Media Age*, 5 May.

Kellner, P. (1991) 'Nobody trusts us and that's bad news', *Independent*, 7 August.

McKay, J. (1998) 'Dear Tony, can reading stuff like this make me pregnant?', *The Scotsman*, 19 November: 16.

Magazine World (2011) 'A licence to print money', Q4, 12–19

Morgan, J. (2000) '"There is money out there", Pollard tells launch hopefuls', *Press Gazette*, 25 February: 9.

O'Hagan, A. (1998) 'A floral tribute', *The Guardian Weekend*, 2 May: 10.

Porter, B. (1999) 'Boarder or day boy', *London Review of Books*, 15 July.

Pugh, A. (2011) 'Could accepting freebies land journalists in jail?'. Available online at: www.pressgazette.co.uk/story.asp?storycode=47771 (accessed 28 June 2012).

Reeves, I. (2005) 'Say it loud, I work in mags and I'm proud', *Press Gazette*, 14 January: 22–3.

Ronson, J. (1999) 'Zoë and an ordinary dream', *The Guardian Weekend*, 25 September: 8.

Shewen, P. (1999) 'Spice is nice, but war's a bore', *New Internationalist*, October: 317.

Smith, L. (1999) 'Why gossip is good for us', *Brill's Content*, May: 107.

Index